EUGEN EHRLICH

BIBLIOGRAPHIC INDEX

Sergiy Nezhurbida
&
Maria Diachuk

Vernon Series in Law

VERNON PRESS

www.vernonpress.com

In the Americas:
Vernon Press
1000 N West Street,
Suite 1200, Wilmington,
Delaware 19801
United States

In the rest of the world:
Vernon Press
C/Sancti Espiritu 17,
Malaga, 29006
Spain

Vernon Series in Law

Library of Congress Control Number: 2018930915

ISBN: 978-1-62273-377-4

Authors

Ass. Prof. **Sergiy NEZHURBIDA**, LL.D.
&
M. Ec. **Maria DIACHUK**
Yuriy Fedkovych Chernivtsi National University

Introductory article

Eugen Ehrlich: Life and Work of the Founder of Sociology of Law
Prof. Dr. **Manfred REHBINDER**
University of Zürich

Editor

Doc. Mgr. **Slávka TOMAŠČÍKOVÁ**, PhD.
Pavol Jozef Šafárik University in Košice

Translation

	Foreword
Doc. Mgr. **Slávka TOMAŠČÍKOVÁ**, PhD.	Main Dates of Eugen Ehrlich's Life and Activity
	Parts 1, 2, 3
Mgr. **Július ROZENFELD**, PhD. & Mgr. **Ulrika STRÖMPLOVÁ**, PhD. Pavol Jozef Šafárik University in Košice	*Eugen Ehrlich: Life and Work of the Founder of Sociology of Law* by Prof. Dr. Manfred Rehbinder

Graphic design

Roman SABADASH

Picture 1. Eugen Ehrlich, Rector of Czernowitz University, 1907 (a section).

Source: Rehbinder, Manfred. *Rechtssoziologie.* 8. Aufl., C. H. Beck Publ., 2014, S. XIV.

(reprinted by kind permission of Manfred Rehbinder)

Picture 2. Eugen Ehrlich, Rector of Czernowitz University, 1907.

Source: Rehbinder, Manfred. *Rechtssoziologie.* 8. Aufl., C. H. Beck Publ., 2014, S. XIV.

(reprinted by kind permission of Manfred Rehbinder)

Picture 3. Eugen Ehrlich, undated (a section).

Source: *Guide to the Papers of Hugo Sinzheimer (1875-1945) undated, 1893-2010*, p. 196, Hugo Sinzheimer Collection, Leo Baeck Institute, New York and Berlin (reprinted by kind permission of Leo Baeck Institute)

Picture 4. Eugen Ehrlich, undated.

Source: *Guide to the Papers of Hugo Sinzheimer (1875-1945) undated, 1893-2010*, p. 196, Hugo Sinzheimer Collection, Leo Baeck Institute, New York and Berlin (reprinted by kind permission of Leo Baeck Institute)

Picture 5. Eugen Ehrlich, undated.

Source: Rehbinder, Manfred. *Die Begründung der Rechtssoziologie durch Eugen Ehrlich.* 2., völlig neu bearb. Aufl., Berlin : Duncker und Humblot, 1986 (reprinted by kind permission of Manfred Rehbinder)

Picture 6. Franz Joseph University in Czernowitz, undated.

Source: *Die k. k. Franz-Josephs-Universität in Czernowitz im ersten Vierteljahrhundert ihres Bestandes : Festschrift / hrsg. vom akademischen Senate.* Czernowitz : Bukowinaer Vereinsdruck, 1900
(reprinted by kind permission of Scientific Library of Yuriy Fedkovych Chernivtsi National University)

Table of Contents

ACKNOWLEDGMENT

or How the EUGEN EHRLICH Bibliographic Index came to life

In 2015 the walls of Yuriy Fedkovych Chernivtsi National University witnessed the presentation of the first ever compiled *HANS GROSS Bibliographic Index* – the text containing data and information about life, scientific, pedagogic, juridical and community work and activities of the Austrian lawyer and criminologist, the founder of world criminology, and the Professor (1899-1902) and the Dean (1899-1900) of the Faculty of Law of Franz Joseph University in Czernowitz – Hans Gustav Adolf Gross.

When working on the bibliographic index the Authors collected and analyzed numerous published sources that included a great amount of so far unknown information about Eugen Ehrlich – the lawyer, founder of sociology of law, Professor at Franz Joseph University in Czernowitz in years 1906-1907.

The uncovered authority of Eugen Ehrlich in the world of science represented the decisive element in the effort of the Authors to assemble the bibliographic index dedicated to this personality. Another important factor having a strong impact on the compilation of the bibliographic index came with the regular visits of Professor Dr. Manfred Rehbinder paid to Chernivtsi. It was the "academic blessing" about the topicality of the bibliographic index provided by Professor Rehbinder who also agreed to write an introductory chapter for the index.

Two years were taken by the titanic work of the two Authors before the *EUGEN EHRLICH Bibliographic Index* has seen the light of life. Its birth would not have been possible without help of our friends, the philologists at Pavol Jozef Šafárik University in Košice, Slovakia – Associate Professor Dr. Slávka Tomaščíková, who took the burden of translating annotations and editing the volume, and Dr. Július Rozenfeld and Dr. Ulrika Strömplová who translated the introductory chapter.

The book contains photographs of Eugen Ehrlich and photographs of materials linked to his life and activities. They have made the bibliographic index more attractive and more interesting for readers. The Authors would like to express their special gratitude: to Professor Dr. Manfred Rehbinder and to Leo Baeck Institute (New York | Berlin) for their kind permission to use pictures of Eugen Ehrlich; to Yuriy Fedkovych Chernivtsi National University for agreeing to use pictures of Czernowitz University, pictures of covers and title pages of Eugen Ehrlich's works, sources about Eugen Ehrlich's research and education activities at Czernowitz University, archival documents, and books with commemorative inscriptions for Eugen Ehrlich.

Last but not least the Authors are grateful to the Vernon Press Publisher for their interest in publishing the result of the Authors' work, and for their professional approach to the process of preparing the manuscript for publication. We, the Authors, want to thank each other for the continuous support and the mutual respect that have lasted for two years of joint effort resulting in this book. Finally, we would like to ask the readers to express their wishes and criticism directly to us.

The Authors

FOREWORD

The **Bibliographic Index EUGEN EHRLICH** is a guide through available materials containing information about the life, scientific, educational, legislative and social activities of the Austrian lawyer and university professor in the period of 1896-1918. Eugen Ehrlich was the Dean in 1901-1902 and 1908-1909 and the Vice-Dean of the Faculty of Law in 1902-1903 and 1909-1910, the Vice-Rector in 1907-1908, and the Rector of Franz Joseph University in Czernowitz in 1906-1907 (now Ukrainian: Chernivtsi). Moreover, *ex officio*, he was a member of the local parliament.

The Index includes the foreword of the compilers, an introductory article, a selected basic chronology with the dates of the life and work of Eugen Ehrlich, and the four main structural parts: "List of works by Eugen Ehrlich", "Eugen Ehrlich as editor", "Literature about Eugen Ehrlich's life and activity" and "Appendices: Documents from Chernivtsi University Scientific Library holdings".

The first part "List of works by Eugen Ehrlich" consists of two thematic units. The first unit "Monographs, articles, reviews" includes publications of Eugen Ehrlich, his reviews of the works of the then leading lawyers, and numerous reprinted articles written in world languages. The second unit of the first part is entitled "Translations of Eugen Ehrlich's works into Ukrainian and Russian". The first section of material is arranged by the year of publication, and within each year, works are grouped alphabetically. Eugen Ehrlich is not specified as the author in bibliographic descriptions of the Index. Reviews of Eugen Ehrlich's works placed in the first unit are presented after the bibliographic description in alphabetical order by the titles of publications and the names of reviewers.

Materials of the second part "Eugen Ehrlich as editor" reflecting the publishing, editorial, and compiling activities of Eugen Ehrlich are arranged chronologically.

Publications in the third part "Literature about Eugen Ehrlich's life and activity" are organized alphabetically (first in Russian and Ukrainian, and then in other foreign languages). The content of collections follows their bibliographic descriptions that carry important information about the life and scientific approaches of Eugen Ehrlich. A significant part of the third part is represented by the news and newspaper chronicles of the late 19th and the first quarter of the 20th century, such as *Bukowinaer Post, Bukowinaer Rundschau, Bukowiner Nachrichten, Czernowitzer Allgemeine Zeitung, Czernowitzer Tagblatt, Czernowitzer Zeitung*, etc. These reflect the chronology of Eugen Ehrlich's everyday life.

The Appendices part contains four sections: "Eugen Ehrlich's works: covers and title pages", "Sources about Eugen Ehrlich's research and education activities at Czernowitz University", "Eugen Ehrlich in archival documents" and "Books with commemorative inscriptions for Eugen Ehrlich".

To avoid duplication, the Index uses 'Ibidem' (for documents in Ukrainian 'Там само' [There] and for the document languages that use the Latin alphabet 'Ibidem').

The elementary source base for the Index was created by catalogues and card indexes (including the library systematic catalogues and archival documents from the period when Bukovina belonged to either Austro-Hungary or Romania), and the domestic and foreign holdings of the Scientific Library of Chernivtsi National University. Indexed materials have been processed *de visu*. Each of them, except for articles from periodicals after the 1945 edition, is presented with the storage code of the Scientific Library of Yuriy Fedkovych Chernivtsi National University. Bibliographic descriptions are sequentially numbered. Some bibliographic descriptions are accompanied by annotations with further references and explanations. Surnames in annotations in English, for authenticity, are indicated in German.

"List of works by Eugen Ehrlich", "Periodicals with Eugen Ehrlich's publications", "List of used periodicals", and "Name index" are all provided for the convenience of users. The "Name index" includes all the names recorded in the main text of the publication (numbers of bibliographic records of works devoted to individual persons are enclosed in parentheses).

The publication of the Bibliographic Index EUGEN EHRLICH neither completes nor finishes the process of search and selection of materials on his academic achievements. The work with foreign holdings of the Scientific Library of Yuriy Fedkovych Chernivtsi National University continues, so the Index is not exhaustive.

We hope that the Index can help users find necessary documents and verify the accuracy of existing information, that it becomes a prerequisite for further research, and finally, it will be useful to all who are interested in Eugen Ehrlich's life journey and scientific legacy.

The Authors

EUGEN EHRLICH: LIFE AND WORK OF THE FOUNDER OF SOCIOLOGY OF LAW

Prof. Dr. Manfred REHBINDER

1. After World War II, when an increased interest about the sociology of law as a scientific discipline arose, German-speaking countries turned to the easternmost corner of the old Austro-Hungarian Monarchy: to Czernowitz, the regional capital of the Duchy of Bukovina. For some, then around the turn of the 20th century, it was the end of the civilized world, for others, it was the cradle of rich multicultural development.

After two World Wars and fundamental revolutionary changes, primarily of ethnic character, the remains of the traditional lifestyle of the then existent society were hard to find and this particularly concerned the life and works of the founder of the sociology of law: Eugen Ehrlich; though, in the years before World War I, he was a prominent personality not only at his university, but well-known far beyond the borders of Bukovina. Ehrlich was a multilingual, much-travelled and many-sided person. Data in the birth register of the local synagogue indicate that he was born on 14 September 1862, named Elias, a son of a doctor of law Simon Ehrlich and his wife Eleonora Donnenfeld. As early as 1865, the young family moved to Sambor (now Ukrainian: Sambir), a small provincial town about 70 km from Lemberg (now Ukrainian: Lviv), the then capital of the Kingdom of Galicia and Lodomeria, which also belonged, like Bukovina before World War I, to the Austro-Hungarian federation. Ehrlich's father was an advocate, and the young Elias, together with his younger brother, the later physician Oswald Ehrlich, spent his youth in Sambor. In 1879, at the age of seventeen, Elias passed his school-leaving exams and acquired his school-leaving certificate at the humanist secondary grammar school with Polish as the language of instruction, founded by the Jesuit order in the 16th century.

2. Ehrlich decided to study law and went back to his birthplace, Czernowitz, where he completed his first year of studies at the Faculty of Law of the young, recently established Franz Joseph University in Czernowitz with German as the language of instruction. Then he moved to the University of Lemberg with Polish as the language of instruction for the second year of his studies. After the death of his father, the family moved to Vienna, where Ehrlich enrolled in the 1881/82 winter term in the 5th year of his studies. He was registered as: "*Elias Ehrlich, Israelite, from Sambor (Galicia), mother tongue Polish*". He graduated as Doctor of Jurisprudence in 1886, and in 1894 he was awarded the academic title of 'Privatdozent' in Roman law at the University of Vienna for his work *Die stillschweigende Willenserklärung* [Tacit Consent]. The habilitation files describe him as "*Eugene (Elias) Ehrlich, son of a lawyer's widow Eleonore*" and indicate his religion as "*Catholic*".

While changing religious affiliation, useful for a scientific career, was acceptable for Ehrlich without reservation as he did not show any religious tendencies anywhere in his extensive writings, he chose his new first name, as he later wrote, in a conscious commitment to the spiritual heritage of Prince Eugene.

3. After obtaining a doctoral degree, Ehrlich completed a court practice and worked as a lawyer in a law firm for several years, and from 1893 to 1896 he was an independent lawyer in Schwechat near Vienna. During this period, he belonged to the circle of friends around Anton Menger and joined – also through his essays - the ongoing debates on socialism. He became active in the political sphere in 1895 when, for social reasons, he intervened in the discussion on the new Austrian Code of Civil Procedure and, with a speech before the society of Austrian economists, brought about a compromise in circumscribing the scope of competence among the stock exchange representatives. A year later he became Associate Professor (senior lecturer) of Roman law at his birthplace Czernowitz, and was promoted to Full Professor in January 1900.

4. Here in Czernowitz, interrupted only by his frequent visits abroad to procure materials for his publications, he developed the foundations for his life work at a feverish pace until his flight from the invasion of the Russians in the autumn of 1914. In addition to a number of works on Roman law, in his extensive publications, Ehrlich focused on sociological jurisprudence, which brought him an international reputation: (1) for his juridical method, which he named Freirechtslehre [free legal theory], and for which he received an

honorary doctorate together with the Swiss Eugen Huber and the French François Gény and Leon Duguit, which was awarded to him on the 300th anniversary of the Rijksuniversiteit Groningen, Holland in 1914, (2) for his efforts and research into the role of 'living law' (lebendes Recht) in Bukovina, (3) and for his work *Grundlegung der Soziologie des Rechts* [Fundamental Principles of the Sociology of Law], which had appeared just before the outbreak of the war.

The German Council of Judges asked him for an opinion on the reform of the Court of Justice, and the German Association of Lawyers (Deutscher Juristentag) asked him for his expert opinion on the reform of legal training, which he finished in 1912. Unfortunately, because of the outbreak of war, he could not accept an invitation from the United States to hold a seminar on living law for the United States Association of American Law Schools at the 1914 Annual General Meeting in Chicago and to report and lecture at Harvard University.

5. In August 1914, Czernowitz University was closed for the first time due to the advance of Russian troops. Ehrlich, leaving behind most of his belongings, travelled to Vienna. He wrote to partners and publishers during the summer months, which he spent in a boarding house in Küb near Semmering and Bad Ischl. He untiringly deepened his doctrine of freedom of law to a theory of judicial law, which was conceived as a continuation of the foundations of the sociology of law. Due to the absence of publication possibilities, his manuscript had to be divided between two periodicals. The first part was published in the *Archiv für die civilistische Praxis* (AcP) [Archives for Civilian Practice] in 1914, and later was also printed as a monograph under the title *Die Juristische Logik* [The Juridical Logic]. The second, even more important part, which appeared under the title *Die richterliche Rechtsfindung aufgrund des Rechtssatzes* [Judicial Jurisdiction According to the Law] in *Jherings Jahrbüchern* [Jhering's Yearbook], was however hardly recognized. Similarly, Ehrlich's scientific debate with Hans Kelsen on the epistemological limits of the sociology of law appeared in the *Archiv für Sozialwissenschaften und Sozialpolitik* [Archives for Social Sciences and Social Policy] in the first years of the war.

6. In addition to Ehrlich's scholar work, his active engagement in the peace movement began during the war, and this led to a considerable series of political writings. Before the war, as he later wrote, he had occupied himself with other work and did not write any political articles. However, as a

member of the Study Commission on Nationality Problems of the Central Organization for a Lasting Peace (Nationaliätenprobleme), which was launched in the Netherlands, he wrote an expert report published in 1917 at The Hague in English under the title *The National Problems in Austria.* His aim was to persuade the allies not to divide the defeated Austro-Hungarian Monarchy, as was demanded because of her supposedly failed nationality policy, namely the suppression of her national minorities. The Austrian Ministry of Foreign Affairs classified the Central Organization as 'extremely pacifist' and therefore dangerous to Austria and argued that it was financed by the American Henry Ford. The participation of the Austrian side in foreign peace conferences of this kind, according to Ehrlich, was therefore undesirable. When losing the war seemed unavoidable, Ehrlich was commissioned by the Ministry of Education during the 1918/1919 winter term to travel to Switzerland 'for scientific purposes', and the Ministry of Foreign Affairs appointed him (by then far too late) to the League of Nations to publish a detailed French version of his Hague opinion on the nationality question with the aim of advocating the Austro-Hungarian national policies. After censorship by the Ministry of Foreign Affairs, the work was published in Geneva at the end of 1918 under the title *Quelques aspects de la question nationale autrichienne* [Some Aspects of the Austrian National Question].

7. Ehrlich was in Switzerland at the end of July 1918 and witnessed the end of the old Austria. In November 1918, Bukovina was annexed by the Kingdom of Romania. In the course of the 'romanianization' of public life, which began in October 1919, Franz Joseph University in Czernowitz originally with German as the language of instruction was converted into a Romanian university with Romanian as the language of instruction and was officially opened in the presence of the king.

Ehrlich stayed first in Switzerland and applied for retirement in a letter to Vienna from June 1920. At the same time, he was looking for a way to stay in Switzerland. When he was not able to achieve his goal, in August 1920, Ehrlich travelled from Bern to his brother in Naples and from there via Vienna back to his home in Romania.

In November 1920, the *Czernowitzer Morgenblatt* [Chernivtsi Morning News] announced his arrival in Czernowitz and voiced the general request that he resume his teaching activities. He, however, had to face strong resistance from the then rector, the historian Ion Nistor, who was a proponent of the unification of Bukovina and Romania. For his services, 'for the rapid unification of Romania' and for the romanianization of Bukovina, Nistor later became a minister of Bukovina. Nistor staged a press campaign of Romanian nationalists against the recall of Ehrlich. Formally, Ehrlich was removed because he was accused of not reporting back in due time after his leave of absence by the Austrian Ministry of Education and because he purportedly did not apply for a post in the Romanian state service. Moreover, he was accused of having always been a 'champion of Austrianism' (so-called Josephinism) and even having demanded the definite abolition of the university during the war, and thus proved to be the 'enemy of the Romanian people'. Hidden antisemitism of Romanian nationalists as an important motive for opposing to Ehrlich, however, remained well-concealed.

8. Ehrlich travelled to Bucharest in November 1920 to negotiate with the Romanian Ministry of Education. There, a few months later after a change of government, he was offered a newly founded chair of Legal Philosophy and Sociology in Czernowitz. He enjoyed thereby the strong support of well-known Romanian personalities such as the agronomist and sociologist, founder of the sociological school of Bucharest, Dimitrie Gusti, the famous historian in Bucharest Nicolae Lorga, and even King Ferdinand I, who all recognized Ehrlich's high scientific rank and wide international reputation.

But the protests against Ehrlich did not stop in Czernowitz, even after Ehrlich's reappointment in July 1921. In October 1921, a new wave of Romanian student protests threatened to forcefully prevent Ehrlich from resuming his teaching activity. In December 1921, the newspaper *Glasul Bucovinei*, which was controlled by Nistor, published a long article from an anonymous author criticizing Ehrlich's appointment as an intervention in the university autonomy that ran counter to the interests of Romanians. Ehrlich therefore never returned to Czernowitz. He spent the summer months of 1921 in Olâneşti, a spa town in rural Wallachia. He stayed with his relatives in Bucharest and worked at the Institute of Gusti on publications in Romanian, mainly not of sociological but of political character, during the rest of his life until impairment of his health in the spring of 1922. Among these works, there are extensive writings on the reasons for the decline of the Donau monarchy (The Austro-Hungarian Monarchy) and his treatise on the demerits of the German generals Ludendorff and Hindenburg in connection to the lost First World War. In April 1922, Ehrlich travelled from Bucharest to Vienna, where he died on the 2 May 1922 at the age of 59, in the hospital of Viennese Kaufmannschaft after the amputation of his leg in the final stage of then incurable diabetes.

9. Finally, a few remarks on the present, so far most comprehensive, bibliography presented by Sergei Nezhurbida and Maria Diachuk. My efforts to develop a complete list of the publications of Ehrlich's works began more than half a century ago. This work was based on an analysis of the files available in library collections at that time, which were limited to independent publications and did not contain any reference to contributions, essays or reviews. These, therefore, had to be supplemented by the analysis of quotations in Ehrlich's works and primarily in the publications of other authors. Besides legal journals, other cultural journals also had to be considered. It turned out that correspondence with publishers and literature available in Switzerland, Romania and mostly in Japan were of great use in this research. But even the second edition of my Ehrlich monograph of 1986 contained an insufficient bibliography (pp. 143-147).

A great breakthrough was the so far unsurpassed study of Stefan Vogl (*Soziale Gesetzgebungspolitik, Freie Rechtsfindung, and Sozialpolitische Rechtswissenschaftschaft*; Eugen Ehrlich, Baden-Baden, 2003, pp. 359-395), not only in its content, but also in the systematic outline of the list of sources and literature. The greatest progress has been achieved by the decision to evaluate the daily newspapers in Ehrlich's times. This was a tremendously time-consuming undertaking, since the relevant newspapers have not been digitized yet except for the *Neues Wiener Tagblatt*. As it can be inferred from the bibliography, in addition to the *Wiener Tagblatt*, the analysis of the (*Viennese*) *Neue Freie Presse* and, primarily, the analysis of the Czernowitz daily newspapers were extremely successful. Today, in the age of the decline of newspapers, it is astonishing to notice that five daily newspapers in German, the *Czernowitzer Zeitung*, the *Czernowitzer Allgemeine Zeitung*, the *Czernowitzer Tagblatt*, the *Bukowiner Rundschau* and the *Bukowiner Nachrichten*, appeared in Ehrlich's days in Czernowitz alone. Nezhurbida and Diachuk not only found an abundance of essays in these newspapers, which have not been published in legal literature, but also registered many newspaper articles on public lectures given by Ehrlich, which have not been published. These newspapers also reported on Ehrlich's public appearances on different occasions, especially during the time when he was the dean of the law faculty and the rector of the university. We do hope that this research on Ehrlich's works will be appreciated by the editors for the surprisingly rich database produced by the meticulous work on newspapers and for the superabundant references in secondary literature in other than German language. The following list of literature is indispensable for further research on Ehrlich's works.

10. Should anyone look for the details of my previous report on the life and work of Eugene Ehrlich, data are available in my publications listed below. However, it is important to note, that with the increasing accessibility of new material, the documents in their chronological sequence also contain numerous corrections and necessary additions, so newer publications are to be preferred to the older ones.

1. Die Grundlegung der Rechtssoziologie durch Eugen Ehrlich, *Kölner Zeitschrift für Soziologie und Sozialphilosophie* 15, 1963, S. 338-353.
2. Neues über Leben und Werk von Eugen Ehrlich, *Festschrift (FS) für Helmut Schelsky*, Berlin 1978, S. 403-418.
3. Die Begründung der Rechtssoziologie durch Eugen Ehrlich. *Schriftenreihe zur Rechtssoziologie und Rechtstatsachenforschung* Bd. 7, 2. Aufl. Berlin 1986.
4. Die rechts- und staatswissenschaftliche Fakultät der Franz-Joseph-Universität Czernowitz. Ihr Beitrag zur Erforschung des Rechts in einer multikulturellen Gesellschaft, in *FS Hans Stoll*, Tübingen 2001, S. 327-344.
5. Aus den letzten Jahren im Leben und Schaffen von Eugen Ehrlich, in *FS Ernst-Joachim Lampe*, Berlin 2003, S. 199-210.
6. Die politischen Schriften des Rechtssoziologen Eugen Ehrlich auf dem Hintergrund seines bewegten Lebens, in *FS Elmar Wadle*, Berlin 2008, S. 901-915.

MAIN DATES OF EUGEN EHRLICH'S LIFE AND ACTIVITY

14/09/1862	Date of Eugen Ehrlich's birth (Czernowitz)
08/04/1886	Doctor of Jurisprudence
1888	*Über die Lücken im Rechte* [On Loopholes in Law]
1893-1896	Independent lawyer in Schwechat near Vienna
1893	*Die stillschweigende Willenserklärung* [Tacit Consent]
1894	'Privatdozent' in Roman law at the University of Vienna
1896	Associate Professor of Roman law at Franz Joseph University in Czernowitz
1896-1914	Activities at Franz Joseph University in Czernowitz
1900	Full Professor of Roman law at Franz Joseph University in Czernowitz
1901-1902	Dean of the Faculty of Law at Franz Joseph University in Czernowitz
1903	*Freie Rechtsfindung und freie Rechtswissenschaft* [Free Finding of the Law and Free Science of Law]
1906	*Die Tatsachen des Gewohnheitsrechts* [Facts of Customary Law] (Rector's inauguration speech)
1906-1907	Rector of Franz Joseph University in Czernowitz
1909	*Die Rechtsfähigkeit* [Capability of Law]
10/10/1909	First mention of Eugen Ehrlich's conducting a seminar in *'Living Law'*
1911	*Über das lebende Recht* [On Living Law]
1913	*Grundlegung der Soziologie des Rechts* [Fundamental Principles of the Sociology of Law]
1914	Honorary Doctor's Degree at the University of Groningen
1917	*The National Problems in Austria*
1918	*Die Juristische Logik* [The Juridical Logic]
2/05/1922	Date of Eugen Ehrlich's death (Vienna)

PART 1.

LIST OF WORKS BY EUGEN EHRLICH

1.1. Monographs, articles, reviews

1887

1. **Ueber Facturenbeisätze.** *Juristische Blätter.* 1887. 31. Juli (Nr. 31, Jg. 16). S. 365–368 ; 7. Aug. (Nr. 32, Jg. 16). S. 377–379 ; 14. Aug. (Nr. 33, Jg. 16). S. 389–391.

IN 2810 86A6

1888

2. **Ueber Lücken** im Rechte. *Ibidem.* 1888. 16. Sept. (Nr. 38, Jg. 17). S. 447–449 ; 23. Sept. (Nr. 39, Jg. 17). S. 459–461 ; 30. Sept. (Nr. 40, Jg. 17). S. 471–473 ; 7. Oct. (Nr. 41, Jg. 17). S. 483–485 ; 14. Oct. (Nr. 42, Jg. 17). S. 495–498 ; 21. Oct. (Nr. 43, Jg. 17). S. 510–512 ; 28. Oct. (Nr. 44, Jg. 17). S. 522–525 ; 4. Nov. (Nr. 45, Jg. 17). S. 535–536 ; 11. Nov. (Nr. 46, Jg. 17). S. 546–547 ; 18. Nov. (Nr. 47, Jg. 17). S. 558 ; 25. Nov. (Nr. 48, Jg. 17). S. 569–570 ; 2. Dec. (Nr. 49, Jg. 17). S. 581–583 ; 9. Dec. (Nr. 50, Jg. 17). S. 594–597 ; 16. Dec. (Nr. 51, Jg. 17). S. 603–605 ; 23. Dec. (Nr. 52, Jg. 17). S. 618–620 ; 30. Dec. (Nr. 53, Jg. 17). S. 627–630.

IN 2820 86A6

1889

3. **Das Stillschweigen** im Handelsverkehre. *Kaufmännische Zeitschrift.* 1889. 1. Dec. (Nr. 23, Jg. 15). S. 202–204.

1890

4. **Die Arische** Urgesellschaft. *Deutsche Worte.* 1890. Jg. 10. S. 353–374.

5. **Der Entwurf** eines bürgerlichen Gesetzbuchs und die socialpolitischen Bestrebungen der Gegenwart. *Unsere Zeit.* 1890. Bd. 2. S. 21–35.

IN 23113 81D1

6. **Sociale** Gesetzgebungspolitik auf dem Gebiete des Deutschen Privatrechts. *Ibidem.* 1890. Bd. 1. S. 433–451.

IN 23112 81D1

1891

7. **Arbeiterschutz** im Privatrechte. *Arbeiterschutz.* 1891. Jg. 2. S. 209–243.

8. **Die sociale** Frage und die Rechtsordnung. *Die Neue Zeit.* 1890/1891. Nr. 40 (Jg. 9, Bd. 2). S. 430–438 ; Nr. 41 (Jg. 9, Bd. 2). S. 476–480 ; Nr. 43 (Jg. 9, Bd. 2). S. 539–544.

9. **[Rezension]**. *Zeitschrift für das Privat- und öffentliche Recht der Gegenwart.* 1891. Bd. 18. S. 286–287. Rez. : Klewitz, Adolf. *Die Verpflichtung zur Rechnungsstellung.* Berlin : Puttkammer & Mühlbrecht, 1890.

IN 23747 16F1

10. **[Rezension]**. *Ibidem.* 1891. Bd. 18. S. 197–198. Rez. : Lastig, Gustav. *Markenrecht und Zeichenregister : ein Beitrag zur Handelsrechtsgeschichte : Festschrift.* Halle a. s. : Max Niemayer, 1889.

IN 23747 16F1

11. **[Rezension]**. *Ibidem.* 1891. Bd. 18. S. 198. Rez. : Weber, Max. *Zur Geschichte der Handelsgesellschaften im Mittelalter : nach südeuropäischen Quellen.* Stuttgart : Ferdinand Enke, 1889.

IN 23747 16F1

1892

12. **[Rezension]**. *Ibidem.* 1892. Bd. 19. S. 535–536. Rez. : Kishi, Kossaburo. “Das Erbrecht Japans, insbesondere Kritik des Intestaterbrechts der Codification vom Jahre 1890.“ Inaug.-Diss. Göttingen : Druck der Univ.-Buchdruck. von W. Fr. Kastner. 1891. 66 S.

IN 23748 16F1

13. **[Rezension]**. *Ibidem.* 1892. Bd. 19. S. 537. Rez. : Menger, Anton. *Das Recht auf den vollen Arbeitsertrag, in geschichtlicher Darstellung.* 2., verbess. Aufl. Stuttgart : Verl. der J. G. Cotta'schen Buchh. Nachf., 1891. [X, 178 S.].

IN 23748 16F1

14. **[Rezension]**. *Ibidem.* 1892. Bd. 19. S. 696. Rez. : Pappenheim, Wilhelm. *Über die fortdauernde Giltigkeit der einberufenen Staatsnoten mit dem Datum 7. Juli 1866 und 25. August 1866.* Wien : Alfred Hölder, 1891. 29 S.

IN 23748 16F1

15. **Die sociale** Frage im Privatrechte. *Juristische Blätter.* 1892. 28. Febr. (Nr. 9, Jg. 21). S. 97–99 ; 6. März. (Nr. 10, Jg. 21). S. 109–111 ; 13. März. (Nr. 11, Jg. 21). S. 121–123 ; 20. März. (Nr. 12, Jg. 21). S. 133–135.

IN 2844 86A6

1893

16. **[Rezension]**. *Zeitschrift für das Privat- und öffentliche Recht der Gegenwart.* 1893. Bd. 20. S. 239. Rez. : Francken, Oscar. *Die Liquidatur der offenen Handelsgesellschaft in geschichtlicher Entwicklung.* Stuttgart : Ferdinand Enke, 1891. 172 S.

IN 23749 16F1

17. **Die stillschweigende** Willenserklärung. Berlin : Carl Heymanns Verl., 1893. XII, 296 S.

IN 19503 5aM31

1895

18. **Arbeitende** Damen. *Neue Revue.* 1895. Jg. 6. S. 1185–1191.

19. **Die Börsenschiedsgerichte**. Wien : M. Engel & Söhne, [1895]. 14 S. Sep.-Abdr. aus : *Neue Revue.* 1895. Jg. 6. S. 262–269, 305–310.

20. **Zur Frage** des Frauenstudiums. *Deutsche Worte.* 1895. Jg. 15. S. 703–712.

1896

21. **Der Gang** der Cultur-Entwicklung : Vortrag, gehalten im Wissenschaftlichen Club. *Neue Revue.* 1896. Jg. 7, Nr. 23. S. 690–696.

22. **[Rezension]**. *Zeitschrift für das Privat- und öffentliche Recht der Gegenwart.* 1896. Bd. 23. S. 368–372. Rez. : Adler, Karl. *Zur Entwicklungslehre und Dogmatik des Gesellschaftsrechts.* Berlin : Carl Heymann's Verl., 1895. [VI, 153 S.].

IN 23751 16F1

23. **Der schweizerische** Erbrechtsentwurf. *Archiv für soziale Gesetzgebung und Statistik.* 1896. Bd. 9. S. 174–186.

IN 244283 14V1

1897

24. [**Rezension**]. *Kritische Vierteljahresschrift für Gesetzgebung und Rechtswissenschaft.* 1897. 3. F., Bd. 3, Heft 3/4 (der ganzen F. Bd. 39). S. 421–428. Rez. : Pfaff, Ivo. *Zur Lehre vom sogenannten in fraudem legis agere.* Wien : Manz'sche k. u. k. Hof.-Verl. und Univ.-Buchh., 1892. VI, 170 S. ; Neff, Paul. *Beiträge zur Lehre von der fraus legi facta in den Digesten.* Berlin : A. L. Prager, 1895. X, 75 S.

IN 23910 16O2

1899

25. [**Rezension**]. *Juristisches Litteraturblatt.* 1899. 15. Aug. (Nr. 107 ; Bd. 11, Nr. 7). S. 161–162. Rez. : Isay, Hermann. "Die Willenserklärung im Thatbestande des Rechtsgeschäfts nach dem Bürgerlichen Gesetzbuch für das Deutsche Reich." In *Abhandlungen zum Privatrecht und Civilprozess des Deutschen Reiches : in zwanglosen Heften,* hrsg. Otto Fischer. Jena : Gustav Fischer, 1899. Bd. 2, Heft 2. VIII, 110 S.

IN 19797 86B2

26. **Das zwingende** und nichtzwingende Recht im Bürgerlichen Gesetzbuch für das Deutsche Reich. In *Abhandlungen zum Privatrecht und Civilprozess des Deutschen Reiches : in zwanglosen Heften,* hrsg. Otto Fischer. Jena : Gustav Fischer, 1899. Bd. 2, Heft 4. VII, 278 S.

IN 24114 16B1

Rez. : Hölder, E. [Rezension]. *Kritische Vierteljahresschrift für Gesetzgebung und Rechtswissenschaft.* 1900. 3. F., Bd. 6, Heft 3/4 (der ganzen F. Bd. 42). S. 477–502.

IN 18840 16O2

Oertmann, Paul. [Rezension]. *Juristisches Litteraturblatt.* 1899. 1. Nov. (Nr. 109 ; Bd. 11, Nr. 8). S. 210–211.

IN 19797 86B2

[Rezension]. *Literarisches Centralblatt für Deutschland.* 1900. 20. Oct. (Nr. 42, Jg. 51). S. 1731–1732. Die Unterschrift : O....

IN 36309 85

1900

27. **Arbeitende** Damen. *Dokumente der Frauen.* 1900. 1. Juli (Nr. 7, Bd. 3). S. 227–236.

28. **Aus guter** Familie. *Czernowitzer Zeitung.* 1900. 8. Apr. (Nr. 81, Jg. 33). S. 1–3.

IN 1928 90A1

29. **Eine Hochschule** für Gesellschaftswissenschaften : Denkschrift. Wien : Selbstverl. des Verf., [1900]. 21 S. Als Manuskript gedruckt!

30. **[Rezension]**. *Zeitschrift für das Privat- und öffentliche Recht der Gegenwart.* 1900. Bd. 27. S. 509–511. Rez. : Bloch, Alfred. *Zur Anwendung des Ratengesetzes. Die Mittel der Civilprocessordnung zur Bekämpfung des illegitimen Ratenhandels.* Wien : Manz'sche k. u. k. Hof.-Verl. und Univ.-Buchh., 1899. S.-Abdr. aus : *Allgemeine österreichische Gerichts-Zeitung.*

IN 23755 16F1

31. **[Rezension]**. *Ibidem.* 1900. Bd. 27. S. 509–511. Rez. : Lazarus, Johann. *Das Recht der Abzahlungsgeschäfte. Nach geltendem Recht und nach dem bürgerlichen Gesetzbuch. Nach geltendem Recht und nach dem bürgerlichen Gesetzbuch.* Berlin : Otto Liebmann, 1898.

IN 23755 16F1

1902

32. **Die Anfänge** der Frauenfrage : [Vortragsbericht]. *Bukowinaer Rundschau.* 1902. 25. Febr. (Nr. 3850, Jg. 21). S. 3.

IN 2089 90A13

33. **Beiträge** zur Theorie der Rechtsquellen. Berlin : Carl Heymanns Verl., 1902. Theil 1, *"Das ius civile, ius publicum, ius privatum."* VII, 258 S.

IN 185745aN66

Rez. : Meyer H. [Rezension]. *Das Recht : Rundschau für den deutschen Juristenstand.* 1902. 10. Nov. (Nr. 21, Jg. 6). S. 537.

IN 3099 86A8

[Rezension]. *Literarisches Centralblatt für Deutschland.* 1903. 21. März (Nr. 12, Jg. 54). S. 421–423.

IN 36333 85

1903

34. **Freie** Rechtsfindung und freie Rechtswissenschaft : Vortrag, gehalten in der juristischen Gesellschaft in Wien am 4. März 1903. Leipzig : C. L. Hirschfeld, 1903. VI, 40 S.

IN 109144 19C13

35. **[Rezension]**. *Juristisches Litteraturblatt.* 1903. 14. März (Nr. 143 ; Bd. 15, Nr. 3). S. 62–63. Rez. : Goldschmidt, L. *Vermischte Schriften.* Hrsg., Einl. von Hermann Veit Simon. Berlin : J. Guttentag, 1901. Bd. 1. XVI, 681 S. ; Bd. 2. II, 535 S.

IN 19787 86B2

1904

36. **Die Anfänge** des testamentum per Aes et Libram. In *Atti del Congresso internazionale di scienze storiche, Roma, Aprilie 1–9, 1903.* Roma : Tip. della R. Accademia dei Lincei, 1904. Vol. 9, *"Atti della sezione V: Storia del diritto. Storia delle scienze economiche e sociali."* S. 329–337.

37. **Recht** und Prätor : eine Entgegnung. Wien : Alfred Hölder, 1904. 34 S. ; *Zeitschrift für das Privat- und öffentliche Recht der Gegenwart.* 1904. Bd. 31. S. 331–364.

IN 23758 16F1

38. **Ulpians** ΌΥΣΙΑ Theorie. Prato : Tip. Giachetti, 1904. 12 S. S.-Abdr. aus : *Studi in onore di Vittorio Scialoja.*

IN 271108 20

1905

39. **Die Anfänge** des testamentum per aes et libram : Bericht erstattet dem Historikercongress in Rom (Rechtshistorische Abtheilung) 1903. *Zeitschrift für vergleichende Rechtswissenschaft.* 1905. Bd. 17. S. 99–109.

IN 24236 16U1

40. **Griechische** Eindrücke. *Czernowitzer Allgemeine Zeitung.* 1905. 22. Okt. (Nr. 543). S. 1–2 ; 24. Okt. (Nr. 544). S. 1–2 ; 25. Okt. (Nr. 545). S. 1–2 ; 26. Okt. (Nr. 546). S. 1–2 ; 27. Okt. (Nr. 547). S. 1–2 ; 28. Okt. (Nr. 548). S. 1–2 ; *Neue Freie Presse.* 1905. 15. Aug. (Nr. 14719). S. 25–30.

IN 90

41. **Die Krise** im Gemeinderate. *Ibidem.* 1905. 10. Dez. (Nr. 582). S. 1–2.

IN 90

42. **Recht** und Prätor : eine Entgegnung. *Zeitschrift für das Privat- und öffentliche Recht der Gegenwart.* 1905. Bd. 32. S. 599–611.

IN 23758 16F1

43. **Vor Allem** erkläreersich… : [Stellungnahme zur geplanten Konzipientensperre : Bericht]. *Czernowitzer Tagblatt.* 1905. 24. Dez. (Nr. 869, Jg. 3). S. 8.

IN 1965 90A45

44. **Ulpians** οὐσία-Theorie. *Österreichische Richter-Zeitung.* 1905. 10. März (Nr. 5, Jg. 2). S. 129–135.

IN 2944 86B21

45. **Volkstümliche** Hochschulkurse. *Czernowitzer Allgemeine Zeitung.* 1905. 24. Dez. (Nr. 594). S. 2–3.

IN 90

1906

46. **Anton Menger**. 1906. Stuttgart : Adolf Bonz & Comp., [1906]. 34 S. S.-Abdr. aus : *Süddeutsche Monatshefte.* 1906. Jg. 3, Heft 9 (Sept.) ; *Czernowitzer Tagblatt.* 1906. 25. Dez. (Nr. 1166, Jg. 4). S. 6 ; *Neues Frauenleben.* 1906. Febr. (Nr. 2, Jg. 18). S. 1–4 ; *Süddeutsche Monatshefte.* 1906. Jg. 3, Bd. 2, Heft 9 (Sept.). S. 285–318.

IN 221370 14aE71

IN 1967 90A45

47. **Anton Menger** : [Vortrag]. *Czernowitzer Allgemeine Zeitung.* 1906. 18. Febr. (Nr. 635). S. 4.

IN 90

48. **Die freie** Rechtsfindung. *Das Recht : volkstümliche Zeitschrift für österreichisches Rechtsleben.* 1906. Jg. 4/5. S. 35–41.

49. **Internationales** Privatrecht. *Deutsche Rundschau.* 1906. Jg. 32, Bd. 126 (März). S. 419–433.

IN 20397 84C1

50. [**Die Neugestaltung** des Vertragsrechtes : Vortragsbericht]. *Czernowitzer Allgemeine Zeitung.* 1906. 11. Jänner (Nr. 605). S. 3–4 ; *Czernowitzer Tagblatt.* 1906. 9. Jänner (Nr. 878, Jg. 4). S. 4–5.

IN 1966 90A45

51. **Das siebente** Gebot : [betr. die Entwendung des sog. Baubuches, das der Kontrolle der Handwerker bei der Errichtung des Czernowitzer Theaters dient]. *Czernowitzer Allgemeine Zeitung.* 1906. 7. März (Nr. 649). S. 3 ; 14. März (Nr. 655). S. 3.

IN 90

52. **Soziologie** und Jurisprudenz. *Österreichische Richter-Zeitung.* 1906. 10. März (Nr. 3, Jg. 3). S. 57–72 ; *Die Zukunft.* 1906. 10. Febr., Bd. 54. S. 231–240.

IN 32708 86B21

IN 3934 84E5

53. **Die Tatsachen** des Gewohnheitsrechts : Inaugurationsrede, gehalten am 2. Dezember 1906. In *Die feierliche Inauguration des Rectors der k. k. Franz-Josephs-Universität in Czernowitz für das Studienjahr 1906/1907.* Czernowitz : Selbstverl. der k. k. Universität, 1906. S. 25–66 ; *Czernowitzer Zeitung.* 1906. 8. Dez. (Nr. 281, Jg. 41). S. 1–2 ; 11. Dez. (Nr. 282, Jg. 41). S. 1–2 ; 13. Dez. (Nr. 284, Jg. 41). S. 1–2.

IN 193510 90K126

IN 1941 90A1

Rez. : Brie. [Rezension]. *Zeitschrift für das Gesamte Handelsrecht und Konkursrecht.* 1908. Bd. 61 (3. F. Bd. 2). S. 499–500.

IN 27275 10D1

54. **Die Überfüllung** der gelehrten Berufe. *Bukowiner Beamten-Zeitung.* 1906. 28. Okt. (Nr. 18, Jg. 1). S. 1–3 ; 4. Nov. (Nr. 19, Jg. 1). S. 1–4.

IN 2164 90A60

55. **Die Zukunft** des Römischen Rechtsunterrichts in Österreich. *Czernowitzer Allgemeine Zeitung.* 1906. 6. Apr. (Nr. 675). S. 1–2 ; 7. Apr. (Nr. 676). S. 1–2 ; *Österreichische Rundschau.* 1906. Bd. 6, Heft 74 (März). S. 386–392.

IN 22936 81B22

1907

56. **Bericht** über das Studienjahr 1906/1907 : erstattet am 9. Dezember 1907 von dem abtretenden Rektor. In *Die feierliche Inauguration des Rectors der k. k. Franz-Josephs-Universität in Czernowitz für das Studienjahr 1907/1908.* Czernowitz : Selbstverl. der k. k. Universität, 1907. S. 3–14.

IN 193513 90K126

57. **Das Leben** als Gesetzgeber. *Czernowitzer Tagblatt.* 1907. 1. Aug. (Nr. 1341, Jg. 5). S. 1–2 ; 8. Aug. (Nr. 1347, Jg. 5). S. 1–2 ; *Neues Wiener Tagblatt.* 1907. 5. Aug. (Nr. 212, Jg. 41). S. 1–2.

IN 1969 90A45

58. **Ein neues** Wein- und Bierverschleissgesetz. *Czernowitzer Allgemeine Zeitung.* 1907. 22. Okt. (Nr. 1134). S. 4.

IN 90

59. **Der Raimundtheaterfall** (zur ultra vires-Lehre bei der juristischen Person). *Das Recht : volkstümliche Zeitschrift für österreichisches Rechtsleben.* 1907/1908. Jg. 6/7. S. 225–229.

60. **[Rezension]**. *Juristisches Literaturblatt.* 1907. 15. Okt. (Nr. 188 ; Bd. 19, Nr. 8). S. 187. Rez. : Mauczka, Josef. *Altes Recht im Volksbewusstsein.* Wien : Manz'sche k. u. k. Hof-Verl. und Univ.-Buchh., 1907. 21 S. S.-Abdr. aus : *Allgemeine österreichische Gerichts-Zeitung.* 1907. Jg. 58.

IN 19792 86B2

61. **Statistisches** zur Universitätsrede des Grafen Thun. *Czernowitzer Allgemeine Zeitung.* 1907. 5. Dez. (Nr. 1171). S. 1–2 ; *Czernowitzer Tagblatt.* 1907. 5. Dez. (Nr. 1447, Jg. 5). S. 1–2 ; *Neue Freie Presse.* 1907. 3. Dez. (Nr. 15548). S. 1–2.

IN 1969 90A45

62. **Die Tatsachen** des Gewohnheitsrechts : Inaugurationsrede, gehalten am 2. Dez. 1906. Leipzig ; Wien : Franz Deuticke, 1907. 42 S.

IN 332517

Rez. : Buchka v. [Rezension]. *Deutsche Juristen-Zeitung.* 1907. 15. Sept. (Nr. 18, Jg. 12). S. 1033.

IN 19883 86B1

Hedemann, J. W. [Rezension]. *Archiv für Bürgerliches Recht.* 1908. Bd. 31. S. 307–308.

IN 24277 16U2

Kantorowicz, Hermann U. [Rezension]. *Jahrbuch für Gesetzgebung, Verwaltung und Volkswirtschaft im Deutschen Reich.* 1908. Jg. 32, Heft 3. S. 351–352.

IN 22494 16D1

63. **Zur Frage** der juristischen Person : Vortrag, gehalten in der Juristisch-staatswissenschaftlichen Gesellschaft in Czernowitz : Nach einer stenographischen Aufnahme. Czernowitz, 1907. 20 S. S.-Abdr. aus : *Österreichische Richter-Zeitung.* 1907. 1. Juni (Nr. 5, Jg. 4). S. 115–127.

IN 19895 86B21

1908

64. **Eine Arbeit** Gurschners in Czernowitz : [über den Wiener Bildhauer Gustav Gurschner]. *Czernowitzer Allgemeine Zeitung.* 1908. 20. März (Nr. 1258). S. 3.

IN 90

65. **Les tendances** actuelles du droit international privé. Trad. de l'allemand Robert Caillemer. *Revue de droit international privé et*

de droit pénal international. 1908. A. 4, № 6 (nov./déc.). S. 902–924. Extr. de la : *Deutsche Rundschau.* 1906. März (Bd. 126). S. 419–433.

IN 20397 84C1

66. [**Zivilrechtspflege** in England : Vortragsberichte]. *Czernowitzer Allgemeine Zeitung.* 1908. 25. Nov. (Nr. 1462). S. 4.

IN 90

1909

67. **Die Aufgaben** der Sozialpolitik im österr. Osten, insbesondere in der Bukowina : mit besonderer Beleuchtung der Juden- und Bauernfrage : Vortrag, gehalten im Sozialwissenschaftlichen Akadem. Vereine an der Czernowitzer Universität im Wintersemester 1908/9. Czernowitz : Im Selbstverl. des Vereines, 1909. 31 S. (*Vorträge und Abhadlungen,* hrsg. vom Sozialwissen schaftlichen akademischen Vereine in Czernowitz ; Nr. 1).

IN 251035 86C118

Rez. : Asenstorfer. [Rezension]. *Allgemeines Literaturblatt.* 1910. 31. Mai (Nr. 10, Jg. 19). S. 312.

IN 1849 22J3

Lederer. [Rezension]. *Archiv für Sozialwissenschaft und Sozialpolitik.* 1910. Bd. 30. S. 901.

IN 244304 14V1

Schiff, W. [Rezension]. *Zeitschrift für Volkswirtschaft, Socialpolitik und Verwaltung.* 1910. Bd. 19. S. 211–212.

IN 244230 14R8

68. **Bericht** über eine englische Studienreise : [Protokoll eines Vortrags vor der Wiener Juristischen Gesellschaft. (Redner hat fünf Monate in England verbracht und hierbei ausschliesslich die englische Zivilrechtspflege studiert) Redner hat fünf Monate in England verbracht und hierbei ausschliesslich die englische Zivilrechtspflege studiert)]. *Allgemeine österreichische Gerichts-Zeitung.* 1909. Jg. 60. S. 94–95.

IN 1221 16R1

69. **Der englische** Richter. *Neues Wiener Tagblatt.* 1909. 27. Febr. (Nr. 58, Jg. 43). S. 7.

IN 93

70. [**Das festländische** und das englische System der Altersfürsorge : Vortragsberichte]. *Czernowitzer Allgemeine Zeitung.* 1909. 19. Mai

(Nr. 1603). S. 4 ; *Bukowinaer Post.* 1909. 23. Mai (Nr. 2386, Jg. 16). S. 5.

IN 2063 90J26

71. **Die Grabrede** auf die Turia. [Wien : Buchdruck. Holzwarth & Berger, 1909]. 6 S. Sep.-Abdr. aus : *Neues Frauenleben.* 1909. Okt. [(Nr. 10, Jg.21)] ; *Czernowitzer Zeitung.* 1909. 31. Okt. (Nr. 249, Jg. 44). S. 1–4.

IN 646 90

IN 1947 90A1

72. **The old-age** pension scheme. *The Economic Review.* 1909. Vol. 19, Jan. pp. 49–53.

73. **Die Rechtsfähigkeit.** In *Das Recht : Sammlung von Abhandlungen für Juristen und Laien,* hrsg. von Franz Kobler. Berlin : Puttkammer & Mühlbrecht, 1909. Bd. 1. XVI, 106 S.

IN 30080 86C120

Rez. : Biermann. [Rezension]. *Zentralblatt für Rechtswissenschaft.* 1910. Apr. (2. R. Bd. 4, Heft 7 ; ganzen R. Bd. 29). S. 112–113.

IN 2932 86C1

Bovensiepen. [Rezension]. *Juristisches Literaturblatt.* 1910. 15. Febr. (Nr. 212 ; Bd. 22, Nr. 2). S. 44–45.

IN 19799 86B2

Dressler, Oskar. [Rezension]. *Allgemeines Literaturblatt.* 1912. 31. Okt. (Nr. 20, Jg. 21). S. 632.

IN 1839 22J3

Pollak. [Rezension]. *Rheinische Zeitschrift für Zivil- und Prozessrecht.* 1911. Jg. 3. S. 150–151.

IN 3237 86C119

[Rezension]. *Archiv für Sozialwissenschaft und Sozialpolitik.* 1910. Bd. 30. S. 278.

IN 244304 14V1

[Rezension]. *Österreichisches Zentralblatt für die juristische Praxis.* 1910. Bd. 27, *"1909."* S. 907.

IN 241269 16E2

74. **Reglementierung** oder Abolition? (Zur Bekämpfung der Geschlechtskrankheiten bei Prostituierten). *Das Recht : volkstümliche Zeitschrift für österreichisches Rechtsleben.* 1908/1909. Jg. 6/7. S. 353–360.

75. **Les tendances** actuelles du droit international privé. Trad. de l'allemand par Robert Caillemer. Paris : L. Larose & L. Tenin, 1909. 27 p.

1910

76. **Frauenberufe** : Feuilleton. *Czernowitzer Zeitung*. 1910. 6. Jänner (Nr. 4, Jg. 45). S. 1–2 ; 8. Jänner (Nr. 5, Jg. 45). S. 1–2 ; 9. Jänner (Nr. 6, Jg. 45). S. 1–2.

IN 1948 90A1

77. **Lebendes** Recht : [Vortragsbericht]. *Czernowitzer Tagblatt*. 1910. 2. März (Nr. 2111, Jg. 8). S. 3–4. Die Unterschrift : Ph. Z.

IN 1974 90A45

78. **Die Klage** gegen den Herrn Baudirektor. *Czernowitzer Allgemeine Zeitung*. 1910. 16. Okt. (Nr. 2025). S. 1.

IN 90

1911

79. **Ein Institut** für lebendes Recht. *Juristische Blätter*. 1911. 14. Mai (Nr. 20). S. 229–231 ; 21. Mai (Nr. 20). S. 241–244.

IN 2841 86A6

80. **Die Erforschung** des lebendes Rechts. *Jahrbuch für Gesetzgebung, Verwaltung und Volkswirtschaft im Deutschen Reich*. 1911. Jg. 35, Heft l. S. 129–147.

IN 22529 16D1

1912

81. **Die Entstaatlichung** der Kollegiengelder. *Czernowitzer Tagblatt*. 1912. 29. Mai (Nr. 2773, Jg. 10). S. 1–2 ; *Neues Wiener Tagblatt*. 1912. 25. Mai (Nr. 142, Jg. 46). S. 1–2.

IN 1978 90A45

82. **Eskorte**: [über die "Eskorte" durch uniformierte Polizisten bei der Verhaftung prostitutionsverdächtiger Personen : Notizen]. *Czernowitzer Allgemeine Zeitung*. 1912. 28. Aug. (Nr. 2578). S. 4.

IN 90

83. **Konzert** Yvette Guilbert : Feuilleton. *Czernowitzer Zeitung*. 1912. 13. Febr. (Nr. 34, Jg. 47). S. 1–2.

IN 1952 90A1

84. **Das lebende** Recht der Völker der Bukowina. *Recht und Wirtschaft*. 1912. Jg. 1. S. 273–279, 322–324.

85. **Die Neuordnung** der Gerichtsverfassung. *Deutsche Richterzeitung.* 1912. 1. Juni (Nr. 11, Jg. 4). S. 436–465 ; 1. Juli (Nr. 13, Jg. 4). S. 563.

IN 267 86B38

86. **Die Überlastung** des Obersten Gerichtshofes. *Mitteilungen der Vereinigung der österreichischen Richter.* 1912. 1. Jänner (Nr. 5, Jg. 5). S. 5–15.

IN 3261 86A20

87. **Der verweigerte** Koupeeschlüssel. *Mährisches Tagblatt.* 1912. 21. Mai (Nr. 115, Jg. 33). S. 1–3.

88. **Was kann** geschehen, um bei der Ausbildung (vor oder nach Abschluß des Universitätsstudiums) das Verständnis des Juristen für psychologische, wirtschaftliche und soziologische Fragen in erhöhtem Maße zu fördern? : Gutachten über die Frage. In *Verhandlungen des 31. Deutschen Juristentages,* hrsg. von dem Schriftführer-Amt der Ständigen Deputation. Berlin : F. Guttentag, 1912. Bd. 2, "*Gutachten.*" S. 200–220.

IN 16W1

1913

89. [**Gedenkrede** für Joseph Unger]. *Czernowitzer Allgemeine Zeitung.* 1913. 1. Juni (Nr. 3016). S. 5.

IN 90

90. **Grundlegung** der Soziologie des Rechts. München ; Leipzig : Duncker & Humblot, 1913. VI, 409 S.

Rez. : Кельзен, Ганс. Основоположение социологии права. В Эрлих, Ойген. *Осново положение социологии права,* пер. с нем. М. В. Антонов. Санкт-Петербург. : Унив. издат. консорциум, 2011. С. 595–638. [Review: Kelsen, Hans. Foundations of the Sociology of Law. In Ehrlich, Eugen. *Foundations of the Sociology of Law,* translated from German to Russian by M. V. Antonov. Saint Petersburg : University Publishing Consortium, 2011. pp. 595–638.]

Butte, George C. [Rezension]. *The American Journal of International Law.* 1915. Vol. 9, No. 2 (Apr.). pp. 569–572.

Davidsohn, Joseph. [Rezension]. *National økonomisk tidsskrift.* 1914. Bd. 52. S. 302–306.

Kelsen, Hans. "Eine Grundlegung der Rechtssoziologie." *Archiv für Sozialwissenschaft und Sozialpolitik.* 1915. Bd. 39. S. 839–876.

IN 244313 14V1

Liepmann, Moritz. [Rezension]. *Weltwirtschaftliches Archiv.* 1918. Bd. 13. S. 75–83.

IN 14

Neukamp. [Rezension]. *Zeitschrift für die gesamte Staatswissenschaft.* 1917. Jg. 73, Heft 1/2. S. 226–232.

IN 16P1

Renner, Karl. [Rezension]. *Archiv für Sozialwissenschaft und Sozialpolitik.* 1930. Bd. 63. S. 185–187.

IN 244335 14V1

[Rezension]. *Giornale degli Economisti e Rivista di Statistica. Serie terza.* 1914. Vol. 48 (a. 25, febbr.). p. 160.

[Rezension]. *Literarisches Zentralblatt für Deutschland.* 1915. 4. Dez. (Nr. 49, Jg. 66). S. 1228–1229.

IN 36370 85

Wenger, L. [Rezension]. *Kritische Vierteljahresschrift für Gesetzgebung und Rechtswissenschaft.* 1914. 3. F., Bd. 16, Heft 4 (der ganzen F. Bd. 52). S. 502–518.

IN 16O2

Wolf, Erik. [Rezension]. *Deutsche Literaturzeitung.* 1929. 15. Juni (Heft 24, N. F. Jg. 6). S. 1162–1165.

IN 1806 22J3

91. **Das lebende** Recht der Völker der Bukowina : Fragebogen für das Seminar für lebendes Rechtmit Einlietung. Czernowitz: Allg. Druck., 1913. 16 S.

92. **Nationalität** und Rasse : [Vortragsbericht]. *Czernowitzer Allgemeine Zeitung.* 1913. 7. Dez. (Nr. 3334). S. 4.

IN 90

93. **Der praktische** Rechtsbegriff : [einleitender Abschnitt des Werkes "Grundlegung der Soziologie des Rechts"]. In *Festschrift für Ernst Zitelmann : zu seinem 60. Geburtstage,* überreicht von Verehrern und Schülern. München ; Leipzig : Duncker & Humblot, 1913. S. 1–20.

IN 22606 16C7

94. **Soziologie** des Rechts. *Die Geisteswissenschaften.* 1913/14. Jg. 1. S. 202–205, 230–234.

1914

95. **Ein Abschiedswort** : [an Theaterdirektor Marius Faber]. *Czernowitzer Allgemeine Zeitung.* 1914. 21. Juli (Nr. 3501). S. 3.

IN 90

96. **Franz Klein** : anlässlich des sechzigsten Geburtstages. *Czernowitzer Zeitung.* 1914. 26. Apr. (Nr. 75, Jg. 49). S. 4–5 ; *Neue Freie Presse.* 1914. 24. Apr. (Nr. 17838). S. 3–4.

IN 1956 90A1

97. **Goudy, Henry.** *Dreiteiligkeit im römischen Recht,* aus dem engl. übertr. von Eugen Ehrlich. München ; Leipzig : Duncker & Humblot, 1914. VI, 71 S.

Rez. : Denzler. [Rezension]. *Archiv des öffentlichen Rechts.* 1918. Bd. 38, Heft 2/4. S. 419–421.

IN 16U7

98. **Neugestaltung** der Gerichtsverfassung : [Vortragsbericht]. *Neue Freie Presse.* 1914. 29. März (Nr. 17813). S. 7.

99. **Soziologie** des Rechts. *Czernowitzer Tagblatt.* 1914. l. Jänner (Nr. 3337, Jg. 12). S. 7–8 ; 4. Jänner (Nr. 3339, Jg. 12). S. 7–8.

IN 1984 90A45

100. **Zur Soziologie** des Rechts : [Entgegnung auf eine Rezension von Friedrich Hahn]. *Der Kampf : Sozialdemokratische Monatsschrift.* 1914. 1. Juli (Heft 10, Jg. 7). S. 461–463.

Response by E. Ehrlich to the article written by Friedrich Hahn: Hahn, Friedrich. "Eine Soziologie des Rechts." *Der Kampf : Sozialdemokratische Monats schrift.* 1914. 1. Juni (Heft 9, Jg. 7). S. 401–407.

IN 371102 14T32

1915

101. **Englische** Rechtspflege. *Österreichische Richter-Zeitung.* 1915. Jg. 8. S. 77–79.

IN 86B21

102. **Die Gesellschaft**, der Staat und ihre Ordnung. [S. l. : s. n., 1915. 23 S. Als Manuskript gedruckt].

1916

103. **Die Aufgaben** der Sozialpolitik im österreichischen Osten (Juden- und Bauernfrage). 4. Aufl. München ; Leipzig : Duncker & Humblot, 1916. 48 S. (*Schriften des Sozialwissen schaftlichen Akademischen Vereins in Czernowitz* ; Heft l).

Rez. : Feuchtwanger, Sigbert. "Sozialpolitik und die Ostjudenfrage." *Neue Jüdische Monatshefte.* 1916. 25. Nov. (Heft 4, Jg. 1). S. 112–114.

104. **Eine Hochschule** für Gesellschaftswissenschaften: Denkschrift. Wien: Selbstverl. des Verf., [1916]. 21 S.

Rez.: Ein aufsehenerregendes Werk des Czernowitzer Universitätsprofessors Ehrlich: Vorschlag zum Gründung einer Hochschule für Gesell schaftswissenschaft. *Czernowitzer Tagblatt.* 1916. 16. März (Nr. 3799, Jg. 14). S. 3.

IN 1988 90A45

105. **Entgegnung.** *Archiv für Sozialwissenschaft und Sozialpolitik.* 1916. Bd. 41. S. 844–849.

Dispute of E. Ehrlich with H. Kelsen. Response by E. Ehrlich to the critical review written by H. Kelsen: Kelsen, Hans. "Eine Grundlegungder Rechtssoziologie." *Archiv für Sozialwissenschaft und Sozialpolitik.* 1915. Bd. 39. S. 839–876.

IN 244315 14V1

106. **Montesquieu** and Sociological Jurisprudence. *Harvard Law Review.* 1916. Vol. 29, № 6 (Apr.). pp. 582–600.

107. **Das Recht** und die Gesellschaft. *Zeitschrift für Notariat und freiwillige Gerichtsbarkeit in Österreich.* 1916. Jg. 58. S. 208–210.

IN 16A4

108. **Die Rechtsvereinheitlichung** zwischen dem Deutschen Reiche und der Monarchie: die Anschauungen hervorragender Juristen: [E. Ehrlich. Das Zivilrecht: Grund sätzliches]. *Neues Wiener Tagblatt.* 1916. 9. Apr. (Nr. 99, Jg. 50). S. 8–9.

IN 93

109. **Replik.** *Archiv für Sozialwissenschaft und Sozialpolitik.* 1916/1917. Bd. 42. S. 609–610.

Dispute of E. Ehrlich with H. Kelsen. Response by E. Ehrlich to: Kelsen, Hans. "Eine Grundlegung der Rechtssoziologie." *Archiv für Sozialwissenschaft und Sozialpolitik.* 1915. Bd. 39. S. 839–876, *and also to:* Kelsen, Hans. "Replik." *Archiv für Sozialwissenschaft und Sozialpolitik.* 1916. Bd. 41. S. 850–853.

IN 244315 14V1

1917

110. **Judicial** Freedom of Decision: Its Principles and Objects. In *Science of Legal Method: Select Essays by Various Authors,* transl. by Ernest Bruncken, and Layton B. Register; with introd. by Henry N. Sheldon, and John W. Salmond. Boston: The Boston Book Co., 1917. pp. 47–84. (*The Modern Legal Philosophy Series*; Vol. 9).

111. **Die juristische** Logik. *Archiv für die civilistische Praxis.* 1917. Bd. 115. Heft 2/3. S. 125–439.

IN 16Z1

112. **Schumpeter, Josef,** Josef Mauczka, und Eugen Ehrlich. "Der Kampf gegen die Czernowitzer Universität." *Bukowiner Bote.* 1917. 24. Jänner (Nr. 16). S. 13–14. *Beilage der Bohemia,* Nr. 22.

IN 90

113. **The National** Problems in Austria. In *International Congress for the study of the principles of a durable peace (Berne, 1916).* The Hague : Martinus Nijhoff, 1917. 45 p.

114. **Die richterliche** Rechtsfindung auf Grund des Rechtssatzes. Vier Stücke aus dem in Vorbereitung begriffenen Werke : Theorie der richterlichen Rechtsfindung. *Jherings Jahrbücher für die Dogmatik des bürgerlichen Rechts.* 1917. Bd. 67 (2. F. Bd. 31). S. 1–80.

IN 24082 16S3

1918

115. **Die Amnestie.** *Der Friede.* 1918. 1. März (Heft 6, Bd. 1). S. 126–127.

116. **Die historischen** Grundlagen der Friedensbewegung. *Der Friede.* 1918. Bd. 1. S. 467–469.

117. **Die juristische** Logik. Tübingen : J. C. B. Mohr (Paul Siebeck), 1918. VIII, 337 S.

Rez. : Hellwig, Albert. [Rezension]. *Literarisches Zentralblatt für Deutschland.* 1919. 23. Okt. (Nr. 43, Jg. 70). S. 833–834.

IN 36319 85

118. **Quelques** aspects de la question nationale autrichienne, avec une lettre de M. Georges Brandès. Genève : Atar, [1918]. 123 p.

119. **Die sittlichen** Voraussetzungen der Friedensbewegung. *Der Friede.* 1918. Bd. 1. S. 515–517, 541–543.

1919

120. **Die bewährte** Lehre und Überlieferung (Art. 1 ZGB) : [Leitgedanken eines Referats Ehrlichs vor dem Zürcher Juristenverein, aufgez. von H. Schmid]. *Schweizerische Juristen-Zeitung.* 1919/1920. Nr. 16. S. 225–226.

121. **Das Kunstwerk** und die Umwelt. Zur Soziologie der Kunst. *Das neue Europa.* 1919. Jg. 5, Nr. 10/11. S. 70–72.

122. **Die Schuldfrage.** *Ibidem.* 1919. Jg. 5, Nr. 4. S. 14–17.

123. **Von der Zukunft** des Völkerbundes. *Die Friedens-Warte.* 1919. Mai, Jg. 21. S. 89–93.

1920

124. **Bismarck** und der Weltkrieg. Zürich: Orell Füssli, 1920. 32 S. S.-Abdr. aus : *Neuen Schweizer Zeitung.*

125. **Die Valutaschwierigkeiten** der Schweiz. *Schweizerische Zeitschrift für Volkswirtschaft und Sozialpolitik.* 1920. Jg. 26, Bd. 1. S. 321–339, 353–369.

IN 18468 14Z7

1921

126. **Judicial** Freedom of Decision: Its Principles and Objects. In *Science of Legal Method: Select Essays by Various Authors,* transl. by Ernest Bruncken, and Layton B. Register ; with introd. by Henry N. Sheldon, and John W. Salmond. New York: The Macmillan Co., 1921. pp. 47–84. *(The Modern Legal Philosophy Series).*

127. **Memoriomania** Generalibor. *Arhiva pentru ştiinţa şi reforma sociala.* 1921. An. 3. pp. 369–383.

IN 86C191

128. **Sfârşitul** unei mari impărăţii. Bucureşti : Inst. de ed. "Reforma sociala", 1921. 46 S. Extr. din : *Arhiva pentru ştiinţa şi reforma sociala.* 1921. An. 3. pp. 80–124.

IN 290339

1922

129. **Karl Marx** şichestia socială. *Arhiva pentru ştiinţa şi reforma sociala.* 1922. An. 4. pp. 651–658.

IN 86C191

130. **La Sociologia** del Diritto. *Rivista internazionale di filosofia del diritto.* 1922. A. 2. pp. 96–110.

131. **The Sociology** of Law, transl. Nathan Isaacs. *Harvard Law Review.* 1922. Vol. 36, No. 2 (Dec.). pp. 130–145.

1925

132. **Die juristische** Logik. 2., photomech. gedr. Aufl. Tübingen: J. C. B. Mohr (Paul Siebeck), 1925. VIII, 337 S.

IN 292116

Rez. : [Rezension]. *Annalen der Philosophie und philosophischen Kritik.* 1926. Bd. 5, Heft 8. S. 247–248. Die Unterschrift : B.

1929

133. **Grundlegung** der Soziologie des Rechts. Unveränd. Neudr. (Manuldr.) der 1. Aufl. 1913. München ; Leipzig : Duncker & Humblot, 1929. IV, 409 S.

IN 291377

Rez. : Darmstaedter, Friedrich. [Rezension]. *Archiv für Rechts- und Wirtschaftsphilosophie.* 1929. Bd. 23, Heft 1 (Okt.). S. 97.

IN 86C128

Kraft, Julius. [Rezension]. *Zeitschrift für die gesamte Staatswissenschaft.* 1929. Jg. 87. S. 156–157.

IN 16P1

[Rezension]. *The American Journal of Sociology.* 1929. Vol. 35, Nr. 1 (Juli). pp. 159–160.

Wolf, Erik. [Rezension]. *Deutsche Literaturzeitung.* 1929. 15. Juni (Heft 24, N. F. Jg. 6). S. 1162–1165.

IN 1806 22J3

1936

134. **Fundamental** Principles of the Sociology of Law. Transl. by Walter L. Moll ; with an introd. by Roscoe Pound. Cambridge : Harvard University Press ; London : Oxford University Press, 1936. XXXVI, 541 p. (*Harvard studies in jurisprudence* ; vol. 5).

Rez. : Ginsberg, Morris. [Rezension]. *The Modern Law Review.* 1937. Vol. 1, Nr. 2 (Sept.). pp. 169–171.

Husserl, Gerhart. [Rezension]. *The University of Chicago Law Review.* 1938. Vol. 5, Nr. 2 (Febr.). pp. 330–340.

Kidd, A. M. [Rezension]. *Columbia Law Review.* 1938. Vol. 38, No. 2 (Febr.). pp. 383–386.

Neumann, Franz. [Rezension]. *The American Journal of Sociology.* 1937. Vol. 43, Nr. 2 (Sept.). pp. 351–353.

Simpson, Sidney Post. [Rezension]. *Harvard Law Review.* 1937. Vol. 51, No. 1 (Nov.). pp. 190–194.

1962

135. **Fundamental** Principles of the Sociology of Law. Transl. by Walter L. Moll ; with an introd. by Roscoe Pound. New York : Russell & Russell, 1962. 541 p.

1966

136. **Die juristische** Logik. Aalen : Scientia-Verl., 1966. VII, 337 S. Neudr. der 2. Aufl. Tubingen 1925.

137. **Law** and the Inner Order of Social Associations. In *The nature of law : readings in legal philosophy,* ed. by Martin P. Golding. New York : Random House, [1966]. p. 208.

1967

138. **Grundlegung** der Soziologie des Rechts. 3. Aufl., unverand. Nachdr. der 1. Aufl. 1913. Berlin : Duncker & Humblot, 1967. 409 S.

139. **Recht** und Leben : gesammelte Schriften zur Rechtstatsachenforschung und zur Freirechtslehre. Ausgew., eingel., [Einl.] von Manfred Rehbinder. Berlin : Duncker & Humblot, 1967. 252 S. (*Schriftenreihe des Instituts für Rechtssoziologie und Rechtstatsachenforschung der Freien Universität Berlin* ; Bd. 7).

Inhaltsverzeichnis enth. u. a.:

Die Erforschung des lebenden Rechts. S. 11–27; Ein Institut für lebendes Recht. S. 28–42; Das lebende Recht der Völker der Bukowina. S. 43–60; Gutachten über die Frage: Was kann geschehen, um bei der Ausbildung (vor oder nach Abschluß des Universitätsstudiums) das Verständnis des Juristen für psychologische, wirtschaftliche und soziale Fragen in erhöhtem Maße zu fördern? S. 61–79; Über Lücken im Rechte. S. 80–169; Freie Rechtsfindung und freie Rechtswissenschaft. S. 170–202; Die richterliche Rechtsfindung auf Grund des Rechtssatzes: vier Stücke aus dem in Vorbereitung begriffenen Werke: Theorie der richterlichen Rechtsfindung. S. 203–252.

1969

140. **Judicial** Freedom of Decision : Its Principles and Objects. In *Science of Legal Method : Select Essays by Various Authors,* transl. by Ernest Bruncken, and Layton B. Register ; with introd. by Henry N. Sheldon, and John W. Salmond. New York : A. M. Kelley, 1969. pp. 47–84. Repr. of the 1917 ed.

1970

141. **Beiträge** zur Theorie der Rechtsquellen. Aalen : Scientia, 1970. Theil 1, *"Das ius civile, ius publicum, ius privatum."* VI, 258 S. Neudr. d. Ausg. Berlin 1902.

142. **Die stillschweigende** Willenserklärung. Aalen : Scientia, 1970. XII, 296 S. Neudr. d. Ausg. Berlin 1893.

143. **Das zwingende** und nichtzwingendeRecht im Burgerlichen Gesetzbuch fur das Deutsche Reich. Aalen : Scientia, 1970. VII, 278 S. (*Abhandlungen zum Privatrecht und Zivilprozess des Deutschen Reiches* ; Bd. 2, Heft 4). Neudr. d. Ausg. Jena 1899.

1973

144. **Freie** Rechtsfindung und Freie Rechtswissenschaft (1903) ; Soziologie und Jurisprudenz (1906). 2. Neudruckausg. in einem Bd. Aalen : Scientia, 1973. VI, 40, 23 S.

145. **Die Rechtsfähigkeit**. Aalen : Scientia Verl., 1973. XVI, 100 S. Neudr. d. Ausg. Berlin 1909.

1975

146. **Fundamental** Principles of the Sociology of Law. Transl. by Walter L. Moll ; with an introd. by Roscoe Pound. New York : Arno Press, 1975. XXXVI, 541 p. (*Harvard studies in jurisprudence* ; 5).

1976

147. **I fondamenti** della sociologia del diritto, a curadi Alberto Febbrajo. Milano : A. Giuffrè, 1976. LIV, 614 p. (*Civiltà del diritto* ; 35).

1986

148. **Gesetz** und lebendes Recht : vermischte kleinere Schriften. Hrsg., [Einl.] von Manfred Rehbinder. Berlin : Duncker & Humblot, 1986. 259 S. (*Schriftenreihe zur Rechtssoziologie und Rechtstatsachenforschung* ; Bd. 61).

Inhaltsverzeichnis enth. u. a.:

Arbeiterschutz im Privatrechte. S. 11–23; Die soziale Frage im Privatrechte. S. 24–47; Anton Menger. S. 48–87; Soziologie und Jurisprudenz. S. 88–103; Die Tatsachen des Gewohnheitsrechts: Inaugurationsrede. S. 104–132; Zur Frage der juristischen Person. S. 133–145; Die Neuordnung der Gerichtsverfassung. S. 146–178; Soziologie des Rechts. S. 179–194; Montesquieu and Sociological jurisprudence. S. 195–210; Eine Hochschule für Gesellschaftswissenschaften. S. 211–227; Gesetz und lebendes Recht. S. 228–240; Die Soziologie des Rechts. S. 241–253.

Rez. : Troje, Hans Erich. [Rezension]. *Zeitschrift der Savigny-Stiftung für Rechtsgeschichte. Romanistische Abteilung.* 1996. Bd. 113. S. 605–607.

1987

149. **Freie** Rechtsfindung und freie Rechtswissenschaft (1903) ; Soziologie und Jurisprudenz (1906). 2. Neudruckausg. in einem Bd. Aalen : Scientia Verl., 1987. VI, 40, 23 S.

1989

150. **Grundlegung** der Soziologie des Rechts, durchges. und hrsg. Manfred Rehbinder. 4. Aufl. Berlin : Duncker & Humblot, 1989. 439 S. (*Schriftenreihe zur Rechtssoziologie und Rechtstatsachenforschung*; Bd. 69).

1992

151. **Die Gesellschaft**, der Staat und ihre Ordnung. *Zeitschrift für Rechtssoziologie.* 1992. Jg. 13, Heft 1 (Jun.). S. 3–15.

1994

152. **Fundamental** Principles of the Sociology of Law, [transl. by Walter L. Moll] ; with an introd. by Roscoe Pound. Holmes Beach : Gaunt, 1994. XXXVI, 541 p.

1996

153. **Die Tatsachen** des Gewohnheitsrechts : Inaugurationsrede, gehalten am 2. Dezember 1906. In Wagner, Rudolf. *Vom Halbmond zum Doppeladler : ausgewählte Beiträge zur Geschichte der Bukowina und Czernowitzer Universität "Francisco-Josephina" : Festgabezum 120. Jahrestag 1995.* Augsburg : Der Südostdeutsche, 1996. S. 296–323.

IN 384051 9(c287)W14

1999

154. **Beiträge** zur Theorie der Rechtsquellen. Dillenburg : Gruber, 1999. Theil 1, *"Das ius civile, ius publicum, ius privatum."* VI, 258 S. Unveränd. reprograph. Nachdr. [d.Ausg.] Berlin, 1902.

2002

155. **Fundamental** Principles of the Sociology of Law, [transl. by Walter L. Moll] ; with an introd. by Roscoe Pound ; with a new introd. by Klaus A. Ziegert. New Brunswick : Transaction Publ., [2002]. LXVIII, 539 p. (*Law and Society Series*).

2003

156. **Internationales** Privatrecht. *Milletlerarası Hukuk ve Milletlerarası Özel Hukuk Bülteni.* 2003. Yıl 23, Sayi 1/2. S. 622–641.

157. **Kelsen, Hans,** und Eugen Ehrlich. Rechtssoziologie und Rechtswissenschaft : eine Kontroverse (1915/17), mit einer Einf. von Klaus Lüderssen. Baden-Baden : Nomos Verl.-Ges., 2003. XXI, 78 S. (*Juristische Zeitgeschichte : kleine R.* ; 7)

158. **Sfârşitul** unei mari impărăţii. *Revista Română de Sociologie.* 2003. An. 14, Nr. 1/2. pp. 105–141.

2005

159. **Escritos** sobre sociología y jurisprudencia. Trad., notas y estudios prelim. de Juan Antonio Gómez García, José Luis Muñoz de Baena, Gregorio Robles Morchón. Madrid : Marcial Pons, 2005. 123 p. (*Politopías* ; 3).

160. **Escritos** polémicos. In Ehrlich, Eugen. *Escritos sobre sociología y jurisprudencia.* Madrid : Marcial Pons, 2005. pp. 109–123. (*Politopías* ; 3).

161. **Libre** investigación del derecho y ciencia del derecho libre**.** *Ibidem.* pp. 53–88.

162. **Sociología** y Jurisprudencia. *Ibidem.* pp. 89–107.

2006

163. **Karl Marx** und die soziale Frage. Vorbem. v. Dimitrie Gusti ; Nachw. v. Manfred Rehbinder. Berlin : Duncker & Humbolt, 2006. 25 S.

2007

164. **Politische** Schriften, hrsg. und eingel. von Manfred Rehbinder. Berlin : Duncker & Humblot, 2007. 206 S. (*Schriftenreihe zur Rechtssoziologie und Rechtstatsachen forschung,* hrsg. Manfred Rehbinder, und Andreas Vosskuhle ; Bd. 88).

Inhaltsverzeichnis enth. u. a.:

Einleitung des Herausgebers. S. 7–16;

I. ZUR ZEITGESCHICHTE DES ERSTEN WELTKRIEGES.

Das Ende eines grossen Reiches (1921). S. 19–80; Die Memoirenmanie der Generäle (1921). S. 81–104; Bismarck und der Weltkrieg (1920). S. 105–119; Die Schuldfrage (1919). S. 121–123; Die Amnestie (1918). S. 125–128;

II. ZUR SOZIALPOLITIK.

Die Aufgaben der Sozialpolitik im österreichischen Osten (Juden- und Bauernfrage) (1916). S. 131–151; Karl Marx und die soziale Frage (1922). S. 153–162;

III. ZUR FRIEDENSBEWEGUNG.

Die historischen Grundlagen der Friedensbewegung (1918). S. 165–171; Die sittlichen Voraussetzungen der Friedensbewegung (1918). S. 173–181; Von der Zukunft des Völkerbundes (1919). S. 183–190;

ANHANG.

Über das "lebende Recht" (1921). S. 191–200.

IN316R36

Rez. : Augsberg, Steffen. [Rezension]. *ARSP: Archiv für Rechts- und Sozialphilosophie.* 2010. Vol. 96, No. 2. pp. 270–271.

Meder, Stephan. [Rezension]. *Zeitschrift der Savigny-Stiftung für Rechtsgeschichte.* 2009. Bd. 126, *"Germanistische Abteilung."* Iss. 1 (Aug.). S. 780–786.

2009

165. **Fundamental** Principles of the Sociology of Law, [transl. by Walter L. Moll] ; with an introd. by Roscoe Pound ; with a new introd. by Klaus A. Ziegert. New Brunswick ; London : Transaction Publ., [2009]. LXVII, 540 p.

2013

166. **Die Aufgaben** der Sozialpolitik im österreichischen Osten (Juden- und Bauernfrage). München ; Leipzig : Duncker & Humblot, 2013. 48 S. (*Schriften des Sozialwissenschaftlichen Akademischen Vereins in Czernowitz* ; Heft l). Repr.

1.2. Translations of Eugen Ehrlich's works into Ukrainian and Russian

1905

167. **Кріза** в черновецкій раді мійскій : (з виступу Є. Ерліха в Чернівецькій міській раді). *Буковина.* 1905. 30 листоп. (13 груд., ч. 142, рочник 21). С. 1. [Crisis in Czernowitz Municipality Council : (from E. Ehrlich's presentation at the Czernowitz Municipality Council meeting). *Bukovina.* 1905. November 30 (December 13, Nr. 142, Vol. 21). p. 1.]

1909

168. **Задачі** социяльної політики на Буковині : (з викладу проф. др-а Е. Ерліха). *Там само.* 1909. 6 лип. (ч. 143, річник 25). С. 2 ; 7 лип. (ч. 144, річник 25). С. 1–2 ; 10 лип. (ч. 146, річник 25). С. 2 ; 14 лип. (ч. 148, річник 25). С. 2–3. [Tasks of the Social Policy at Bukovina : (from the lecture by Prof. Dr. E. Ehrlich). *Ibidem.* 1909. July 6 (Nr. 143, Vol. 25). p. 2 ; July 7 (Nr. 144, Vol. 25). pp. 1–2 ; July 10 (Nr. 146, Vol. 25). p. 2 ; July 14 (Nr. 148, Vol. 25). pp. 2–3.]

1911

169. **Про живуче** право. Львів : Товариство Українсько-Руських правників, 1911. 14 с. ; *Правничий вісник.* 1911. Р. 2, Ч. 3/4. С. 191–204. [On Living Law. Lviv : Society of Ukrainian-Russian Lawyers, 1911. 14 p. ; *Legal Newsletter.* 1911. Vol. 2, Chap. 3/4. pp. 191–204.]

2005

170. **Вільне** правознаходження і вільне правознавство : [доповідь, зроблена на засіданні Юридичного товариства у Відні, 4 березня 1903 р. д-ром Євгеном Ерліхом, професором права у Чернівцях], пер. з нім. Д. С. Дороша. В *Проблеми філософії права.* Київ ; Чернівці : Рута, 2005. Т. 3, № 1/2. С. 168–184. [Free Finding of the Law and Free Science of Law : report given on the meeting of the Law Society in Vienna, on 4 March 1903, by Dr. Eugen Ehrlich, Professor of law in Czernowitz, translated from German into Ukrainian by D. S. Dorosh. In *Problems of the Philosophy of Law.* Kyiv ; Chernivtsi : Ruta, 2005. Vol. 3, Nr. 1/2. pp. 168–184.]

171. **Карл Маркс** та суспільне питання, пер. з рум. І. Ж. Торончука. *Там само.* Київ ; Чернівці : Рута, 2005. Т. 3, № 1/2. С. 221–226. Передм. с. 221. [Karl Marx and Social Issue, translated from Romanian into Ukrainian by I. Zh. Toronchuk. *Ibidem.* Kyiv ; Chernivtsi : Ruta, 2005. Vol. 3, Nr. 1/2. pp. 221–226. Introd. p. 221.]

В 70701 34П781

172. **Основи** соціології права. XX.I. Дослідження живого права, пер. з нім. В. В. Трутня. *Там само.* Київ ; Чернівці : Рута, 2005. Т. 3, № 1/2. С. 211–220. Бібліогр.: с. 219–220. [Fundamental Principles of the Sociology of Law. XX.I. The Studies of Living Law, translated from German into Ukrainian by V. V. Truten. *Ibidem.* Kyiv ; Chernivtsi : Ruta, 2005. Vol. 3, Nr. 1/2. pp. 211–220. Bibliogr.: pp. 219–220.]

В 70701 34П781

173. **Про живе** право : [передрук за : Ерліх Евген. Про живуче право. Львів : Товариство Українсько-Руських правників, 1911. 14 с., мовна ред. В. С. Бігуна]. *Там само.* Київ ; Чернівці : Рута, 2005. Т. 3, № 1/2. С. 194–200. [On Living Law: [reprint of : Eugen Ehrlich. On Living Law. Lviv: Society of Ukrainian-Russian Lawyers, 1911. 14 p., language editing by V. S. Bihun]. *Ibidem.* Kyiv ; Chernivtsi : Ruta, 2005. Vol. 3, Nr. 1/2. pp. 194–200.]

В 70701 34П781

174. **Соціологія** і юриспруденція, пер. з нім. В. С. Бігуна. *Там само.* Київ ; Чернівці : Рута, 2005. Т. 3, № 1/2. С. 185–193. [Sociology and Jurisprudence, translated from German into Ukrainian by V. S. Bihun. *Ibidem.* Kyiv ; Chernivtsi : Ruta, 2005. Vol. 3, Nr. 1/2. pp. 185–193.]

В 70701 34П781

175. **Соціологія** права, пер. В. С. Бігуна. *Там само.* Київ ; Чернівці : Рута, 2005. Т. 3, № 1/2. С. 161–167. [Sociology of Law, translated by V. S. Bihun. *Ibidem.* Kyiv; Czernowitz : Ruta, 2005. Vol. 3, Nr. 1/2. pp. 161–167.]

В 70701 34П781

176. **Юридична** логіка. Розділ IV. Уявлення про єдність права, пер. з нім. Д. С. Дороша. *Там само.* Київ ; Чернівці : Рута, 2005. Т. 3, № 1/2. С. 201–210. [The Juridical Logic. Chapter IV. The Idea of the Unity of Law, translated from German into Ukrainian by D. S. Dorosh. *Ibidem.* Kyiv ; Chernivtsi : Ruta, 2005. Vol. 3, Nr. 1/2. pp. 201–210.]

В 70701 34П781

2006

177. **Факти** звичаєвого права: інавгураційна ректорська промова, виголошена 2 грудня 1906 р. Звіт про 1906/1907 навчальний рік, зроблений 9-го грудня 1907 року ректором, який передає свою посаду, проф. др. Євгеном Ерліхом, пер. з нім. І. Я. Яцюка; пер. з латині Т. Д. Попової; передм., наук. ред. пер. М. В. Никифорака. В *Науковий вісник Чернівецького університету: зб. наук. пр.* Чернівці: Рута, 2006. Вип. 311, *"Правознавство."* С. 5–23. [The Facts of Common Law: rector's inauguration speech delivered on the 2nd of December 1906. A report on the 1906/1907 academic year, made on the 9th December 1907 by the Rector, prof. Dr. Eugen Ehrlich, who passed his post, translated from German into Ukrainian by I. Ya. Yatsiuk; translated from Latin into Ukrainian by T. D. Popova; introduction; scientific editing by M. V. Nykyforak. In *The Scientific Herald of Chernivtsi University: Collection of Scientific Works.* Chernivtsi: Ruta, 2006. Issue 311, *"Science of Law."* pp. 5–23.]

2009

178. **Возражение,** пер. с нем. М. В. Антонова. В *Российский ежегодник теории права. № 1, 2008.* Санкт-Петербург: Унив. издат. Консорциум "Юридическая книга", 2009. С. 634–639. [Objection, translated from German into Russian by M. V. Antonov. In *Russian Yearbook of the Theory of Law. Nr. 1, 2008.* Saint Petersburg: Universal Publishing Consortium "Juridical Book", 2009. pp. 634–639.]

> *Dispute of E. Ehrlich with H. Kelsen. Response by E. Ehrlich to the critical review written by H. Kelsen:* Kelsen, Hans. "Eine Grundlegung der Rechtssoziologie." *Archiv für Sozialwissenschaft und Sozialpolitik.* 1915. Bd. 39. S. 839–876.

179. **Реплика,** пер. с нем. М. В. Антонова. *Там же.* Санкт-Петербург: Унив. издат. Консорциум "Юридическая книга", 2009. С. 642–643. [Remark, translated from German into Russian by M. V. Antonov. *Ibidem.* Saint Petersburg: Universal Publishing Consortium "Juridical Book", 2009. pp. 642–643.]

> *Dispute of E. Ehrlich with H. Kelsen. Response by E. Ehrlich to the critical review written by H. Kelsen:* Kelsen, Hans. "Eine Grundlegungder Rechtssoziologie." *Archiv für Sozialwissenschaft und Sozialpolitik. 1915. Bd. 39. S. 839–876, and also to:* Kelsen, Hans. lik." *Archiv für Sozialwissenschaft und Sozialpolitik.* 1916. Bd. 41. S. 850–853.

180. **Социология** права, пер. с нем. М.В. Антонова. *Там же.* Санкт-Петербург : Унив. издат. Консорциум "Юридическая книга", 2009. С. 593–603. [Sociology of Law, translated from German into Russian by M.V. Antonov. *Ibidem.* Saint Petersburg : Universal Publishing Consortium "Juridical Book", 2009. pp. 593–603.]

2011

181. **Возражение,** пер. с нем. М. В. Антонова. В *Эрлих, Ойген. Основоположение социологии права.* Санкт-Петербург : Унив. издат. консорциум, 2011. С. 638–645. [Objection, translated from German into Russian by M. V. Antonov. In Ehrlich, Eugen. *Fundamental Principles of the Sociology of Law.* Saint Petersburg : Universal Publishing Consortium, 2011. pp. 638–645.]

Dispute of E. Ehrlich with H. Kelsen. Response by E. Ehrlich to the critical review written by H. Kelsen : Kelsen, Hans. "Eine Grundlegung der Rechtssoziologie.“ *Archiv für Sozialwissenschaft und Sozialpolitik. 1915. Bd. 39. S. 839–876.*

182. **Основоположение** социологии права, пер. с нем. М. В. Антонова ; под. ред. В. Г. Графского, и Ю. И. Гревцова ; авт. вступ. ст. Ю. И. Гревцов. Санкт-Петербург : Унив. издат. консорциум, 2011. 704 с. [Fundamental Principles of the Sociology of Law, translated from German into Russian by M. V. Antonov ; edited by V. G. Grafskii, and Yu. I. Grevtsov ; author's introductory article by Yu. I. Grevtsov. Saint Petersburg : Universal Publishing Consortium, 2011. 704 p.]

183. **Реплика,** пер. с нем. М. В. Антонова. В *Эрлих, Ойген. Основоположение социологии права.* Санкт-Петербург : Унив. издат. консорциум, 2011. С. 650–651. [Remark, translated from German into Russian by M. V. Antonov. In Ehrlich, Eugen. *Fundamental Principles of the Sociology of Law.* Saint Petersburg : Universal Publishing Consortium, 2011. pp. 650–651.]

Dispute of E. Ehrlich with H. Kelsen. Response by E. Ehrlich to the critical review written by H. Kelsen : Kelsen, Hans. "Eine Grundlegung der Rechtssoziologie.“ *Archiv für Sozialwissenschaft und Sozialpolitik.* 1915. Bd. 39. S. 839–876, *and also to :* Kelsen, Hans. "Replik.“ *Archiv für Sozialwissenschaft und Sozialpolitik.* 1916. Bd. 41. S. 850–853.

184. **Социология** права, пер. с нем. М. В. Антонова. *Там же.* С. 580–594. [Sociology of Law, translated from German into Russian by M. V. Antonov. *Ibidem.* pp. 580–594.]

185. **Судейское** нахождение права на основании правового предложения. Четыре отрывка из незавершенной работы “Теория судейского нахождения права”, пер. с нем. М. В. Антонова. В Эрлих, Ойген. *Основоположение социологии права.* Санкт-Петербург : Унив. издат. консорциум, 2011. С. 520–579 ; *Российский ежегодник теории права. № 2, 2009.* Санкт-Петербург : Унив. издат. Консорциум “Юридическая книга”, 2011. С. 332–375. [Law in Court on the Basis of Legal Proposal. Four excerpts from an unfinished work “Theory of Law in Court”, translated from German into Russian by M. V. Antonov. In Ehrlich, Eugen. *Fundamental Principles of the Sociology of Law.* Saint Petersburg : Universal Publishing Consortium, 2011. pp. 520–579 ; *Russian Yearbook on Theory of Law. Nr. 2, 2009.* Saint Petersburg : Universal Publishing Consortium “Juridical Book”, 2011. pp. 332–375.]

2012

186. **Інститут** живого права, пер. з нім. І. Я. Яцюка ; наук. ред. М. В. Никифорака. В *Науковий вісник Чернівецького університету : зб. наук. пр.* Чернівці : ЧНУ, 2012. Вип. 636, *“Правознавство.”* С. 5–13. [Institute of Living Law, translated from German into Ukrainian by I. Ya. Yatsiuk; scientific editing by M. V. Nykyforak. In *Scientific Herald of Chernivtsi University: Collection of Scientific Works.* Chernivtsi : Chernivtsi National University, 2012. Issue 636, *“Law Science.”* pp. 5–13.]

IN 73987 061Ч492

2013

187. **Соціологія** та юриспруденція, пер. з нім. І. Я. Яцюка ; наук. ред. перекл. М. В. Никифорака. *Там само.* Чернівці : ЧНУ, 2013. Вип. 644, *“Правознавство.”* С. 5–11. [Sociology and Jurisprudence, translated from German into Ukrainian by I. Ya. Yatsiuk; translated and edited by M. V. Nykyforak. *Ibidem.* Chernivtsi : Chernivtsi National University, 2013. Issue 644, *“Science of Law.”* pp. 5–11.]

IN 74151 061Ч492

2014

188. **Монтеск’є** та соціологічна юриспруденція, пер. з анг., передм. С. І. Нежурбіди. *Там само.* Чернівці : ЧНУ, 2014. Вип. 728, *“Правознавство.”* С. 5–14. Бібліогр.: 18 назв. [Montesquieu and Sociological Jurisprudence, translated from English, preface S. I. Nezhurbida. *Ibidem.* Chernivtsi : ChNU, 2014. Issue 728, *“Science of Law.”* pp. 5–14. Bibliogr.: 18 titl.]

2015

189. **Інститут** живого права, пер. з нім. І. Я. Яцюка ; наук. ред. пер. М. В. Никифорак. В *Никифорак, Михайло. Чернівецький юридикум: історія та сьогодення : вибране (1994–2015).* Чернівці : РОДОВІД, 2015. С. 206–224. [Institute of Living Law, transl. from German by I. Ya. Yatsiuk; scient. edit. transl. M. V. Nykyforak. In Nykyforak, Mykhailo. *Chernivtsi Juridicum: History and Contemporaneity: Selected (1994–2005).* Chernivtsi : RODOVID, 2015. pp. 206–224.]

Б 559487 34Н627

190. **Соціологія** та юриспруденція, пер. з нім. І. Я. Яцюка ; наук. ред. пер. М. В. Никифорака. *Там само.* Чернівці : РОДОВІД, 2015. С. 225–239. [Sociology and Jurisprudence, transl. from German by I. Ya. Yatsiuk; scient. edit. transl. M. V. Nykyforak. *Ibidem.* Chernivtsi : RODOVID, 2015. pp. 225–239.]

Б 559487 34Н627

191. **Факти** звичаєвого права : інавгураційна ректорська промова, виголошена 2 грудня 1906 р., пер. з нім. І. Я. Яцюка ; пер. з латині Т. Д. Попової ; передм., наук. ред. пер. М. В. Никифорака. *Там само.* Чернівці : РОДОВІД, 2015. С. 129–170. [Facts of Customary Law: the rector's inauguration speech delivered on the 2nd of December 1906, trans. from German by I. Ya. Yatsiuk; transl. from Latin by T. D. Popova; preface scient. edit. transl. M. V. Nykyforak. *Ibidem.* Chernivtsi : RODOVID, 2015. pp. 129–170.]

Б 559487 34Н627

PART 2.

EUGEN EHRLICH AS EDITOR

1899

192. **Juristisches** Litteraturblatt. [Hrsg. und verantw. Red. von A. Keil]. Berlin : Carl Heymanns Verl., 1899. Jg. 11. VIII, 248 S.

Professor of Czernowitz University Dr. E. Ehrlich – a contributor to the Berlin journal "Juristisches Litteraturblatt" ["Journal of Legal Literature"] – p. VII.

IN 19797 86B2

1903

193. **Juristisches** Literaturblatt, hrsg. von A. Keil. Berlin : Carl Heymanns Verl., 1903. Jg. 15. IX, 252 S.

Professor of Czernowitz University Dr. E. Ehrlich – a contributor to the Berlin journal "Juristisches Literaturblatt" ["Journal of Legal Literature"] – p. VIII.

IN19787 86B2

1905

194. **Österreichische** Richter-Zeitung, red. von Anton Nevečeřel, und Alfred Handl. Czernowitz : Buchdruck. "Gutenberg", 1905. Jg. 2. IV, 648 S.

Professor Dr. E. Ehrlich – a contributor to the Czernowitz newspaper "Österreichische Richter-Zeitung" ["Austrian Judicial Newspaper"] – p. I.

IN2944 86B21

1907

195. **Juristisches** Literaturblatt, begr. von Otto Loewenstein; hrsg. von A. Keil. Berlin : Carl Heymanns Verl., 1907. Jg. 19. IX, 248 S.

Full Professor of Czernowitz University Dr. E. Ehrlich – a contributor to the Berlin journal "Juristisches turblatt" ["Journal of Legal Literature"] – p. VIII.

IN 19792 86B2

1910

196. **Sozialwissenschaftliche** Ecke : [redigiert vom "sozialwissenschaftlichen akad. Verein" ; unter Mitw. der Eugen Ehrlich, und Josef Schumpeter]. *Czernowitzer Allgemeine Zeitung.* 1910. 18. Dez. (Nr. 2077). S. 6–8.

Speech at the meeting of the Social-Scientific Academic Society with the participation of Eugen Ehrlich and Josef Schumpeter.

IN 90

1911

197. **Sozialwissenschaftliche** Ecke : [redigiert vom "Sozialwissenschaftlichen akad. Verein" ; unter Mitw. der Eugen Ehrlich, und Josef Schumpeter]. *Ibidem.* 1911. 19. Febr. (Nr. 2128). S. 5–6.

Speech at the meeting of the Social-Scientific Academic Society with the participation of Eugen Ehrlich and Josef Schumpeter.

IN 90

1912

198. **Sozialwissenschaftliche** Ecke : [redigiert vom "Sozialwissenschaftlichen akad. Verein" ; unter Mitw. der Eugen Ehrlich, und Josef Schumpeter]. *Ibidem.* 1912. 20. Okt. (Nr. 2654). S. 7–9.

Speech at the meeting of the Social-Scientific Academic Society with the participation of Eugen Ehrlich and Josef Schumpeter.

IN 90

1913

199. **Archiv** für Rechts- und Wirtschaftsphilosophie, mit besonderer Berücksichtigung der Gesetzgebungsfragen : Organ der Internationalen Vereinigung für Rechts- und Wirtschaftsphilosophie samt den Gesetzgebungsfragen, hrsg. von Josef Kohler, und Fritz Berolzheimer. Berlin ; Leipzig : Verl.-Buchh. Walther Rothschild, 1913. Bd. 7, Heft 1 (Okt.). VII, 172 S.

Professor of Czernowitz University Dr. E. Ehrlich – a contributor to the German journal "Archiv für Rechts- und Wirtschaftsphilosophie" ["Archive of Philosophy of Law and Economics"] – p. II.

86C128

200. **Mitteilungen** des Sozialwissenschaftlichen akademischen Vereines : [redigiert von Eugen Ehrlich et al.]. *Czernowitzer Tagblatt.* 1913. 30. Nov. (Nr. 3228, Jg. 11). S. 3–4.

Eugen Ehrlich as an editor of the publication.

IN 1983 90A45

1914

201. **Mitteilungen** des Sozialwissenschaftlichen akademischen Vereines : [redigiert von Eugen Ehrlich et al.]. *Ibidem.* 1914. 1. Jänner (Nr. 3337, Jg. 12). S. 7–8 ; 11. Jänner (Nr. 3344, Jg. 12). S. 7–8 ; 18. Jänner (Nr. 3350, Jg. 12). S. 9–10 ; 25. Jänner (Nr. 3356, Jg. 12). S. 9–10 ; 1. Febr. (Nr. 3362, Jg. 12). S. 9–10 ; 8. Febr. (Nr. 3368, Jg. 12). S. 9–10 ; 22. Febr. (Nr. 3380, Jg. 12). S. 9–10 ; 1. März (Nr. 3386, Jg. 12). S. 9–10 ; 8. März (Nr. 3392, Jg. 12). S. 9–10 ; 15. März (Nr. 3398, Jg. 12). S. 9–10 ; 22. März (Nr. 3404, Jg. 12). S. 9–10 ; 29. März (Nr. 3409, Jg. 12). S. 9–10 ; 5. Apr. (Nr. 3415, Jg. 12). S. 9–10 ; 12. Apr. (Nr. 3421, Jg. 12). S. 17–21 ; 26. Apr. (Nr. 3432, Jg. 12). S. 9–10 ; 3. Mai (Nr. 3437, Jg. 12). S. 9–10 ; 17. Mai (Nr. 3449, Jg. 12). S. 9–10 ; 24. Mai (Nr. 3454, Jg. 12). S. 10 ; 7. Juni (Nr. 3465, Jg. 12). S. 10–11 ; 14. Juni (Nr. 3470, Jg. 12). S. 9–10 ; 21. Juni (Nr. 3476, Jg. 12). S. 9–10 ; 28. Juni (Nr. 3482, Jg. 12). S. 9–11 ; 12. Juli (Nr. 3493, Jg. 12). S. 9–10.

Eugen Ehrlich as an editor of the publication.

IN 1984 90A45

IN 1985 90A45

IN 1986 90A45

PART 3.

LITERATURE ABOUT EUGEN EHRLICH'S LIFE AND ACTIVITY

202. **Андрусяк, І. П.** Правове вчення Євгена Ерліха та розвиток ідеї гендерної рівності в Австро-Угорській монархії. В *Ерліхівський збірник. Юридичний факультет Чернівецького національного університету ім. Ю. Федьковича : наук. доп. та повідомл.* Чернівці : ЧНУ, 2012. Вип. 6. С. 115–119. Бібліогр.: 10 назв. [Andrusiak, I. P. The Legal Doctrine of Eugen Ehrlich and the Development of the Idea of Gender Equality in the Austro-Hungarian Monarchy. In *Ehrlich Collection. Faculty of Law of Yuriy Fedkovych Chernivtsi National University: Scient. Research and Report.* Chernivtsi : ChNU, 2012. Vol. 6. pp. 115–119. Bibliogr.: 10 titl.]

   В 74131 34Е719

203. **Андрусяк, Т. Г.** Євген Ерліх та його вплив на розвиток української правової думки кінця XIX – початку XX ст. *Там само.* Чернівці : ЧНУ, 2012. Вип. 6. С. 78–82. Бібліогр.: 10 назв. [Andrusiak, T. H. Eugen Ehrlich and his Influence on the Development of the Ukrainian Legal Thought of the late XIX – early XX centuries. *Ibidem.* Chernivtsi : ChNU, 2012. Vol. 6. pp. 78–82. Bibliogr.: 10 titl.]

   В 74131 34Е719

204. **Андрусяк, Тарас.** *Історія політичних та правових вчень : навч. посіб.* Львів : Видавн. центр ЛНУ ім. Івана Франка, 2001. 220 с. Бібліогр.: с. 214. [Andrusiak, Taras. *History of Political and Legal Doctrines: Teaching Manual.* Lviv : Publishing Center of Ivan Franko National University of Lviv, 2001. 220 p. Bibliogr.: 214 p.]

   E. Ehrlich. – pp. 207–209.

   Б 484443 34(091)А663

205. **Антонов, М. В.** Запоздавшая реплика: об одной из последних работ Ойгена Эрлиха. В *Российский ежегодник теории права. № 2, 2009.* Санкт-Петербург : Унив. издат. Консорциум "Юридическая книга", 2011. С. 320–331. Библиогр. в подстроч.

примеч. [Antonov, M. V. The Late Replica: On One of the Last Works by Eugen Ehrlich. In *Russian Annual of Theory of Law. № 2, 2009.* Saint Petersburg : Univ. Publ. Consortium "Juridical Book", 2011. pp. 320–331. Bibliogr. in the footnotes.]

206. **Антонов, Михаил Валерьевич.** "Интеграция знания о праве и обществе в творчестве Ойгена Эрлиха." *Государство и право.* 2011. № 1. С. 79–87. Библиогр. в подстроч. примеч. [Antonov, Mikhail Valerievich. "Integration of Knowledge about the Law and Society in the Works of Eugen Ehrlich." *State and Law.* 2011. Nr. 1. pp. 79–87. Bibliogr. in the footnotes.]

207. **Антонов, М. В.** "Кілька слів про життя і творчість Ойгена Ерліха." *Філософія права і загальна теорія права.* 2012. № 2. С. 350–355. Бібліогр.: 16 назв. [Antonov, M. V. "A Few Words about the Life and Work of Eugen Ehrlich," *Philosophy of Law and General Theory of Law.* 2012. № 2. pp. 350–355. Bibliogr.: 16 titl.]

208. **Антонов, М. В.** "Ойген Эрлих: живое право против правового плюрализма?" *Известия высших учебных заведений. Правоведение.* 2013. № 1. С. 151–175. Библиогр. в подстроч. примеч. [Antonov, M. V. "Eugen Ehrlich: Living Law against Legal Pluralism?" *Newsletter of Higher Educational Institutions. Jurisprudence.* 2013. Nr. 1. pp. 151–175. Bibliogr. in the footnotes.]

209. **Антонов, М. В.** "Ойген Ерліх про закон і правосуддя." *Філософія права і загальна теорія права.* 2012. № 2. С. 356–368. [Antonov, M. V. "Eugen Ehrlich about Law and Justice." *Philosophy of Law and General Theory of Law.* 2012. Nr. 2. pp. 356–368.]

210. **Антонов, М. В.** "Путь и перспективы правового учения Ойгена Эрлиха." *Право. Журнал Высшей школы экономики.* 2012. № 4. С. 39–50. [Antonov, M. V. "The Way and the Prospects of the Legal Doctrine of Eugen Ehrlich." *Law. Journal of the Higher School of Economics.* 2012. Nr. 4. pp. 39–50.]

211. **Антонов, М. В.** "Соціологія права і чиста теорія права: складний взаємозв'язок." *Філософія права і загальна теорія права.* 2012. № 1. С. 250–256. Бібліогр.: с. 254–255. [Antonov, M. V. "Sociology of Law and Pure Theory of Law: Complex Interconnection." *Philosophy of Law and General Theory of Law.* 2012. Nr. 1. pp. 250–256. Bibliogr: pp. 254–255.]

212. **Антонов, М. В.** "Социология права Ойгена Эрлиха." *Известия высших учебных заведений. Правоведение.* 2008. № 6 (281). С. 128–137. [Antonov, M. V. "Sociology of Law of Eugen Ehrlich." *Proceedings of Higher Educational Institutions. Jurisprudence.* 2008. Nr. 6 (281). pp. 128–137.]

213. **Антонов, М. В.** Социология права: рождение новой научной дисциплины. В Эрлих, Ойген. *Основоположение социологии права.* Санкт-Петербург : Унив. издат. консорциум, 2011. С. 9–63. Библиогр. в подстроч. примеч. [Antonov, M. V. Sociology of

Law: The Creation of New Scientific Discipline. In Ehrlich, Eugen. *Fundamental Principles of the Sociology of Law.* Saint Petersburg : Univ. Publish. Consortium, 2011. pp. 9–63. Bibliogr. in the footnotes.]

214. **Антонов, М. В.** Социолого-правовая концепция Ойгена Эрлиха в контексте современных дебатов о правовом плюрализме. В *Ерліхівський збірник. Юридичний факультет Чернівецького національного університету ім. Ю. Федьковича : наук. доп. та повідомл.* Чернівці : ЧНУ, 2012. Вип. 6. С. 8–13. Бібліогр.: 28 назв. [Antonov, M. V. The Sociological-Legal Concept of Eugen Ehrlich in the Context of Contemporary Debates on Legal Pluralism. In *Ehrlich Collection. Faculty of Law of Yuriy Fedkovych Chernivtsi National University : Scient. Research and Report.* Chernivtsi : ChNU, 2012. Issue 6. pp. 8–13. Bibliogr.: 28 titl.]

B 74131 34E719

215. **Антонов, М. В.** У истоков социологии права: Ойген Эрлих. В *Российский ежегодник теории права. № 1, 2008.* Санкт-Петербург : Унив. издат. Консорциум "Юридическая книга", 2009. С. 565–592. Библиогр. в подстроч. примеч. [Antonov, M. V. Origins of the Sociology of Law: Eugen Ehrlich. In *Russian Annual of Theory of Law. Nr. 1, 2008.* Saint Petersburg : Univ. Publish. Consortium "Juridical Book", 2009. pp. 565–592. Bibliogr. in the footnotes.]

216. **Балабанова, Даріна.** Становлення поняття "живе право" в сучасній філософії права. В *Актуальні проблеми державного управління : зб. наук. пр. Одес. регіон. ін-ту держ. упр.* [Одеса] : ОРІДУ НАДУ, 2012. Вип. 3 (51). С. 10–13. Бібліогр.: 11 назв. [Balabanova, Darina. Development of the Concept of "Living Law" in the Modern Philosophy of Law. In *Contemporary Problems of Public Administration: Collect. of Scient. Works of Odesa Regional Institute of Public Administration.* [Odesa] : ORIDU NADU, 2012. Issue 3 (51). pp. 10–13. Bibliogr.: 11 titl.]

217. **Балинська, О. М.** Людина як аксіоматичне начало сучасного праворозуміння. В *Ерліхівський збірник. Юридичний факультет Чернівецького національного університету ім. Ю. Федьковича : наук. доп. та повідомл.* Чернівці : ЧНУ, 2012. Вип. 6. С. 133–134. Бібліогр.: 4 назви. [Balynska, O. M. Human Being as Axiomatic Beginning of the Modern Legal Consciousness. In *Ehrlich Collection. Faculty of Law of Yuriy Fedkovych Chernivtsi National University: scientifically enlarged and inform.* Chernivtsi : ChNU, 2012. Issue 6. pp. 133–134. Bibiliogr.: 4 titl.]

E. Ehrlich. – p. 134.

B 74131 34E719

218. **Бачинин, В. А.,** и Ю. А. Сандулов. *История западной социологии : учебник.* Санкт-Петербург : Лань, 2002. 384 с. (*Мир культуры, истории и философии*). [Bachinin, V. A., and Yu. A. Sandulov. *History of Western Sociology: Textbook.* Saint Petersburg : Lan, 2002. 384 p. *(World of culture, history and philosophy).*]

E. Ehrlich. – pp. 214–215.

219. **Бігун, В. С.** Євген Ерліх: життя і правознавча спадщина (актуальний наукознавчий нарис). В *Проблеми філософії права.* Київ; Чернівці : Рута, 2005. Т. 3, № 1/2. С. 105–126 : фото. Бібліогр.: с. 118–126. [Bihun, V. S. Eugen Ehrlich: Life and Jurisprudence Legacy (Latest Scientific Outline). In *Problems of Philosophy of Law.* Kyiv; Chernivtsi; Ruta, 2005. Vol. 3., Nr. 1/2. pp. 105–126 : photos. Bibliogr.: pp. 118–126.]

В 70701 34П781

220. **Бігун, В. С.** Ребіндеру Манфреду – 70 років : [німецький вчений правознавець, дослідник соціології права, життя й творчої спадщини Євгена Ерліха]. *Там само.* Київ ; Чернівці : Рута, 2005. Т. 3, № 1/2. С. 401–402. Бібліогр.: 4 назви. [Bihun, V. S. For Manfred Rehbinder – 70 years old [German scientist of law, researcher of the sociology of law, life and creative heritage of Eugene Ehrlich). *Ibidem.* Kyiv; Chernivtsi : Ruta, 2005. Vol. 3, Nr. 1/2. pp. 401–402. Bibliogr.: 4 titl.]

В 70701 34П781

221. **Бігун, В. С.** Соціологія права. В *Юридична енциклопедія : у 6 т.* Київ : Укр. енцикл., 2003. Т. 5, *"П–С."* С. 561–563. [Bihun, V. S. Sociology of Law. In *Juridical Encyclopedia: in 6 volumes.* Kyiv : Ukr. Encycl., 2003, Vol. 5, *"P–S."* pp. 561–563.]

E. Ehrlich. – pp. 561, 563.

Б 492509 34Ю704

222. **Бігун, В. С.** *Філософія правосуддя: ідея та здійснення : монографія.* Київ : [б. в.], 2011. 303 с. *(Бібліотека Міжнародного часопису "Проблеми філософії права").* Бібліогр.: с. 235–281. [Bihun, V. S. *Philosophy of Justice: Idea and Effectuation: monograph.* Kyiv : [s. n.], 2011. 303 p. *(The Library of International Journal "Problems of Philosophy of Law").* Bibiliogr.: pp. 235–281.]

E. Ehrlich. – pp. 14–15, 22, 25, 72–80, 118, 137, 187, 201, 220.

223. **Бігун, В. С.** Філософія правосуддя: ідея та здійснення (огляд окремих висновків філософсько-правового дослідження). В *Проблеми філософії права.* Київ ; Чернівці : Чернів. нац. ун-т, 2010–2011. Т. 8/9. С. 262–275. [Bihun, V. S. Philosophy of Justice: Idea and Effectuation (Survey of some Conclusions of Philosophic-Legal Investigation). In *Problems of Philosophy of Law.* Kyiv ;

Chernivtsi : Cherniv. Nation. Univ., 2010–2011. Vol. 8/9. pp. 262–275.]

E. Ehrlich. – pp. 270, 274, 275.

B 74161 34П781

224. **Боботов, С. В.** *Буржуазная социология права.* Москва : Юрид. лит., 1978. 224 с. [Bobotov, S. V. *Bourgeois Sociology of Law.* Moscow : Jurid. Lit., 1978. 224 p.]

E. Ehrlich. – pp. 13–14, 18, 48.

Б 330013 34Б723

225. **Ботушанський, В. М.** Чернівецький університет: історія й сучасність. В *Матеріали IV Буковин. міжнар. іст.-краєзн. наук. конф., присвяченої 125-річчю заснування ЧНУ ім. Ю. Федьковича, Чернівці, Жовтень 5, 2000.* Чернівці : Золоті литаври, 2001. С. 12–16. [Botushanskyi, V. M. Chernivtsi University: History and Reality. In *Materials of the IV Bukovin. Internat. Historic-Cultural Study Scient. Conferen. dedicated to the 125th anniversary of the Foundation of Yuriy Fedkovych Chernivtsi National University, Chernivtsi, October 5, 2000.* Chernivtsi : Golden Tympany, 2001. pp. 12–16.]

E. Ehrlich. – p. 13.

Б 481335 9(с287)Б906

226. **Братасюк, М. Г.** Значення поглядів Є. Ерліха на особливості юридичного мислення в контексті правової культури постмодерну. В *Проблеми філософії права.* Київ ; Чернівці : Рута, 2005. Т. 3, № 1/2. С. 152–156. Бібліогр.: 25 назв. [Bratasiuk, M. H. Significance of E. Ehrlich's Views on Peculiarities of Juridical Thinking in the Context of Legal Culture of Postmodernity. In *Problems of Philosophy of Law.* Kyiv ; Chernivtsi : Ruta, 2005. Vol. 3, Nr. 1/2. pp. 152–156. Bibliogr.: 25 titl.]

B 70701 34П781

227. **Буджетова** дебата. *Буковина.* 1907. 28 верес. (11 жовт., ч. 114, рочник 23). С. 1–2. [Budget debate. *Bukovina.* 1907. September 28 (October 11, Nr. 114, Vol. 23). pp. 1–2.]

About the meeting of Bukovina Council, including information about the participation of the Rector Ehrlich.

90

228. **Буковиньский** Сойм. *Буковина.* 1907. 5 (18) верес. (ч. 104, рочник 23). С. 1. [Bukovina Council. *Bukovina.* 1907. September 5 (18) (Nr. 104, Vol. 23). p. 1.]

About the first meeting of Bukovina Council, including information about the first point on the agenda, namely, "ambassadorial oath" that was supposed to be performed by Dr. Ehrlich.

90

229. **Буковиньский** Сойм. *Буковина.* 1907. 12 (25) верес. (ч. 107, рочник 23). С. 3. [Bukovina Council. *Bukovina.* 1907. September 12 (25) (Nr. 107, Vol. 23). p. 3.]

About the second meeting of the Bukovina Council at which Dr. Ehrlich performed his "ambassadorial oath".

90

230. **Бунчук, О. Б.** Погляди Івана Франка на сутність права. В *Науковий вісник Чернівецького університету: зб. наук. пр.* Чернівці : ЧНУ, 2010. Вип. 550, *"Правознавство."* С. 20–23. Бібліогр.: 8 назв. [Bunchuk, O. B. Ivan Franko's Views on the Nature of Law. In *Scientific Newsletter of Chernivtsi University: Coll. of Scient. Works.* Chernivtsi : ChNU, 2010. Issue 550, *"Jurisprudence."* pp. 20–23. Bibliogr.: 8 titl.]

E. Ehrlich. – p. 21.

B 72858 061Ч492

231. **Бунчук, О. Б.** Соціологічна юриспруденція та її напрямки. В *Ерліхівський збірник. Юридичний факультет Чернівецького національного університету ім. Ю. Федьковича : наук. доп. та повідомл.* Чернівці : ЧНУ, 2012. Вип. 6. С. 130–132. Бібліогр.: 13 назв. [Bunchuk, O. B. Sociologic Jurisprudence and its Branches. In *Ehrlich Collection. Faculty of Law of Yuriy Fedkovych Chernivtsi National University: Scien. Add. and Inform.* Chernivtsi : ChNU, 2012. Issue 6. pp. 130–132. Bibliogr.: 113 titl.]

B 74131 34E719

232. **Бурдяк, В. І.** *Становлення і розвиток соціологічних концепцій права : навч. посіб.* Чернівці : Рута, 2001. 84 с. Бібліогр.: с. 79–83. [Burdiak, V. I. *Establishment and Development of Sociological Conceptions of Law: Textbook.* Chernivtsi : Ruta, 2001. 84 p. Bibliogr.: pp. 79–83.]

E. Ehrlich. – pp. 14, 15, 26, 32, 42–47.

A 402527 34Б912

233. **Бутирська, І. А.** Судовий прецедент як складова принципу "живого права". В *Ерліхівський збірник. Юридичний факультет Чернівецького національного університету ім. Ю. Федьковича : наук. доп. та повідомл.* Чернівці : ЧНУ, 2012. Вип. 6. С. 149–150. Бібліогр.: 3 назви. [Butyrska, I. A. Juridical Case as a Part of Living Law Principle. In *Ehrlich Collection. Faculty of Law of Yuriy Fedkovych Chernivtsi National University: Scien. Add. and Inform.* Chernivtsi : ChNU, 2012. Issue 6. pp. 149–150. Bibliogr.: 3 titl.]

B 74131 34E719

234. **Бутирський, А. А.** Реалізація принципу "живого права" у суддівській діяльності. *Там само.* Чернівці : ЧНУ, 2012. Вип. 6. С. 147–148. Бібліогр.: 4 назви. [Butyrskyi, A. A. Realisation of a "Living Law" Case in Court Practice. *Ibidem.* Chernivtsi : ChNU, 2012. Issue 6. pp. 147–148. Bibliogr.: 4 titl.]

B 74131 34E719

235. **Буткевич, О. В.** Правова концепція професора Є. Ерліха і міжнародне право. *Там само.* Чернівці : ЧНУ, 2012. Вип. 6. С. 160–167. Бібліогр.: 18 назв. [Butkevych, O. V. Professor E. Ehrlich's Legal Conception and International Law. *Ibidem.* Chernivtsi : ChNU, 2012. Issue 6. pp. 160–167. Bibliogr. : 18 titl.]

B 74131 34E719

236. **Вакарюк, Л. В.** Основні концептуальні підходи до інституціоналізації пострадянського вітчизняного фінансового права у світлі доктрини правопізнання Євгена Ерліха. *Там само.* Чернівці : ЧНУ, 2012. Вип. 6. С. 59–63. Бібліогр.: 26 назв. [Vakariuk, L. V. The Main Conceptual Approaches to the Institutionalization of Post-Soviet National Financial Law in Terms of Doctrine of Legal Science of Eugen Ehrlich. *Ibidem.* Chernivtsi : ChNU, 2012. Issue 6. pp. 59–63. Bibiliogr.: 26 titl.]

B 74131 34E719

237. **Васильчук, В. О.** Категорія справедливості у концепції "живого права" Євгена Ерліха. *Там само.* Чернівці : ЧНУ, 2012. Вип. 6. С. 110–112. Бібліогр.: 2 назви. [Vasylchuk, V. O. Category of Justice in the Concept of "Living Law" by Eugen Ehrlich. *Ibidem.* Chernivtsi : ChNU, 2012. Issue 6. pp. 110–112. Bibliogr.: 2 titl.]

B 74131 34E719

238. **Вишневська, М.** "Люди зі світовим ім'ям працювали у Чернівцях : [про Чернів. ун-т; про Є. Ерліха – засновника сучасної соціології права; Г. Гросса – засновника сучасної наукової криміналістики]." *Свобода слова.* 2008. 15 трав. (чис. 18). С. 17. [Vyshnevska, M. "Worldwide-known Personalities who Worked in Chernivtsi : [About Chernivtsi Univ.; about E. Ehrlich – the Founder of Modern Sociology of Law; H. Gross – the Founder of Modern Scientific Criminalistics]." *Freedom of Speech,* 2008, May 15 (numb. 18). p. 17.]

239. **Вишневська, М.** "Право не в законах, а в суспільстві" – стверджував класик філософії і соціології права, чернівчанин, доктор права, професор Євген Ерліх. Цьогоріч минає 150 років від дня народження і 90 років від дня смерті засновника сучасної соціології права." *Буковинське віче.* 2012. 14 верес. (№ 37). С. 1 ; 21 верес. (№ 38). С. 2. [Vyshnevska, M. "The Law is not in Laws, but in Society" – Stated by the Classic of

the Philosophy and Sociology of Law, Chernivtsi Citizen, Doctor of Law, Professor Eugen Ehrlich. This Year Marks the 150th Anniversary of the Birth and the 90th Anniversary of the Death of the Founder of Contemporary Sociology of Law." *Bukovynske Viche*, 2012, September 14 (Nr. 37). p. 1 ; September 21 (Nr. 38). p. 2.]

240. **Відкрили** пам'ятні дошки світовому вченому. *Молодий буковинець*. 2017. 12–13 трав. (№ 38). С. 2. [Memorial plaques dedicated to the world famous scientist revealed. *Molodyi Bukovynets*. 2017. May 12–13 (№ 38). p. 2.]

On the ceremonial revelation of two memorial plaques dedicated to the outstanding scientist, lawyer, founder of the sociology of law in Chernivtsi – Eugen Ehrlich. The CV of Ehrlich is provided.

241. **Воднік, В. Д.,** Ю. І. Золотарьова, Г. П. Клімова, Н. П. Осипова, та О. В. Сердюк. *Соціологія права : навч. посіб.*, за ред. Н. П. Осипової. Харків : Право, 2007. 234 с. [Vodnik, V. D., Yu. I. Zolotariova, G. P. Klimova, N. P. Osypova, and O. V. Serdiuk. *Sociology of Law: Teach. Manual*, ed. by N. P. Osipova. Kharkiv : Pravo, 2007. 234 p.]

E. Ehrlich. – pp. 76–77.

A 421295 316C693

242. **Возняк, Н. В.** Соціологічний метод у праві. В *Ерліхівський збірник. Юридичний факультет Чернівецького національного університету ім. Ю. Федьковича : наук. доп. та повідомл.* Чернівці : ЧНУ, 2012. Вип. 6. С. 64–66. Бібліогр.: 6 назв. [Vozniak, N. V. The Sociological Method in Law. In *Ehrlich Collection. Faculty of Law of Yuriy Fedkovych Chernivtsi National University: Scientific Report and Inform.* Chernivtsi : ChNU, 2012. Issue 6. pp. 64–66. Bibliogr.: 6 titl.]

B 74131 34E719

243. **Гаврилюк, Р. А.** Эмпириокритицизм как формула правопознания Евгения Эрлиха. *Там само.* Чернівці: ЧНУ, 2012. Вип. 6. С. 14–32. Бібліогр.: 30 назв. [Havriliuk, R. A. Empiric Criticism as a Clue to the Understanding of E. Ehrlich's Theory. *Ibidem.* Chernivtsi : ChNU, 2012. Issue 6. pp. 14–32. Bibliogr.: 30 titl.]

B 74131 34E719

244. **Гаджиев, Г. А.** *Онтология права : (критическое исследование юридического концепта действительности) : монография.* Москва : Норма ; ИНФРА-М, 2013. 320 с. [Gadzhiev, G. A. *Ontology of Law : (Critical Study of the Legal Concept of Reality): monograph.* Moscow : Norma ; INFRA-M, 2013. 320 p.]

E. Ehrlich. – pp. 35, 182–187, 206, 314, 318.

245. **Георгіца, А.,** та С. Меленко. "Євген Ерліх – основоположник соціологічного праворозуміння (до 150-річчя від дня народження)." *Право України.* 2012. № 9. С. 445–454. Бібліогр.: 19 назв. [Georgitsa, A., and S. Melenko. "Eugene Ehrlich – the Founder of Sociological Legal Thinking (for the 150th Anniversary of his Birth)." *The Law of Ukraine.* 2012. Nr. 9. pp. 445–454. Bibliogr.: 19 titl.]

246. **Георгіца, А. З.** та М. В. Никифорак. З історії юридичного факультету Чернівецького університету у 1918–1940 рр. В *Науковий вісник Чернівецького університету : зб. наук. пр.* Чернівці : Рута, 2006. Вип. 333, *"Правознавство."* С. 5–8. Бібліогр.: 11 назв. [Georgitsa, A. Z., and M. V. Nykyforak. From the History of the Faculty Law of Chernivtsi University in the Years 1918–1940. In *Scientific Bulletin of Chernivtsi University: Collection of Scientific Works.* Chernivtsi : Ruta, 2006. Issue 333, *"Jurisprudence."* pp. 5–8. Bibliogr.: 11 titl.]

E. Ehrlich. – pp. 5, 7.

B 71450 061Ч492

247. **Георгіца, А. З.** та М. В. Никифорак. "Маловідомі сторінки історії юридичного факультету Чернівецького університету." *Бюлетень Міністерства юстиції України.* 2004. № 6 (32). С. 5–12. Бібліогр.: 18 назв. [Georgitsa, A. Z. and M. V. Nykyforak. "Unknown Periods of the History of the Faculty of Law of Chernivtsi University." *Bulletin of the Ministry of Justice of Ukraine.* 2004. Nr. 6 (32). pp. 5–12. Bibliogr.: 18 titl.]

E. Ehrlich. – pp. 5–7, 12.

248. **Георгіца, А. З.** Соціологія права Євгена Ерліха: на шляху до інтеграційного праворозуміння. В *Ерліхівський збірник. Юридичний факультет Чернівецького національного університету ім. Ю. Федьковича : наук. доп. та повідомл.* Чернівці : ЧНУ, 2012. Вип. 6. С. 72–77. Бібліогр.: 28 назв ; В *Науковий вісник Чернівецького університету : зб. наук. пр.* Чернівці : ЧНУ, 2012. Вип. 618, *"Правознавство."* С. 7–12. Бібліогр.: 28 назв. [Georgitsa, A. Z. Sociology of Law of Eugene Ehrlich: Towards an Integrated Comprehension of Law. In *Ehrlich Collection. Faculty of Law of Yuriy Fedkovych Chernivtsi National University: Scient. Report and Inform.* Chernivtsi : ChNU, 2012. Issue 6. pp. 72–77. Bibliogr.: 28 titl.; In *Scientific Bulletin of Chernivtsi University: Collection of Scientific Works.* Chernivtsi : ChNU, 2012. Issue 618, *"Jurisprudence."* pp. 7–12. Bibliogr.: 28 titl.]

B 74131 34E719

B 73807 061Ч492

249. **Георгіца, А. З.,** В. П. Марчук, М. В. Никифорак, та П. С. Пацурківський. Юридичний факультет Чернівецького

університету : історичний нарис. В *Ерліхівський збірник : наук. ст. та повідомл. викл., аспірантів та співроб. юридич. ф-тів Чернів. та Київ. ун-тів.* Чернівці, 1995. Вип. 2. С. 3–20. [Georgitsa, A. Z., V. P. Marchuk, M. V. Nykyforak, and P. S. Patsurkivskyi. Faculty of Law of Chernivtsi University: Historical Essay. In *Ehrlich Collection: Scientific art. and inform. of professors, post-graduates and graduates of the faculties of law of Chernivtsi and Kyiv universities.* Chernivtsi, 1995. Issue 2. pp. 3–20.]

E. Ehrlich. – pp. 4, 6–10.

А 396555 34Е719

250. **Графский, В. Г.,** Н. М. Золотухина, Л. С. Мамут, и др. *История политических и правовых учений : учеб. для вузов,* под общ. ред. В. С. Нерсесянца. 4-е изд., перераб. и доп. Москва : Норма, 2003. 933 с. [Grafskii, V. H., N. M. Zolotukhina, L. S. Mamut, et al. *History of the Political and Law Studies : Manual for the Institutions of Higher Education,* general edition of V. S. Nersesiants. 4th Ed., modif. and added. Moscow : Norma, 2003. 993 p.]

E. Ehrlich. – pp. 758–759.

Б 491178 34(09)И907

251. **Гриценко, І.,** М. Никифорак, та Л. Гіждіван "Професорсько-викладацький склад юридичного факультету університету Франца Йосифа в Чернівцях : формування і діяльність." Матеріали III Міжнар. іст.-краєзн. наук. конф., присвяченої 120-річчю заснування Чернівецького університету, (Чернівці, 29 верес. – 1 жовт. 1995 р.). Чернівці : Рута, 1995. С. 106–111. [Hrytsenko, I., M. Nykyforak, and L. Hizhdivan. "Professors and Teachers of Faculty of Law of Franz Joseph University in Czernowitz: Formation and Activity." Materials of the Third International Scientific Conference of Local History Marking the 120th anniversary of the Foundation of Chernivtsi University, Chernivtsi, September 29 – October 1, 1995. Chernivtsi : Ruta, 1995. pp. 106–111.]

E. Ehrlich. – pp. 107–109.

Б 499239 378М581

252. **Гураленко, Н. А.** Антиномічна природа права : соціологічно-правовий аналіз. В *Ерліхівський збірник. Юридичний факультет Чернівецького національного університету ім. Ю. Федьковича : наук. доп. та повідомл.* Чернівці : ЧНУ, 2012. Вип. 6. С. 46–49. Бібліогр.: 11 назв. [Huralenko, N. A. The Antynomic Nature of Law: Sociological-Legal Analyses. In *Ehrlich Collection. Faculty of Law of Yuriy Fedkovych Chernivtsi National University: Scient. Rep. and Inform.* Chernivtsi : ChNU, 2012. Issue 6. pp. 46–49. Bibliogr.: 11 titl.]

E. Ehrlich. – pp. 47, 49.

В 74131 34Е719

253. **Гураленко, Н. А.** Детермінація розвитку вчення про судову правотворчість : ретроспективний аналіз західної традиції права. В *Науковий вісник Чернівецького університету : зб. наук. пр.* Чернівці : ЧНУ, 2011. Вип. 597, *"Правознавство."* С. 25–28. Бібліогр.: 11 назв. [Huralenko, N. A. Determination of the Doctrine of Judicial Law-making: Retrospective Analysis of Western Law Tradition. In *Scientific Bulletin of Chernivtsi University: Collection of Scientific Works.* Chernivtsi : ChNU, 2011. Issue 597, *"Jurisprudence."* pp. 25–28. Bibliogr.: 11 titl.]

E. Ehrlich. – pp. 25–26, 28.

B 73548 061Ч492

254. **Гурвич, Г. Д.** Теория источников права Ойгена Эрлиха и идея социального права, [пер. с фр. М. В. Антонова] ; под общ. ред. : В. Графского, и Ю. Гревцова. В Эрлих, Ойген. *Основоположение социологии права.* Санкт-Петербург : Унив. издат. консорциум, 2011. С. 653–666. Библиогр. в подстрочных примеч. [Gurvich, G. D. Theory of the Sources of Eugen Ehrlich's Law and the Idea of Social Law, [translation from French by M. V. Antonov]; under the joint edition: V. Grafskii, and Yu. Grevtsov. In Ehrlich, Eugen. *Fundamental Principles of the Sociology of Law.* Saint Petersburg : Univ. Publ. Consortium, 2011. pp. 653–666. Bibliogr. in footnotes.]

255. **Гусар, Ю.** "Календар "Буковинського віча": учений юрист зі світовим ім'ям : [14 верес. – 150 р. від дня народж. засн. сучасної соціології права Є. Ерліха (1862–1922)]." *Буковинське віче.* 2012. 7 верес. (№ 36). С. 4. [Husar, Yu. "Calendar of "Bukovinske Viche": Renowned Scholar and Lawyer: [14 September the 150th anniversary of the birthday of the founder of the modern sociology of law E. Ehrlich (1862–1922)]." *Bukovinske Viche,* 2012, September 7 (Nr. 36). p. 4.]

256. **Данилюк, М. І.** Доктрина "суддівського права" Є. Ерліха. В *Ерліхівський збірник. Юридичний факультет Чернівецького національного університету ім. Ю. Федьковича : наук. доп. та повідомл.* Чернівці : ЧНУ, 2012. Вип. 6. С. 143–146. Бібліогр.: 6 назв. [Danyliuk, M. I. E. Ehrlich's Doctrine of "Judiciary Law". *In Ehrlich Collection. Faculty of Law of Yuriy Fedkovych Chernivtsi National University: Scient. Reports and Inform.* Chernivtsi : ChNU, 2012. Issue 6. pp. 143–146. Bibliogr.: 6 titl.]

B 74131 34E719

257. **Джонстон, Вільям М.** "Три письменники (Франко, Францоз, Целан) та три мислителі (Ерліх, Бубер, Чаргаф) реагують на соціокультурні контрасти в Чернівцях і Східній Галичині з 1867 року." Міні-космос Буковини. Культурні здобутки регіону : матеріали Міжнар. наук. конф., присвяч. 130-річчю

Чернів. ун-ту, (Чернівці, 3–4 жовт., 2005 р.). Чернівці : Зелена Буковина, 2006. С. 42–57. Бібліогр. в підрядк. прим. [Johnston, William M. "Three Writers (Franko, Franzos, Celan) and Three Thinkers (Ehrlich, Buber, Chargaff) React to the Social-Cultural Contrasts in Chernivtsi and Eastern Galicia since 1867." Microcosmos of Bukovina. Cultural Achievements of the Region: Materials of the International Scientific Conference Dedicated to the 130th Anniversary of Chernivtsi University, Chernivtsi, October 3–4, 2005. Chernivtsi : Green Bukovina, 2006. pp. 42–57. Bibliogr. in footnotes.]

E. Ehrlich. – pp. 42, 46, 49–50, 57.

Б 502731 9(с287)М618

258. **Джужа, О. М.,** І. Г. Кириченко, В. С. Ковальський, С. М. Корецький, та ін. *Соціологія права : навч. посіб.*, за заг. ред. О. М. Джужи. Київ : Юрінком Інтер, 2004. 288 с. Бібліогр.: с. 276–283. [Dzhuzha, O. M., I. H. Kyrychenko, V. S. Kovalskyi, S. M. Koretskyi, et al. *Sociology of Law: Teach. Manual,* ed. O. M. Dzhuzha. Kyiv: Yurinkom Inter, 2004. 288 p. Bibliogr.: pp. 276–283.]

E. Ehrlich. – pp. 13, 29, 45–46, 57–64, 81.

Б 491317 316С693

259. **Дорош, Д. С.** Розуміючи Ерліха сьогодні. В *Проблеми філософії права.* Київ ; Чернівці : Рута, 2005. Т. 3, № 1/2. С. 157–159. Бібліогр.: 10 назв. [Dorosh, D. S. Understanding Ehrlich Today. In *Problems of the Philosophy of Law.* Kiev ; Chernivtsi : Ruta, 2005. Vol. 3, Nr. 1/2. pp. 157–159. Bibliogr.: 10 titl.]

В 70701 34П781

260. **Дубовицкий, В. Н.** *Социология права : предмет, методология и методы.* Минск : Право и экономика, 2010. 174 с. *(Гуманитарные науки).* Библиогр. в конце глав. [Dubovitskii, V. N. *Sociology of Law: Subject, Methodology and Methods.* Minsk: Law and Economics, 2010. 174 p. *(Humanities).* Bibliograf. at the end of chapters.]

E. Ehrlich. – pp. 3, 12, 21–22, 27, 73.

261. **Ерышев, А. А.** *История политических и правовых учений : учеб. Пособие.* 3-е изд., стереотип. Киев : МАУП, 2002. 152 с. Библиогр.: с. 148–149. [Yeryshev, A. A. *History of Political and Legal Studies: Textbook.* 3rd ed., stereotype. Kiev : IAPM, 2002. 152 p. Bibliogr.: pp. 148–149.]

E. Ehrlich. – pp. 143–144.

262. **Євген Ерліх** (1862–1922): вчений-юрист, ректор університету. В Павлюк, О. М, авт.-упоряд. *Буковина. Визначні постаті: 1774–1918 : біогр. довід.* Чернівці : Золоті литаври, 2000. С. 119–121. [Eugen Ehrlich (1862–1922): Scientist-Lawyer, Rector of the University. In Pavliuk, O. M., author-compiler. *Bukovina.*

Famous figures: 1774–1918 : biogr. refer. Chernivtsi : Zoloti Litavri, 2000. pp. 119–121.]

Б 495666 9(с287)Б906

263. **Євген Ерліх**: [вчений-юрист, юрид. ф-т ЧНУ ім. Ю. Федьковича]. *Молодий буковинець.* 2013. 18 квіт. (№ 45). С. 15. [Eugen Ehrlich: [Scientist-Lawyer, Faculty of Law of Yuriy Fedkovych Chernivtsi National University]. *Molodyi Bukovynets,* 2013, April 18 (Nr. 45). p. 15.]

264. **Євген Ерліх** (1862–1922). Учений-юрист, ректор Чернівецького університету. В Матвійчук, О., та Н. Струк, авт.-упоряд. *Серцем з Буковиною : імена славних сучасників : довід.-біогр. вид.* 3-тє вид. Київ: Світ успіху, 2011. С. 29. [Eugen Ehrlich (1862-1922). Scientist-Lawyer, Rector of Yuriy Fedkovych Chernivtsi National University. In Matviichuk, O., and N. Struk, authors-compilers. *With Heart in Bukovina : Names of Famous Contemporaries : refer. biography. publishing house.* 3 ed. Kyiv : The World of Success, 2011. p. 29.]

В 73179 9(с287)С331

265. **Євген Ерліх**. В Струк, Н., та О. Матвійчук, авт.-упоряд. *Чернівецький національний університет імені Юрія Федьковича : імена славних сучасників : довід.-біогр. вид.* Київ : Світ Успіху, 2005. С. 43. [Eugen Ehrlich. In Struk, N., and O. Matviichuk, authors-compilers. *Yuriy Fedkovych Chernivtsi National University: The Names of Famous Contemporaries: biography publ.* Kyiv : The World of Success, 2005. p. 43.]

Б 497383 378Ч490

266. **"Ерліхівські** студії "живого права": погляд зі Швейцарії", подав Василь Дуган. *Буковинське віче.* 2005. 16 берез. (№ 19). С. 3. ["Ehrlich's Studies of "Living Law": The View from Switzerland", sent by Vasyl Duhan. *Bukovynske Viche,* 2005, March 16 (Nr. 19). p. 3.]

267. **Жоль, К. К.** *Соціологія : навч. посіб. для студ. вищ. навч. закладів.* Київ : Либідь, 2005. 440 с. [Zhol, K. K. *Sociology: Educ. Tutor. for Students of Institutions of Higher Education.* Kyiv : Lybid, 2005. 440 p.]

E. Ehrlich. – pp. 257, 259–260.

Б 497456 316Ж798

268. **Жоль, К. К.** *Философия и социология права : учеб. пособие.* Киев : Юринком Интер, 2000. 480 с. *(Bibliotheca Studiorum).* Библиогр.: с. 444–479. [Zhol, K. K. *Philosophy and Sociology of Law : Manual.* Kyiv: Yurinkom Inter, 2000. 480 p. *(Bibliotheca Studiorum).* Bibliogr.: pp. 444–479.]

E. Ehrlich. – pp. 9, 369, 388–392, 428.

Б 478905 1Ф798

269. **З буковиньского** Сойму. *Буковина.* 1907. 21 верес. (4 жовт., ч. 111, рочник 23). С. 1–2. [From the Bukovina Council. *Bukovina.* 1907. September 21 (October 4, Nr. 111, Vol. 23). pp. 1–2.]

About the meeting of Bukovina Council at which the Rector, Prof. Ehrlich called for "propynational bill".

90

270. **Задорожна, С. М.** Природно-правовий характер принципів міжнародного права. В *Науковий вісник Чернівецького університету: зб. наук. пр.* Чернівці: ЧНУ, 2013. Вип. 660, *"Правознавство."* С. 49–56. [Zadorozhna, S. M. Natural-Legal Nature of the Principles of International Law. In *Science Newsletter of Chernivtsi University : Collection of Scientific Works.* Chernivtsi : ChNU, 2013. Issue 660, *"Science of Law."* pp. 49–56.]

E. Ehrlich. – pp. 49, 52–54, 56.

IN 74338 061Ч492

271. **Карбонье, Жан.** *Юридическая социология,* пер. с фр., вступ. ст. В. А. Туманова. Москва : Прогресс, 1986. 352 с. [Carbonnier, Jean. *Law* Sociology, trans. from French, introd. article by V. A. Tumanov. Moscow : Progress, 1986. 352 p.]

E. Ehrlich. – pp. 74, 109–114, 117, 120, 122, 137, 171–172, 180, 208, 225, 228.

Б 400581 1фБК217

272. **Карвацька, С. Б.** Інтерпретація історико-правової реальності у рамках соціологічного підходу до права. В *Ерліхівський збірник. Юридичний факультет Чернівецького національного університету ім. Ю. Федьковича: наук. доп. та повідомл.* Чернівці : ЧНУ, 2012. Вип. 6. С. 127–129. Бібліогр.: 16 назв. [Karvatska, S. B. The Interpretation of Historical-Legal Reality within the Sociological Approach to Law. In *Ehrlich Collection. Yuriy Fedkovych Chernivtsi National University, Faculty of Law : Scient. Res. and Report.* Chernivtsi : ChNU, 2012. Issue 6. pp. 127–129. Bibliogr.: 16 titl.]

B 74131 34E719

273. **Кельзен, Г.** Заключительное слово, [пер. с нем. М. В. Антонова]. В *Российский ежегодник теории права. № 1, 2008.* Санкт-Петербург : Унив. издат. Консорциум "Юридическая книга", 2009. С. 643–644 ; В Эрлих, Ойген. *Основоположение социологии права.* Санкт-Петербург : Унив. издат. консорциум, 2011. С. 651–652. [Kelsen, H. Concluding Remarks, [transl. from German by M. V. Antonov]. In Russian Yearbook of the Theory of *Law. № 1, 2008.* Saint Petersburg : Univers. Publ. Consortium "Legal book", 2009. pp. 643–644; In Ehrlich, Eugen. *Fundamental Principles of the Sociology of Law.* Saint Petersburg: Univers. Publ. Consortium, 2011. pp. 651–652.]

Dispute of E. Ehrlich with H. Kelsen. Closing remarks – response by H. Kelsen to the objections written by E. Ehrlich : "Entgegnung." *Archiv für Sozialwissenschaft und Sozialpolitik.* 1916. Bd. 41. S. 844–849, *and also to* : "Replik." *Archiv für Sozialwissenschaft und Sozialpolitik.* 1916/1917. Bd. 42. S. 609–610.

274. **Кельзен, Г.** Основоположение социологи и права, [пер. с нем. М. В. Антонова]. В *Российский ежегодник теории права. № 1, 2008.* Санкт Петербург : Унив. издат. Консорциум "Юридическая книга" 2009. С. 604–634 ; В Эрлих, Ойген. *Основоположение социологии права.* Санкт-Петербург : Унив. издат. консорциум, 2011. С. 595–638. [Kelzen, H. Fundamental Principles of Sociology and Law, [transl. from German by M. V. Antonov]. In Russian Yearbook of the Theory of *Law. № 1, 2008.* Saint Petersburg : Univers. Publ. Consortium "Juridicial Book", 2009. pp. 604–634; In Ehrlich, Eugen. *Fundamental Principles of the Sociology of Law.* Saint Petersburg : Univers. Publ. Consortium, 2011. pp. 595–638.]

Dispute of E. Ehrlich with H. Kelsen. Criticism by H. Kelsen of the work written by E. Ehrlich : Grundlegung der Soziologie des Rechts. München ; Leipzig : Duncker & Humblot, 1913. 409 S.

275. **Кельзен, Г.** Реплика, [пер. с нем. М. В. Антонова]. В *Российский ежегодник теории права. № 1, 2008.* Санкт-Петербург : Унив. издат. Консорциум "Юридическая книга", 2009. С. 639–642 ; В Эрлих, Ойген. *Основоположение социологии права.* Санкт-Петербург : Унив. издат. консорциум, 2011. С. 645–649. [Kelzen, H. Remark, [transl. from German by M. V. Antonov]. In *Russian Yearbook of the Theory of Law. № 1, 2008.* Saint Petersburg : Univ. Publ. Consortium "Juridical Book", 2009. pp. 639–642 ; In Ehrlich, Eugen. *Fundamental Principles of the Sociology of Law.* Saint Petersburg: Univ. Publ. Consortium, 2011. pp. 645–649.]

Dispute of E. Ehrlich with H. Kelsen. Response by H. Kelsen to the objections written by E. Ehrlich : "Entgegnung." *Archiv für Sozialwissenschaft und Sozialpolitik.* 1916. Bd. 41. S. 844–849.

276. **Кобан, О. Г.** "Можливості використання соціологічного підходу Євгена Ерліха у здійсненні правосуддя." *Бюлетень Міністерства юстиції України.* 2014. № 4. С. 56–62. Бібліогр.: 13 назв. [Koban, O. G. "Possibilities of Using Eugen Ehrlich's Sociological Approach in the Administration of Justice." *Bulletin of the Ministry of Justice of Ukraine.* 2014. Nr. 4. pp. 56–62. Bibliogr.: 13 titl.]

277. **Кобан, О. Г.** Онтологічний плюралізм права Є. Ерліха. В *Науковий вісник Ужгородського національного університету. Сер. Право.* – Ужгород, 2014. Вип. 25. С. 27–31. Бібліогр.:

15 назв. [Koban, O. G. Ontological Pluralism of Law of E. Ehrlich. In *Scientific Newsletter of Uzhgorod National University. Ser. Law.* Uzhgorod, 2014. Issue 25. pp. 27–31. Bibliogr.: 15 titl.]

278. **Кобан, О. Г.** Основні положення вчення Є. Ерліха про вільне правознаходження та його значення. В *Науковий вісник Херсонського державного університету. Серія : Юридичні науки.* Херсон : Гельветика, 2013. Вип. 5, Т. 1. С. 44–48. Бібліогр.: с. 47–48. [Koban, O. G. The Basic Grounds of the Doctrine of E. Ehrlich on the Free Legal Process and its Significance. In *Scientific Newsletter of Kherson State University. Series : Law Science.* Kherson : Helvetica, 2013. Issue 5, Volume 1. pp. 44–48. Bibliogr.: pp. 47–48.]

279. **Кобан, О.** "Разработка Е. Эрлихом учения о живом праве и его значении в правопонимании." *Закон и жизнь.* 2013. № 8/3 (260). С. 118–120. Библиогр.: 11 наим. [Koban, O. "Development of the Doctrine by E. Ehrlich about the Living Law and its Meaning for the Understanding of Law." *Law and Life.* 2013. Nr. 8/3 (260). pp. 118–120. Bibliogr.: 11 titl.]

280. **Кобан, Ольга Геннадіївна.** "Соціологічна теорія права Є. Ерліха." Автореф. дис... канд. юрид. наук : 12.00.01 "Теорія та історія держави і права; історія політичних і правових учень." Київ : Київ. нац. ун-т ім. Т. Шевченка, 2014. 24 с. [Koban, Olha. "Sociological Theory of Law of E. Ehrlich." Author's Abstract of the Candidate of Law Science Dissertation : 12.00.01 "Theory and History of State and Law; History of Political and Legal Studies." Kyiv : Kyiv Taras Schevchenko National University, 2014. 24 p.]

281. **Коваль, А. Ф.** Витоки соціологічних поглядів Євгена Ерліха та Станіслава Дністрянського, В *Ерліхівський збірник. Юридичний факультет Чернівецького національного університету ім. Ю. Федьковича : наук. доп. та повідомл.* Чернівці : ЧНУ, 2012. Вип. 6. С. 83–87. Бібліогр.: 6 назв. [Koval, A. F. The Origins of Sociological Thoughts of Eugene Ehrlich and Stanislav Dnistrianskyi. In *Ehrlich Collection. Faculty of Law of Chernivtsi National University : Scientific Res. and Report.* Chernivtsi : ChNU, 2012. Issue 6. pp. 83-87. Bibliogr.: 6 titl.]

B 74131 34E71

282. **Ковальчук, Олександр,** та Володимир Хаврук. Цінність права в соціологічному підході до праворозуміння. В *Про українське право. Київ. нац. ун-т ім. Т. Шевченка, юридич. ф-т,* за ред. І. Безклубого. Київ, 2011/2012. Число 6/7. С. 103–111. [Kovalchuk, Oleksandr, and Volodymyr Khavruk. The Meaning of Law in the Sociological Approach to the Legal Consciousness. In *About the Ukrainian Law. Kyiv T. Shevchenko National University, Faculty of Law,* edited by I. Bezklubyi. Kyiv, 2011/2012. Number 6/7. pp. 103–111.]

E. Ehrlich. – p. 107.

283. **Козловський, А. А.** Курс "Філософії права" на юридичному факультеті Чернівецького університету. В *Науковий вісник Чернівецького університету : зб. наук. пр.* Чернівці : ЧДУ, 1996. Вип. 4/5, *"Правознавство."* С. 3–25. Бібліогр.: 20 назв. [Kozlovskyi, A. A. The Course of Philosophy of Law at the Faculty of Law of Chernivtsi University. In *Scientific Newsletter of Chernivtsi University : Collect. of Scient. Works.* Chernivtsi : ChNU, 1996. Issue 4/5, *"Law."* pp. 3–25. Bibliogr.: 20 titl.]

E. Ehrlich. – pp. 3, 11, 12, 22, 23.
Б 472979 061Ч492

284. **Козловський, А. А.** *Право як пізнання : вступ до гносеології права.* Чернівці : Рута, 1999. 295 с. Бібліогр.: с. 275–284. [Kozlovskyi, A. A. *Law as Perception : Introduction to the Gnosiology of Law.* Chernivtsi : Ruta, 1999. 295 p. Bibliogr.: pp. 275–284.

E. Ehrlich. – pp. 28, 118, 214, 235–237.

Б 477445 34К592

285. **Козловський, А. А.** Предмет та історичні етапи розвитку юридичної логіки. В *Ерліхівський збірник : наук. ст. викл., аспірантів та співроб. юридич. ф-тів Чернів. та Київ. ун-тів.* Чернівці, 1994. Вип. 1. С. 52–55. [Kozlovskyi, A. A. The Subject and Historical Periods of the Development of the Logic of Law. In *Ehrlich Collection : scient. degrees of prof., candidates and the staff memb. of the faculties of law of Chernivtsi and Kyiv universities.* Chernivtsi, 1994. Issue 1. pp. 52–55.]

E. Ehrlich. – pp. 53–54.

А 395963 34Е719

286. **Козловський, А. А.** Соціально-історичні константи правового пізнання. В *Науковий вісник Чернівецького університету : зб. наук. пр.* Чернівці : ЧДУ, 1999. Вип. 55, *"Правознавство."* С. 5–11. Бібліогр.: 3 назви. [Kozlovskyi, A. A. Social-Historical Constants of the Juridical Knowledge. In *Scientific Newsletter of Chernivtsi University : collect. of scient. works.* Chernivtsi : ChNU, 1999. Issue 55, *"Law."* pp. 5–11. Bibliogr.: 3 titl.]

E. Ehrlich. – pp. 5, 11.

В 66924 061Ч492

287. **Козьмук, Я. Р.** Особливість європейської самоідентифікації Буковини: досвід минулого – основа майбутнього : (до 130-х роковин від дня народження ректора Чернів. ун-ту Є. Ерліха). В *До витоків назви краю Буковина (600-річчя першої писемної згадки) : тези доп. та повідомл. 2-ої Буковин. іст.-краєзн. конф., (Чернівці, 2–3 жовт., 1992 р.).* Чернівці : ЧДУ, 1992. С. 68–69. [Kozmuk, Y. R. The Features of the European Self-Definition of Bukovina: Past Experience – Basis for Future: (on the occasion of the 130th anniversary of the date of birth of the Rector

of Chernivtsi University E. Ehrlich). In *Back to the Grounds of the Denomination of the Bukovina Area (the 600th anniversary of the first record) : theses of the report and the notes of the 2nd Bukovina hist.-area studies conf., Chernivtsi, October 2–3, 1992.* Chernivtsi : ChNU, 1992. pp. 68–69.]

Б 467165 9(с2)Д55

288. **Колодій, А. М.,** В. В. Копєйчиков, та С. Л. Лисенков. *Теорія держави і права : навч. посіб.,* за заг. ред. С. Л. Лисенкова, та В. В. Копєйчикова. Київ : Юрінком Інтер, 2003. 368 с. Бібліогр.: с. 358–364. [Kolodii, A. M., V. V. Kopeichykov, and S. L. Lysenkov. *State and Law Theory: Teach. Manual,* ed. by S. L. Lysenkov, and V. V. Kopeichykov. Kyiv : Yurinkom Inter, 2003. 368 p. Bibliogr.: pp. 358–364.]

E. Ehrlich. – pp. 284–285.

Б 487593 34Т338

289. **Копєйчиков, В. В.** Живе право. В *Юридична енциклопедія : у 6 т.* Київ : Укр. енцикл., 1999. Т. 2, *"Д–Й."* С. 429–430. [Kopeichykov, V. V. Living Law. In *Encyclopedia of Law : in 6 vol.* Kyiv : Ukr. Encyclop., 1999. Vol. 2, *"D–J."* pp. 429–430.]

E. Ehrlich. – p. 429.

Б 482330 34Ю704

290. **Косович, В.** "Живе право" як джерело формування досконалих нормативно-правових актів України. В *Ерліхівський збірник. Юридичний факультет Чернівецького національного університету ім. Ю. Федьковича : наук. доп. та повідомл.* Чернівці : ЧНУ, 2012. Вип. 6. С. 178–183. Бібліогр.: 23 назви. [Kosovych, V. "Living Law" as a Formation Source of the Flawless Legislative and Regulatory Acts of Ukraine. In *Ehrlich Collection. Faculty of Law of Y. Fedkovych Chernivtsi National University: Scient. Report and Inform.* Chernivtsi : ChNU, 2012. Issue 6. pp. 178–183. Bibliogr.: 23 titl.]

E. Ehrlich. – p. 178.

В 74131 34Е719

291. **Косович, В. М.** "Живе право" як джерело формування досконалих нормативно-правових актів України. В *Науковий вісник Чернівецького університету : зб. наук. пр.* Чернівці : ЧНУ, 2012. Вип. 628, *"Правознавство."* С. 34–40. Бібліогр.: 23 назви. [Kosovych, V. M. "Living Law" as a Formation Source of the Flawless Legislative and Regulatory Acts of Ukraine. In *Scientific Newsletter of Chernivtsi University : collect. of scient. works.* Chernivtsi : ChNU, 2012. Issue 628, *"Law."* pp. 34–40. Bibliogr.: 23 titl.]

E. Ehrlich. – p. 34.

В 73982 061Ч492

292. **Костишин, С. С.** Юридичний факультет Чернівецького національного університету – кузня правничих кадрів. В *Ерліхівський збірник. Юридичний факультет Чернівецького національного університету ім. Ю. Федьковича : наук. доп. та повідомл.* Чернівці : Рута, 2002. Вип. 3. С. 3–4 ; В *Науковий вісник Чернівецького університету : зб. наук. пр.* Чернівці : Рута, 2000. Вип. 100, *"Правознавство."* С. 5–6. [Kostyshyn, S. S. Faculty of Law of Chernivtsi National University as a Forge of Law Staff Members. In *Ehrlich Collection. Faculty of Law of Y. Fedkovych Chernivtsi National University : scientif. report and inform.* Chernivtsi : Ruta, 2002. Issue 3. pp. 3–4 ; In *Scientific Newsletter of Chernivysi University : collect. of scient. works.* Chernivtsi : Ruta, 2000. Issue 100, *"Law."* pp. 5–6.]

В 66982 061Ч492

293. **Коттеррелл, Роджер.** Эрлих на окраине Империи: центры и периферии в правовых исследованиях, [пер. с англ. М. В. Антонова]. В *Российский ежегодник теории права. № 1, 2008.* Санкт-Петербург : Унив. издат. Консорциум "Юридическая книга", 2009. С. 546–564. Библиогр. в подстроч. примеч. ; В Эрлих, Ойген. *Основоположение социологии права.* Санкт-Петербург : Унив. издат. консорциум, 2011. С. 673–699. Библиогр. в подстроч. примеч. [Cotterell, Roger. Ehrlich at the Edge of the Empire : Focuses and Peripheries in the Juridical Investigations, [transl. from English by M. V. Antonov]. In *Russian Annual of the Theory of Law. № 1, 2008.* Saint Petersburg : Univ. Publish. Consortium "Juridicial Book" 2009. pp. 546–564. Footnote Bibliogr. ; In Ehrlich, Eugen. *Fundamental Principles of the Sociology of Law.* Saint Petersburg : Univ. Publ. Consortium, 2011. pp. 673–699. Bibliogr. in footnotes.]

294. **Кульчар, Кальман.** *Основы социологии права,* [пер. с венг. В. Гусева] ; предисл., общ. ред. В. П. Казимирчука. Москва : Прогресс, 1981. 256 с. *(Логика и методология науки).* Библиогр. в подстроч. примеч. [Kulchar, Kalman. *Fundamental Principles of the Sociology of Law,* [transl. from Hungarian by V. Gusev] ; foreword of the editor V. P. Kazimirchuk. Moscow : Progress, 1981. 256 p. *(Logic and Methodology of Science).* Bibliogr. in footnotes.]

E. Ehrlich. – pp. 36, 39–40, 69, 79–85, 142, 165, 196.

Б 357524 34К906

295. **Курко, Я. С.** Деякі питання становлення соціології права. В *Науковий вісник Чернівецького університету : зб. наук. пр.* Чернівці : ЧДУ, 1996. Вип. 4/5, *"Правознавство."* С. 113–117. Бібліогр.: 20 назв. [Kurko, Ya. S. Some Issues of the Development of the Sociology of Law. In *Scientific Newsletter of Chernivtsi University : collect. of scient. works.* Chernivtsi : ChNU, 1996. Issue 4/5, *"Law."* pp. 113–117. Bibliogr.: 20 titl.]

Б 472979 061Ч492

296. **Лапаева, В. В.** *Типы правопонимания: правовая теория и практика : монография.* Москва : Российская академия правосудия, 2012. 580 с. Библиогр. в подстроч. примеч. [Lapaieva, V. V. *The Types of Legal Consciousness: Theory and Practice of Law : monograph.* Moscow : Russian Academy of Justice, 2012. 580 p. Bibliogr. in footnotes.]

E. Ehrlich. – pp. 62–64.

297. **Маковецький, Адам.** "Соціологія в ЧНУ та її тернистий шлях розвитку". *Університетський вісник.* 2007. Квіт./трав. (№ 5/6). С. 10. [Makovetskyi, Adam. "Sociology at ChNU and its Thorny Way od Development". *University Newsletter,* 2007, April/May (№ 5/6). p. 10.]

298. **Максимюк, О. Д.** Мізерне значення карного примусу (за Є. Ерліхом). В *Ерліхівський збірник. Юридичний факультет Чернівецького національного університету ім. Ю. Федьковича : наук. доп. та повідомл.* Чернівці : ЧНУ, 2012. Вип. 6. С. 102–103. Бібліогр.: 5 назв. [Maksymiuk, O. D. Poor Meaning of Criminal Compulsion (after E. Ehrlich). In *Ehrlich Collection. Faculty of Law of Y. Fedkovych Chernivtsi National University: scient. report and inform.* Chernivtsi : ChNU, 2012. Issue 6. pp. 102–103. Bibliogr.: 5 titl.]

B 74131 34E719

299. **Манелис, Б.** "Школа "свободного права" и её место в буржуазной юридической науке." *Вестник Коммунистической академии.* 1928. Кн. 28 (4). С. 199–231. [Manelis, B. "The School of "Free Law" and its Place in the Bourgeois Science of Law." *Newsletter of Communist Academy.* 1928. Book 28 (4). pp. 199–231.]

E. Ehrlich. – pp. 211–212, 215–219, 223, 225, 230–231.

31394

300. **Манык, Алена.** "Актуализация проблемы свободного правоопределения в творчестве Е. Эрлиха." *Legea şiviaţa.* 2014. Nr. 7/2 (271). P. 88–91. Библиогр.: 9 наим. [Manyk, Alena. "Representation of the Problem of the Free Law Defined in the Works by E. Ehrlich." *Legea şi viaţa.* 2014. Nr. 7/2 (271). pp. 88–91. Bibliogr.: 9 titl.]

301. **Мартьянова, Т. С.** Роль теорії "живого права" в обґрунтуванні інституту розсуду. В *Ерліхівський збірник. Юридичний факультет Чернівецького національного університету ім. Ю. Федьковича : наук. доп. та повідомл.* Чернівці : ЧНУ, 2012. Вип. 6. С. 151–154. Бібліогр.: 12 назв. [Martianova T. S. The Role of the Theory of "Living Law" in Justification of the Institute of Discretion. *In Ehrlich Collection. Faculty of Law of Yuriy Fedkovych Chernivtsi National University: scientific report.* Chernivtsi : ChNU, 2012. Issue 6. pp. 151–154. Bibliogr.: 12 titl.]

E. Ehrlich. – pp. 151, 154.

B 74131 34E719

302. **Марчук, В. П.,** та В. П. Скоткіна. Ерліх (Ehrlich) Євген. В *Юридична енциклопедія: у 6 т.* Київ : Укр. енцикл., 1999. Т. 2, *"Д–Й."* С. 364–365. [Marchuk, V. P., and V. P. Skotkina. Ehrlich Eugene. In *Legal Encyclopedia: in 6 Vol.* Kyiv : Ukr. Encyclopedia, 1999. Vol. 2, *"D –J."* pp. 364–365.]

Б 482330 34Ю704

303. **Марчук, В.** "Ерліх, ще нами незнаний : [інтерв'ю із доц. ЧДУ В. Марчуком про проф. права Чернів. ун-ту Є. Ерліха]", інтерв'ю записав Василь Дуган. *Буковина.* 1998. 8 лип. (№ 53). С. 2. [Marchuk, V. "Ehrlich, Still Unknown to Us: [interview with V. Marchuk, the associate professor of ChNU about prof. of law of Chernivtsi University E. Ehrlich", interview was recorded by Vasyl Duhan. *Bukovina,* 1998, July 8 (Nr. 53). p. 2.]

304. **Марчук, В. П.** Євген Ерліх – основоположник соціології права. В *Проблеми філософії права.* Київ; Чернівці : Рута, 2005. Т. 3, № 1/2. С. 147–151. Бібліогр.: с. 151. [Marchuk, V. P. Eugene Ehrlich – the Founder of the Sociology of Law. In *Problems of the Philosophy of Law.* Kiev ; Chernivtsi : Ruta, 2005. Vol. 3, Nr. 1/2. pp. 147–151. Bibliogr.: p. 151.]

В 70701 34П781

305. **Марчук, В. П.** Євген Ерліх: сторінки життя і творчості. В *Ерліхівський збірник : наук. ст. викл., аспірантів та співроб. юридич. ф-тів Чернів. та Київ. ун-тів.* Чернівці, 1994. Вип. 1. С. 5–10. [Marchuk, V. P. Eugene Ehrlich: Pages of Life and Scientific Work. In *Ehrlich Collection: scientific articles of teachers, postgraduate students and staff of faculties of law of Chernivtsi and Kyiv universities.* Chernivtsi, 1994. Vol. 1. pp. 5–10.]

А 395963 34Е719

306. **Марчук, В. П.** "Идеи "свободного права" в концепции Е. Эрлиха и их роль в буржуазной юриспруденции". Автореф. дисс. ... канд. юрид. наук : специальность № 12.710 "Теория и история государства и права". Киев : Киев. ордена Ленина гос. ун-т им. Т. Г. Шевченко, 1971. 24 с. [Marchuk, V. P. "The Ideas of "Free Law" in the Conception of E. Ehrlich and their Role in Bourgeois Jurisprudence." Synopsis of dissertation ... candidate of Legal Science: specialty Nr. 12.710 "Theory and History of State and Law". Kiev : Kiev State Order of Lenin T. G. Shevchenko State University, 1971. 24 p.]

Ав 38893

307. **Марчук, В. П.** "Идеи "свободного права" Е. Эрлиха." *Советское государство и право.* 1972. № 6. С. 130–133. [Marchuk, V. P. "Ideas of "free law" E. Ehrlich." *Soviet State and Law.* 1972. Nr. 6. pp. 130–133.]

308. **Марчук, В. П.** Концепція "живого права" Є. Ерліха та її вплив на сучасну буржуазну юриспруденцію. В *Проблеми правознавства: міжвідом. наук. зб.* Київ: Вид-во КДУ, 1970. Вип. 16. С. 124–130. [Marchuk, V. P. The Conception of "Living Law" of E. Ehrlich and its Influence on Modern Bourgeois Jurisprudence. In *Problems of Jurisprudence: Interdepartmental Scientific Collected Volume.* Kyiv : KSU Publishing House, 1970. Vol. 16. pp. 124–130.]

309. **Марчук, В. П.,** Н. С. Прозорова, В. В. Хірсін, та Т-во "Знання" Української РСР. *Критика сучасних буржуазних теорій права.* Київ, 1981. 48 с. (Сер. *"Юридична"*, XIII, № 9). [Marchuk, V. P., N. S. Prozorova, V. V. Khirsin, and Society "Knowledge" of the Ukrainian SSR. *Criticism of Modern Bourgeois Theories of Law.* Kyiv, 1981. 48 p. (Series, *"Legal"*, XIII, Nr. 9).]

E. Ehrlich. – pp. 19–22, 24–25.

А 312159 34БМ30

310. **Марчук, В. П.** *"Свободное право" в буржуазной юриспруденции: критика концепций Е. Эрлиха.* Киев: Вища шк., 1977. 167 с. Библиогр. в подстроч. примеч. [Marchuk, V. P. *"Free Law" in Bourgeois Jurisprudence: Criticism of the Conception of E. Ehrlich.* Kiev : Vyshcha shkola, 1977. 167 p. Bibliogr. in footnotes.]

А 273961 34БМ30

311. **Марчук, В. П.** *Соціологічні теорії права в Німеччині: історія і сучасність.* Чернівці: ЧДУ, 1998. 128 с. [Marchuk, V. P. *Sociological Theories of Law in Germany: History and Modernity.* Chernivtsi: ChNU, 1998. 128 p.]

Б 476308 34М30

312. **Марчук, В.** "Учений-юрист європейського рівня: [розмова з доц. юрид. ф-ту Віталієм Марчуком про проф. Чернів. ун-ту Євгена Ерліха", розмову вів Василь Дуган]. *Юридичний вісник України.* 1998. 15 квіт. (№ 15). С. 7. [Marchuk, V. P. "Law-Scholar of European Level: Conversation with V. Marchuk, the associate professor of the Faculty of Law about prof. of Chernivtsi University E. Ehrlich", the conversation was conducted by Vasyl Duhan. *Legal Newsletter of Ukraine*, 1998, April 15 (Nr. 15). p. 7.]

313. **Масіян, Н. Б.** "Ректори університету: [1875–2000]." *Буковинське віче.* 2000. 4 жовт. (№ 76). С. 2. [Masiian, N. B. "Rectors of the University: [1875–2000]." *Bukovynske Viche*, 2000, October 4 (Nr. 76). p. 2.]

314. **Місевич, С. В.** Живе право церкви: проблема змінності церковних канонів. В *Ерліхівський збірник. Юридичний факультет Чернівецького національного університету ім. Ю. Федьковича: наук. доп. та повідомл.* Чернівці: ЧНУ, 2012. Вип. 6. С. 187–191. Бібліогр.: 9 назв. [Misevych, S. V. Living

Law of Church: The Problem of the Variability of Church Canons. In *Ehrlich Collection. Faculty of Law of Yuriy Fedkovych Chernivtsi National University: scientific report.* Chernivtsi : ChNU, 2012. Issue 6. pp. 187–191. Bibliogr.: 9 titl.]

E. Ehrlich. – p. 187.

B 74131 34E719

315. **Мироненко, О. М.,** та В. П. Горбатенко. *Історія вчень про державу і право : навч. посіб.* Київ : Академія, 2010. 454 с. *(Альма-матер).* Бібліогр. в кінці розд. [Myronenko, O. M., and V. P. Horbatenko. *History of the Doctrines about the State and Law: Teach. Manual.* Kyiv : Akademiya, 2010. 454 p. *(Alma Mater).* Bibliogr. at the end of chapters.]

E. Ehrlich. – pp. 341–342.

Б 541168 34M641

316. **Музика, І. В.** Розвиток соціології права на Україні у першій половині XX століття. В *Юридична наука та освіта: історія, сучасність, перспективи : матеріали IX іст.-прав. конф., (Рівне, 6–8 черв., 2003 р.).* Київ, 2004. С. 56–62. Бібліогр.: 15 назв. [Muzyka, I. V. Development of the Sociology of Law in Ukraine in the First Half of the XX century. In *Law Science and Education: History, Present and Prospects: Materials of IX Historical-Legal Conference, Rivne, June 6–8, 2003.* Kyiv, 2004. pp. 56–62. Bibliogr.: 15 titl.]

E. Ehrlich. – pp. 56–57.

317. **Музика, Л. А.** Вчення Є. Ерліха та цивільно-правова політика. В *Ерліхівський збірник. Юридичний факультет Чернівецького національного університету ім. Ю. Федьковича : наук. доп. та повідомл.* Чернівці : ЧНУ, 2012. Вип. 6. С. 192–194. Бібліогр.: 15 назв. [Muzyka, L. A. Doctrine of E. Ehrlich and Civil Law Politics. In *Ehrlich Collection. Faculty of Law of Yuriy Fedkovych Chernivtsi National University: scientific report.* Chernivtsi: ChNU, 2012. Issue 6. pp. 192–194. Bibliogr.: 15 titl.]

E. Ehrlich. – pp. 192, 193.

B 74131 34E719

318. **Настасяк, І. Ю.** Проблема залежності змісту правового впливу від типу праворозуміння. *Там само.* Чернівці : ЧНУ, 2012. Вип. 6. С. 50–54. Бібліогр.: 9 назв. [Nastasiak, I. Yu. The Problem of the Dependence of Content of Legal Influence on the Type of Legal Thinking. *Ibidem.* Chernivtsi: ChNU, 2012. Issue 6. pp. 50–54. Bibliogr.: 9 titl.]

E. Ehrlich. – p. 52.

B 74131 34E719

319. **Нежурбіда, Сергій.** *Етіологія злочину: теорії, аналіз, результат : монографія.* Чернівці : Друк Арт, 2013. 431 с. [Nezhur-

bida, Sergii. *Etiology of Crime: Theory, Analysis, Result: monograph.* Chernivtsi: Druk Art, 2013. 431 p.]

E. Ehrlich. – p. 205.

Б 551123 343.2Н439

320. **Нежурбіда, С. І.** Теорії культурної девіантності як теорії причин злочинності від Євгена Ерліха до Елайджі Андерсона. В *Ерліхівський збірник. Юридичний факультет Чернівецького національного університету ім. Ю. Федьковича : наук. доп. та повідомл.* Чернівці : ЧНУ, 2012. Вип. 6. С. 39–45. Бібліогр.: 59 назв. [Nezhurbida, S. I. Theories of Cultural Deviance as the Causes of Crime Theory from Eugene Ehrlich to Ellidge Anderson. In *Ehrlich Collection. Faculty of Law of Yuriy Fedkovych Chernivtsi National University : scientifical report and inform.* Chernivtsi : ChNU, 2012. Issue 6. pp. 39–45. Bibliogr.: 59 titl.]

В 74131 34Е719

321. **Нестеренко, Л. Б.** Вплив Євгена Ерліха на формування соціологічних поглядів Йозефа Алоїза Шумпетера. *Там само.* Чернівці : ЧНУ, 2012. Вип. 6. С. 113–114. Бібліогр.: 7 назв. [Nesterenko, L. B. Eugene Ehrlich's Influence on the Formation of Joseph Alois Schumpeter's Sociological Views. *Ibidem.* Chernivtsi : ChNU, 2012. Issue 6. pp. 113–114. Bibliogr.: 7 titl.]

В 74131 34Е719

322. **Никифорак, В. М.** Договір в концепції "живого права" Євгена Ерліха. В *Ерліхівський збірник. Юридичний факультет Чернівецького національного університету ім. Ю. Федьковича : наук. доп. та повідомл.* Чернівці : ЧНУ, 2012. Вип. 6. С. 97–101. Бібліогр.: 16 назв. [Nykyforak, B. M. Agreement in the Conception of "Living Law" of Eugene Ehrlich. In *Ehrlich Collection. Faculty of Law of Yuriy Fedkovych Chernivtsi National University : scientifical report and inform.* Chernivtsi : ChNU, 2012. Issue 6. pp. 97–101. Bibliogr.: 16 titl.]

В 74131 34Е719

323. **Никифорак, М. В.** "Відродження юридичного : [розмова з доц. каф. теорії та історії держави і права М. В. Никифораком]." *Університетський вісник.* 1992. Берез. (№ 4). С. 2. [Nykyforak, M .V. "The Revival of Legal : [conversation with the associate professor of the Department of Theory and History of State and Law M.V. Nykyforak]." *University Newsletter,* 1992, March (№ 4). p. 2.]

324. **Никифорак, Михайло Васильович.** *Буковина в державно-правовій системі Австрії (1774–1918).* Чернівці : Рута, 2004. 384 с. [Nykyforak, Mikhailo. *Bucovyna in the State-Legal System of Austria (1774-1918).* Chernivtsi : Ruta, 2004. 384 p.]

E. Ehrlich. – pp. 268–269, 305, 313–315, 321–324, 349, 359, 374.

Б 497984 34(с287)Н627

325. **Никифорак, М. В.,** та Л. А. Марчук. В. П. Марчук – дослідник творчості Євгена Ерліха. В *Ерліхівський збірник. Юридичний факультет Чернівецького національного університету ім. Ю. Федьковича : наук. доп. та повідомл.* Чернівці : ЧНУ, 2012. Вип. 6. С. 88–91. Бібліогр.: 40 назв. [Nykyforak, M. V., and L. A. Marchuk. V. P. Marchuk – Eugene Ehrlich Investigator of Creativity. In *Ehrlich Collection. Faculty of Law of Yuriy Fedkovych Chernivtsi National University : scientifical report and inform.* Chernivtsi : ChNU, 2012. Issue 6. pp. 88–91. Bibliogr.: 40 titl.]

В 74131 34Е719

326. **Никифорак, М. В.** До питання про джерела державного права на Буковині у 1775–1918 рр. В *Науковий вісник Чернівецького університету : зб. наук. пр.* Чернівці : Рута, 2000. Вип. 75, *"Правознавство."* С. 23–26. Бібліогр.: 19 назв. [Nykyforak, M. V. On the Question about Sources of State Law in Bukovina in 1775–1918. In *Scientific Newsletter of the Chernivtsi University: Collection of scientific works.* Chernivtsi : Ruta, 2000. Issue 75, *"Science of Law."* pp. 23–26. Bibliogr.: 12 titl.]

E. Ehrlich. – pp. 23, 26.

В 66952 061Ч492

327. **Никифорак, М.** "З історії вищої правничої освіти на Буковині." *Юридический вестник.* 2000. № 3. С. 135–140. Бібліогр.: 20 назв. [Nykyforak, M. "From the History of Higher Education in Law in Bukovina." *Law Newsletter.* 2000. № 3. pp. 135–140. Bibliogr.: 20 titl.]

E. Ehrlich. – pp. 136–140.

328. **Никифорак, М. В.** З історії Чернівецького магістрату. В *Науковий вісник Чернівецького університету : зб. наук. пр.* Чернівці : ЧДУ, 1999. Вип. 55, *"Правознавство."* С. 21–26. Бібліогр.: 21 назва. [Nykyforak, M. V. From the History of Chernivtsi Town Hall. In *Scientific Newsletter of Chernivtsi University: Collection of scientific papers.* Chernivtsi : ChNU, 1999. Issue 55, *"Science of Law."* pp. 21–26. Bibliogr.: 21 titl.]

E. Ehrlich. – p. 24.

В 66924 061Ч492

329. **Никифорак, Михайло.** "Кафедра філософії та теорії права юридичного факультету Чернівецького національного університету імені Юрія Федьковича." *Буковинське віче.* 2015. 19 берез. (№ 11). С. 3 ; 26 берез. (№ 12). С. 2. [Nykyforak, Mykhailo. "Department of Philosophy and Theory of Law of the Faculty Law of Yuriy Fedkovych Chernivtsi National University." *Bukovinske Viche,* 2015, March 19 (№ 11). p. 3 ; March 26 (№ 12). p. 2.]

330. **Никифорак,** Михайло Васильович. *Правничий факультет університету Франца-Йосифа у Чернівцях (1875–1918 рр.).*

Чернівці : Рута, 2003. 32 с. [Nykyforak, Mykhailo. *Faculty of Law of Franz Joseph Czernowitz University (1875–1918).* Chernivtsi: Ruta, 2003. 32 p.]

E. Ehrlich. – pp. 10, 20–22, 25–29.

331. **Никифорак, М. В.** Р. Ф. Кайндль як історик права. В *Науковий вісник Чернівецького університету : зб. наук. пр.* Чернівці : Рута, 2003. Вип. 187, *"Правознавство."* С. 122–124. Бібліогр.: 15 назв. [Nykyforak, M. V. R. F. Kaindl as a Historian of Law. In *Scientific Newsletter of Chernivtsi University: - collection of scientific works.* Chernivtsi : Ruta, 2003. Issue 187, *"Science of Law."* pp. 122–124. Bibliogr.: 15 titl.]

E. Ehrlich. – p. 122.

B 68636 061Ч492

332. **Никифорак, М. В.** Становлення вищої юридичної освіти на Буковині. В *Ерліхівський збірник : наук. ст. викл., аспірантів та співроб. юридич. ф-тів Чернів. та Київ. ун-тів.* Чернівці, 1994. Вип. 1. С. 11–16. [Nykyforak, M. V. The Establishment of the Higher Education in Law in Bukovina. In *Ehrlich Collection: scientific papers of teachers, candidates of science and staff of faculties of law of Chernivtsi and Kyiv Universities.* Chernivtsi, 1994. Issue 1. pp. 11–16.]

E. Ehrlich. – pp. 11, 14, 15.

A 395963 34E719

333. **Никифорак, М. В.** Три портрети з історії правничого факультету університету Франца-Йосифа у Чернівцях : [Ерліх Є., Гросс Г., Шумпетер Й. А.]. В *Ерліхівський збірник. Юридичний факультет Чернівецького національного університету ім. Ю. Федьковича : зб. наук. ст.* Чернівці : Рута, 2005. Вип. 4/5. С. 26–30. Бібліогр.: 18 назв. [Nykyforak, M. V. Three Portraits from the History of Franz Joseph Czernowitz University: [Ehrlich E., Gross H., Schumpeter J. A.]. In *Ehrlich Collection. Faculty of Law of Yuriy Fedkovych Chernivtsi National University: Collection of scientific reports.* Chernivtsi : Ruta, 2005. Issue 4/5. pp. 26–30. Bibliogr.: 18 titl.]

B 69563 34E719

334. **Никифорак, Михайло.** *Чернівецький юридикум: історія та сьогодення : вибране (1994–2015).* Чернівці : РОДОВІД, 2015. 239 с. [Nykyforak, Mykhailo. *Chernivtsi Law School: History and Present: selected (1994-2015).* Chernivtsi : Rodovid, 2015. 239 p.]

Contents:

Пацурківський, П. С. Зразок синтезу і моста правових культур народів Заходу і Сходу. С. 5–7 *(Є. Ерліх – С. 5, 6)* [Patsurkivskyi, P. S. Examples of Synthesis and

Bridge of Legal Cultures of the Peoples from the West and the East. pp. 5–7 *(E. Ehrlich – pp. 5, 6)*];

СТАТТІ З ІСТОРІЇ ФАКУЛЬТЕТУ [ARTICLES FROM THE HISTORY OF THE FACULTY.]

Никифорак, М. В. Становлення вищої юридичної освіти на Буковині. С. 9–11 *(E. Ehrlich. – pp. 9, 13)* [Nykyforak, M. V. The Establishment of Higher Education in Law in Bukovina. pp. 9–11 *(E. Ehrlich – pp. 9, 13)*]; Никифорак, М. В. З історії вищої правничої освіти на Буковині. С. 16–26 *(E. Ehrlich. – pp. 18, 21–23)* [Nykyforak, M. V. From the History of Law Education in Bukovina. pp. 16–26 *(E. Ehrlich. – pp. 18, 21–23)*]; Никифорак, М. В. Правничий факультет університету Франца-Йосифа у Чернівцях (1875–1918 рр.). С. 27–51 *(E. Ehrlich. – pp. 32, 41–43, 45–50)* [Nykyforak, M. V. Faculty of Law of Franz-Joseph Czernowitz University (1875–1918). pp. 27–51 *(E. Ehrlich. – pp. 32, 41–43, 45–50)*]; Никифорак, М. В., та А. З. Георгіца. З історії юридичного факультету Чернівецького університету у 1918–1940 рр. С. 52–59 *(E. Ehrlich. – pp. 53, 57)* [Nykyforak, M. V., and A. Z. Georhitsa. From the History of the Faculty of Law of Chernivtsi University in 1918–1940. pp. 52–59 *(E. Ehrlich. – pp. 53, 57)*]; Никифорак, М. В., та П. С. Пацурківський. Сучасні проблеми університетської підготовки юристів (із досвіду юридичного факультету Чернівецького національного університету імені Юрія Федьковича). С. 60–68 *(E. Ehrlich. – pp. 60, 65)* [Nykyforak, M. V., and P. S. Patsurkivskyi. Current Problems of University Lawyers Training (From the Experience of the Faculty of Law of Yuriy Fedkovich Chernivtsi National University). pp. 60–68 *(E. Ehrlich. – pp. 60, 65)*]; Никифорак, М. В. Кафедра філософії та теорії права юридичного факультету Чернівецького національного університету імені Юрія Федьковича). С. 69–73 *(E. Ehrlich. – pp. 71, 72)* [Nykyforak, M. V. Department of Philosophy and Theory of Law, Faculty of Law, Yuriy Fedkovich Chernivtsi National University. pp. 69–73 *(E. Ehrlich. – pp. 71, 72)*];

ПЕРСОНАЛІЇ ЮРИСТІВ [PERSONALITIES OF LAWYERS.] Никифорак, М. В. Р. Ф. Кайндль як історик права. С. 81–85 *(E. Ehrlich. – p. 82)* [Nykyforak, M. V. R. F. Kaindl as a Law Historian. pp. 81–85 *(E. Ehrlich. – p. 82)*]; Никифорак, М. В., та А. З. Георгіца. Маловідомі сторінки історії юридичного факультету Чернівецького університету. С. 86–94 *(E. Ehrlich. – pp. 86–88, 93)* [Nykyforak, M. V., and A. Z. Georhitsa. Unknown Pages of History of the Faculty of Law of Chernivtsi University. pp. 86–94 *(E. Ehrlich. – pp. 86–88, 93)*]; Никифорак, М. В. Три портрети з історії правничого факультету Франца-Йосифа у Чернівцях. С. 95–103

(E. Ehrlich. – pp. 95–97, 102–103) [Nykyforak, M. V. Three Portraits from the History of Franz-Joseph Czernowitz University. pp. 95–103 *(E. Ehrlich. – pp. 95–97, 102–103)*]; Никифорак, М. В., та Л. А. Марчук. В. П. Марчук – дослідник творчості Євгена Ерліха. С. 120–128. [Nykyforak, M. V., and L. A. Marchuk. V. P. Marchuk –Investigator of Eugen Ehrlich Creativity. pp. 120–128.]

Б 559487 34Н627

335. **Никифорак, М. В.** Юридична освіта на Буковині в період її перебування у складі Австрії та Австро-Угорщини. В *Юридична наука та освіта: історія, сучасність, перспективи : матеріали IX іст.-прав. конф., (Рівне, 6–8 черв., 2003 р.).* Київ, 2004. С. 44–50. Бібліогр. : 14 назв. [Nykyforak, M. V. Law Education in Bukovina during its Periods of Belonging to Austria and Austria-Hungary. In *Juridical Science and Education: History, Presence, Perspectives: Materials of the IX History-Law Conference, Rivne, June 6–8, 2003).* Kyiv, 2004. pp. 44–50. Bibliogr.: 14 titl.]

E. Ehrlich. – pp. 45–50.

336. **Никифорак, М.,** та С. Нежурбіда. "Юридичний факультет Чернівецького національного університету імені Юрія Федьковича." *Право України.* 2013. № 1/2. С. 442–447. [Nykyforak, M., and S. Nezhurbida. "Faculty of Law of Yuriy Fedkovych Chernivtsi National University." *Ukrainian Law.* 2013. № 1/2. pp. 442–447.]

E. Ehrlich. – pp. 442–444.

337. **Новинки.** Чернівці, 6 грудня 1906 р.: із черн. університету. *Буковина.* 1906. 7 груд. (ч. 140, рочник 22). С. 3. [News. Chernivtsi, 6 December 1906 : from Chernivtsi University. *Bukovina,* 1906, December 7 (Nr. 140, Vol. 22). p. 3.]

Information about the report of the Vice-Rector Dr. Herzberg-Frenkel related to the growth in numbers of students in the faculties in the period of 1875–1899, and also about the inaugural speech of the recently elected Rector E. Ehrlich on "The Facts of Customary Law".

90

338. **Новинки.** Чернівці, 27 червня 1907: з універзитету. *Буковина.* 1907. 15 (28) черв. (ч. 69, рочник 23). С. 3. [News. Chernivtsi, 27 June 1907: from the University. *Bukovina,* 1907, June 15 (28) (Nr. 69, Vol. 23). p. 3.]

Composition of the Academic Senate for the academic year 1907/1908. Dr. Eugen Ehrlich – the Vice-Rector of the Czernowitz University.

90

339. **Новинки.** Чернівці, 28 вересня 1907: признанє жидівскої народности на черновецкім унїверзитетї. *Буковина.* 1907. 16 (29) верес. (ч. 109, рочник 23). С. 3. [News. Chernivtsi, 28 September 1907: recognition of Jews at the Czernowitz University. *Bukovina.* 1907. September 16 (29) (Nr. 109, Vol. 23). p. 3.]

About the appeal of the representatives of the academic societies "Emuna", "Gebroniya" and "Zephyra" to the Rector of the University Dr. Ehrlich about recognition of 300 Jewish students.

90

340. **Новинки.** Чернівцї, 23 червня 1909: із штуки і лїтератури. Prof. Dr. Eugen Ehrlich. *Буковина.* 1907. 24 черв. (ч. 133, рочник 25). С. 3. [News. Chernivtsi, 23 June 1909: from issue and literature. Prof. Dr. Eugen Ehrlich. *Bukovina*, 1907, June 24 (Nr. 133, Vol. 25). p. 3.]

About the publication of the research work of Professor Dr. Eugen Ehrlich "The Task of Social Policy in Austrian East" ("Die Aufgaben der Sozialpolitik im österreichischen Osten") by the Social-Scientific Academic Society in Czernowitz. The brief outline of the work is also provided.

90

341. **Павлюк, А. Г.** "Мовчазне волевиявлення" Є. Ерліха з погляду теорії цивільно-правового відведення. В *Ерліхівський збірник. Юридичний факультет Чернівецького національного університету ім. Ю. Федьковича: наук. доп. та повідомл.* Чернівці: ЧНУ, 2012. Вип. 6. С. 120–122. Бібліогр.: 3 назви. [Pavliuk, A. H. "The Silent Will Expression" of E. Ehrlich from the Point of View of Civil-Legal Assignment Theory. In *Ehrlich Collection. Faculty of Law of Y. Fedkovych Chernivtsi National University: sci rep. and inform.* Chernivtsi: ChNU, 2012. Issue 6. pp. 120–122. Bibliogr.: 3 titl.]

B 74131 34E719

342. **Пам'яті** Євгена Ерліха. *Буковинське віче.* 2017. 11 трав. (№ 16). С. 1. [Memories of Eugen Ehrlich. *Bukovinske viche.* 2017. May 11 (№ 16). p. 1.]

On the revelation of the memorial plaques dedicated to the outstanding scientist, lawyer, researcher, founder of the sociology of law, the Dean of the Faculty of Law, the Rector of the Czernowitz University – Eugen Ehrlich, on the 10th of May 2017 in Chernivtsi. The CV of Ehrlich is provided.

343. **Панов, М. І.,** Н. П. Осипова, Л. М. Герасіна, Г. П. Клімова, та О. В. Сердюк. *Соціологія права: підруч. для студ. юрид. спец.*, за ред. Н. П. Осипової. Київ: Ін-Юре, 2003. 276 с. Бібліогр.:

c. 270–273. [Panov, M. I., N. P. Osypova, L. M. Herasina, G. P. Klimova, and O. V. Serdiuk. *Sociology of Law: Manual for Students of Law,* ed. N. P. Osypova. Kyiv: In-Yur, 2003. 276 p. Bibliogr.: pp. 270–273.]

E. Ehrlich. – pp. 23, 25, 30, 31, 38, 39, 128–129.

Б 502574 316С693

344. **Паунд, Р.** Вшанування Євгена Ерліха, пер. з англ. В. С. Бігуна. В *Проблеми філософії права.* Київ ; Чернівці : Рута, 2005. Т. 3, № 1/2. С. 160. [Pound, R. In Honour of Eugen Ehrlich, translated from English by B. S. Bihun. In *Problems of the Philosophy of Law.* Kyiv ; Chernivtsi : Ruta, 2005. Volume 3, Nr. 1/2. p. 160.]

В 70701 34П781

345. **Пацурківський, П. С.** Інтегративний підхід в системі методів пізнання права. В *Науковий вісник Чернівецького університету : зб. наук. пр.* Чернівці : Рута, 2000. Вип. 75, *"Правознавство."* С. 10–18. Бібліогр.: 44 назви. [Patsurkivskyi, P. S. Integrative Approach to the System of Methods of Law Cognition. In *Scientific Newsletter of Chernivtsi University : scientific collect. of works.* Chernivtsi : Ruta, 2000. Issue 75, *"Science of Law."* pp. 10–18. Bibliogr.: 44 titl.]

E. Ehrlich. – pp. 12, 18.

В 66952 061Ч492

346. **Пацурківський, П. С.,** та Р. О. Гаврилюк. Методологія правопізнання Євгена Ерліха: неокласична парадигма. *Там само.* Чернівці : ЧНУ, 2012. Вип. 628, *"Правознавство."* С. 27–33. Бібліогр.: 22 назви. [Patsurkivskyi, P. S., and R. O. Havryliuk. Methodology of Eugen Ehrlich's Legal Recognition: Neoclassical Paradigm. *Ibidem.* Chernivtsi : ChNU, 2012. Issue 628, *"Science of Law."* pp. 27–33. Bibliogr.: 22 titl.]

В 73982 061Ч492

347. **Пацурківський, П.** та Р. Гаврилюк. "Методологія правопізнання Євгена Ерліха: неокласична парадигма." *Право України.* 2012. № 9. С. 383–391. Бібліогр.: 17 назв. [Patsurkivskyi, P. and R. Havryliuk. "Methodology of Eugen Ehrlich's Legal Recognition: Neoclassical Paradigm." *The Law of Ukraine.* 2012. № 9. pp. 383–391. Bibliogr.: 17 titl.]

348. **Пацурківський, П. С.,** та Р. О. Гаврилюк. "Парадигмально-методологічний підхід Євгена Ерліха до правопізнання як прояв наукової раціональності неокласичного типу." *Соціологія права.* 2012. № 2/3 (4/5). С. 13–19. [Patsurkivskyi, P. S., and R. O. Havryliuk. "Paradigmal – Methodological Approach of Eugen Ehrlich to Legal Recognition as a Manifestation of the Neoclassical Scientific Rationality." *Sociology of Law.* 2012. Nr. 2/3 (4/5). pp. 13–19.]

349. **Пацурківський, П. С.** Співвідношення змісту категорій "об'єкт науки фінансового права" та "предмет науки фінансового права". В *Науковий вісник Чернівецького університету : зб. наук. пр.* Чернівці : Рута, 2003. Вип. 187, *"Правознавство."* С. 5–13. Бібліогр.: 46 назв. [Patsurkivskyi, P. S. Correlation of Contents of Categories "Object of Financial Law" and "Subject of Financial Law". In *Scientific Newsletter of Chernivtsi University: scientific collect. of works.* Chernivtsi : Ruta, 2003. Issue 187, *"Science of Law."* pp. 5–13. Bibliogr.: 46 titl.]

E. Ehrlich. – pp. 10, 13.

B 68636 061Ч492

350. **Пацурківський, П. С.,** та Р. О. Гаврилюк. Чому Євген Ерліх "мовчазно відмовився" від класичних критеріїв науковості правопізнання? В *Ерліхівський збірник. Юридичний факультет Чернівецького національного університету ім. Ю. Федьковича : наук. доп. та повідомл.* Чернівці : ЧНУ, 2012. Вип. 6. С. 135–139. Бібліогр.: 8 назв. [Patsurkivskyi, P. S., and R. O. Havryliuk. Why Eugen Ehrlich "Silently Rejected" Classical Criteria of Legal Knowledge Scientificity? In *Ehrlich Collection. Faculty of Law of Y. Fedkovych Chernivtsi National University: scient. report and inform.* Chernivtsi : ChNU, 2012. Issue 6. pp. 135–139. Bibliogr.: 8 titl.]

B 74131 34E719

351. **Ребіндер, М.** Євген Ерліх: деякі сторінки з останніх років життя та творчості, пер. з нім. В. С. Бігуна. В *Проблеми філософії права.* Київ ; Чернівці : Рута, 2005. Т. 3, № 1/2. С. 127–134. Бібліогр.: 9 назв. [Rebinder, M. Eugen Ehrlich: Some Pages from the Last Years of Life and Creativity, translated from German by B. S. Bihun. In *Problems of the Philosophy of Law.* Kyiv ; Chernivtsi : Ruta, 2005. Volume 3, Nr. 1/2. pp. 127–134. Bibliogr.: 9 titl.]

B 70701 34П781

352. **Ребіндер, Манфред.** Семінар Євгена Ерліха про "живе право". В *Судово-правова реформа в Україні: проблеми та перспективи : матеріали Міжнар. наук.-практ. конф., присвяч. 200-річчю Крайового суду Буковини, (Чернівці, 26–28 трав., 2004 р.).* Чернівці : Рута, 2004. С. 87–89. [Rebinder, Manfred. Seminar by Eugen Ehrlich "Living Law". In *Ukrainian Judicial – Legal Reform: Problems and Prospects : materials from scientific – practical conference, dedicated to the 200th anniversary of Bukovinian Regional Court, Chernivtsi, May 26–28, 2004.* Chernivtsi : Ruta, 2004. pp. 87–89.]

Б 494754 342.5С892

353. **Савайда, О. І.** Соціологічні погляди Є. Ерліха в енциклопедії права. В *Ерліхівський збірник. Юридичний факультет*

Чернівецького національного університету ім. Ю. Федьковича : наук. доп. та повідомл. Чернівці : ЧНУ, 2012. Вип. 6. С. 104–106. Бібліогр.: 6 назв. [Savaida, O. I. Sociological Views of E. Ehrlich in the Encyclopedia of Law. In *Ehrlich Collection. Faculty of Law of Y. Fedkovych Chernivtsi National University: scient. report and inform.* Chernivtsi : ChNU, 2012. Issue 6. pp. 104–106. Bibliogr.: 6 titl.]

В 74131 34Е719

354. **Савчук, С.** "Велике бачиться на відстані." *Право України.* 2012. № 9. С. 457–460. [Savchuk, S. "The Great is Seen at a Distance." *The Law of Ukraine.* 2012. Nr. 9. pp. 457–460.]

355. **Савчук, С. В.** Передумови виникнення та формування юридичної соціології. В *Науковий вісник Чернівецького університету: зб. наук. пр.* Чернівці: Рута, 2003. Вип. 187, *"Правознавство."* С. 27–32. Бібліогр.: 28 назв. [Savchuk, S. V. Prerequisites for the Emergence and Formation of the Sociology of Law. In *Scientific Newsletter of Chernivtsi University: scient. collect. of works.* Chernivtsi : Ruta, 2003. Issue 187, *"Science of Law."* pp. 27–32. Bibliogr.: 28 titl.]

E. Ehrlich. – pp. 28–30, 32.

В 68636 061Ч492

356. **Савчук, С. В.** Юридична соціологія і філософія права. В *Проблеми філософії права.* Київ ; Чернівці : Рута, 2003. Т. 1. С. 176–181. Бібліогр.: 30 назв. [Savchuk, S. V. Legal Sociology and Philosophy of Law. In *Problems of the Philosophy of Law.* Kyiv ; Chernivtsi : Ruta, 2003. Volume 1. pp. 176–181. Bibliogr.: 30 titl.]

E. Ehrlich. – pp. 179, 181.

В 69400 34П781

357. **Савчук, С. В.** *Юридична соціологія: предмет та місце в системі юридичних наук.* Чернівці : Рута, 2003. 240 с. Бібліогр.: с. 190–226. [Savchuk, S. V. *Legal Sociology: Subject and Place in the System of Legal Sciences.* Chernivtsi : Ruta, 2003. 240 p. Bibliogr.: pp. 190–226.]

E. Ehrlich. – pp. 5, 17, 48, 50–51, 53, 70, 116, 149, 166, 175, 182, 225.

Б 486570 316.3С137

358. **Світові** вчені, які викладали в Чернівецькому університеті : [Є. Ерліх, Г. Гросс, Й. Шумпетер, Г. Е. Мюллер]. *Молодий буковинець.* 2013. 18 квіт. (№ 45). С. 15. [World Scientists Who Taught at Chernivtsi University: [E. Ehrlich, H. Gross, J. Schumpeter, G. E. Müller]. *Young Bucovinian,* 2013, April 18 (Nr. 45). p. 15.]

359. **Скакун, О. Ф.** Теорія "живого права" Євгена Ерліха і сучасний підхід до типології правових систем світу. В *Ерліхівський збірник. Юридичний факультет Чернівецького національного*

університету ім. Ю. Федьковича : наук. доп. та повідомл. Чернівці : ЧНУ, 2012. Вип. 6. С. 155–159. Бібліогр.: 12 назв. [Skakun, O. F. Theory of "Living Law" by Eugen Ehrlich and Modern Approach to the Typology of World Legal Systems. In *Ehrlich Collection. Faculty of Law of Yu. Fedkovych Chernivtsi National University: scient. report and inform.* Chernivtsi : ChNU, 2012. Issue 6. pp. 155–159. Bibliogr.: 12 titl.]

В 74131 34Е719

360. **Смородинський, В. С.** Співвідношення права і держави: сучасний погляд на дискусію Євгена Ерліха і Ганса Кельзена. *Там само.* Чернівці : ЧНУ, 2012. Вип. 6. С. 175–177. [Smorodynskyi, V. S. The Interrelation of Law and State: A Modern View on the Discussion of Eugene Ehrlich and Hans Kelsen. *Ibidem.* Chernivtsi : ChNU, 2012. Issue 6. pp. 175–177.]

В 74131 34Е719

361. **Струк, Н.,** та О. Матвійчук, авт.-упоряд. *Чернівецький національний університет імені Юрія Федьковича : імена славних сучасників : довід.-біогр. вид.* Київ : Світ Успіху, 2005. 287 с. : ілюстр. [Struk, N., and O. Matviichuk, authors-compilers. *Yuriy Fedkovych Chernivtsi National University: The Names of Famous Contemporaries: biography publ.* Kyiv : The World of Success, 2005. 287 p. : Illustr.]

E. Ehrlich. – pp. 8, 9, 17, 43, 170, 171, 187.

Б 497383 378Ч490

362. **Тимашев, Н. С.** Рецензия, пер. с англ. М. В. Антонова. В Эрлих, Ойген. *Основоположение социологии права.* Санкт-Петербург : Унив. издат. консорциум, 2011. С. 667–672. Библиогр. в подстроч. примеч. [Timasheff, N. S. Review, trans. from English by M. V. Antonov. In Ehrlich, Eugen. *Fundamental Principles of the Sociology of Law.* Sankt-Petersburg : Univ. Pub. Consortium, 2011. p. 667–672. Bibliogr. in footnotes.]

363. **Тимошина, О.** "Методологічні підстави соціології права: Л. Петражицький vs Є. Ерліх." *Право України.* 2014. № 1. С. 195–202. Бібліогр. в кінці ст. [Timoshina, O. "Methodological Grounds of the Sociology of Law: L. Petrazhytsky vs E. Ehrlich." *The Law of Ukraine.* 2014. Nr. 1. pp. 195–202. Bibliogr. at the end of chapters.]

364. **Торончук, І. Ж.** та Т. А. Грекул-Ковалик. Основні етапи формування концепції "живого права" Євгена Ерліха. В *Ерліхівський збірник. Юридичний факультет Чернівецького національного університету ім. Ю. Федьковича : наук. доп. та повідомл.* Чернівці : ЧНУ, 2012. Вип. 6. С. 107–109. Бібліогр.: 16 назв. [Toronchuk, I. Zh., and T. A. Hrekul-Kovalyk. The Main Stages of the Formation of the Concept of "Living Law"

of Eugene Ehrlich. In *Ehrlich Collection. Faculty of Law of Chernivtsi National University: scient. report and inform.* Chernivtsi: ChNU, 2012. Issue 6. pp. 107–109. Bibliogr.: 16 titl.]

B 74131 34E719

365. **Трофимов, В. В.** "Проблема микросоциальных истоков права в юридической науке." *Ленинградский юридический журнал.* 2007. № 1 (7). С. 5–20. [Trofimov, V. V. "The Problem of Microsocial Sources of Law in Legal Science." *Leningrad Juridical Journal.* 2007. Nr. 1 (7). pp. 5–20.]

E. Ehrlich. – pp. 6–7.

366. **Трутень, В. В.** Постерліхівська методологія цивільного права. В *Ерліхівський збірник. Юридичний факультет Чернівецького національного університету ім. Ю. Федьковича: наук. доп. та повідомл.* Чернівці: ЧНУ, 2012. Вип. 6. С. 195–200. Бібліогр.: 11 назв. [Truten, V. V. Post-Ehrlich Methodology of Civil Law. In *Ehrich Collection. Faculty of Law of Yuriy Fedkovych Chernivtsi National University : scient. report and inform.* Chernivtsi: ChNU, 2012. Issue 6. pp. 195–200. Bibliogr.: 11 titl.]

B 74131 34E719

367. **Туманов, В. А.** *Буржуазная правовая идеология: к критике учений о праве.* Москва: Наука, 1971. 382 с. [Tumanov, V. A. *Bourgeois' Legal Ideology: On the Criticism of the Doctrines of Law.* Moscow: Science, 1971. 382 p.]

E. Ehrlich. – pp. 51–52, 85, 115, 153, 244, 245, 247, 252–259, 261, 266, 272, 285, 287, 288, 312.

Б 252789 34БТ83

368. **Туманов, В. А.** Эрлих (Ehrlich) Евгений. В *Современная западная социология: словарь.* Москва: Политиздат, 1990. С. 420. [Tumanov, V. A. Ehrlich Eugene. In *Contemporary Western Sociology: A Dictionary.* Moscow: Politizdat, 1990. p. 420.]

Б 452744 316С568

369. **Фещук, Наталія.** "Ректор, який знав десяток іноземних мов." *Чернівці.* 2017. 11 трав. (№ 19). С. 2. [Feshchuk, Nataliya. "Rector who spoke dozen foreign languages." *Chernivtsi.* 2017. May 11 (№ 19). p. 2.]

On the revelation of two memorial plaques dedicated to the Dean of the Faculty of Law and the Rector of the Czernowitz University – Eugen Ehrlich. The CV of Ehrlich is provided.

370. **Чернівецький** університет. 1875–1995: сторінки історії. Чернівці: Рута, 1995. 208 с. [Chernivtsi University. 1875-1995: History Pages. Chernivtsi: Ruta, 1995. 208 p.]

E. Ehrlich. – pp. 3, 18, 41–46, 92, 179, 195, 198.

B66244 378Ч498

371. **Черновський, О. К.,** та А. В. Федіна. Вплив концепції "живого права" Є. Ерліха на здійснення правосуддя в Україні. В *Ерліхівський збірник. Юридичний факультет Чернівецького національного університету ім. Ю. Федьковича : наук. доп. та повідомл.* Чернівці : ЧНУ, 2012. Вип. 6. С. 140–142. Бібліогр.: 7 назв. [Chernovskyi, O. K., and A. V. Fedina. The Influence of E. Ehrlich's Conception of the "Living Law" on the Administration of Justice in Ukraine. In *Ehrlich Collection. Faculty of Law of Yuriy Fedkovych Chernivtsi National University : scient. report and inform.* Chernivtsi : ChNU, 2012. Issue 6. pp. 140–142. Bibliogr.: 7 titl.]

В 74131 34Е719

372. **Штейнберг, И. З.** *Что такое "движение свободного права"? (Закон и судья) : доклад, читанный в Московском юридическом обществе.* Москва : [б. и.], 1914. 29 с. Библиогр.: с. 27–29. [Shteinberg, I. Z. *What is the "Free-Law Movement"? (Law and a judge): a report read in the Moscow Juridical Society.* Moscow : [s. n.], 1914. 29 p. Bibliogr.: pp. 27–29.]

E. Ehrlich. – pp. 5, 15, 27.

373. **Шульженко, Ф. П.,** та Т. Г. Андрусяк. *Історія політичних і правових вчень : навч. посіб.* 3-є вид., стер. Київ : Юрінком Інтер, 2002. 304 с. [Shulzhenko, F. P., and T. H. Andrusiak. *History of Political and Legal Doctrines: Teach. Manual.* 3rd Ed., ster. Kyiv : Yurinkom Inter, 2002. 304 p.]

E. Ehrlich. – pp. 266–267.

Б 487619 34(091)Ш957

374. **Щербанюк, О. В.** Соціологічний підхід до дослідження принципу народного суверенітету. В *Ерліхівський збірник. Юридичний факультет Чернівецького національного університету ім. Ю. Федьковича : наук. доп. та повідомл.* Чернівці : ЧНУ, 2012. Вип. 6. С. 55–58. Бібліогр.: 7 назв. [Shcherbaniuk, O. V. Sociological Approach to the Study of the Principle of the National Sovereignty. In *Ehrlich Collection. Faculty of Law of Yuriy Fedkovych Chernivtsi National University: scient. report and inform.* Chernivtsi : ChNU, 2012. Issue 6. pp. 55–58. Bibliogr.: 7 titl.]

E. Ehrlich. – pp. 55, 58.

В 74131 34Е719

375. **Юсов, С. Л.** Ерліх (Ehrlich) Євген. В НАН України, та Ін-т історії України. *Енциклопедія історії України.* Київ : Наук. думка, 2005. Т. 3, *"Е–Й."* С. 46. [Yusov, S. L. Ehrlich Eugene. In National Academy of Sciences of Ukraine, and Institute of History of Ukraine. *Encyclopedia of the History of Ukraine.* Kyiv : Science. thought, 2005. T. 3, *"E–J."* p. 46.]

В 69985 9(с2)Е644

376. **Adler, Karl.** "Ueber weltfremde und weltkluge Juristen im Juristenjahr 1911." *Czernowitzer Zeitung,* 1912, 6. Jänner (Nr. 4, Jg. 47). – S. 1–3.

Information about Eugen Ehrlich as a lawyer – p. 2.

IN 1952 90A1

377. **Adressbuch** von Czernowitz samt Vorstädtenzusammengestellt nach Daten der k. k. Polizeidirektion sowie der Städte Radautz und Suczawa : Schematismus sämtlicher Behörden und Privatanstalten der Bukowina, Ortschaftsverzeichnis der Bukowina, Verzeichnis der protokollierten Firmen etc. Kalender 1908 mit Termin- und Vormerkbuch. Czernowitz : Druk und Verl. der Bukowinaer Vereinsdruck., [1907]. XXIV, 336, 30 S.

Information about Eugen Ehrlich in the address book of Czernowitz – pp. 125, 254, 274, 275, 276.

IN 103675 90S1

378. **Adressbuch** von Czernowitz samt Vorstädtenzusammengestellt nach Daten der k. k. Polizeidirektion sowie der Städte Radautz und Suczawa : Schematismus sämtlicher Behörden und Privatanstalten der Bukowina, Ortschaftsverzeichnis der Bukowina, Verzeichnis der protokollierten Firmen etc. Kalender 1909 mit Termin- und Vormerkbuch. Czernowitz : Druk und Verl. der Bukowinaer Vereinsdruck., [1908]. XXVIII, 368, 34 S.

Information about Eugen Ehrlich in the address book of Czernowitz – pp. 125, 299, 300, 301.

IN 194139 90S

379. **Adressbuch** von Czernowitz samt Vorstädtenzusammengestellt nach Daten der k. k. Polizeidirektion sowie der Städte Radautz und Suczawa : Schematismus sämtlicher Behörden und Privatanstalten der Bukowina, Ortschaftsverzeichnis der Bukowina, Verzeichnis der protokollierten Firmen etc. Kalender 1910 mit Termin- und Vormerkbuch. Czernowitz : Druk und Verl. der Bukowinaer Vereinsdruck., [1909]. XXVIII, 369, 25 S.

Information about Eugen Ehrlich in the address book of Czernowitz – pp. 125, 304, 305.

IN 103683 90S1

380. **Adressbuch** von Czernowitz samt Vorstädtenzusammengestellt nach Daten der k. k. Polizeidirektion sowie der Städte Radautz und Suczawa : Schematismus sämtlicher Behörden und Privatanstalten der Bukowina, Ortschaftsverzeichnis der Bukowina, Verzeichnis der protokollierten Firmen etc. Kalender 1911 mit Termin- und Vormerkbuch. Czernowitz : Druk und Verl. der Bukowinaer Vereinsdruck., [1910]. XXIV, 378, 28 S.

Information about Eugen Ehrlich in the address book of Czernowitz – pp. 124, 307, 308.

IN 103684 90S1

381. **Adressbuch** von Czernowitz samt Vorstädtenzusammengestellt nach Daten der k. k. Polizeidirektion sowie der Städte Radautz und Suczawa : Schematismus sämtlicher Behörden und Privatanstalten der Bukowina, Ortschaftsverzeichnis der Bukowina, Verzeichnis der protokollierten Firmen etc. Kalender 1912 mit Termin- und Vormerkbuch. Czernowitz : Druk und Verl. der Bukowinaer Vereinsdruck., [1911]. XXIV, 378, 252 S.

Information about Eugen Ehrlich in the address book of Czernowitz – pp. 124, 304, 306.

IN 108611 90S1

382. **Adressbuch** von Czernowitz samt Vorstädtenzusammengestellt nach Daten der k. k. Polizeidirektion sowie der Städte Radautz und Suczawa : Schematismus sämtlicher Behörden und Privatanstalten der Bukowina, Ortschaftsverzeichnis der Bukowina, Verzeichnis der protokollierten Firmen etc. Kalender 1913 mit Termin- und Vormerkbuch. Czernowitz : Druk und Verl. der Bukowinaer Vereinsdruck., [1912]. XXIV, 376, 26 S.

Information about Eugen Ehrlich in the address book of Czernowitz – pp. 124, 303, 306.

IN 103674 90S1

383. **Adressbuch** von Czernowitz samt Vorstädtenzusammengestellt nach Daten der k. k. Polizeidirektion sowie der Städte Radautz und Suczawa : Schematismus sämtlicher Behörden und Privatanstalten der Bukowina, Ortschaftsverzeichnis der Bukowina, Verzeichnis der protokollierten Firmen etc. Kalender 1914 mit Termin- und Vormerkbuch. Czernowitz : Druk und Verl. der Bukowinaer Vereinsdruck., [1913]. XXIV, 381, 21 S.

Information about Eugen Ehrlich in the address book of Czernowitz – pp. 125, 315, 316.

IN 103673 90S1

384. **Akademischen** Senate der k.k. Franz-Josephs-Universität in Czernowitz, hrsg. *Die k. k. Franz-Josephs-Universität in Czernowitz im ersten Vierteljahrhundert ihres Bestandes : Festschrift.* Czernowitz : Bukowinaer Vereinsdruck., 1900. LXXVII, 179 S.

Information about Eugen Ehrlich as the university professor in the publication – p. 72.

IN 194066 90S9

385. **Allerlei.** *Die Wahrheit.* 1909. 14. Mai (Nr. 48/49, Jg. 3). S. 19–27.

Note about information that was surprising for the newspaper "Czernowitzer Tagblatt", about the creation of a committee composed of several young educated people of Jewish origin under the supervision of University Professor Dr. Erlich, who want to study "Issues of Peasants and Jews" ("Bauern- und Judenfrage") at Bukovina – pp. 24–25.

IN 90O50

386. **Amtlicher** Theil. Seine k. und k. Apostolische Majestät haben mit Allerhöchster Entschliessung vom 23. Janner d. J. ... *Wiener Zeitung.* 1900. 14. Febr. (Nr. 35). S. 1.

Information about the Resolution of His (Franz Joseph) Imperial and Royal Apostolic Majesty from the 23rd January 1900 who graciously appoints the Extraordinary (associate) Professor of Roman law, Dr. Eugen Ehrlich to the position of a Full Professor of Czernowitz University.

IN 1675 93A1

387. **Antonov,** Mikhail. "Eugen Ehrlich – State Law and Law Enforcement in Societal Systems." *Rechtstheorie.* 2013. Vol. 44, Iss. 3 (Sept.). p. 287–313.

388. **Antonov,** Mikhail. "History of Schidsm: the Debates between Hans Kelsen and Eugen Ehrlich." *ICL Journal : Vienna Journal on International Constitutional Law.* 2011. Vol. 5, № 1. p. 5–21.

389. **Ascherson, F.,** hrsg. *Deutscher Universitäts-Kalender für das Sommer-Semester 1895.* [47. Ausg.]. Berlin : Leonhard Simion, 1895. 50, 337, 24 S.

Information about Eugen Ehrlich in the publication – p. 282.

IN 313062 85H1

390. **Ascherson, F.,** hrsg. *Deutscher Universitäts-Kalender für das Winter-Semester 1895/1896.* [48. Ausg.]. Berlin : Leonhard Simion, 1895. 56, 340, 28 S.

Information about Eugen Ehrlich in the publication – p. 237.

IN 313063 85H1

391. **Ascherson, F.,** hrsg. *Deutscher Universitäts-Kalender für das Sommer-Semester 1896.* [49. Ausg.]. Berlin : Leonhard Simion, 1896. 50, 354, 29 S.

Information about Eugen Ehrlich in the publication – p. 250.

IN 313064 85H1

392. **Ascherson, F.,** hrsg. *Deutscher Universitäts-Kalender für das Winter-Semester 1896/1897.* [50. Ausg.]. Berlin : Leonhard Simion, 1896. 58, 364, 35 S.

Information about Eugen Ehrlich in the publication – p. 254.

IN 313065 85H1

393. **Ascherson, F.,** hrsg. *Deutscher Universitäts-Kalender für das Sommer-Semester 1897.* [51. Ausg.]. Berlin : Leonhard Simion, 1897. 50, 364, 24 S.

Information about Eugen Ehrlich in the publication – p. 226.

IN 313066 85H1

394. **Ascherson, F.,** hrsg. *Deutscher Universitäts-Kalender für das Winter-Semester 1897/1898.* [52. Ausg.]. Berlin : Leonhard Simion, 1897. 58, 377, 32 S.

Information about Eugen Ehrlich in the publication – p. 233.

IN 313067 85H1

395. **Ascherson, F.,** hrsg. *Deutscher Universitäts-Kalender für das Sommer-Semester 1898.* [53. Ausg.]. Berlin : Leonhard Simion, 1898. 50, 372, 28 S.

Information about Eugen Ehrlich in the publication – p. 232.

IN 313068 85H1

396. **Ascherson, F.,** hrsg. *Deutscher Universitäts-Kalender für das Sommer-Semester 1899.* [55. Ausg.]. Berlin : Leonhard Simion, 1899. 54, 388, 24 S.

Information about Eugen Ehrlich in the publication – p. 241.

IN 313069 85H1

397. **Ascherson, F.,** hrsg. *Deutscher Universitäts-Kalender für das Winter-Semester 1900/1901.* [58. Ausg.]. Berlin : Leonhard Simion, 1900. 62, 410, 35 S.

Information about Eugen Ehrlich in the publication – p. 236.

IN 313070 85H1

398. **Ascherson, F.,** hrsg. *Deutscher Universitäts-Kalender für das Sommer-Semester 1901.* [59. Ausg.]. Berlin : Leonhard Simion, 1901. 54, 420, 23 S.

Information about Eugen Ehrlich in the publication – p. 262.

IN 313071 85H1

399. **Ascherson, F.,** hrsg. *Deutscher Universitäts-Kalender für das Winter-Semester 1903/04.* [64. Ausg.]. Leipzig : K. G. Th. Scheffer, 1903. 62, 443, 24 S.

Information about Eugen Ehrlich in the publication. – p. 269.

IN 313072 85H1

400. **Ascherson, F.,** begr. *Deutscher Universitäts-Kalender. Winter-Semester 1906/07,* hrsg. von Th. Scheffer, und G. Zieler. 70. Ausg. Leipzig : Johann Ambrosius Barth, 1906. Teil 1, *"Die Universitäten im Deutschen Reich."* 8, 4, 339 S. ; Teil 2, *"Die Universitäten im benachbarten Auslande."* 7, 341–571, 16, 40 S.

Information about Eugen Ehrlich in the publication – pp. 341, 342.

IN 313073 85H1

401. **Ascherson, F.,** begr. *Deutscher Universitäts-Kalender. Sommer-Semester 1907,* hrsg. von Th. Scheffer, und G. Zieler. 71. Ausg. Leipzig : Johann Ambrosius Barth, 1907. Teil 1, *"Die Universitäten im Deutschen Reich."* VIII, 6, 333, XXIII S. ; Teil 2, *"Die Universitäten im benachbarten Auslande."* 6, 334–570, 16, 16, 24 S.

Information about Eugen Ehrlich in the publication – pp. 335, 336.

IN 287872 85H1

402. **Ascherson, F.,** begr. *Deutscher Universitäts-Kalender. Sommer-Semester 1908.* 73. Ausg. Leipzig : Johann Ambrosius Barth, 1908. Teil 2, *"Die Universitäten im benachbarten Auslande."* 7, 323–553, 16, 32, VIII, 16 S.

Information about Eugen Ehrlich in the publication – p. 324.

IN 287871 85H1

403. **Ascherson, F.,** begr. *Deutscher Universitäts-Kalender. Sommer-Semester 1909.* 75. Ausg. Leipzig : Johann Ambrosius Barth, 1909. Teil 2, *"Die Universitäten im benachbarten Auslande."* 4, 321–544, 16, 24, 16, VIII S.

Information about Eugen Ehrlich in the publication – pp. 321, 322.

IN 287874 85H1

404. **Ascherson, F.,** begr. *Deutscher Universitäts-Kalender. Winter-Semester 1909/10.* 76. Ausg. Leipzig : Johann Ambrosius Barth, 1909. Teil 2, *"Die Universitäten im benachbarten Auslande."* 4, 327–554 S.

Information about Eugen Ehrlich in the publication – p. 328.

IN 287876 85H1

405. **Ascherson, F.,** begr. *Deutscher Universitäts-Kalender. Sommer-Semester 1910.* 77. Ausg. Leipzig : Johann Ambrosius Barth, 1910. Teil 2, *"Die Universitäten im benachbarten Auslande."* 4, 329–561 S.

Information about Eugen Ehrlich in the publication – p. 330.

IN 287875 85H1

406. **Ascherson, F.,** begr. *Deutscher Universitäts-Kalender. Winter-Semester 1911/12.* 80. Ausg. Leipzig: Johann Ambrosius Barth, 1911. Teil 1, *"Die Universitäten im Deutschen Reiche."* VIII, 6, 340 S. ; Teil 2, *"Die Universitäten im benachbarten Auslande."* 4, 341–576, 16, 24, 20, 16 S.

Information about Eugen Ehrlich in the publication – pp. 341, 342.

IN 287836 85H1

407. **Aus Stadt**, Provinz und den Nachbarländern. Czernowitz, 22. Juni. Der akademische Senat. *Bukowiner Nachrichten.* 1912. 23. Juni (Nr. 6875, Jg. 25). S. 4.

Composition of the Academic Senate of Czernowitz University for the academic year 1912/1913. Dr. Eugen Ehrlich – Vice-Dean of the Faculty of Law.

IN 2045 90J6

408. **Aus Stadt**, Provinz und den Nachbarländern. Czernowitz, 19. März. Akademische Studienreise. *Ibidem.* 1912. 20. März (Nr. 6836, Jg. 25). S. 3–4.

Participation of the Dean of the Faculty of Law Professor Dr. Eugen Ehrlich in the meeting of students on the 17th of March 1912.

IN 2045 90J6

409. **Aus Stadt**, Provinz und den Nachbarländern. Czernowitz, den 26. Juni. Akademischer Senat. *Ibidem.* 1909. 27. Juni (Nr. 6198, Jg. 22). S. 4.

Composition of the Academic Senate of Czernowitz University for the academic year 1909/1910. Professor Dr. Eugen Ehrlich – Vice-Dean of the Faculty of Law.

IN 2040 90J6

410. **Aus Stadt**, Provinz und den Nachbarländern. Czernowitz, 24. Juni. Akademischer Senat unserer Universität. *Ibidem.* 1911. 25. Juni (Nr. 6727, Jg. 24). S. 4.

Composition of the Academic Senate of Czernowitz University for the academic year 1911/1912. Dr. Eugen Ehrlich – Dean of the Faculty of Law.

IN 2044 90J6

411. **Aus Stadt**, Provinz und den Nachbarländern. Czernowitz, den 13. Juli. Der Bater als Promotor des Sohnes. Ibidem. 1909. 14. Juli (Nr. 6211, Jg. 22). S. 3.

Participation of the Dean Professor Dr. Ehrlich in the defense procedure of Ludwig Kleinwächter applying for the degree of doctor of law.

IN 2041 90J6

412. **Aus Stadt**, Provinz und den Nachbarländern. Czernowitz, 23. Dezember. Czernowitzer Herrenfecht-Societe. *Ibidem.* 1910. 24. Dez. (Nr. 6644, Jg. 23). S. 3.

In the elections of the 19th of December 1910 University Professor Dr. Ehrlich was elected as Head of the Czernowitz Society of Fencing.

IN 2043 90J6

413. **Aus Stadt**, Provinz und den Nachbarländern. Czernowitz, 1. Dezember. Juristisch-staatswissenschaftliche Gesellschaft. *Ibidem.* 1910. 2. Dez. (Nr. 6626, Jg. 23). S. 3.

Request of the Juridical-Political Scientific Society for Prof. Ehrlich to continue in lecturing on law.

IN 2043 90J6

414. **Aus Stadt**, Provinz und den Nachbarländern. Czernowitz, 20. Juni. Landeszentrale für Kinderschutz. *Ibidem.* 1911. 21. Juni (Nr. 6725, Jg. 24). S. 4.

Participation of University Professor Dr. Ehrlich in the meeting of the Regional Centre for Child Protection.

IN 2044 90J6

415. **Aus Stadt**, Provinz und den Nachbarländern. Czernowitz, den 21. Juni. Das Leichenbegängnis. *Ibidem.* 1909. 22. Juni (Nr. 6193, Jg. 22). S. 2.

Information about the funeral of University Professor Dr. Johann Wrobel attended by the Dean Dr. Ehrlich.

IN 2040 90J6

416. **Aus Stadt**, Provinz und den Nachbarländern. Czernowitz, 6. April. Promotion. *Ibidem.* 1911. 7. Apr. (Nr. 6693, Jg. 24). S. 4.

Prof. Ehrlich – promoter of the graduation ceremony of new doctors of law at Czernowitz University – Theodor Czechowski, Konstantin Lewandowski and Emilian Berthold Winkler.

IN2044 90J6

417. **Aus Stadt**, Provinz und den Nachbarländern. Czernowitz, 1. Dezember. Promotion. *Ibidem.* 1909. 2. Dez. (Nr. 6329, Jg. 22). S. 4.

Professor Dr. Ehrlich – promoter of the graduation ceremony of a new doctor of law at Czernowitz University – Otto Ernst.

IN 2041 90J6

418. **Aus Stadt**, Provinz und den Nachbarländern. Czernowitz, 11. März. Promotion. *Ibidem.* 1910. 12. März (Nr. 6410, Jg. 23). S. 3.

Professor Dr. Ehrlich – promoter of the graduation ceremony of a new doctor of law at Czernowitz University – Apollonarius Argasinski.

IN 2042 90J6

419. **Aus Stadt**, Provinz und den Nachbarländern. Czernowitz, 18. Dezember 1909. Promotionen. *Ibidem.* 1909. 19. Dez. (Nr. 6343, Jg. 22). S. 4.

Prof. Dr. Ehrlich – promoter of the graduation ceremony of a new doctor of law at Czernowitz University – Arthur Füllenbaum.

IN 2041 90J6

420. **Aus Stadt**, Provinz und den Nachbarländern. Czernowitz, 30. Juni. Promotionen. *Ibidem.* 1910. 2. Juli (Nr. 6499, Jg. 23). S. 2.

Professor Dr. Ehrlich – promoter of the graduation ceremony of a new doctor of law at Czernowitz University – Julius Hruder.

IN 2043 90J6

421. **Aus Stadt**, Provinz und den Nachbarländern. Czernowitz, 2. November. Promotionen. *Ibidem.* 1910. 3. Nov. (Nr. 6601, Jg. 23). S. 3.

Professor Dr. Ehrlich – promoter of the graduation ceremony of new doctors of law at Czernowitz University – Erich Ebermann and Hermann Altmann.

IN 2043 90J6

422. **Aus Stadt**, Provinz und den Nachbarländern. Czernowitz, 20. Oktober. Das Seminar über "Lebendes Recht". *Ibidem.* 1909. 21. Okt. (Nr. 6294, Jg. 22). S. 3.

Information that Professor Dr. Eugen Ehrlich and Professor Dr. Ferdinand Kogler will hold a seminar "On Living Law" for graduate lawyers on the 26th of October 1909.

IN 2041 90J6

423. **Aus Stadt**, Provinz und den Nachbarländern. Czernowitz, 21. Februar. Sozialwissenschaftlicher akademischer Verein. *Ibidem.* 1910. 22. Febr. (Nr. 6394, Jg. 23). S. 3.

Information about the lecture of University Professor Dr. Eugen Ehrlich entitled "Living Law" ("Lebendes Recht"), that will be held on the 23rd of February 1910 in the Hall of "House of Merchants" on Petersplatz, Nr. 2.

IN 2042 90J6

424. **Aus Stadt**, Provinz und den Nachbarländern. Czernowitz, 1. Juni. Die Standeserhöhung des Landespräsidenten. *Ibidem.* 1911. 2. Juni (Nr. 6717, Jg. 24). S. 3.

Participation of University Professor Dr. Ehrlich in the formal welcoming ceremony for the Regional President Dr. von Bleyleben.

IN 2044 90J6

425. **Aus Stadt**, Provinz und den Nachbarländern. Czernowitz, 5. September. Volkstümliche Universitätskurse. *Ibidem.* 1911. 6. Sept. (Nr. 6756, Jg. 24). S. 3.

Information about the first series of the popular university courses for the academic year 1911/1912 beginning on the 21st of October 1911 including four stages of the course on "Theories of Karl Marx in the light of present times" ("Die Theorien von Karl Marx im Lichte der wirtschaftlichen Entwicklung der Gegenwart") by Professor Dr. Eugen Ehrlich.

IN 2044 90J6

426. **Aus Stadt**, Provinz und den Nachbarländern. Czernowitz, 12. November. Volkstümliche Universitätskurse. *Ibidem.* 1911. 12. Nov. (Nr. 6785, Jg. 24). S. 4.

Information about the cancelled lecture by Professor Dr. Eugen Ehrlich announced for the 11th of November 1911 on "Theories of Karl Marx in the light of present times" ("Die Theorien von Karl Marx im Lichte der wirtschaftlichen Entwicklung der Gegenwart") due to his business trip. The new date will be announced in newspapers.

IN 2044 90J6

427. **Aus Stadt**, Provinz und den Nachbarländern. Czernowitz, 25. November. Volkstümliche Universitätskurse. *Ibidem.* 1911. 26. Nov. (Nr. 6791, Jg. 24). S. 5.

Information about time and place of the previously cancelled lecture by Professor Dr. Eugen Ehrlich on "Theories of Karl Marx in the light of present times" ("Die Theorien von Karl Marx im Lichte der wirtschaftlichen Entwicklung der

Gegenwart") set for the 30th of November 1911 and the 7th of December 1911.

IN 2044 90J6

428. **Aus Stadt**, Provinz und den Nachbarländern. Czernowitz, 22. Juni. Von unserer Universität. *Ibidem.* 1911. 22. Juni (Nr. 6726, Jg. 24). S. 3.

In the elections of the 20th June 1911 Professor of Roman law Dr. Eugen Ehrlich elected the Dean of the Faculty of Law of Czernowitz University for the academic year 1911/1912.

IN 2044 90J6

429. **Aus Stadt**, Provinz und den Nachbarländern. Czernowitz, 27. Jänner. Von unserer Universität. *Ibidem.* 1912. 28. Jänner (Nr. 6814, Jg. 25). S. 3.

Participation of the Dean Professor Dr. Eugen Ehrlich in the Matriculation ceremony for the new students of the university registered for the winter semester of the academic year 1911/1912.

IN 2045 90J6

430. **Aus Stadt**, Provinz und den Nachbarländern. Czernowitz, 14. November. Vorträge des Professors Ehrlich. *Ibidem.* 1910. 16. Nov. (Nr. 6612, Jg. 23). S. 3.

Information about the intention of University Professor Dr. Ehrlich to hold a series of lectures for the Juridical-Political Scientific Society entitled "On Science of Law" ("Ueber Rechtswissenschaft"). It also points out that the first lecture will be on the 18th of November 1910 in the large hall of the Palace of Justice.

IN2043 90J6

431. **Aus Stadt** und Land. Czernowitz, 9. Oktober. Dem Vereine deutscher Alkoholgegner... *Ibidem.* 1907. 10. Okt. (Nr. 5688, Jg. 20). S. 5.

Information of the German Society against Alcoholism about the speech of the Rector of Czernowitz University Professor Dr. Ehrlich on how to combat alcoholism at the meeting of the Bukovina Sejm.

IN 2037 90J6

432. **Aus Stadt** und Land. Czernowitz, 8. Oktober. Diner beim Herrn k. k. Landespräsidenten. *Ibidem.* 1907. 9. Okt. (Nr. 5687, Jg. 20). S. 4.

Participation of the Rector Dr. Ehrlich in the Sunday lunch event organized by the Regional President Dr. Octavian von Bleyleben.

IN 2037 90J6

433. **Aus Stadt** und Land. Czernowitz, 20. September. Fremder Orden. *Ibidem.* 1907. 21. Sept. (Nr. 5672, Jg. 20). S. 4.

The Rector of Czernowitz University Professor Dr. Eugen Ehrlich awarded the Commander's Cross of the Greek Order of the Saviour.

IN 2037 90J6

434. **Aus Stadt** und Land. Czernowitz, 23. September. K. k. Franz Josefs-Universität. *Ibidem.* 1907. 24. Sept. (Nr. 5674, Jg. 20). S. 2.

Information related to the death of the Rector Elect Dr. Basil Gaina: until the new elections, the acting Rector Professor Dr. Eugen Ehrlich and the acting Vice-Rector Professor Dr. Sigmund Herzberg-Fränkel, remain in their positions with the possibility of re-election to their positions.

IN 2037 90J6

435. **Aus Stadt** und Land. Czernowitz, 15. Juli. Personalnachrichten. *Ibidem.* 1907. 16. Juli (Nr. 5615, Jg. 20). S. 2.

Information about a long vacation of the Rector Professor Dr. Eugen Ehrlich as of the 14th of July 1907, and about his trip to Vienna.

IN 2037 90J6

436. **Aus Stadt** und Land. Czernowitz, den 24. Oktober. Rektorswahl. *Ibidem.* 1907. 25. Okt. (Nr. 5701, Jg. 20). S. 3.

Information about the elections of the rector of Czernowitz University for the coming academic year organized under the supervision of Dr. Eugen Ehrlich.

IN 2037 90J6

437. **Aus Stadt** und Land. Czernowitz, 15. Juli. Ein Unfug. *Ibidem.* 1907. 16. Juli (Nr. 5615, Jg. 20). S. 2–3.

A note on a street accident involving the Rector of Czernowitz University Professor Dr. Eugen Ehrlich.

IN 2037 90J6

438. **Aus Stadt** und Land. Czernowitz, den 29. Oktober. Von unserer Universität. *Ibidem.* 1907. 30. Okt. (Nr. 5705, Jg. 20). S. 4.

Composition of the Academic Senate in the current academic year. Dr. Eugen Ehrlich – Vice-Rector of Czernowitz University.

IN 2037 90J6

439. **Autonomie** universitară. *Glasul Bucovinei.* 1921. 23 dec. (Nr. 878, An. 4). p. 1. Fără semnătură.

Criticism of Eugen Ehrlich by Romanian nationalists in the Romanian language newspaper Glasul Bucovinei.

IN 733 90A89

440. **Ball-Chronik.** Wohltätigkeitsfechtakademie. *Czernowitzer Tagblatt.* 1914. 4. Febr. (Nr. 3363, Jg. 12). S. 6.

Detailed chronicle of the Society of Fencing's charity ball within formation about the participation of Professor Dr. Ehrlich in the event including his fight with the fencing master Tonioni.

IN 1984 90A45

441. **Banakar, Reza.** Sociological Jurisprudence. In *An Introduction to Law and Social Theory,* ed. by Reza Banakar, and Max Travers. Oxford ; Portland Oregon : Hart Publ., 2002. p. 33–49.

E. Ehrlich. – pp. 33–36, 40–49.

442. **Behlert, Wolfgang.** "An den Gründen der Rechtssoziologie. Zu Semen V. Pachman und Eugen Ehrlich." *Archiv für Rechts- und Sozialphilosophie.* 1990. Vol. 76. S. 400–406.

About Eugen Ehrlich as a founder of the Sociology of Law.

443. **Bihun, V. S.** Revival of Philosophy of Law in Contemporary Ukraine. В *Проблеми філософії права.* Київ ; Чернівці : Рута, 2003. Т. 1. С. 210–212. [Bihun, V. S. Revival of Philosophy of Law in Contemporary Ukraine. In *Problems of the Philosophy of Law.* Kyiv ; Chernivtsi : Ruta, 2003. Vol. 1. pp. 210–212.]

E. Ehrlich. – p. 210.

B 69400 34П781

444. **Bukowinaer** Landtag. 2. Sitzung vom 24. September. *Bukowinaer Volks-Zeitung.* 1907. 25. Sept. (Nr. 167, Jg. 1). S. 1–2.

About the meeting of Bukovina Landtag with the participation of Professor Dr. Ehrlich – p. 1.

IN 2166 90A64

445. **Bukowinaer** Landtag. 3. Sitzung vom 1. Oktober. *Ibidem.* 1907. 3. Okt. (Nr. 174, Jg. 1). S. 1–2.

About the meeting of Bukovina Landtag with the participation of the Rector of Czernowitz University Dr. Ehrlich – p. 2.

IN 2166 90A64

446. **Bukowinaer** Landtag. 5. (Schluss)-Sitzung vom 8. Oktober. *Ibidem.* 1907. 10. Okt. (Nr. 180, Jg. 1). S. 2.

About the meeting of Bukovina Landtag with the participation of Dr. Ehrlich – p. 2.

IN 2166 90A64

447. **Bürgermeister** Dr. Eduard Reiss. Czernowitz, 30. April. *Czernowitzer Tagblatt.* 1907. 1. Mai (Nr. 1269, Jg. 5). S. 1–3.

Participation of the University Rector Professor Dr. Ehrlich in the mourning activities on the death of Dr. Eduard Reiss – the government advisor, Chevalier Officer of the Order of Franz Josef, Vice-President of the Bukovina Colledge of Barristers, a member of the State Examination Commission, Deputy-Mayor and Mayor of Czernowitz – p. 1.

IN 1968 90A45

448. **Bürgermeister** Dr. Eduard Reiss. *Czernowitzer Zeitung.* 1907. 1. Mai (Nr. 100, Jg. 42). S. 2–4.

Participation of the University Rector Professor Dr. Ehrlich in the mourning activities on the death of Dr. Eduard Reiss – the government advisor, Chevalier Officer of the Order of Franz Josef, Vice-President of the Bukovina Colledge of Barristers, a member of the State Examination Commission, Deputy-Mayor and Mayor of Czernowitz.

IN 1942 90A1

449. **Bürgermeister** Dr. Eduard Reiss. *Ibidem.* 1907. 3. Mai (Nr. 102, Jg. 42). S. 3–6.

Condolences on behalf of the Academic Senate and the entire university signed by the Rector Ehrlich on the death of Dr. Eduard Reiss – p. 5.

IN 1942 90A1

450. **Cardozo, Benjamin N.** *The Nature of the Judicial Process.* New Haven : Yale University Press, 1921. 180 p.

E. Ehrlich. – pp. 19, 49, 69–70, 74, 79, 101, 104, 112, 116–117, 121, 137, 169.

451. **Carrino, Agostino.** *Eugen Ehrlich e Hans Kelsen : una controversia sulla sociologia del diritto.* Barcelona : Inst. de Ciènices Polítiques i Socials, 1993. 52 p. (*Workingpapers* ; núm. 79).

On the polemics of Eugen Ehrlich with Hans Kelsen.

452. **Cebeira Moro, Ana.** Pluralismo jurídico y Derecho vivo : la concepción sociológica de Ehrlich. In *Hacia un paradigma cosmopolita del derecho?: Pluralismo jurídico, ciudadanía y resolución de conflictos,* coords. Nuria Belloso Martín, and Alfonso de Julios-Campuzano. Madrid : Dykinson, 2008. p. 79–98. Bibliogr.: p. 97–98.

On Eugen Ehrlich's concept of 'living law'.

453. **Cotterrell, Roger.** *The Sociology of Law : An Introduction.* 2 ed. New York : Oxford University Press Inc., 1992. XV, 398 p.

E. Ehrlich. – pp. 26–32, 34, 35, 37–40, 44–45, 49, 52, 55, 79–80, 96, 119, 128, 131, 167, 205, 245, 270, 285, 361, 388.

454. **Czeban, Galina,** und Elmar Lechner, Hrsg. Deutschsprachige Quellen zur Geschichte des Bildungswesen der Bukowina um 1900 (I). In *Retrospektiven in Sachen Bildung.* R. 5. (*Historico-paedagogic Europaea,* № 2). Klagenfurt, 1994. 43 S.

Information about Eugen Ehrlich in the publication – p. 9.

IN 382437 37R46

455. **Czernowitzer** Angelegenheiten. Czernowitz, 17. Februar. Anton Menger : [Zeitungsbericht über die Trauerfeier]. *Czernowitzer Allgemeine Zeitung.* 1906. 18. Febr. (Nr. 635). S. 4.

Information about the commemorative speech by the University Professor Dr. Eugen Ehrlich for the late Honorary Professor of the University of Vienna, Dr. Anton Menger on the meeting of the Juridical-Political Scientific Society. The full text of the speech is provided.

IN 90

456. **Czernowitzer** Angelegenheiten. Czernowitz, 20. September. Auszeichnung des Rektors Dr. Ehrlich. *Ibidem.* 1907. 21. Sept. (Nr. 1108). S. 5.

The Rector, University Professor Dr. Eugen Ehrlich was awarded the Commander's Cross of the Greek Order of the Saviour.

IN 90

457. **Czernowitzer** Angelegenheiten. Czernowitz, 15. Juli. Eine Czernowitzer Strassenszene : [über den Bettel mit fremden Kindern]. *Ibidem.* 1907. 16. Juli (Nr. 1051). S. 5.

On an incident in the street of Czernowitz with the participation of Eugen Ehrlich, the Rector of Czernowitz University.

IN 90

458. **Czernowitzer** Angelegenheiten. Czernowitz, 18. Mai. Das festländische und das englische System der Altersfürsorge. *Ibidem.* 1909. 19. Mai (Nr. 1603). S. 4.

Information about the speech of Professor Dr. Eugen Ehrlich at the meeting of Social-Scientific Academic Society on "Continental and English Retirement Systems" ("das festländische und das englische System der Altersfürsorge"). The summary of the speech is provided.

IN 90

459. **Czernowitzer** Angelegenheiten. Czernowitz, 12. Dezember. Die Krise im Gemeinderate. *Ibidem.* 1905. 13. Dez. (Nr. 584). S. 3.

Participation of Prof. Ehrlich in solving a municipality crisis.

IN 90

460. **Czernowitzer** Angelegenheiten. Czernowitz, 6. Dezember. Nationalität und Rasse. *Ibidem.* 1913. 7. Dez. (Nr. 3334). S. 4.

Information about the report by Professor Dr. Eugen Ehrlich at the meeting of Social-Scientific Academic Society on the topic: "Nationalism and Race" ("Nationalität und Rasse"). The summary of the report is provided.

IN 90

461. **Czernowitzer** Angelegenheiten. Czernowitz, 23. Juni. Das neue Rektor der Universität. *Ibidem.* 1906. 24. Juni (Nr. 738). S. 5.

The election of the Professor of Roman law Dr. Eugen Erhlich for the Rector of Czernowitz University for the academic year 1906/1907. The CV of the new Rector is provided.

IN 90

462. **Czernowitzer** Angelegenheiten. Czernowitz, 10. Jänner. Die Neugestaltung des Vertragsrechtes. *Ibidem.* 1906. 11. Jänner (Nr. 605). S. 3–4.

Information about the speech of Professor of Czernowitz University Dr. Eugen Ehrlich at the plenary session of Lower Austrian Commercial Society in Vienna on the 8th of January 1906 entitled: "Restructuring Contract Law" ("Die Neugestaltung des Vertragsrechtes"). The summary of the speech is also provided.

IN 90

463. **Czernowitzer** Angelegenheiten. Czernowitz, 30. Juni. Universitätsprofessor Dr. Ehrlich – Ehrendoktor der Universität Groningen. *Ibidem.* 1914. 1. Juli (Nr. 3484). S. 6.

Information about the celebration of the 300th anniversary of the foundation of the University of Groningen in Amsterdam where Professor Dr. Eugen Ehrlich representing Czernowitz University was awarded the honorary doctorate.

IN 90

464. **Czernowitzer** Angelegenheiten. Czernowitz, 24. November. Zivilrechtspflege in England. *Ibidem.* 1908. 25. Nov. (Nr. 1462). S. 4.

Information about the report of Professor Dr. Ehrlich at the meeting of the Czernowitz Juridical-

Political Scientific Society on the 21st of November 1908 on "Civil Justice in England" ("Zivilrechtspflege in England"). The summary of the report is provided.

IN 90

465. **Czernowitzer** "Austria" Kalender für das Jahr 1904. Czernowitz: Druck u. Verl. Der Buchdruck.-Ges. "Austria", 1904. Jg. 1. 158, 52 S.

Information about Eugen Ehrlich in the publication – C. 136, 137.

IN 103699 90S18

466. **Czernowitzer** "Austria" Kalender für das Jahr 1906. Czernowitz: Druck u. Verl. der Buchdruck.-Ges. "Austria", 1906. Jg. 3. 4, 160, 32 S.

Information about Eugen Ehrlich in the publication – pp. 135, 136.

IN 103693 90S18

467. **Czernowitzer** "Austria" Kalender für das Jahr 1907. Czernowitz: Druck u. Verl. der Buchdruck.-Ges. "Austria", 1907. Jg. 4. 4, 178, 32 S.

Information about Eugen Ehrlich in the publication – pp. 126, 159, 160.

IN 103694 90S18

468. **Czernowitzer** "Austria-Kalender" für das Jahr 1908. Czernowitz: Druck u. Verl. der Buchdruck.-Ges. "Austria", 1908. Jg. 5. 2, 185, 25 S.

Information about Eugen Ehrlich in the publication – pp. 132, 163.

IN 103695 90S18

469. **Czernowitzer** "Austria"-Kalender für das Jahr 1909. Czernowitz: Druck u. Verl. der Buchdruck.-Ges. "Austria", 1909. Jg. 6. 4, 189, 23 S.

Information about Eugen Ehrlich in the publication – pp. 151, 152.

IN 103696 90S18

470. **Czernowitzer** "Austria"-Kalender für das Jahr 1910. Czernowitz: Druck u. Verl. der Buchdruck.-Ges. "Austria", 1910. Jg. 7. 2, 195, 21 S.

Information about Eugen Ehrlich in the publication – pp. 157, 158.

IN 103689 90S18

471. **Czernowitzer** "Austria"-Kalender für das Jahr 1911. Czernowitz: Druck u. Verl. der Buchdruck.-Ges. "Austria", 1911. Jg. 8. 2, 190, 34 S.

Information about Eugen Ehrlich in the publication – p. 158.

IN 103690 90S18

472. **Czernowitzer** "Austria"-Kalender für das Jahr 1912. Czernowitz: Druck u. Verl. der Buchdruck.-Ges. "Austria", 1912. Jg. 9. 2, 210, 18 S.

Information about Eugen Ehrlich in the publication – pp. 159, 160.

IN 103691 90S18

473. **Czernowitzer** "Austria"-Kalender für das Jahr 1913. Czernowitz: Druck u. Verl. der Buchdruck.-Ges. "Austria", 1913. Jg. 10. 2, 230, 24 S.

Information about Eugen Ehrlich in the publication – pp. 170, 171.

IN 103692 90S18

474. **Czernowitzer** "Austria"-Kalender für das Jahr 1914. Czernowitz: Druck u. Verl. der Buchdruck.-Ges. "Austria", 1914. Jg. 11. 2, 220, 28 S.

Information about Eugen Ehrlich in the publication – p. 161.

IN 103697 90S18

475. **Desiderate**: [1911–1940]. Czernowitz: K. k. Franz-Josephs-Universität, [1911–1940]. 378 S.

Journal of pre-orders for books from lecturers of Czernowitz University in the years 1911–1940. – pp. 16, 28, 121, 127.

INMs 49

476. **Desideratenbuch**: 1895–1902. Czernowitz: K. k. Franz-Josephs-Universität, 1895–1902. 322 S.

Journal of pre-orders for books from lecturers of Czernowitz University in the years 1895–1902. – pp. 61, 64, 80–81, 115–117, 120, 122, 139, 145, 164, 171, 223, 226, 230–231, 243, 247, 252, 262, 263, 269, 273–275. 279–280, 283, 286, 288, 290, 291, 309, 313.

IN Ms 49 (V, 3)

477. **Desideratenbuch**: 1902–1905. Czernowitz: K. k. Franz-Josephs-Universität, 1902–1905. 112 S.

Journal of pre-orders for books from lecturers of Czernowitz University in the years 1902–1905. – pp. 20, 25, 27, 44, 50, 56, 66, 75, 80, 81, 83, 88, 93, 95, 97, 108, 110.

IN Ms 49 (V, 4)

478. **Desideratenbuch**: 1905–1911. Czernowitz: K. k. Franz-Josephs-Universität, 1905–1911. 392 S.

Journal of pre-orders for books from lecturers of Czernowitz University in the years 1905–1911. – pp. 8, 10, 17, 23, 26, 28, 29, 42, 50, 52, 55, 66, 82, 105, 123, 157, 159, 160, 180, 185–186, 194, 197, 200, 241, 256, 258, 263, 264, 267, 271, 276, 280, 286, 288, 309, 328, 337, 339, 365, 367, 373, 374, 382, 391.

IN Ms 49 (V, 5)

479. **Doboş, F.** "D-nii Last şi Ehrlich la universitatea noastră?" *Glasul Bucovinei.* 1921. 10 mar. (Nr. 652, An. 4). P. 1.

Criticism of Eugen Ehrlich by Romanian nationalists in the Romanian language newspaper Glasul Bucovinei.

IN 73290A89

480. **Döhring, Erich.** Eugen Ehrlich. In *Neue Deutsche Biographie*, hrsg. von der hist. Kommiss. bei der Bayerischen Akad. der Wiss. Berlin: Duncker & Humblot, 1959. Bd. 4, *"Dittel–Falck."* S. 362.

481. **30jähriges** Jubelfest der akadem. Burschenschaft "Arminia". *Bukowiner Nachrichten.* 1907. 12. Juli (Nr. 5612, Jg. 20). S. 2–3.

Information about the festive event on the occasion of the 30th anniversary of the Academic Society "Arminia", with the information about the Rector of Czernowitz University Dr. Eugen Ehrlich taking part in the event among other dignitaries.

IN 2037 90J6

482. **Eugen Ehrlich.** In *The Great Legal Philosophers: Selected Readings in Jurisprudence*, ed. Clarence Morris. Philadelphia: Univ. of Pennsylvania Press, 1959. p. 437–464.

483. **Ehrlich, Eugen.** In Österreichischen Nationalbibliothek, hrsg. *Handbuch österreichischer Autorinnen und Autoren jüdischer Herkunft: 18. bis 20. Jahrhundert.* München: K. G. Saur, 2002. Bd. 1, *"A–I."* S. 254.

484. **Ehrlich, Eugen.** In *The New Encyclopaedia Britannica: Micropaedia: Ready Reference.* 15th ed. Chicago, et al.: Encycl. Britannica, Inc., 1993. Vol. 4, *"Delusion–Frenssen."* p. 394.

IN 382344 031E54

485. **Ehrlich Eugen.** In *Österreichisches Biographisches Lexikon 1815–1950.* 2., unveränd. Aufl. Wien : Österreichischen Akademie der Wissenschaften, 1993. Bd. 1, *"A–Glä."* S. 229.

5288АБ

486. **Ehrlich Eugen.** In Bruckmüller, Ernst, hrsg. *Personen Lexikon Österreich.* Wien : Verlagsgemeinschaft Österreich-Lexikon, 2001. S. 100.

11031 АБ

487. **Ehrlich Eugen.** In Degener, Herrmann A. L., begr., hrsg., red. *Wer ist's? Unsere Zeitgenossen.* 6. Ausg. Leipzig : H. A. Ludwig Degener, 1912. S. 352.

IN 1166 03D31

488. **[Ehrlich Eugen]** : Nachrichten. *Literarisches Centralblatt für Deutschland.* 1896. 21. Nov. (Nr. 47). S. 1716.

Appointment of the privatdozent from Vienna Dr. Eugen Ehrlich an Extraordinary (associate) Professor of Roman law in Czernowitz.

IN 36318 85

489. **[Ehrlich Eugen]** : Nachrichten. *Ibidem.* 1900. 3. März (Nr. 9, Jg. 51). S. 410.

Appointment of Dr. E. Ehrlich (Roman law) from Czernowitz a Full Professor.

IN 3630985

490. **Einreichung** Protokoll der k. k. Franz-Josephs-Universität in Czernowitz : 1910–1911. Rektor : Dr. Matthias Friedwagner ; Rektor : Dr. Johannes Kromayer. Czernowitz : k. k. Franz-Jozeph Universität, 1910/1911. 140 S.

Journal of appeals to Czernowitz University. Records № 330 of 12.12.1910, № 358 of 19.12.1910, № 813 of 29.05.1911, № 930 of 30.06.1911, № 1002 of 15. 07.1911, № 1013 of 18.07.1911 containing information about Prof. Dr. Ehrlich – pp. 42, 45, 102, 117, 126, 127

IN 372857 60

491. **Der 31. Deutsche** Juristentagin Wien. *Czernowitzer Zeitung.* 1912. 6. Sept. (Nr. 204, Jg. 47). S. 2–4.

About the work of the 31st assembly of the German Lawyers in Vienna with the participation of Prof. Dr. Ehrlich – p. 3.

IN 1953 90A1

492. **Der 31. Deutsche** Juristentagin Wien. *Ibidem.* 1912. 7. Sept. (Nr. 205, Jg. 47). S. 1–5.

Detailed information about the work of the 31st assembly of the German Lawyers in Vienna with the participation of Czernowitz Professor Dr. Ehrlich – pp. 4, 5.

IN 1953 90A1

493. **Enthüllung** des Schillerdenkmals. Czernowitz, 11. November. *Czernowitzer Tagblatt.* 1907. 12. Nov. (Nr. 1427, Jg. 5). S. 1–2.

Inauguration of the monument to Schiller – the first monument dedicated to the poet in Bukovina. Participation, among other dignitaries, of the Vice-Rector of University Dr. Ehrlich in the event – p. 1.

IN 1969 90A45

494. **Fasching 1910**. Der Ruthenenball. *Bukowinaer Post.* 1910. 8. Febr. (Nr. 2497, Jg. 17). S. 1–2.

Participation of the University Professor Dr. Ehrlich in the ball organized by Czernowitz Academic Society "Soyuz" on the 6th of February 1910 – p. 1.

IN 2064 90J26

495. **Feier** an der k. k. Franz-Josefs-Universität. *Czernowitzer Zeitung.* 1897. 6. Okt. (Nr. 228, Jg. 30). S. 3.

The inaugural speech of the Rector of Czernowitz University Professor Dr. Röshmann-Hörburh, in which it is stated that Prof. Ehrlich is the successor of Prof. Ernst Hruza in the given discipline for the academic year 1896/1897.

IN 1923 90A1

496. **Feier** an der k. k. Franz-Josefs-Universität. *Ibidem.* 1898. 5. Oct. (Nr. 227, Jg. 31). S. 3–4.

Information about the stay of the Rector of Czernowitz University and the Dean of the Faculty of Law with other Austrian and foreign lawyers in Vienna on the 2nd of July 1898 celebrating the 70th anniversary of Dr. Joseph Unger. It is noted that Dr. Unger was awarded the honorary doctorate of the Faculty of Law of Czernowitz University based on the proposal by Professor Dr. Eugen Ehrlich – p. 4.

IN 1925 90A1

497. **Feier** des 60jährigen Regierungsjubiläums Sr. Majestät des Kaisers in Czernowitz. Kaiserkommers der akademischen Korps "Alemannia", "Austria" und "Gothia". *Ibidem.* 1908. 8. Dez. (Nr. 283, Jg. 43). S. 2–3.

Participation of the Dean Professor Dr. Ehrlich, among other dignitaries, in the celebration events dedicated to the Emperor by the societies of "Alemannia", "Austria" and "Gothia".

IN 1945 90A1

498. **Feier** im Kaiser Franz-Joseph-Universitäts-Studentenheim. *Ibidem.* 1904. 3. Juli (Nr. 150, Jg. 39). S. 4–5.

Participation of the Vice-Dean Professor Dr. Ehrlich in the celebration event of the opening of Czernowitz University hostel.

IN 1937 90A1

499. **Fleck, Christian.** *Rundum "Marienthal": von den Anfängen der Soziologie in Österreich bis zu ihrer Vertreibung.* Wien : Verl. für Gesellschaftskritik, 1990. 270 S. (*Österreichische Texte zur Gesellschaftskritik* ; Bd. 51).

Information about Eugen Ehrlich in the publication – pp. 13, 16, 21, 24, 35, 55–64, 82–87, 90, 117, 206, 207, 211, 212, 239.

500. **Gedächtnisfeier** für Professor v. Löwl. *Czernowitzer Zeitung.* 1909. 5. Mai (Nr. 101, Jg. 44). S. 3–4.

Information about the participation of the Dean o the Faculty of Law Professor Dr. Eugen Ehrlich in the commemorative events dedicated to the University Professor Dr. Ferdinand Löwl von Lenkenthal on the 1st of May 1909.

IN 1946 90A1

501. **Gedenkfeier** für Unger. *Czernowitzer Allgemeine Zeitung.* 1913. 1. Juni (Nr. 3016). S. 5.

Information about the commemorative event organized by the Juridical-Political Scientific Society in connection with the death of the President of Imperial Court Dr. Joseph Unger, with the participation of Professor Dr. Ehrlich who delivered a speech (text of the speech is provided).

IN 90

502. **Gestions-Protokoll** des akademischen Senates der k. k. Universitätin Czernowitz : 1900–1901. Rektor : Dr. Franz Hauke. Czernowitz : k. k. Franz-Josephs-Universität, 1900–1901. 258 S.

Journal of appeals to the Academic Senate of Czernowitz University for the years 1900–1901. Records № 351 of 23.01.1901, № 371 of 5.03.1901, № 403 of 19.03.1901. They contain information about Professor Dr. Ehrlich – pp. 116, 122, 134.

IN 60

503. **Goldenberg, Max.** "Die Entwirrung im Gemeinderate." *Czernowitzer Allgemeine Zeitung.* 1905. 22. Dez. (Nr. 592). S. 1–2.

E. Ehrlich. – p. 1.

Information about Eugen Ehrlich's participation in the activities of the Czernowitz Municipality Council.

IN 90

504. **Gómez García, Juan Antonio.** Derecho, vida y derecho vivo en el pensamiento ius filosófico de Eugen Ehrlich. In Ehrlich, Eugen. *Escritos sobre sociología y jurisprudencia.* Madrid : Marcial Pons, 2005. P. 11–25. (*Politopías* ; 3).

On Eugen Ehrlich's concept of 'living law'.

505. **Gurvitch, Georges.** *Sociology of Law,* with a pref. by Roscoe Pound. London : Kegan Paul, French, Trubner & Co., LTD, [1947]. XV, 248, 12 p.

E. Ehrlich. – pp. 51, 52, 77, 116-122, 127, 132.

506. **Hafner, Josef.** "Zur Konzipientensperre : [Lokal- und Provinznachrichten. Czernowitz, 27. Dezember]." *Czernowitzer Tagblatt.* 1905. 28. Dez. (Nr. 870, Jg. 3). S. 2–3.

About consideration of issues related to the barriers to training lawyers including a proposal by Professor Dr. Ehrlich who addressed the problem.

IN 1965 90A45

507. **Hahn, Friedrich.** "Eine Soziologie des Rechts." *Der Kampf: Sozialdemokratische Monatsschrift.* 1914. 1. Juni (Heft 9, Jg. 7). S. 401–407.

On Eugen Ehrlich's concept of the Sociology of Law.

IN 371102 14T32

508. **Hensel, Isabell.** Eugen Ehrlich (1862-1922). Verbindungslinien zwischen Leben und Recht. In *Streitbare Juristinnen : eine andere Tradition.* Hrsg. Kritische Justiz. 1. Aufl. Baden-Baden : Nomos, 2016. Bd. 2. S. 162–185.

On Eugen Ehrlich's concept of the Sociology of Law.

509. **Herget, James E.,** and Stephen Wallace. "The German Free Law Movement as the Source of American Legal Realism." *Virginia Law Review.* 1987. Vol. 73, Nr. 2 (Mar.). pp. 399–455.

510. **Hertogh, Marc.** "A "European" Conception of Legal Consciousness: Rediscovering Eugen Ehrlich." *Journal of Law and Society.* 2004. Vol. 31, Nr. 4 (Dec.). pp. 457–481.

511. **Hertogh, Marc,** and Oñati Institute for the Sociology of Law, eds. *Living Law: Reconsidering Eugen Ehrlich.* Oxford ; Portland Oregon : Hart Publ., 2009. X, 280 p. *(Oñati International Series in Law and Society).*

Contents:

Marc Hertogh. From "Men of Files" to "Men of the Senses": A Brief Characterisation of Eugen Ehrlich's Sociology of Law. pp. 1–17;

PART I. EUGEN EHRLICH: LIFE, WORK AND CONTEXT. Monica Eppinger. Governing in the Vernacular: Eugen Ehrlich and Late Habsburg Ethnography. pp. 21–47;

Assaf Likhovski. Venus in Czernowitz: Sacher-Masoch, Ehrlich and the Fin-de-siècle Crisis of Legal Reason. pp. 49–71;

PART II. EHRLICH'S SOCIOLOGY OF LAW. Roger Cotterrell. Ehrlich at the Edge of Empire: Centres and Peripheries in Legal Studies. pp. 75–94; Stefan Vogl. Eugen Ehrlich's Linking of Sociology and Jurisprudence and the Reception of his Work in Japan. pp. 95–123;

PART III. EHRLICH AND HIS CONTEMPORARIES. Bart van Klink. Facts and Norms: The Unfinished Debate between Eugen Ehrlich and Hans Kelsen. pp. 127–155; Salif Nimaga. Pounding on Ehrlich. Again? pp. 157–175; Franz and Keebet von Benda-Beckmann. The Social Life of Living Law in Indonesia. pp. 177–197;

PART IV. EHRLICH AND CONTEMPORARY SOCIO-LEGAL STUDIES. Jeremy Webber. Naturalism and Agency in the Living Law. pp. 201–221; Klaus A Ziegert. World Society, Nation State and Living Law in the Twenty-first Century. pp. 223–236; David Nelken. Ehrlich's Legacies: Back to the Future in the Sociology of Law? pp. 237–272.

512. **Hof- und Staats-Handbuch** der Österreichisch-Ungarischen Monarchie für 1894. Wien : K. K. Hof- und Staatsdruckerei, [1894]. IV, XX, 1276 S.

Information about Eugen Ehrlich in the publication – p. 363.

IN 24677 89C1

513. **Hof- und Staats-Handbuch** der Österreichisch-Ungarischen Monarchie für 1895. Wien : K. K. Hof- und Staatsdruckerei, [1895]. IV, XX, 1282 S.

Information about Eugen Ehrlich in the publication – pp. 343, 372.

IN 24672 89C1

514. **Hof- und Staats-Handbuch** der Österreichisch-Ungarischen Monarchie für 1896. Wien : K. K. Hof- und Staatsdruckerei, [1896]. IV, XXIII, 1310 S.

Information about Eugen Ehrlich in the publication – pp. 349, 379.

IN 24656 89C1

515. **Hof- und Staats-Handbuch** der Österreichisch-Ungarischen Monarchie für 1897. Wien : K. K. Hof- und Staatsdruckerei, [1897]. IV, XXIII, 1312 S.

Information about Eugen Ehrlich in the publication – pp. 354, 359, 383, 769.

IN 24624 89C1

516. **Hof- und Staats-Handbuch** der Österreichisch-Ungarischen Monarchie für 1898. Wien : K. K. Hof- und Staatsdruckerei, [1898]. IV, XXIII, 1324 S.

Information about Eugen Ehrlich in the publication – pp. 388, 782, 783.

IN 24637 89C1

517. **Hof- und Staats-Handbuch** der Österreichisch-Ungarischen Monarchie für 1899. Wien : K. K. Hof- und Staatsdruckerei, [1899]. XX, 1335 S.

Information about Eugen Ehrlich in the publication – pp. 813, 814.

IN 24635 89C1

518. **Hof- und Staats-Handbuch** der Österreichisch-Ungarischen Monarchie für 1900. Wien : K. K. Hof- und Staatsdruckerei, [1900]. IV, XX, 1364 S.

Information about Eugen Ehrlich in the publication – pp. 809, 810.

IN 24633 89C1

519. **Hof- und Staats-Handbuch** der Österreichisch-Ungarischen Monarchie für1901. Wien : K. K. Hof- und Staatsdruckerei, [1901]. IV, XX, 1386 S.

Information about Eugen Ehrlich in the publication – pp. 826, 828.

IN 24636 89C1

520. **Hof- und Staats-Handbuch** der Österreichisch-Ungarischen Monarchie für 1902. Wien : K. K. Hof- und Staatsdruckerei, [1902]. IV, XX, 1412 S.

Information about Eugen Ehrlich in the publication – pp. 844, 846.

IN 24634 89C1

521. **Hof- und Staats-Handbuch** der Österreichisch-Ungarischen Monarchie für das Jahr 1903. Wien : K. K. Hof- und Staatsdruckerei, [1903]. Jg. 29. VI, XX, 1448 S.

Information about Eugen Ehrlich in the publication – pp. 843, 845.

IN 24627 89C1

522. **Hof- und Staats-Handbuch** der Österreichisch-Ungarischen Monarchie für das Jahr 1905. Wien : K. K. Hof- und Staatsdruckerei, 1905. Jg. 31. VI, XX, 1414 S.

Information about Eugen Ehrlich in the publication – pp. 837, 838.

IN 24629 89C1

523. **Hof- und Staats-Handbuch** der Österreichisch-Ungarischen Monarchie für das Jahr 1906. Wien : K. K. Hof- und Staatsdruckerei, 1906. Jg. 32. VI, XX, 1438 S.

Information about Eugen Ehrlich in the publication – pp. 858, 859.

IN 24630 89C1

524. **Hof- und Staats-Handbuch** der Österreichisch-Ungarischen Monarchie für das Jahr 1907. Wien : K. K. Hof- und Staatsdruckerei, 1907. Jg. 33. VI, XX, 1464 S.

Information about Eugen Ehrlich in the publication – pp. 871, 875, 876, 877.

IN 24625 89C1

525. **Hof- und Staats-Handbuch** der Österreichisch-Ungarischen Monarchie für das Jahr 1908. Wien : K. K. Hof- und Staatsdruckerei, 1908. Jg. 34. VI, XXXIV, 1499 S.

Information about Eugen Ehrlich in the publication – pp. 907, 908, 909.

IN 24623 89C1

526. **Hof- und Staats-Handbuch** der Österreichisch-Ungarischen Monarchie für das Jahr 1909. Wien : K. K. Hof- und Staatsdruckerei, 1909. Jg. 35. IV, XXXIV, 1501, XXIV S.

Information about Eugen Ehrlich in the publication – pp. 943, 945.

IN 24631 89C1

527. **Hof- und Staats-Handbuch** der Österreichisch-Ungarischen Monarchie für das Jahr 1910. Wien : K. K. Hof- und Staatsdruckerei, 1910. Jg. 36. VIII, XXXVI, 1531, LII S.

Information about Eugen Ehrlich in the publication – pp. 967, 969.

IN 24632 89C1

528. **Hof- und Staats-Handbuch** der Österreichisch-Ungarischen Monarchie für das Jahr 1913. Wien : K. K. Hof- und Staatsdruckerei, 1913. Jg. 39. XXXIII, 1616, 72 S.

Information about Eugen Ehrlich in the publication – pp. 1030, 1031, 1032.

IN 24675 89C1

529. **Hof- und Staats-Handbuch** der Österreichisch-Ungarischen Monarchie für das Jahr 1914. Wien : K. K. Hof- und Staatsdruckerei, 1914. Jg. 40. XXXIII, 1651, 84 S.

Information about Eugen Ehrlich in the publication – pp. 1047, 1049.

IN 24666 89C1

530. **Horowitz, Mayer.** "Was die neue Stadtanleihe kostet." *Bukowinaer Volks-Zeitung.* 1907. 10. Dez. (Nr. 231, Jg. 1). S. 1–3.

Information about Eugen Ehrlich in the publication – p. 2.

IN 2166 90A64

531. **Hrycenko, Ivan,** Aurel Georgica, Mychajlo Nykyforak, Petro Pacurkivs`kiyj, und Lubomyr Hyzdyvan. Die Professoren der juridischen Fakultätin Czernowitz. In *Glanz und Elend der Peripherie : 120 Jahre Universität Czernowitz : eine Veröffentlichung des Österreichischen Ost- und Südosteuropa-Instituts,* hrsg. von Ilona Slawinski, und Joseph P. Strelka. Bern ; Berlin ; Frankfurt a. M. ; New York ; Paris ; Wien : Peter Lang, 1998. S. 101–122.

Information about Eugen Ehrlich, as the Professor of the Faculty of Law at Czernowitz University – pp. 107, 110–112, 120.

АБ 8495 В

532. **Jahrbuch** des höheren Unterrichtswesens in Österreich. Jg. 10, bearb. von Johann Neubauer, und Josef Diviš. Wien ; Prag : F. Tempsky, 1897. X, 439 S.

Yearbook of higher education in Austria. The list of schools, faculties and lecturers.

E. Ehrlich. – p. 67.

IN 245035 60B132

Jg. 12, bearb. von Johann Neubauer, und Josef Diviš. Wien ; Prag : F. Tempsky, 1899. X, 396 S.

Yearbook of higher education in Austria. The list of schools, faculties and lecturers.

E. Ehrlich. – p. 69.

IN 316 81N17

Jg. 13, bearb. von Johann Neubauer, und Josef Diviš. Wien ; Prag : F. Tempsky, 1900. X, 410 S.

Yearbook of higher education in Austria. The list of schools, faculties and lecturers.

E. Ehrlich. – p. 70.

IN 315 81N17

Jg. 15, bearb. von Josef Diviš. [Wien : F. Tempsky], 1902. 439 S.

Yearbook of higher education in Austria. The list of schools, faculties and lecturers.

E. Ehrlich – pp. 73, 74.

IN 245038 60B132

Jg. 16, bearb. von Josef Diviš. Wien : F. Tempsky, 1903. VIII, 488 S.

Yearbook of higher education in Austria. The list of schools, faculties and lecturers.

E. Ehrlich. – pp. 77, 78.

IN 298 81N17

Jg. 19, bearb. von Josef Diviš. Wien : F. Tempsky, 1906. X, 580 S.

Yearbook of higher education in Austria. The list of schools, faculties and lecturers.

E. Ehrlich. – p. 92.

IN 297 81N17

Jg. 20, bearb. von Josef Diviš. Wien : F. Tempsky,1907. VIII, 594 S.

Yearbookof higher education in Austria. The list of schools, faculties and lecturers.

E. Ehrlich. – pp. 94, 95.

IN 296 81N17

Jg. 21, bearb. von Josef Diviš. Wien : F. Tempsky,1908. VIII, 511 S.

Yearbook of higher education in Austria. The list of schools, faculties and lecturers.

E. Ehrlich. – pp. 83, 84.

IN 295 81N17

Jg. 23, bearb. von Erwin Lauppert von Peharnik. Wien : F. Tempsky, 1910. X, 592 S.

Yearbook of higher education in Austria. The list of schools, faculties and lecturers.

E. Ehrlich. – pp. 87, 88.

IN 310 81N18

Jg. 24, bearb. von Erwin Lauppert von Peharnik. Wien : F. Tempsky, 1911. VIII, 628 S.

Yearbook of higher education in Austria. The list of schools, faculties and lecturers.

E. Ehrlich. – p. 88.

IN 299 81N18

Jg. 26, hrsg. von Richard Wengraf. Wien : F. Tempsky, 1913. 566 S.

Yearbook of higher education in Austria. The list of schools, faculties and lecturers.

E. Ehrlich. – pp. 110, 111.

IN 311 81N19

Jg. 27, hrsg. von Heinrich Löwner. Wien : F. Tempsky, 1914. 601 S.

Yearbook of higher education in Austria. The list of schools, faculties and lecturers.

E. Ehrlich. – p. 113.

IN 300 81N20

533. **Johnston, William M.** *The Austrian Mind: An Intellectual and Social History, 1848–1938.* Berkeley ; Los Angeles ; London : University of California Press, 1983. XVI, 519 p.

E. Ehrlich. – pp. 88–90, 417–418.

534. **Der Jubiläumscommers** der "Hasmonaea". 30. November 1901 : Feuilleton. *Bukowinaer Post.* 1901. 5. Dec. (Nr. 1233, Jg. 9). S. 1–3.

On the ceremony of the Society "Hasmonaea" with the participation of Professor Dr. Eugen Ehrlich.

IN 2055 90J26

535. **Jüdische** Volksversammlung. *Bukowinaer Volks-Zeitung.* 1907. 10. Dez. (Nr. 231, Jg. 1). S. 1–3.

About the Jewish National Assembly including the information about the chapter by University Professor Dr. Eugen Ehrlich entitled "Statistisches zur Universitätsrede des Grafen Thun" ["Statistics on the university speech of Count Thun"] published in the newspaper "Neue Freie Presse" related to the "Judaisation" of university – p. 1.

IN 2166 90A64

536. **Juristische** Gesellschaft. *Allgemeine Juristen-Zeitung.* 1892. 10. März (Nr. 17, Jg. 15). S. 159.

Information about the lecture of Dr. E. Ehrlich at the meeting of the Society of Lawyers in Vienna on the 9th of March 1892.

IN 2030 90J6 BPK

537. **Kaindl, Raimund Friedrich.** Bericht über das Studienjahr 1912/1913, erstattet am 2. Dezember 1913 von dem abtretenden Rektor. In *Die feierliche Inauguration des Rectors der k. k. Franz-Josephs-Universität in Czernowitz für das Studienjahr 1913/1914 am 2. Dezember 1913.* Czernowitz : Selbstverl. der k. k. Universität, 1913. S. 3–15.

Eugen Ehrlich mentioned in the inauguration speech of professor Raimund Friedriech Kaindl – p. 13.

IN 379634 90K126

538. **K. k. Franz-Josephs-Universität.** *Czernowitzer Zeitung.* 1912. 23. Aug. (Nr. 192, Jg. 47). S. 1–2.

The list of public lectures for the winter semester of the academic year 1912/1913 issued by the Academic Senate, including a note about Prof. Ehrlich's vacation in this semester, and indicating that information about the lecture course on Roman law will be published later.

IN 1953 90A1

539. **Kaiserkommers** der Czernowitzer akad. Korps. *Bukowinaer Post.* 1908. 8. Dez. (Nr. 2316, Jg. 16). S. 2.

Participation of University Prof. Ehrlich, among other dignitaries, in the celebration events dedicated to the Emperor by the societies of "Alemannia", "Austria" and "Gothia".

IN 2062 90J26

540. **Kalender** Termin- und Vormerkbuch. 1900. Dr. Nussbaum's Wohnungs-Anzeiger Schematismus, Verzeichnis der protokollirten Firmen, sowie Handels- und Gewerbe-Adressen. Czernowitz : Druk und Verl. der Bukowinaer Vereinsdruck., 1899. 262, 34 S.

Information about Eugen Ehrlich in the publication – pp. 155, 202.

IN 103718 90S1

541. **Kalender** Termin- und Vormerkbuch. 1901. Dr. Nussbaum's Wohnungs-Anzeiger von Czernowitz sammt Vorstädten und dem Verzeichnisse der Hauseigenthümer von Radautz, Sereth und Suczawa. Ortschafts-Verzeichnis Schematismus, Verzeichnis der protokollirten Firmen, sowie Handels- und Gewerbe-Adressen. Czernowitz : Druk und Verl. der Bukowinaer Vereinsdruck., 1900. 8, IV, 291, 45 S.

Information about Eugen Ehrlich in the publication – pp. 127, 257, 258.

IN 103710 90S1

542. **Kalender** Termin- und Vormerkbuch. 1902. Dr. Nussbaum's Wohnungs-Anzeiger von Czernowitz sammt Vorstädten, ferner von Radautz und Suczawa. Ortschafts-Verzeichnis Schematismus, Verzeichnis der protokollirten Firmen, sowie Handels- und Gewerbe-Adressen. Czernowitz : Druk und Verl. der Bukowinaer Vereinsdruck., 1901. 8, 308, 36 S.

Information about Eugen Ehrlich in the publication – pp. 119, 261,262.

IN 103711 90S1

543. **Kalender** Termin- und Vormerkbuch. 1903. Dr. Nussbaum's Wohnungs-Anzeiger von Czernowitz sammt Vorstädten, ferner von Radautz und Suczawa. Ortschafts-Verzeichnis Schematismus, Verzeichnis der protokollirten Firmen, sowie Handels- und Gewerbe-Adressen. Czernowitz : Druk und Verl. der Bukowinaer Vereinsdruck., 1902. 2, XIV, 304, 60 S.

Information about Eugen Ehrlich in the publication – pp. 118, 267, 268.

IN 103682 90S1

544. **Kalender** Termin- und Vormerkbuch. 1904. Dr. Nussbaum's Wohnungs-Anzeiger von Czernowitz samt Vorstädten, ferner von Radautz und Suczawa. Ortschafts-Verzeichnis Schematismus, Verzeichnis der protokollirten Firmen, sowie Handels- und Gewerbe-Adressen. Czernowitz : Druk und Verl. der Bukowinaer Vereinsdruck., 1903. 2, XVIII, 306, 74 S.

Information about Eugen Ehrlich in the publication – pp. 117, 266, 267.

IN 103681 90S1

545. **Kalender** Termin- und Vormerkbuch. 1905. Dr. Nussbaum's Wohnungs-Anzeiger von Czernowitz samt Vorstädten, ferner von Radautz und Suczawa. Ortschafts-Verzeichnis Schematismus, Verzeichnis der protokollirten Firmen, sowie Handels- und Gewerbe-Adressen. Czernowitz : Druk und Verl. der Bukowinaer Vereinsdruck., 1904. 6, XVIII, 328, 40 S.

Information about Eugen Ehrlich in the publication – pp. 120, 286, 287.

IN 103709 90S1

546. **Kalender** Termin- und Vormerkbuch. 1906. Dr. Nussbaum's Wohnungs-Anzeiger von Czernowitz samt Vorstädten, ferner von Radautz und Suczawa. Ortschafts-Verzeichnis Schematismus, Verzeichnis der protokollirten Firmen, sowie Handels- und Gewerbe-Adressen. Czernowitz : Druk und Verl. der Bukowinaer Vereinsdruck., 1905. 2, XXII, 354, 40 S.

Information about Eugen Ehrlich in the publication – pp. 125, 310, 311.

IN 103677 90S1

547. **Kalender** Termin- und Vormerkbuch. 1907. Dr. Nussbaum's Wohnungs-Anzeiger von Czernowitz samt Vorstädten, ferner von Radautz und Suczawa. Ortschafts-Verzeichnis Schematismus, Verzeichnis der protokollirten Firmen, sowie Handels- und Ge-

werbe-Adressen. Czernowitz : Druk und Verl. der Bukowinaer Vereinsdruck., 1906. XVI, 358, 38 S.

Information about Eugen Ehrlich in the publication – pp. 109, 129, 130, 208.

IN 103676 90S1

548. **Kantorowicz, Hermann U.** *Rechtswissenschaft und Soziologie.* Tübingen : J. C. B. Mohr (Paul Siebeck), 1911. 35 S.

Information about Eugen Ehrlich in the publication – pp. 9–12, 28–29.

549. **Kassner, S.** Ehrlich, Eugen. In *Jüdisches Lexikon : ein enzyklopädisches Handbuch des jüdischen Wissens : in 4. Bd.*, hrsg. von Georg Herlitz, und Bruno Kirschner ; unter red. Mithilfe Ismar Elbogen, et al. Berlin : Jüdischer Verl., 1928. Bd. 2, *"D–H."* "S. 281.

Chapter about Eugen Ehrlich in the publication.

550. **Kelsen, Hans.** "Eine Grundlegung der Rechtssoziologie." *Archiv für Sozialwissenschaft und Sozialpolitik.* 1915. Bd. 39. S. 839–876.

Dispute of E. Ehrlich with H. Kelsen. Critical review by H. Kelsen of the work written by E. Ehrlich: Grundlegung der Soziologie des Rechts. München ; Leipzig : Duncker & Humblot, 1913. 409 S.

IN 244313 14V1

551. **Kelsen, Hans.** "Replik." *Ibidem.* 1916. Bd. 41. S. 850–853.

Dispute of E. Ehrlich with H. Kelsen. Response of H. Kelsen to the objections written by E. Ehrlich: "Entgegnung." *Archiv für Sozialwissenschaft und Sozialpolitik.* 1916. Bd. 41. S. 844–849.

IN 244315 14V1

552. **Kelsen, Hans.** "Schlusswort." *Ibidem.* 1916/1917. Bd. 42. S. 611.

Dispute of E. Ehrlich with H. Kelsen. Concluding remarks-answers by H. Kelsen to the objections written by E. Ehrlich : "Entgegnung." *Archiv für Sozialwissenschaft und Sozialpolitik.* 1916. Bd. 41. S. 844–849, *and also to :* "Replik." *Archiv für Sozialwissenschaft und Sozialpolitik.* 1916/1917. Bd. 42. S. 609–610.

IN 244315 14V1

553. **Kelsen, Hans.** *Werke,* hrsg. Matthias Jestaedt in Kooperation mit Hans Kelsen-Institut. Tübingen : Mohr (Siebeck), 2010. Bd. 3, *"Veröffentlichte Schriften 1911–1917."* "X, 871 S.

Information about Eugen Ehrlich in the publication – pp. VIII, 79, 80–81, 85, 91, 317–346, 348–357, 424, 530, 548, 576–577, 584, 600, 603, 607–614, 648, 654–658, 713, 715–722, 733, 755, 810, 833, 851.

554. **Kininger, Ewald.** *Die Realität der Rechtsnorm : eine empirische Studie.* Berlin : Duncker & Humblot, [1971]. 230 S. (*Schriftenreihe zur Rechtssoziologie und Rechtstatsachenforschung*; Bd. 24).

Information about Eugen Ehrlich in the publication – p. 25–26.

555. **Kleine** Chronik. Die "akademische Lesehalle"... *Bukowinaer Rundschau.* 1901. 12. Dec. (Nr. 3790, Jg. 20). S. 3.

Participation of the Dean Prof. Ehrlich, among other dignitaries, in the ceremony of the "Academic Reading Hall" that took place on the 7th of December 1901.

IN 2088 90A13

556. **Kleine** Chronik. Czernowitz, 14. December. Die "Akademische Lesehalle"... *Bukowiner Nachrichten.* 1901. 15. Dec. (Nr. 3959, Jg. 14). S. 4.

Participation of the Dean Prof. Ehrlich, among other dignitaries, in the ceremony of the "Academic Reading Hall" that took place on the 7th of December 1901.

IN 2031 90J6

557. **Kleine** Chronik. Czernowitz, 8. März. Akademische Lesehalle. *Ibidem.* 1902. 9. März (Nr. 4027, Jg. 15). S. 4.

Participation of University Professor Dr. Ehrlich in the Committee for the organization of the 15th March 1902 grand celebration in the Academic Reading Hall of the 40th anniversary of the award of the doctor of sciences diploma by Prague University on the 31st of March 1902 to Honorary Professor Dr. Kleinwächter who was popular in all segments of the population of Bukovina.

IN 2032 90J6

558. **Kleine** Chronik. Czernowitz, 26. Juni. Akademischer Senat. *Ibidem.* 1902. 27. Juni (Nr. 4115, Jg. 15). S. 3.

Composition of the Academic Senate of Czernowitz Univerity in the academic year 1902/1903. Dr. Eugen Ehrlich – Vice-Dean of the Faculty of Law and Public Administration.

IN 2032 90J6

559. **Kleine** Chronik. Czernowitz, 30. September 1903. Akademischer Senat. *Ibidem.* 1903. 1. Okt. (Nr. 4490, Jg. 16). S. 2.

Composition of the Academic Senate of Czernowitz Univerity in the current academic year. Dr. Eugen Ehrlich – Vice-Dean of the Faculty of Law and Public Administration.

IN 2033 90J6

560. **Kleine** Chronik. Czernowitz, 24. Juni. Akademischer Senat im Studienjahr 1901/1902. *Ibidem.* 1901. 25. Juni (Nr. 3813, Jg. 14). S. 2.

Composition of the Academic Senate of Czernowitz Univerity in the academic year 1901/1902. Dr. Eugen Ehrlich – Dean of the Faculty of Law and Public Administration.

IN 2031 90J6

561. **Kleine** Chronik. Czernowitz, 30. November. Akad. Corps "Alemannia". *Ibidem.* 1901. 1. Dec. (Nr. 3947, Jg. 14). S. 4.

Participation of Professor Dr. Ehrlich, among other dignitaries, in the celebration of the 50th semester of the Academic Society "Alemannia".

IN 2031 90J6

562. **Kleine** Chronik. Czernowitz, 6. Juni. Akad. Corps Alemannia. *Ibidem.* 1902. 7. Juni (Nr. 4098, Jg. 15). S. 2.

Participation of the Dean of the Facultty of Law Professor Dr. Ehrlich, among other dignitaries, in the celebration of the Academic Society "Alemannia".

IN 2032 90J6

563. **Kleine** Chronik. Czernowitz, 15. November. Der akademische Corps Alemannia... *Ibidem.* 1899. 16. Nov. (Nr. 3338, Jg. 12). S. 3.

Participation of University Professor Dr. Ehrlich, among other dignitaries, in the celebration of the Academic Society "Alemannia" on the 7th of November 1899.

IN 2029 90J6

564. **Kleine** Chronik. Czernowitz, 10. Juni. Akademisches Corps Alemannia. *Ibidem.* 1902. 11. Juni (Nr. 4101, Jg. 15). S. 3.

On the celebration of the Academic Society "Alemannia" including the information about the welcome speech by Professor Dr. Ehrlich.

IN 2032 90J6

565. **Kleine** Chronik. Czernowitz, 14. November. Akademisches Corps "Alemannia". *Ibidem.* 1903. 15. Nov. (Nr. 4529, Jg. 16). S. 3.

Participation of University Professor Dr. Ehrlich, among other dignitaries, in the celebration of the Academic Society "Alemannia" on the 7th of November 1903.

IN 2033 90J6

566. **Kleine** Chronik. Czernowitz, den 22. September 1900. Aus dem deutschen 25. Juristentage... *Bukowinaer Rundschau.* 1900. 23. Sept. (Nr. 3427, Jg. 19). S. 3.

Participation of Czernowitz University Professor Dr. Eugen Ehrlich in the 25th meeting of German lawyers.

IN 2087 90A13

567. **Kleine** Chronik. Czernowitz, 22. September. Deutscher Juristentag. *Bukowiner Nachrichten.* 1900. 23. Sept. (Nr. 3591, Jg. 13). S. 3.

Participation of Professor Dr. Eugen Ehrlich in the meeting of German lawyers in Bamberg.

IN 2030 90J6

568. **Kleine** Chronik. Czernowitz, 7. Juli. Empfang beim Landeshauptmann. *Ibidem.* 1902. 8. Juli (Nr. 4124, Jg. 15). S. 2–3.

On the official admission to the Regional Governor Lupul, including the information about the participation of Prof. Ehrlich as a representative of Czernowitz University.

IN 2032 90J6

569. **Kleine** Chronik. Czernowitz, den 14. Februar 1900. Ernennungen. *Bukowinaer Rundschau.* 1900. 15. Febr. (Nr. 3245, Jg. 19). S. 2.

Information about the appointment of the Associate Professor of Czernowitz University Dr. Eugen Ehrlich a Full Professor.

IN 2087 90A13

570. **Kleine** Chronik. Czernowitz, 26. November. Eröffnungskneipe der akad. Burschenschaft "Arminia". *Bukowiner Nachrichten.* 1901. 27. Nov. (Nr. 3943, Jg. 14). S. 2.

Opening of the socializing basis of the Academic Society "Arminia". Professor Dr. Ehrlich – one of the speakers at the event.

IN 2031 90J6

571. **Kleine** Chronik. Czernowitz, 13. December. Festabend der akad. Verbindung "Hasmonaea". *Ibidem.* 1900. 14. Dec. (Nr. 3658, Jg. 13). S. 2.

Participation of Professor Dr. Ehrlich in the ceremony of the Society "Hasmonaea" on the 8th of December 1900 on the occasion of the 25th anniversary of the foundation of our Alma Mater.

IN 2030 90J6

572. **Kleine** Chronik. Czernowitz, 3. Februar. Festbanket. *Ibidem.* 1897. 4. Febr. (Nr. 2508, Jg. 10). S. 2.

Participation of Dr. Ehrlich together with the local collegium of professors in the celebration of the conferring an honorary doctorate to the Vicar von Repta.

IN 2027 90J6

573. **Kleine** Chronik. Der Festcommers der akad. Verbindung "Hasmonaea". *Bukowinaer Rundschau.* 1901. 5. Dec. (Nr. 3784, Jg. 20). S. 3–4.

Participation of the Dean of the Faculty of Law Professor Dr. Ehrlich in the celebration of the 10th anniversary of the Society "Hasmonaea".

IN 2088 90A13

574. **Kleine** Chronik. Czernowitz, 14. August. Franz-Josefs-Universität. *Bukowiner Nachrichten.* 1897. 15. Aug. (Nr. 2666, Jg. 10). S. 4.

Professor Dr. Ehrlich, a member of the Faculty of Law and Public Administration of Czernowitz University in the winter semester of the academic year 1897/98.

IN 2027 90J6

575. **Kleine** Chronik. Czernowitz, 19. Juni. Franz-Josefs-Universität. *Ibidem.* 1901. 21. Juni (Nr. 3810, Jg. 14). S. 3.

Election of the Dean of the Faculty of Law of Czernowitz University for the academic year 1901/1902 – Professor Dr. Eugen Ehrlich.

IN 2031 90J6

576. **Kleine** Chronik. Czernowitz, 11. März. Franz Josephs-Universität. *Ibidem.* 1901. 12. März (Nr. 3729, Jg. 14). S. 3.

Information about Professor Dr. Eugen Ehrlich's 14-day research trip to archives.

IN 2031 90J6

577. **Kleine** Chronik. Juristisch-staatswissenschaftliche Gesellschaft. *Bukowinaer Rundschau.* 1904. 22. Jänner (Nr. 4398, Jg. 23). S. 2.

Information about the assembly of the members of the Society of Law and Public Administration on the 20th January 1904 and about the lecture by Professor Dr. Ehrlich to be held on the 24th February 1904.

IN 2091 90A13

578. **Kleine** Chronik. Die juristisch-staatswissenschaftliche Gesellschaft... *Ibidem.* 1904. 24. Jänner (Nr. 4400, Jg. 23). S. 2–3.

Information about the 4th annual assembly of the members of the Society of Law and Public Administration on the 20th January 1904, as well as about lectures and discussions including the lecture by Professor Dr. Ehrlich on "Free Finding of the Law and Free Science of Law" ("freie Rechtsfindung und freie Rechtswissenschaft").

IN 2091 90A13

579. **Kleine** Chronik. Juristisch-staatswissenschaftliche Gesellschaft. *Ibidem.* 1904. 23. Febr. (Nr. 4424, Jg. 23). S. 3.

Information about the lecture by Professor Dr. Eugen Ehrlich on "Zittelmann, International Private

Law" ("Zittelmann, internationals Privatrecht"), to be held on the 24th February 1904 in the Town Hall.

IN 2091 90A13

580. **Kleine** Chronik. Czernowitz, 4. Februar. Die juristisch-staatswissenschaftliche Gesellschaft... *Ibidem.* 1905. 5. Febr. (Nr. 4708, Jg. 24). S. 4.

Information about the lecture by Professor Dr. Eugen Ehrlich on "Sociology and Science of Law" ("Sociologie und Rechtswissenschaft"), to be held on the 15th February 1905 in the Town Hall.

IN 2092 90A13

581. **Kleine** Chronik. Czernowitz, 13. Februar. Juristisch-staatswissenschaftliche Gesellschaft. *Ibidem.* 1905. 14. Febr. (Nr. 4715, Jg. 24). S. 3.

Information about the lecture by University Professor Dr. Eugen Ehrlich on "Sociology and Jurisprudence" ("Sociologie und Jurisprudenz"), to be held on the 15th February 1905 in the Town Hall.

IN 2092 90A13

582. **Kleine** Chronik. Czernowitz, 9. Februar. Juristisch-staatswissenschaftliche Gesellschaft. *Bukowiner Nachrichten.* 1903. 10. Febr. (Nr. 4300, Jg. 16). S. 3.

Information about the lecture by Professor Dr. Eugen Ehrlich on "Free Finding of the Law and Free Science of Law" ("freie Rechtsfindung und freie Rechtswissenschaft"), to be held on the 11th February 1903 in the Town Hall.

IN 2033 90J6

583. **Kleine** Chronik. Czernowitz, 22. Februar. Juristisch-staatswissenschaftliche Gesellschaft. *Ibidem.* 1904. 23. Febr. (Nr. 4608, Jg. 17). S. 2.

Information about the lecture by Professor Dr. Ehrlich on "Zittelmann, International Private Law" ("Zittelmann, internationals Privatrecht"), to be held on the 24th February 1904 in the Town Hall.

IN 2034 90J6

584. **Kleine** Chronik. Czernowitz, 23. Juni. Kaiser Franz Joseph-Universitäts-Studentenheim. *Ibidem.* 1902. 24. Juni (Nr. 4112, Jg. 15). S. 3.

Participation of the Dean Professor Dr. Ehrlich in the celebration of the laying the first stone in the foundations of the Czernowitz University dormitory.

IN 2032 90J6

585. **Kleine** Chronik. K. k. Franz-Josefs-Universität. *Czernowitzer Zeitung.* 1896. 22. Nov. (Nr. 271, Jg. 29). S. 4.

Announcement of the beginning of the lecture course as of the 1st of December 1896 by the newly appointed Associate Professor of Roman law at Czernowitz University Dr. Eugen Ehrlich.

IN 1922 90A1

586. **Kleine** Chronik. K. k. Franz-Josefs-Universität. *Ibidem.* 1897. 14. Aug. (Nr. 185, Jg. 30). S. 2.

Information about Professor of the Faculty of Law and Public Administration of Czernowitz University Dr. Ehrlich, who will read lectures according to the list of public lectures at Czernowitz University in the winter semester of the academic year 1897/1898.

IN 1923 90A1

587. **Kleine** Chronik. Czernowitz, 12. Dezember. Die kommunale Krise. *Bukowinaer Rundschau.* 1905. 13. Dez. (Nr. 4961, Jg. 24). S. 2.

About a resonating article by University Professor Dr. Ehrlich published in "Czernowitzer Allgemeine Zeitung", on the topic of municipal crisis with the critical opinions of the members of the municipality.

IN 2092 90A13

588. **Kleine** Chronik. Czernowitz, 27. October. Personalnachricht. *Ibidem.* 1896. 28. Oct. (Nr. 2270, Jg. 15). S. 2.

Information about the appointment of the lawyer from Schwechat and at the same time the privatdozent of the University of Vienna Dr. Ehrlich an Associate Professor of Roman law at Czernowitz University.

IN 2083 90A13

589. **Kleine** Chronik. Czernowitz, 31. Mai. Personalnachricht. *Bukowiner Nachrichten.* 1902. 1. Juni (Nr. 4093, Jg. 15). S. 4.

Information about arrival of the Advisor, Fekete de Belafalva, by an express train from Vienna on the 31st of March 1902. Among the greeters – Professor Dr. Ehrlich.

IN 2032 90J6

590. **Kleine** Chronik. Czernowitz, den 24. Februar. Personalnachrichten. *Bukowinaer Rundschau.* 1900. 25. Febr. (Nr. 3254, Jg. 19). S. 3.

Notice of the departure of University Professor Dr. Eugen Ehrlich for Vienna.

IN 2087 90A13

591. **Kleine** Chronik. Czernowitz, den 24. Februar. Personalnachrichten. *Bukowiner Nachrichten.* 1900. 25. Febr. (Nr. 3419, Jg. 13). S. 3.

Notice of the departure of University Professor Dr. Eugen Ehrlich for Vienna.

IN 2030 90J6

592. **Kleine** Chronik. Czernowitz, 10. Mai. Personalnachrichten. *Ibidem.* 1902. 11. Mai (Nr. 4077, Jg. 15). S. 3.

Notice of the return of University Professor Dr. Ehrlich from vacations.

IN 2032 90J6

593. **Kleine** Chronik. Populärwissenschaftliche Vorträge. *Bukowinaer Rundschau.* 1902. 7. Febr. (Nr. 3835, Jg. 21). S. 3.

Information about the change of the date of the scientific-popular lecture by Professor Dr. Ehrlich on "The Origins of Women's Question" ("Die Anfänge der Frauenfrage") from the 7th of February to the 14th of March 1902.

IN 2089 90A13

594. **Kleine** Chronik. Czernowitz, 6. Februar. Populär-wissenschaftliche Vorträge. *Bukowiner Nachrichten.* 1902. 7. Febr. (Nr. 4001, Jg. 15). S. 4.

Information about the change of the date of the scientific-popular lecture by Professor Dr. Ehrlich on "The Origins of Women's Question" ("Die Anfänge der Frauenfrage") from the 7th of February to the 14th of March 1902.

IN 2032 90J6

595. **Kleine** Chronik. Czernowitz, 20. Februar. Populär-wissenschaftliche Vorträge. *Ibidem.* 1902. 21. Febr.(Nr. 4013, Jg. 15). S. 3.

Announcement of the 21st of February 1902 about the scientific-popular lecture by Professor Dr. Ehrlich on "The Origins of Women's Question" ("Die Anfänge der Frauenfrage") to be held on the 14th of March 1902.

IN 2032 90J6

596. **Kleine** Chronik. Populärwissenschaftliche Vorträge. *Bukowinaer Rundschau.* 1902. 25. Febr. (Nr. 3850, Jg. 21). S. 3.

Announcement of the 21st of February 1902 about the scientific-popular lecture by Professor Dr. Eugen Ehrlich on "The Origins of Women's Question" ("Die Anfänge der Frauenfrage").

IN 2089 90A13

597. **Kleine** Chronik. Die popular-wissenschaftlichen Vorträge der "akad. Lesehalle"... *Ibidem.* 1901. 31. Dec. (Nr. 3804, Jg. 20). S. 3.

Announcement of the upcoming lecture by Professor Dr. Ehrlich planned for the 7th of February 1901, within the framework of scientific-popular lectures in the "Academic Reading Hall".

IN 2088 90A13

598. **Kleine** Chronik. Czernowitz, den 27. Juni. Promotion. *Ibidem.* 1900. 28. Juni (Nr. 3355, Jg. 19). S. 3.

Professor Dr. Ehrlich – promoter of the Czernowitz University graduation ceremony of a new doctor of law, Dragoş Bumbac.

IN 2087 90A13

599. **Kleine** Chronik. Czernowitz, den 3. November. Promotion. *Ibidem.* 1900. 4. Nov. (Nr. 3459, Jg. 19). S. 3.

Professor Dr. Ehrlich – promoter of the Czernowitz University graduation ceremony of a newdoctor of law, Carl Bertoni.

IN 2087 90A13

600. **Kleine** Chronik. Promotion. *Ibidem.* 1904. 11. Febr. (Nr. 4414, Jg. 23). S. 3.

Professor Dr. Ehrlich – promoter of the Czernowitz University graduation ceremony of a new doctor of law, Felix Reik, a journalist from Vienna.

IN 2091 90A13

601. **Kleine** Chronik. Promotion. *Ibidem.* 1904. 12. Juli (Nr. 4538, Jg. 23). S. 2.

Professor Dr. Ehrlich – promoter of the Czernowitz University graduation ceremony of a new doctor of law, Public Administration trainee (Landesregierungs-Konzeptspraktikant) Anton Josefowicz, on the 9th of July 1904.

IN 2091 90A13

602. **Kleine** Chronik. Promotion. *Ibidem.* 1904. 16. Dez. (Nr. 4667, Jg. 23). S. 3.

Professor Dr. Ehrlich – promoter of the Czernowitz University graduation ceremony of a new doctor of law, court secretary (Gerichtsauskultant) Leo Löwner.

IN 2091 90A13

603. **Kleine** Chronik. Czernowitz, 27. Juni. Promotion. *Bukowiner Nachrichten.* 1900. 28. Juni (Nr. 3519, Jg. 13). S. 4.

Professor Dr. Ehrlich – promoter of the Czernowitz University graduation ceremony of a new doctor of law, notary candidate (Notariatscandidaten) Dragoş Bumbac.

IN 2030 90J6

604. **Kleine** Chronik. Czernowitz, 5. November. Promotion. *Ibidem.* 1900. 6. Nov. (Nr. 3626, Jg. 13). S. 3.

Professor Dr. Ehrlich – promoter of the Czernowitz University graduation ceremony of a new doctor of law, junior consul (Consulareleven) Carl Franz Bertoni.

IN 2030 90J6

605. **Kleine** Chronik. Czernowitz, 10. Februar. Promotion. *Ibidem.* 1904. 11. Febr. (Nr. 4598, Jg. 17). S. 4.

Professor Dr. Ehrlich – promoter of the Czernowitz University graduation ceremony of a new doctor of law, Felix Reik.

IN 2034 90J6

606. **Kleine** Chronik. Czernowitz, 11. Juli. Promotion. *Ibidem.* 1904. 12. Juli (Nr. 4722, Jg. 17). S. 2.

Professor Dr. Ehrlich – promoter of the Czernowitz University graduation ceremony of a new doctor of law, Public Administration trainee (Landesregierungs-Konzeptspraktikant) Anton Josefowicz.

IN 2034 90J6

607. **Kleine** Chronik. Czernowitz, 18. Februar. Promotion. *Bukowinaer Rundschau.* 1905. 19. Febr. (Nr. 4720, Jg. 24). S. 3.

Professor Dr. Ehrlich – promoter of the Czernowitz University graduation ceremony of a new doctor of law, Max Singer.

IN 2092 90A13

608. **Kleine** Chronik. Promotion. *Czernowitzer Tagblatt.* 1913. 23. Juli (Nr. 3121, Jg. 11). S. 2.

Professor Dr. Ehrlich – promoter of the Czernowitz University graduation ceremony of a new doctor of law, Otto Sorda, on the 17th July 1913.

IN 1982 90A45

609. **Kleine** Chronik. Czernowitz, den 22. December. Promotionen. *Bukowinaer Rundschau.* 1900. 23. Dec. (Nr. 3500, Jg. 19). S. 3.

Professor Dr. Ehrlich – promoter of the Czernowitz University graduation ceremony of a new doctor of law, Hugo Badian, on the 18th December 1900.

IN 2087 90A13

610. **Kleine** Chronik. Promotionen. *Ibidem.* 1901. 28. Apr. (Nr. 3602, Jg. 20). S. 3.

Professor Dr. Ehrlich – promoter of the Czernowitz University graduation ceremony of new doctors of law, Bernhard Stecher and Jakob Fleischer.

IN 2088 90A13

611. **Kleine** Chronik. Promotionen. *Ibidem.* 1901. 12. Dec. (Nr. 3790, Jg. 20). S. 3.

Professor Dr. Ehrlich – promoter of the Czernowitz University graduation ceremony of a new doctor of law, Max Diamant, on the 13th December 1901.

IN 2088 90A13

612. **Kleine** Chronik. Promotionen. *Ibidem.* 1903. 18. Okt. (Nr. 4321, Jg. 22). S. 3.

Professor Dr. Ehrlich – promoter of the Czernowitz University graduation ceremony of a new doctor of law, Edgar Bucksch, on the 16th October 1903.

IN 2090 90A13

613. **Kleine** Chronik. Czernowitz, 28. Juni. Promotionen. *Ibidem.* 1905. 29. Juni (Nr. 4825, Jg. 24). S. 3.

Professor Dr. Ehrlich – promoter of the Czernowitz University graduation ceremony of a new doctor of law Mordche Deligdisch.

IN 2092 90A13

614. **Kleine** Chronik. Czernowitz, 3. November. Promotionen. *Ibidem.* 1905. 4. Nov. (Nr. 4929, Jg. 24). S. 3.

Professor Dr. Ehrlich – promoter of the Czernowitz University graduation ceremony of a new doctor of law Julius Brüll.

IN 2092 90A13

615. **Kleine** Chronik. Czernowitz, 22. December. Promotionen. *Bukowiner Nachrichten.* 1900. 23. Dec. (Nr. 3666, Jg. 13). S. 4.

Professor Dr. Ehrlich – promoter of the Czernowitz University graduation ceremony of a new doctor of law Hugo Badian, on the 18th December 1900.

IN 2030 90J6

616. **Kleine** Chronik. Czernowitz, 29. April. Promotionen. *Ibidem.* 1901. 30. Apr. (Nr. 3769, Jg. 14). S. 3.

Professor Dr. Ehrlich – promoter of the Czernowitz University graduation ceremony of new doctors of law Jankel Fleischer and Bernhard Stecher, on the 27th April 1901.

IN 2031 90J6

617. **Kleine** Chronik. Czernowitz, von 17. Oktober. Promotionen. *Bukowiner Nachrichten.* 1903. 18. Okt. (Nr. 4505, Jg. 16). S. 3.

Professor Dr. Ehrlich – promoter of the Czernowitz University graduation ceremony of a new doctor of law, Edgar Bucksch.

IN 2033 90J6

618. **Kleine** Chronik. Czernowitz, 28. November. Prüfungscommissionen an unserer Universität. *Bukowinaer Rundschau.* 1899. 29. Nov. (Nr. 3184, Jg. 18). S. 3.

Information about the request of the Minister of Cultus and Education to the President of the Regional Court in Czernowitz to appoint the State Judicial Examination Boards in Czernowitz for the period of the academic years from 1899/1900 to 1901/1902, and to extend the function period of University Professors Dr. Eugen Ehrlich and Alfred von Halban in their positions of members of the State Judicial Examination Board by the end of September 1902.

IN 2086 90A13

619. **Kleine** Chronik. Vierzigjähriges Doktorjubiläum. *Ibidem.* 1902. 7. März (Nr. 3859, Jg. 21). S. 4.

Participation of Professor Dr. Ehrlich in the Committee for the grand celebration of the 40th anniversary of the graduation ceremony of the awarding doctor of sciences diploma to Honorary Professor of Czernowitz University Dr. Friedrich Kleinwächter, on the 15th of March 1902 in the Academic Reading Hall.

IN 2089 90A13

620. **Kleine** Chronik. Czernowitz, 20. Februar. 40-jähriges Doktorjubiläum. *Bukowiner Nachrichten.* 1902. 21. Febr. (Nr. 4013, Jg. 15). S. 3.

Participation of the Dean of the Faculty of Law Professor Dr. Ehrlich in the Committee for the grand celebration of the 40th anniversary of the graduation ceremony of the awarding doctor of sciences diploma to Honorary Professor of Czernowitz University Dr. Kleinwächter.

IN 2032 90J6

621. **Kleine** Chronik. Czernowitz, 11. Februar. Volkstümliche Universitätskurse. *Bukowinaer Rundschau.* 1905. 12. Febr. (Nr. 4714, Jg. 24). S. 4.

The schedule of courses held by professors and associate professors of Czernowitz University in March and April of the current year including the information about the lecture on "General Theory of Law" by Professor Dr. Eugen Ehrlich.

IN 2092 90A13

622. **Kleine** Chronik. Czernowitz, 30. Juni. Volkstümliche Universitätskurse. *Ibidem.* 1905. 1. Juli (Nr. 4826, Jg. 24). S. 3–4.

The schedule of courses and numbers of students enrolled in the courses held by professors and associate professors of Czernowitz University in March and April of the current year including the information about the number of students of the course on "General Theory of Law" by Professor Dr. Eugen Ehrlich. – p. 3.

IN 2092 90A13

623. **Kleine** Chronik. Czernowitz, 10. Oktober. Volkstümliche Universitätskurse. *Ibidem.* 1905. 11. Okt. (Nr. 4909, Jg. 24). S. 4.

The schedule of courses held by professors and associate professors in the academic year 1905/1906 including the information about the course on "General Theory of Law" by Professor Dr. Eugen Ehrlich.

IN 2092 90A13

624. **Kleine** Chronik. Czernowitz, 18. Oktober. Volkstümliche Universitätskurse. *Ibidem.* 1905. 19. Okt. (Nr. 4916, Jg. 24). S. 3.

Information about the opening of the popular university lecture series on "General Theory of Law" by Professor Dr. Eugen Ehrlich that will take place on Friday, the 20th of October 1905 in the lecture hall No. 5.

IN 2092 90A13

625. **Kleine** Chronik. Czernowitz, 25. Oktober. Volkstümliche Universitätskurse. *Ibidem.* 1905. 26. Okt. (Nr. 4922, Jg. 24). S. 3.

Notice about the second lecture within the series on "General Theory of Law" to be held by Professor Dr. Eugen Ehrlich on the 27th of October 1905 in the lecture hall No. 5.

IN 2092 90A13

626. **Kleine** Chronik. Czernowitz, 15. November. Volkstümliche Universitätskurse. *Ibidem.* 1905. 16. Nov. (Nr. 4939, Jg. 24). S. 3.

Notice about the fifth lecture within the series on "General Theory of Law" to be held by Professor Dr. Eugen Ehrlich on the 17th of November 1905 in the lecture hall No. 5.

IN 2092 90A13

627. **Kleine** Chronik. Czernowitz, 23. Oktober. Vom Universitätsstudentenheim. *Ibidem.* 1905. 24. Okt. (Nr. 4920, Jg. 24). S. 2.

Election at the Faculty of Law and Public Administration of the local university in which Professor Dr. Eugen Ehrlich was elected a member of Board of Trustees replacing Professor Dr. von Halban.

IN 2092 90A13

628. **Kleine** Chronik. Czernowitz, 19. Mai. Von akademischen Corps "Alemannia". *Bukowiner Nachrichten.* 1897. 20. Mai (Nr. 2595, Jg. 10). S. 2.

Participation of Professor Dr. Ehrlich in the activities of the Society "Alemannia".

IN 2027 90J6

629. **Kleine** Chronik. Czernowitz, den 19. August. Von der Universität. *Ibidem.* 1896. 20. Aug. (Nr. 2372, Jg. 9). S. 3.

Appointment of the privatdozent of the University of Vienna and the court lawyer Dr. Ehrlich (Bukovina) who enjoys a reputation of the outstanding expert on Roman law, a follower of Prof. Ernst Hruza.

IN 2026 90J6

630. **Kleine** Chronik. Czernowitz, 21. November. Von der Universität. *Bukowinaer Rundschau.* 1896. 22. Nov. (Nr. 2292, Jg. 15). S. 4.

Information about the beginning of the lecture series on "History and Institutions of Roman Law" and "Inheritance in Roman Law" on the 1st of December 1896 by Associate Professor of Roman law at Czernowitz University Dr. Eugen Ehrlich.

IN 2083 90A13

631. **Kleine** Chronik. Czernowitz, 18. Juli. Von der Universität. *Bukowiner Nachrichten.* 1902. 19. Juli (Nr. 4134, Jg. 15). S. 3.

About vacations at the university including the information about vacations of the Dean of the Faculty of Law and Public Administration Professor Dr. Eugen Ehrlich.

IN 2032 90J6

632. **Kleine** Chronik. Czernowitz, 8. Oktober. Von der Universität. *Ibidem.* 1902. 9. Okt. (Nr. 4201, Jg. 15). S. 2.

On the appointment of University Professor Dr. Eugen Ehrlich a member of the State Judicial Examination Board in Czernowitz for the period of the academic years 1902/1903 to 1904/1905 by the Minister of Cultus and Education.

IN 2032 90J6

633. **Kleine** Chronik. Czernowitz, 16. Juli. Von der Universität. *Ibidem.* 1903. 17. Juli (Nr. 4428, Jg. 16). S. 2.

Information about vacations of the Rector Professor Dr. Scharizer, the Dean Professor Dr. Adler, and the Vice-Dean Professor Dr. Ehrlich. Management of the rectorate is taken by the Vice-Rector Professor Dr. Wojucki, and management of the dean's office of the Faculty of Law and Public Administration is taken by the Advisor Professor Dr. Kleinwächter.

IN 2033 90J6

634. **Kleine** Chronik. Czernowitz, 27. April. Von unserer Universität. *Bukowinaer Rundschau.* 1897. 28. Apr. (Nr. 2418, Jg. 16). S. 2.

On the appointment of University Associate Professors Dr. Alfred von Halban and Dr. Eugen Ehrlich members of the State Judicial Examination Board in Czernowitz.

IN 2084 90A13

635. **Kleine** Chronik. Czernowitz, 28. April. Von unserer Universität. *Bukowiner Nachrichten.* 1897. 29. Apr. (Nr. 2578, Jg. 10). S. 3.

On the appointment of University Associate Professor Dr. Eugen Ehrlich a member of the State Judicial Examination Board in Czernowitz.

IN 2027 90J6

636. **Kleine** Chronik. Czernowitz, den 14. Februar. Von unserer Universität. *Ibidem.* 1900. 15. Febr. (Nr. 3410, Jg. 13). S. 3.

On the appointment of Associate Professor of Czernowitz University Dr. Eugen Ehrlich a Full Professor.

IN 2030 90J6

637. **Kleine** Chronik. Von unserer Universität. *Bukowinaer Rundschau.* 1901. 12. März (Nr. 3563, Jg. 20). S. 3.

Information about Professor Dr. Eugen Ehrlich's 14-day research trip to archives in Vienna.

IN 2088 90A13

638. **Kleine** Chronik. Von unserer Universität. *Ibidem.* 1901. 21. Juni (Nr. 3645, Jg. 20). S. 2.

Elections of the 19th of June of the Dean of the Faculty of Law of Czernowitz University for the academic year 1901/1902 – Professor of Roman law Dr. Eugen Ehrlich.

IN 2088 90A13

639. **Kleine** Chronik. Von unserer Universität. *Ibidem.* 1901. 25. Sept. (Nr. 3724, Jg. 20). S. 4.

Elections of the academic management of Czernowitz University for the academic year 1901/1902 – the Dean of the Faculty of Law, Professor Dr. Eugen Ehrlich.

IN 2088 90A13

640. **Kleine** Chronik. Von unserer Universität. *Ibidem.* 1902. 9. Okt. (Nr. 4034, Jg. 21). S. 3.

Appointment of University Professor Dr. Eugen Ehrlich a member of the State Judicial Examination Board in Czernowitz by the Minister of Cultus and Education for the period of the academic years 1902/1903 to 1904/1905.

IN 2089 90A13

641. **Kojder, Andrzej.** Z Czerniowców w szeroki świat... Eugen Ehrlich i narodziny idei socjologii prawa. In *Stawanie się społeczeństwa: szkice ofiarowane Piotrowi Sztompce z okazji 40-lecia pracy naukowej,* pod red. Andrzeja Flisa. Krakow: T-wo aut. i wydaw. prac nauk. Universitas, 2006. S. 125–146. [Kojder, Andrzej. From Czernowitz to the whole world... Eugen Ehrlich and the origin of the idea of the Sociology of Law. In *Development of the society : sketches dedicated to Piotr Sztompce on the occasion of the 40 years of his scientific work,* edited by Andrzej Flis. Krakow: Society of the authors and publishers of scientific works. Universitas, 2006. pp. 125–146]

642. **Kosch, Wilhelm.** "Juden und Deutsche in der Bukowina." *Neue Jüdische Monatshefte.* 1916. 25. Dez. (Heft 6, Jg. 1). S. 143–152.

Information about professor Eugen Ehrlich in the publication pp. 148–149.

643. **Die Krise** im Gemeinderate. Czernowitz, 11. Dezember. *Czernowitzer Allgemeine Zeitung.* 1905. 12. Dez. (Nr. 583). S. 1–4.

About the participation of Professor Dr. E. Ehrlich in solving the municipal crisis – pp. 1, 3.

IN 90

644. **Die Krise** im Gemeinderate. Czernowitz, 13. Dezember. *Ibidem.* 1905. 14. Dez. (Nr. 585). S. 1–4.

About the participation of Professor Dr. E. Ehrlich in solving the municipal crisis – pp. 1, 2.

IN 90

645. **Kronika.** Skład senatu akademickiego... *Gazeta Polska.* 1906. 28. czerw. (nr. 51, r. 24). S. 2.

Composition of the Academic Senate of Czernowitz University for the academic year 1906/1907. Dr. E. Ehrlich – Rector of the University.

IN 2010 90A1

646. **Kronika.** Z uniwersytetów. *Ibidem.* 1901. 23. czerw. (nr. 49, r. 19). S. 2.

Elections of the Dean of the Faculty of Law of Czernowitz University for the academic year 1901/1902 – Professor Dr. Eugen Ehrlich.

IN 2005 90A16

647. **Kronika.** Z uniwersytetu. *Ibidem.* 1900. 18. lutego (nr. 14, r. 18). S. 3.

On the appointment of Dr. E. Ehrlich a full professor of Roman law at Czernowitz University.

IN 2004 90A16

648. **Kronika.** Z uniwersytetu. *Ibidem.* 1901. 27. czerw. (nr. 50, r. 19). S. 2.

Composition of the Academic Senate of Czernowitz University for the academic year 1901/1902. Dr. Eugen Ehrlich – the Dean of the Faculty of Law.

IN 2005 90A16

649. **Kronika.** Z uniwersytetu. *Ibidem.* 1901. 26. wrzes. (nr. 76, r. 19). S. 2.

Composition of the Academic Senate of Czernowitz University for the academic year 1901/1902. Dr. E. Ehrlich – the Dean of the Faculty of Law.

IN 2005 90A16

650. **Kronika.** Z uniwersytetu. *Ibidem.* 1906. 24. czerw. (nr. 50, r. 24). S. 3.

The election of Professor of Roman law Dr. Eugen Ehrlich for the Rector of Czernowitz University for the academic year 1906/1907.

IN 2010 90A16

651. **Kronika.** Zwszechnicy. *Ibidem.* 1896. 15. list. (nr. 92, r. 14). S. 3.

Information about the appointment of the lawyer from Vienna and at the same time the privatdozent Dr. E. Ehrlich an Associate Professor of Roman law at Czernowitz University.

IN 1441 90A16

652. **Letzte** Telegramme. Studienreise des Univ.-Prof. Dr. Eugen Ehrlich nach Albanien. Wien, 17. April. (Priv.-Tel. der "Cz. Allg. Ztg."). *Czernowitzer Allgemeine Zeitung.* 1914. 18. Apr. (Nr. 3425). S. 6.

Information about research visit of Professor Eugen Ehrlich in Albania.

IN 90

653. **Likhovski, Assaf.** "Czernowitz, Lincoln, Jerusalem, and the Comparative History of American Jurisprudence." *Theoretical Inquiries in Law.* 2003. Vol. 4, Nr. 2 (July). pp. 621–657.

E. Ehrlich. – pp. 621, 625–629, 632–633, 636, 637–647, 651–656.

654. **Lokalnachrichten.** Czernowitz, 7. November. Beileidskundgebungen anlätzlich des Ablebens des Erzherzogs Otto. *Bukowiner Nachrichten.* 1906. 8. Nov. (Nr. 5414, Jg. 19). S. 4.

Participation of the Rector Professor Dr. Eugen Ehrlich, together with the deans, in the memorial service dedicated to the late Archduke Otto at the Cathedral Church.

IN 2036 90J6

655. **Lokalnachrichten.** Czernowitz, 13. Oktober. Dejeuner beim Landespräsidenten. *Ibidem.* 1906. 14. Okt. (Nr. 5395, Jg. 19). S. 5.

Participation of the Rector Professor Dr. Eugen Ehrlich in the Sunday lunch organized by the Regional President of Bukovina Dr. von Bleyleben on the 12th of October 1906.

IN 2036 90J6

656. **Lokalnachrichten.** Czernowitz, 8. Oktober. Einweihung und Eröffnung des neuen Ziviljustizpalais. *Ibidem.* 1906. 9. Okt. (Nr. 5390, Jg. 19). S. 2–3.

Participation of the Rector Dr. Ehrlich in the celebration of the opening of the new Palace of Civil Justice.

IN 2036 90J6

657. **Lokalnachrichten.** Czernowitz, 23. Juni. Rektorswahl. *Ibidem.* 1906. 24. Juni (Nr. 5303, Jg. 19). S. 4.

Information about the first round of the elections on the 23rd of June 1906 in which Professor of Roman law Dr. Eugen Ehrlich was unanimously elected the Rector of Czernowitz University.

IN 2036 90J6

658. **Lokal-** und Personal nachrichten. *Hochschul-Nachrichten.* 1900. Febr. (Heft 113, Jg. 10, Nr. 5). S. 107–112.

Information about Professor Eugen Ehrlich in the publication – p. 111.

IN 360375 60A15

659. **Lokal-** und Personalnachrichten. *Ibidem.* 1906. Juni (Heft 189, Jg. 16, Nr. 4). S. 227–234.

Information about Professor Eugen Ehrlich in the publication – p. 232.

IN 19441 60A15

660. **Lokal-** und Provinznachrichten. Czernowitz, 4. Februar. Abschiedsdiner für den Divisionär General-Major v. Hornik. *Czernowitzer Tagblatt.* 1907. 5. Febr. (Nr. 1198, Jg. 5). S. 4.

Participation of University Professor Dr. Ehrlich in a farewell dinner of Divisional General Major von Hornik.

IN 1968 90A45

661. **Lokal-** und Provinznachrichten. Czernowitz, 12. Juli. 80. Geburstag. *Ibidem.* 1911. 13. Juli (Nr. 2515, Jg. 9). S. 3.

Greetings of the Faculty of Law and Public Administration of Czernowitz University to Professor of Law at the University in Halle Dr. Hermann Fitting on the occasion of his 80th birthday, signed by the Faculty collegium of professors including Dr. Eugen Ehrlich.

IN 1977 90A45

662. **Lokal-** und Provinznachrichten. Czernowitz, 11. April. Die Akademie der Herrenfechtsocietee. *Ibidem.* 1910. 12. Apr. (Nr. 2143, Jg. 8). S. 3–4.

About the charity event of the Society of Fencing that took place in Czernowitz at "Deutsches Hause" ["German House"]. The event was attended by Professor Dr. Ehrlich – p. 4.

IN 1974 90A45

663. **Lokal-** und Provinznachrichten. Czernowitz, 26. Juni. Der akademische Senat unserer Universität... *Ibidem.* 1907. 27. Juni (Nr. 1312, Jg. 5). S. 3.

Composition of the Academic Senate for the academic year 1907/1908. Dr. Eugen Ehrlich – the Vice-Rector of Czernowitz University.

IN 1968 90A45

664. **Lokal-** und Provinznachrichten. Czernowitz, 26. Juni. Der akademische Senat unserer Universität... *Ibidem.* 1909. 27. Juni (Nr. 1908, Jg. 7). S. 4.

Composition of the Academic Senate of Czernowitz University for the academic year 1909/1910. Dr. Eugen Ehrlich – the Vice-Dean of the Faculty of Law.

IN 1972 90A45

665. **Lokal-** und Provinznachrichten. Czernowitz, 22. Juni. Der akademische Senat unserer Universität... *Ibidem.* 1912. 23. Juni (Nr. 2794, Jg. 10). S. 4.

Composition of the Academic Senate of Czernowitz University for the academic year 1912/1913. Dr. Eugen Ehrlich – the Vice-Dean of the Faculty of Law.

IN 1978 90A45

666. **Lokal-** und Provinznachrichten. Czernowitz, 18. März. Akademische Studienreise. *Ibidem.* 1912. 19. März (Nr. 2717, Jg. 10). S. 4.

Participation of the Dean of the Faculty of Law Professor Dr. Ehrlich in the students' meeting of the 17th of March 1912.

IN 1978 90A45

667. **Lokal**- und Provinznachrichten. Czernowitz, 26. Jänner. Akademischer Ball. *Ibidem.* 1914. 27. Jänner (Nr. 3357, Jg. 12). S. 3–4.

Information about the Academic Ball organized under the auspices of the Regional President Rudolf von Meran. Participation of University Professor Dr. Eugen Ehrlich in the Ball – p. 3.

IN 1984 90A45

668. **Lokal**- und Provinznachrichten. Czernowitz, 28. Oktober. Akademischer Senat. *Ibidem.* 1907. 29. Okt. (Nr. 1416, Jg. 5). S. 4.

Composition of the Academic Senate for the current academic year. Dr. Eugen Ehrlich – the Vice-Rector of Czernowitz University.

IN 1969 90A45

669. **Lokal**- und Provinznachrichten. Czernowitz, 24. Juni. Akademischer Senat unserer Universität. *Ibidem.* 1911. 25. Juni (Nr. 2501, Jg. 9). S. 5.

Composition of the Academic Senate of Czernowitz University for the academic year 1911/1912. Professor Dr. Eugen Ehrlich – the Dean of the Faculty of Law.

IN 1976 90A45

670. **Lokal**- und Provinznachrichten. Czernowitz, 13. November. Akademisches Korps "Alemannia". *Ibidem.* 1903. 14. Nov. (Nr. 240, Jg. 1). S. 3.

Participation of University Professor Dr. Ehrlich, among other dignitaries, in the celebration of the Academic Society "Alemannia" on the 7th of November 1903.

IN 1961 90A45

671. **Lokal**- und Provinznachrichten. Czernowitz, 3. November. Anerkennung der jüdischen Nationalität. *Ibidem.* 1906. 4. Nov. (Nr. 1124, Jg. 4). S. 5.

Dispute of the Academic Senate led by the Rector Dr. Ehrlich about the recognition of Jews at Czernowitz University.

IN 1967 90A45

672. **Lokal**- und Provinznachrichten. Czernowitz, 12. Februar. Anton Menger. *Ibidem.* 1906. 13. Febr. (Nr. 907, Jg. 4). S. 3.

Information about the commemorative speech by University Professor Dr. Eugen Ehrlich for the late Honorary Professor of the University of Vienna Dr. Anton Menger at the meeting of the Juridical-Political Scientific Society on the 14th of February 1906 at 7 pm. The full text of the speech is provided.

IN 1966 90A45

673. **Lokal**- und Provinznachrichten. Czernowitz, 6. Februar. Archäologischer Kongress in Athen. *Ibidem.* 1905. 7. Febr. (Nr. 606, Jg. 3). S. 4.

Information about the Archaeological Congress to be held from the 7th to the 13th of April 1905 in Athens – Czernowitz University will be represented there by Professor Dr. Ehrlich.

IN 1964 90A45

674. **Lokal**- und Provinznachrichten. Czernowitz, 28. Februar. Auerkennung der jüdischen Nationalität. *Ibidem.* 1907. 1. März (Nr. 1219, Jg. 5). S. 4.

The Rector Dr. Ehrlich about the recognition of Jews at Czernowitz University.

IN 1968 90A45

675. **Lokal**- und Provinznachrichten. Czernowitz, 21. November. Auerkennung der jüd. Nationalität. *Ibidem.* 1907. 22. Nov. (Nr. 1436, Jg. 5). S. 4.

Professor Dr. Ehrlich about the recognition of Jews at Czernowitz University.

IN 1969 90A45

676. **Lokal**- und Provinznachrichten. Czernowitz, 22. Juni. "Die Aufgaben der Sozialpolitik im österreichischen Osten". *Ibidem.* 1909. 23. Juni (Nr. 1904, Jg. 7). S. 3.

Information about the publication of University Professor Dr. Eugen Ehrlich entitled "Die Aufgaben der Sozialpolitik im österreichischen Osten" ["Tasks of Social Politics in Austrian East"] by the Social Scientific Academic Society.

IN 1972 90A45

677. **Lokal**- und Provinznachrichten. Czernowitz, 15. Juli. "Die Aufgaben der Sozialpolitik im österr. Osten". *Ibidem.* 1909. 16. Juli (Nr. 1923, Jg. 7). S. 4.

Information about the second edition of the publication of University Professor Dr. Eugen Ehrlich entitled "Die Aufgaben der Sozialpolitik im österreichischen Osten, insbesondere in der Bukowina, mit besonderer Beleuchtung der Juden- und Bauernfrage" ["Tasks of Social Politicy in Austrian East, especially in Bukovina, with Special Illumination of Issues of Jews and Peasants"] by the Czernowitz Social Scientific Academic Society. It also provides the information about the cost of the brochure and the address where it is available.

IN 1973 90A45

678. **Lokal**- und Provinznachrichten. Czernowitz, 16. März. Ein auf sehen erregendes Werk des Czernowitzer Universitätsprofessors Ehrlich. Vorschlag zum Gründung einer Hochschule für Gesellschaftswissenschaft. *Ibidem.* 1916. 16. März (Nr. 3799, Jg. 14). S. 3.

About the exceptional work of Czernowitz University Professor Dr. Eugen Ehrlich entitled "Eine Hochschule für Gesellschaftswissenschaft" ["High School for Social Science"], in which he proposes the foundation of the higher school of social studies. It also includes a passage from Ehrlich's work.

IN 1988 90A45

679. **Lokal**- und Provinznachrichten. Czernowitz, 20. September. Auszeichnung. *Ibidem.* 1907. 21. Sept. (Nr. 1384, Jg. 5). S. 4.

Information about the award of the Rector Professor Dr. Eugen Ehrlich the Commander's Cross of the Greek Order of the Saviour.

IN 1969 90A45

680. **Lokal**- und Provinznachrichten. Czernowitz, 3. Februar. Das Blumenfest für das Kind. *Ibidem.* 1909. 4. Febr. (Nr. 1792, Jg. 7). S. 2–3.

About the festival of colours for children. The University Professor Ehrlich, a festival guest, among other dignitaries – p. 2.

IN 1972 90A45

681. **Lokal**- und Provinznachrichten. Czernowitz, 12. Februar. "Bucovina"-Ball. *Ibidem.* 1907. 13. Febr. (Nr. 1205, Jg. 5). S. 3–4.

Participation of the University Rector Dr. Ehrlich in the Ball of Academic Society "Bucovina" – "Bucovina-Ball".

IN 1968 90A45

682. **Lokal**- und Provinznachrichten. Czernowitz, 3. Mai. Bürgermeister Dr. Eduard Reiss. *Ibidem.* 1907. 4. Mai (Nr. 1271, Jg. 5). S. 2–3.

Condolences on the death of Dr. Eduard Reiss on behalf of the Academic Senate and the entire University signed by the Rector Ehrlich – p. 2.

IN 1968 90A45

683. **Lokal**- und Provinznachrichten. Czernowitz, 22. Dezember. Czernowitzer Herrenfecht-Societee. *Ibidem.* 1910. 23. Dez. (Nr. 2353, Jg. 8). S. 3.

Election of the 19th of December 1910 of University Professor Dr. Ehrlich the Head of the Czernowitz Society of Fencing.

IN 1975 90A45

684. **Lokal**- und Provinznachrichten. Czernowitz, 31. Jänner. Czernowitzer Herrenfecht-Societe. *Ibidem.* 1911. 1. Febr. (Nr. 2385, Jg. 9). S. 4.

The activities of Professor Dr. Ehrlich as the Head of the Czernowitz Society of Fencing.

IN 1976 90A45

685. **Lokal**- und Provinznachrichten. Czernowitz, 12. Dezember. Czernowitzer Herrenfecht-Societee. *Ibidem.* 1911. 13. Dez. (Nr. 2640, Jg. 9). S. 3.

About Professor Dr. Ehrlich and the Czernowitz Society of Fencing.

IN 1977 90A45

686. **Lokal**- und Provinznachrichten. Czernowitz, 23. März. Czernowitzer Herrenfecht-Société. *Ibidem.* 1912. 24. März (Nr. 2722, Jg. 10). S. 5.

About the Czernowitz Society of Fencing. Professor Dr. Ehrlich – the Head of the Society.

IN 1978 90A45

687. **Lokal**- und Provinznachrichten. Czernowitz, 24. Februar. Czernowitzer Herrenfechtsocietee. *Ibidem.* 1913. 25. Febr. (Nr. 2999, Jg. 11). S. 4.

About the Czernowitz Society of Fencing. Professor Dr. Ehrlich – the Head of the Society.

IN 1980 90A45

688. **Lokal**- und Provinznachrichten. Czernowitz, 27. Februar. Czernowitzer Herrenfechtsocietee. *Ibidem.* 1914. 3. März (Nr. 3387, Jg. 12). S. 3.

About the Czernowitz Society of Fencing. Professor Dr. Ehrlich – the Head of the Society.

IN 1984 90A45

689. **Lokal**- und Provinznachrichten. Czernowitz, 12. Oktober. Dejeuner beim Landespräsidenten. *Ibidem.* 1906. 14. Okt. (Nr. 1107, Jg. 4). S. 4.

Participation of the Rector Dr. Ehrlich in the Sunday lunch event on the 12th of October 1906 organized by the Bukovina Regional President Dr. von Bleyleben.

IN 1967 90A45

690. **Lokal**- und Provinznachrichten. Czernowitz, 7. Oktober. Diner beim Herrn Landespräsidenten. *Ibidem.* 1907. 8. Okt. (Nr. 1398, Jg. 5). S. 3.

Participation of the Rector Professor Dr. Ehrlich in the Sunday lunch organized by the Regional President Dr. Octavian von Bleyleben.

IN 1969 90A45

691. **Lokal**- und Provinznachrichten. Czernowitz, 1. Juli. Doppeljubiläum des Universitätsrofessors Dr. Isidor Hilberg. *Ibidem.* 1912. 2. Juli (Nr. 2806, Jg. 10). S. 4.

Participation of University Professor Dr. Ehrlich in the joint celebration of Professor Dr. Isidor Hilberg, namely his 60th birthday and the 30th anniversary of his tenure as a Full Professor of classical philosophy.

IN 1979 90A45

692. **Lokal**- und Provinznachrichten. Czernowitz, 27. Oktober. Ehrung. *Ibidem.* 1909. 28. Okt. (Nr. 2010, Jg. 7). S. 4.

About the event of conferring an honorary membership of the Social Scientific Academic Society to University Professor Dr. Eugen Ehrich in recognition of the merits for the Society, on the 24th of October 1909.

IN 1973 90A45

693. **Lokal**- und Provinznachrichten. Czernowitz, 28. November. Ehrung Professors Dr. Eugen Ehrlich. *Ibidem.* 1910. 29. Nov. (Nr. 2333, Jg. 8). S. 4.

About an honorary membership of the Social Scientific Academic Society awarded to Professor Dr. Eugen Ehrich in recognition of the merits for the Society.

IN 1975 90A45

694. **Lokal**- und Provinznachrichten. Czernowitz, 2. September. 31. Deutscher Juristentag. *Ibidem.* 1912. 3. Sept. (Nr. 2853, Jg. 10). S. 4.

Departure of University Professor Dr. Eugen Ehrlich to participate in the 31st meeting of German lawyers.

IN 1979 90A45

695. **Lokal**- und Provinznachrichten. Czernowitz, 24. Dezember. Errichtung einer medizinischen Fakultät in Czernowitz : eine Rundfrage. *Ibidem.* 1907. 25. Dez. (Nr. 1464, Jg. 5). S. 10–11.

Discussion about the establishment of a medical faculty in Czernowitz; remarks of Professor Dr. Ehrlich – p. 11.

IN 1969 90A45

696. **Lokal**- und Provinznachrichten. Czernowitz, 6. November. Erzherzogs Otto. *Ibidem.* 1906. 7. Nov. (Nr. 1126, Jg. 4). S. 3–4.

Participation of the Rector Professor Dr. Ehrlich, together with the deans, in the memorial service dedicated to the late Archduke Otto – p. 4.

IN 1967 90A45

697. **Lokal**- und Provinznachrichten. Czernowitz, 22. Juni. Exkursion des sozialw. akad. Vereines. *Ibidem.* 1911. 23. Juni (Nr. 2499, Jg. 9). S. 3.

About the excursion for the members of the Social Scientific Academic Society led by the honorary member of the Society Professor of Roman law Dr. Eugen Ehrlich that took place on the 18th of June 1911.

IN 1976 90A45

698. **Lokal**- und Provinznachrichten. Czernowitz, 20. Jänner. Das Fest der Herren-Fecht-Societee. Zu Gunsten der Landeszentrale für Kinderschutz- und Jugendfürsorge. *Ibidem.* 1914. 21. Jänner (Nr. 3352, Jg. 12). S. 2–3.

About the charity sporting event of the Czernowitz Society of Fencing (Professor Dr. Eugen Ehrlich – Head of the Society) in favour of the State Agency for Child Protection and Supervision of Youth.

IN 1984 90A45

699. **Lokal**- und Provinznachrichten. Czernowitz, 28. Jänner 1907. Festkommers der "Hebronia". *Ibidem.* 1907. 29. Jänner (Nr. 1193, Jg. 5). S. 4.

On the celebration of the Society "Hebronia". The Rector of Czernowitz University Professor Dr. Ehrlich – an honorary guest of the event.

IN 1968 90A45

700. **Lokal**- und Provinznachrichten. Czernowitz, 16. Dezember. Fremde Orden. *Ibidem.* 1907. 17. Dez. (Nr. 1457, Jg. 5). S. 2.

University Professor Dr. Eugen Ehrlich from Czernowitz awarded the Commander's Cross of the Greek Order of the Saviour.

IN 1969 90A45

701. **Lokal**- und Provinznachrichten. Czernowitz, 21. Jänner. Fünf Uhr-Tee an Bord. *Ibidem.* 1914. 22. Jänner (Nr. 3353, Jg. 12). S. 4.

Participation of Professor Dr. Ehrlich in the tea ceremony.

IN 1984 90A45

702. **Lokal**- und Provinznachrichten. Czernowitz, 25. Februar. 25jähriges Doktorjubiläum. *Ibidem.* 1906. 27. Febr. (Nr. 919, Jg. 4). S. 4.

Participation of University Professor Dr. Ehrlich in the solemn commemoration of the 25th anniversary of awarding the degree of doctor to Prof. Emilian Wojucki – the first Doctor of Orthodox Theology.

IN 1966 90A45

703. **Lokal**- und Provinznachrichten. Czernowitz, 3. Mai. Die Gedächtnisfeier für Professor Ferdinand Löwl. *Ibidem.* 1909. 4. Mai (Nr. 1864, Jg. 7). S. 4.

Information about the commemorative events dedicated to the University Professor Ferdinand Löwl von Lenkenthal, with the participation of the Dean of the Faculty of Law Professor Dr. Eugen Ehrlich in the events of the 1st of May 1909.

IN 1972 90A45

704. **Lokal**- und Provinznachrichten. Czernowitz, 28. Mai. Gedenkrede für Professor Dr. Josef Unger. *Ibidem.* 1913. 29. Mai (Nr. 3074, Jg. 11). S. 5.

Information about the commemorative speech for Professor Dr. Joseph Unger by University Professor Dr. Ehrlich to be delivered in the House of Civil Justice on the 30th of May.

IN 1981 90A45

705. **Lokal**- und Provinznachrichten. Czernowitz, 16. Jänner. Generalversammlung der "Czernowitzer Herrenfecht-Societee". *Ibidem.* 1912. 17. Jänner (Nr. 2665, Jg. 10). S. 4.

University Professor Dr. Ehrlich – the Head of the Society of Fencing.

IN 1978 90A45

706. **Lokal**- und Provinznachrichten. Czernowitz, 29. Mai. Die Generalversammlung der "Gesellschaft der Kunstfreunde". *Ibidem.* 1913. 30. Mai (Nr. 3075, Jg. 11). S. 3–4.

Participation of the University Professor Dr. Ehrlich in the General Assembly of the "Society of the Friends of Art" – p. 4.

IN 1981 90A45

707. **Lokal**- und Provinznachrichten. Czernowitz, 1. April. Hofrat Kleinwächter-Jubiläum. *Ibidem.* 1912. 2. Apr. (Nr. 2728, Jg. 10). S. 3–4.

Participation of the Dean of the Faculty of Law and Public Administration of Franz Joseph University Professor Dr. Ehrlich in the celebration of the 50th anniversary of the promotion of the director of "Bukowinaer Sparkasse" Dr. Friedrich von Kleinwächter to the position of doctor of law at Prague University.

IN 1978 90A45

708. **Lokal**- und Provinznachrichten. Czernowitz, 13. Dezember. Immatrikulation. *Ibidem.* 1906. 14. Dez. (Nr. 1157, Jg. 4). S. 3.

Participation of the Rector of Czernowitz University Professor Dr. Eugen Ehrlich, together with the deans, in the Matriculation ceremony of the new students of the University.

IN 1967 90A45

709. **Lokal**- und Provinznachrichten. Czernowitz, 13. Juli. Eine interessante Promotion. *Ibidem.* 1909. 14. Juli (Nr. 1921, Jg. 7). S. 4.

Participation of the Dean Professor Dr. Ehrlich in the defense procedure of Ludwig Kleinwächter applying for the degree of doctor of law.

IN 1973 90A45

710. **Lokal**- und Provinznachrichten. Czernowitz, 3. März. Eine jüdische Studentenversammlung. *Ibidem.* 1907. 5. März (Nr. 1222, Jg. 5). S. 3–4.

Participation of the collegium of professors led by the Rector of Czernowitz University Ehrlich in the general assembly of Jewish students.

IN 1968 90A45

711. **Lokal**- und Provinznachrichten. Czernowitz, 4. März. Jüdische Studentenversammlung an der Universität. *Ibidem.* 1912. 5. März (Nr. 2705, Jg. 10). S. 3–4.

Participation of the Dean of the Faculty of Law Professor Dr. Ehrlich in the meeting of Jewish students of Czernowitz University – p. 4.

IN 1978 90A45

712. **Lokal**- und Provinznachrichten. Czernowitz, 8. Februar. Der "Junimea"-Ball. *Ibidem.* 1907. 9. Febr. (Nr. 1202, Jg. 5). S. 3–4.

Participation of the Rector Professor Dr. Ehrlich in the ball of the Academic Society "Junimea".

IN 1968 90A45

713. **Lokal**- und Provinznachrichten. Czernowitz, 9. Februar. Juristisch-staatswissenschaftliche Gesellschaft. *Ibidem.* 1903. 10. Febr. (Nr. 11, Jg. 1). S. 2.

Information about the lecture on "Freie Rechtsfindung und freie Rechtswissenschaft" ["Free Finding of the Law and Free Science of Law"] to be delivered by Professor Dr. Ehrlich in the Town Hall on the 11th of February 1903.

IN 1960 90A45

714. **Lokal**- und Provinznachrichten. Czernowitz, 21. Jänner. Juristisch-staatswissenschaftliche Gesellschaft. *Ibidem.* 1904. 22. Jänner (Nr. 294, Jg. 2). S. 3.

Information about the meeting of the members of Juridical-Political Scientific Society on the 20th of January 1904 and notification of the lecture by Professor Dr. Ehrlich to be delivered on the 24th of February 1904.

IN 1962 90A45

715. **Lokal**- und Provinznachrichten. Czernowitz, 23. Februar. Juristisch-staatswissenschaftliche Gesellschaft. *Ibidem.* 1904. 24. Febr. (Nr. 321, Jg. 2). S. 3.

Information about the lecture by Professor Dr. Eugen Ehrlich entitled "Zittelmann, internationales Privatrecht" ["Zittelmann, International Law"], to be held in the Town Hall on the 24th of February 1904.

IN 1962 90A45

716. **Lokal**- und Provinznachrichten. Czernowitz, 4. Februar. Die Juristisch-staatswissenschaftliche Gesellschaft. *Ibidem.* 1905. 5. Febr. (Nr. 605, Jg. 3). S. 5.

Notice that Professor Dr. Eugen Ehrlich will read a lecture on "Sociologie und Rechtswissenschaft" ("Sociology and Science of Law") in the Town Hall on the 15th of February 1905.

IN 1964 90A45

717. **Lokal**- und Provinznachrichten. Czernowitz, 13. Februar. Juristisch-staatswissenschaftliche Gesellschaft. *Ibidem.* 1905. 14. Febr. (Nr. 612, Jg. 3). S. 3.

Notice that University Professor Dr. Eugen Ehrlich will read a lecture on "Sociologie und Jurisprudenz" ("Sociology and Jurisprudence") in the Town Hall on the 15th of February 1905.

IN 1964 90A45

718. **Lokal**- und Provinznachrichten. Czernowitz, 27. Jänner. Juristisch-staatswissenschaftliche Gesellschaft. *Ibidem.* 1906. 28. Jänner (Nr. 895, Jg. 4). S. 5.

Information of the Juridical-Political Scientific Society about the lecture by the University Professor Dr. Eugen Ehrlich on the reform of contract law that will be delivered on the 31st of January 1906.

IN 1966 90A45

719. **Lokal**- und Provinznachrichten. Czernowitz, 3. März. Juristisch-staatswissenschaftliche Gesellschaft. *Ibidem.* 1907. 5. März (Nr. 1222, Jg. 5). S. 5.

Information about the report of Professor Dr. Eugen Ehrlich on "Zur Lehre von den juristischen Personen" ("The Doctrine of Legal Persons") to be provided in the hall of the Privincial Court (Civil Law Chamber) on the 8th of March 1907.

IN 1968 90A45

720. **Lokal-** und Provinznachrichten. Czernowitz, 17. November. Juristisch-staatswissenschaftliche Gesellschaft. I*bidem.* 1908. 18. Nov. (Nr. 1731, Jg. 6). S. 3.

Information about the report of University Professor Dr. Eugen Ehrlich on "Englische Zivilrechtspflege" ("The English Civil Law Administration") to be provided in the Civil Law Chamber on the 21st of November 1908.

IN 1971 90A45

721. **Lokal-** und Provinznachrichten. Czernowitz, 1. Dezember. Juristisch-staatswissenschaftliche Gesellschaft. *Ibidem.* 1910. 2. Dez. (Nr. 2336, Jg. 8). S. 3.

Information of the Juridical-Political Scientific Society about a lecture on law by Prof. Ehrlich.

IN 1975 90A45

722. **Lokal-** und Provinznachrichten. Czernowitz, 5. Oktober. Kaiser Franz Joseph-Knabeninternat. *Ibidem.* 1906. 6. Okt. (Nr. 1100, Jg. 4). S. 4.

Participation of the Rector Professor Dr. Ehrlich in the inauguration of the Romanian Boarding School for boys which was established with the help of charity activities of the Society of Romanian Culture and Literature.

IN 1967 90A45

723. **Lokal-** und Provinznachrichten. Czernowitz, 10. Oktober. K. k. Franz Josephs-Universitätin Czernowitz. *Ibidem.* 1906. 11. Okt. (Nr. 1104, Jg. 4). S. 4.

Information about the 2nd of December, the day of the anniversary of the government of the Emperor Franz Joseph I, when the solemn inauguration of the Rector for the academic year 1906/1907 will be held at 11 am with the Rector Professor Dr. Eugen Ehrlich's inaugural address on the subject of "Die Tatsachendes Gewohnheitsrechts" ("Facts of Customary Law").

IN 1967 90A45

724. **Lokal-** und Provinznachrichten. Czernowitz, 13. Februar. Karnevalfest "Die Welt auf Reisen". *Ibidem.* 1908. 14. Febr. (Nr. 1504, Jg. 6). S. 4.

About financial contributions to Karnevalfest "Die Welt auf Reisen" ("World Travel"), including the contribution of 20 crowns by Professor Dr. Ehrlich.

IN 1970 90A45

725. **Lokal-** und Provinznachrichten. Czernowitz, 16. Juni. Kinderschutzund Jugendfürsorge. *Ibidem.* 1911. 17. Juni (Nr. 2494, Jg. 9). S. 4.

Information about the meeting of the Regional Centre for the Child Protection and Child Care with the participation of University Professor Dr. Eugen Ehrlich.

IN 1976 90A45

726. **Lokal**- und Provinznachrichten. Czernowitz, 20. November. Die Klerikalisierung der Universität. *Ibidem.* 1907. 21. Nov. (Nr. 1435, Jg. 5). S. 4.

About the clericalization of Czernowitz University, including the information about the attitude of Professor Dr. Ehrlich to the clericalization.

IN 1969 90A45

727. **Lokal**- und Provinznachrichten. Czernowitz, 6. Februar. Der Krieg im Wandel der Jahrtausende. *Ibidem.* 1914. 7. Febr. (Nr. 3367, Jg. 12). S. 3.

Participation of Professor Dr. Ehrlich in the lecture by the Rector of Czernowitz University Professor Dr. von Frisch announced at the meeting of the Social Scientific Society.

IN 1984 90A45

728. **Lokal**- und Provinznachrichten. Czernowitz, 22. Juni 1904. Landespräsident Prinz Hohenlohe in Wiznitz. *Ibidem.* 1904. 23. Juni (Nr. 419, Jg. 2). S. 3.

About the visit of Vizhnitsa by the Bukovina Regional President Prince Hohenlohe accompanied by Prof. Ehrlich.

IN 1962 90A45

729. **Lokal**- und Provinznachrichten. Czernowitz, 4. November. "Das lebende Recht". *Ibidem.* 1909. 5. Nov. (Nr. 2016, Jg. 7). S. 4.

About the second session of the seminar on "Living Law" by Professors Dr. Ehrlich and Dr. Kogler.

IN 1973 90A45

730. **Lokal**- und Provinznachrichten. Czernowitz, 9. November. "Das lebende Recht". *Ibidem.* 1909. 10. Nov. (Nr. 2020, Jg. 7). S. 3.

About the excursion of the participants of the seminar on "Living Law" organized by Professor Dr. Ehrlich.

IN 1973 90A45

731. **Lokal**- und Provinznachrichten. Czernowitz, 21. Februar. "Lebendes Recht". *Ibidem.* 1910. 22. Febr. (Nr. 2104, Jg. 8). S. 4.

Information about the lecture by University Professor Dr. Eugen Ehrlich on "Lebendes Recht" ("Living Law"), which is organized by the Social-Scientific Academic Society on the 23rd of February 1910 in the hall of "kaufmännischen Vereines" on Petersplatz 2.

IN 1974 90A45

732. **Lokal**- und Provinznachrichten. Czernowitz, 1. März. "Lebendes Recht". *Ibidem.* 1910. 2. März (Nr. 2111, Jg. 8). S. 3–4. – Die Unterschrift : Ph. Z.

Information about the lecture by University Professor Dr. Eugen Ehrlich on "Lebendes Recht" ("Living Law"), which was organized by the Social-Scientific Academic Society on the 23rd of February 1910. The summary of the lecture is provided as well.

IN 1974 90A45

733. **Lokal**- und Provinznachrichten. Czernowitz, 13. Juli. Das Leichenbegängnis des kais. Rates... *Ibidem.* 1912. 14. Juli (Nr. 2811, Jg. 10). S. 4.

Participation of Prof. Ehrlich in the funeral of the Emperor's Advisor and town architect Solomon Salter.

IN 1979 90A45

734. **Lokal**- und Provinznachrichten. Czernowitz, 28. November. "Marxismus und Sozialismus". *Ibidem.* 1910. 29. Nov. (Nr. 2333, Jg. 8). S. 4.

Information of the Social-Scientific Academic Society about the lecture by University Professor Dr. Eugen Ehrlich on the topic of "Marxismus und Sozialismus" ("Marxism and Socialism") on the 4th of December 1910.

IN 1975 90A45

735. **Lokal**- und Provinznachrichten. Czernowitz, 14. März. Mikulicz-Denkmal in Czernowitz. *Ibidem.* 1907. 15. März (Nr. 1231, Jg. 5). S. 4.

On the inaugural meeting of the Committee for the installation of the monument for Professor Johann von Mikulicz-Radecki in his birthplace of Czernowitz (based on the initiative of the Rector of the local University Professor Dr. Eugen Ehrlich who was elected a Chairman of the Committee).

IN 1968 90A45

736. **Lokal**- und Provinznachrichten. Czernowitz, 18. Jänner 1907. Die Mittelschulenquete. *Ibidem.* 1907. 19. Jänner (Nr. 1185, Jg. 5). S. 3–4.

On the speech of the Rector of Czernowitz University Professor Dr. Ehrlich on the reform of secondary schools.

IN 1968 90A45

737. **Lokal**- und Provinznachrichten. Czernowitz, 28. November. Nachruf. *Ibidem.* 1907. 29. Nov. (Nr. 1442, Jg. 5). S. 3.

On the obituary presented by the Vice-Rector of Czernowitz University Professor Dr. Ehrlich for Professor Dr. Basil Gaina. The text of the obituary is also provided.

IN 1969 90A45

738. **Lokal**- und Provinznachrichten. Czernowitz,5. Oktober. Namensfest des Kaisers. *Ibidem.* 1906. 6. Okt. (Nr. 1100, Jg. 4). S. 4.

Participation of the University Rector Professor Dr. Ehrlich, together with academic officials of Czernowitz University, in the worship of His Majesty the Emperor for students of primary and secondary schools in all churches.

IN 1967 90A45

739. **Lokal**- und Provinznachrichten. Czernowitz, 6. Dezember. "Nationalität und Rasse". *Ibidem.* 1913. 7. Dez. (Nr. 3234, Jg. 11). S. 5.

About the lecture on "Nationalität und Rasse" ["Nationalism and Race"] by University Professor Dr. Eugen Ehrlich that took place on the 28th of November 1913 and the 5th of December 1913 (repeated) at the Social-Scientific Academic Society.

IN 1983 90A45

740. **Lokal**- und Provinznachrichten. Czernowitz, 5. November. Ovation für den Rektor unserer Universität. *Ibidem.* 1906. 6. Nov. (Nr. 1125, Jg. 4). S. 4.

Dispute of the Academic Senate led by the Rector Dr. Ehrlich of the issue of recognition of Jews at Czernowitz University.

IN 1967 90A45

741. **Lokal**- und Provinznachrichten. Czernowitz,13. Juli. Personalnachrichten. *Ibidem.* 1907. 16. Juli (Nr. 1327, Jg. 5). S. 3.

Information about a long vacation of the Rector Dr. Eugen Ehrlich as of the 14th of July 1907, and about his trip to Vienna.

IN 1969 90A45

742. **Lokal**- und Provinznachrichten. Czernowitz, 11. Februar. Der Polenball. *Ibidem.* 1907. 12. Febr. (Nr. 1204, Jg. 5). S. 3–4.

Participation of the University Rector Dr. Ehrlich in the ball of the Polish Academic Society.

IN 1968 90A45

743. **Lokal**- und Provinznachrichten. Czernowitz, 12. April. Professor Dr. Ehrlich über die Rechtsgemeinschaft. *Ibidem.* 1916. 12. Apr. (Nr. 3825, Jg. 14). S. 4.

About the work by Professor of Czernowitz University Dr. Eugen Ehrlich published in "Neuen Wiener Tagblatt" dedicated to "Legal Association" ("Rechtsgemeinschaft").

IN 1988 90A45

744. **Lokal**- und Provinznachrichten. Czernowitz, 16. November. Promotio sub auspiciis Imperatoris. *Ibidem*. 1907. 17. Nov. (Nr. 1432, Jg. 5). S. 4.

About the solemn promotion at Czernowitz University. The text of the speech by the Vice-Rector Dr. Ehrlich is also provided.

IN 1969 90A45

745. **Lokal**- und Provinznachrichten. Czernowitz, 11. Juli. Promotion. *Ibidem*. 1904. 12. Juli (Nr. 434, Jg. 2). S. 4.

Professor Dr. Ehrlich – promoter of the Czernowitz University graduation ceremony of a new doctor of law Landesregierungs-Konzeptspraktikant Anton Josefowicz on the 9th of July 1904.

IN 1963 90A45

746. **Lokal**- und Provinznachrichten. Czernowitz, 16. Dezember. Promotion. *Ibidem*. 1904. 17. Dez. (Nr. 565, Jg. 2). S. 4.

Professor Dr. Ehrlich – promoter of the Czernowitz University graduation ceremony of a new doctor of law Leo Löwner.

IN 1963 90A45

747. **Lokal**- und Provinznachrichten. Czernowitz, 17. Februar. Promotion. *Ibidem*. 1905. 18. Febr. (Nr. 616, Jg. 3). S. 3.

Professor Dr. Ehrlich – promoter of the Czernowitz University graduation ceremony of a new doctor of law Max Singer.

IN 1964 90A45

748. **Lokal**- und Provinznachrichten. Czernowitz, 30. Juni. Promotion. *Ibidem*. 1905. 1. Juli (Nr. 723, Jg. 3). S. 3.

Professor Dr. Ehrlich – promoter of the Czernowitz University graduation ceremony of a new doctor of law Mordche Deligdish.

IN 1965 90A45

749. **Lokal**- und Provinznachrichten. Czernowitz,4. November. Promotion. *Ibidem*. 1905. 5. Nov. (Nr. 828, Jg. 3). S. 7.

Professor Dr. Ehrlich – promoter of the Czernowitz University graduation ceremony of a new doctor of law Julius Brüll.

IN 1965 90A45

750. **Lokal**- und Provinznachrichten. Czernowitz, 14. Dezember. Promotion. *Ibidem*. 1907. 15. Dez. (Nr. 1456, Jg. 5). S. 5.

Professor Dr. Ehrlich – promoter of the Czernowitz University graduation ceremony of a new doctor of law Moses Bardach.

IN 1969 90A45

751. **Lokal**- und Provinznachrichten. Czernowitz, 3. Februar. Promotion. *Ibidem.* 1908. 4. Febr. (Nr. 1495, Jg. 6). S. 4.

Professor Dr. Ehrlich – promoter of the Czernowitz University graduation ceremony of a new doctor of law Ruben Geringer.

IN 1970 90A45

752. **Lokal**- und Provinznachrichten. Czernowitz, 16. März. Promotion. *Ibidem.* 1908. 17. März (Nr. 1531, Jg. 6). S. 3.

Professor Dr. Ehrlich – promoter of the Czernowitz University graduation ceremony of a new doctor of law Meier Kinsbrunner.

IN 1970 90A45

753. **Lokal**- und Provinznachrichten. Czernowitz, 17. März. Promotion. *Ibidem.* 1908. 18. März (Nr. 1532, Jg. 6). S. 4.

Professor Dr. Ehrlich – promoter of the Czernowitz University graduation ceremony of new doctors of law Meier Kinsbrunner, M. Fischer and Norbert Sekler.

IN 1970 90A45

754. **Lokal**- und Provinznachrichten. Czernowitz, 3. April. Promotion. *Ibidem.* 1908. 4. Apr. (Nr. 1546, Jg. 6). S. 3.

Professor Dr. Ehrlich – promoter of the Czernowitz University graduation ceremony of a new doctor of law Lazar Pomeranz.

IN 1970 90A45

755. **Lokal**- und Provinznachrichten. Czernowitz, 23. Oktober. Promotion. *Ibidem.* 1909. 24. Okt. (Nr. 2007, Jg. 7). S. 5.

Professor Dr. Ehrlich – promoter of the Czernowitz University graduation ceremony of a new doctor of law Johann Max Tarden.

IN 1973 90A45

756. **Lokal**- und Provinznachrichten. Czernowitz, 27. November. Promotion. *Ibidem.* 1909. 28. Nov. (Nr. 2036, Jg. 7). S. 4.

Professor Dr. Ehrlich – promoter of the Czernowitz University graduation ceremony of a new doctor of law Samuel Rubinger.

IN 1973 90A45

757. **Lokal**- und Provinznachrichten. Czernowitz, 9. Dezember. Promotion. *Ibidem.* 1909. 10. Dez. (Nr. 2045, Jg. 7). S. 4.

Professor Dr. Ehrlich – promoter of the Czernowitz University graduation ceremony of a new doctor of law Ruben Lang on the 7th of December 1909.

IN 1973 90A45

758. **Lokal**- und Provinznachrichten. Czernowitz, 7. Februar. Promotion. *Ibidem.* 1910. 8. Febr. (Nr. 2092, Jg. 8). S. 4.

Professor Dr. Ehrlich – promoter of the Czernowitz University graduation ceremony of a new doctor of law Simon Knopf on the 5th of February 1910.

IN 1974 90A45

759. **Lokal**- und Provinznachrichten. Czernowitz, 16. Februar. Promotion. *Ibidem.* 1910. 17. Febr. (Nr. 2100, Jg. 8). S. 4.

Professor Dr. Ehrlich – promoter of the Czernowitz University graduation ceremony of a new doctor of law Abraham Ber Tamler.

IN 1974 90A45

760. **Lokal**- und Provinznachrichten. Czernowitz, 16. April. Promotion. *Ibidem.* 1910. 17. Apr. (Nr. 2148, Jg. 8). S. 5.

Professor Dr. Ehrlich – promoter of the Czernowitz University graduation ceremony of a new doctor of law Leopold Sekler.

IN 1974 90A45

761. **Lokal**- und Provinznachrichten. Czernowitz, 17. Februar. Promotion. *Ibidem.* 1911. 18. Febr. (Nr. 2399, Jg. 9). S. 3.

Professor Dr. Ehrlich – promoter of the Czernowitz University graduation ceremony of a new doctor of law David Müller on the 18th of February 1911.

IN 1976 90A45

762. **Lokal**- und Provinznachrichten. Czernowitz, 18. Februar. Promotion. *Ibidem.* 1911. 19. Febr. (Nr. 2400, Jg. 9). S. 5.

Professor Dr. Ehrlich – promoter of the Czernowitz University graduation ceremony of a new doctor of law Leib Saul Kula.

IN 1976 90A45

763. **Lokal**- und Provinznachrichten. Czernowitz, 23. Februar. Promotion. *Ibidem.* 1911. 24. Febr. (Nr. 2404, Jg. 9). S. 3.

Professor Dr. Ehrlich – promoter of the Czernowitz University graduation ceremony of a new doctor of law Romuald von Szymonowitz.

IN 1976 90A45

764. **Lokal-** und Provinznachrichten. Czernowitz, 20. Mai. Promotion. *Ibidem.* 1913. 21. Mai (Nr. 3068, Jg. 11). S. 4.

Professor Dr. Ehrlich – promoter of the Czernowitz University graduation ceremony of a new doctor of law Josef Abrahamowicz.

IN 1981 90A45

765. **Lokal-** und Provinznachrichten. Czernowitz, 19. Juni. Promotion. *Ibidem.* 1913. 20. Juni (Nr. 3092, Jg. 11). S. 3.

Professor Dr. Ehrlich – promoter of the Czernowitz University graduation ceremony of a new doctor of law Josef Sommer on the 21st of June 1913.

IN 1981 90A45

766. **Lokal-** und Provinznachrichten. Czernowitz, 17. Oktober. Promotionen. *Ibidem.* 1903. 18. Okt. (Nr. 217, Jg. 1). S. 4.

Professor Dr. Ehrlich – promoter of the Czernowitz University graduation ceremony of a new doctor of law Edgar Bucksch.

IN 1961 90A45

767. **Lokal-** und Provinznachrichten. Czernowitz, 18. Mai. Promotionen. *Ibidem.* 1907. 19. Mai (Nr. 1282, Jg. 5). S. 6.

Professor Dr. Ehrlich – promoter of the Czernowitz University graduation ceremony of a new doctor of law Heinrich Amster.

IN 1968 90A45

768. **Lokal-** und Provinznachrichten. Czernowitz, 1. Dezember. Promotionen. *Ibidem.* 1909. 2. Dez. (Nr. 2039, Jg. 7). S. 3.

Dr. Ehrlich – promoter of the Czernowitz University graduation ceremony of a new doctor of law Otto Ernst.

IN 1973 90A45

769. **Lokal-** und Provinznachrichten. Czernowitz, 18. Dezember. Promotionen. *Ibidem.* 1909. 19. Dez. (Nr. 2053, Jg. 7). S. 5.

Professor Dr. Ehrlich – promoter of the Czernowitz University graduation ceremony of a new doctor of law Arthur Füllenbaum.

IN 1973 90A45

770. **Lokal-** und Provinznachrichten. Czernowitz, 11. März. Promotionen. *Ibidem.* 1910. 12. März (Nr. 2120, Jg. 8). S. 4.

Professor Dr. Ehrlich – promoter of the Czernowitz University graduation ceremony of new doctors of law Ezechiel Rappaport and Appolonarius Argasinski.

IN 1974 90A45

771. **Lokal**- und Provinznachrichten. Czernowitz, 1. Juli. Promotionen. *Ibidem*. 1910. 2. Juli (Nr. 2209, Jg. 8). S. 3.

Professor Dr. Ehrlich – promoter of the Czernowitz University graduation ceremony of a new doctor of law Julius Hruder.

IN 1975 90A45

772. **Lokal**- und Provinznachrichten. Czernowitz, 2. Juli. Promotionen. *Ibidem*. 1910. 3. Juli (Nr. 2210, Jg. 8). S. 4.

Professor Dr. Ehrlich – promoter of the Czernowitz University graduation ceremony of new doctors of law Richard Poras and Moses Krässel.

IN 1975 90A45

773. **Lokal**- und Provinznachrichten. Czernowitz, 2. November. Promotionen. *Ibidem*. 1910. 3. Nov. (Nr. 2311, Jg. 8). S. 4.

Professor Dr. Ehrlich – promoter of the Czernowitz University graduation ceremony of new doctors of law Erich Ebermann and Hermann Altmann on the 5th of November 1910.

IN 1975 90A45

774. **Lokal**- und Provinznachrichten. Czernowitz, 6. April. Promotionen. *Ibidem*. 1911. 7. Apr. (Nr. 2439, Jg. 9). S. 4.

Professor Dr. Ehrlich – promoter of the Czernowitz University graduation ceremony of new doctors of law Theodor Czechowski, Konstantin Lewandowski, Mendel Sekler and Emilian Berthold Winkler.

IN 1976 90A45

775. **Lokal**- und Provinznachrichten. Czernowitz, 12. Februar. Protestversammlung. *Ibidem*. 1909. 13. Febr. (Nr. 1800, Jg. 7). S. 3.

Participation of University Professor Ehrlich together with the Rector Dr. Zelinka in the discussion of consequences of the student protests.

IN 1972 90A45

776. **Lokal**- und Provinznachrichten. Czernowitz, 30. Oktober. Prüfungskommissionen an unserer Universität. *Ibidem*. 1911. 31. Okt. (Nr. 2605, Jg. 9). S. 3.

On the appointment of University Professor Dr. Eugen Ehrlich a member of the State Judicial Examination Board and the examiner of the Austrian private law, commercial law, and exchange law in Czernowitz for the period of the academic years 1911/1912 to 1913/1914 by the Minister of Cultus and Education. It also includes information about the appointment by the Minister of Professor Dr. Eugen Ehrlich a member of the State Historic-Legal Examination Board with the powers of the examiner of German law.

IN 1977 90A45

777. **Lokal**- und Provinznachrichten. Czernowitz, 7. Dezember. Das Regierungsjubiläum des Kaisers. *Ibidem.* 1908. 8. Dez. (Nr. 1748, Jg. 6). S. 3–4.

About the celebration of the anniversary of the Emperor. Participation of Professor Dr. Ehrlich, among other dignitaries, in the celebration events dedicated to the Emperor by the societies of "Alemannia", "Austria", and "Gothia" – p. 3.

IN 1971 90A45

778. **Lokal**- und Provinznachrichten. Czernowitz, 3. Dezember. Rektorsinauguration. *Ibidem.* 1906. 4. Dez. (Nr. 1149, Jg. 4). S. 3.

Information about the inauguration ceremony of the Rector Professor Dr. Eugen Ehrlich for the academic year 1906/1907 held on the 2nd of December 1906 with the Rector's inaugural address on the subject of "Ueber die Tatsachen des Gewohnheitsrechts" ("Facts of Customary Law").

IN 1967 90A45

779. **Lokal**- und Provinznachrichten. Czernowitz, 9. Dezember. Rektorsinauguration. *Ibidem.* 1907. 10. Dez. (Nr. 1451, Jg. 5). S. 3.

Information about the report on the previous academic year by the Vice-Rector of Czernowitz University Professor Dr. Eugen Ehrlich on the occasion of the inauguration of the Rector Dr. Eugen Kozak for the academic year 1907/1908.

IN 1969 90A45

780. **Lokal**- und Provinznachrichten. Czernowitz, 10. Dezember. Rektorsinauguration. *Ibidem.* 1907. 11. Dez. (Nr. 1452, Jg. 5). S. 3–4.

About the inauguration ceremony of the Rector Dr. Eugen Kozak for the academic year 1907/1908 including the information about the report on the previous academic year by the Vice-Rector of Czernowitz University Dr. Eugen Ehrlich. The text of the report by Dr. Ehrlich is provided as well.

IN 1969 90A45

781. **Lokal**- und Provinznachrichten. Czernowitz, 23. Juni. Retorswahl an der Czernowitzer Universität. *Ibidem.* 1906. 24. Juni (Nr. 1015, Jg. 4). S. 4–5.

Information about the election of the 23rd of June 1906 by the Academic Senate of Czernowitz University in which Professor of the Faculty of Law and Public Administra-

tion Dr. Eugen Ehrlich was unanimously elected the Rector of Czernowitz University for the academic year 1906/1907. The CV of the new Rector is also provided.

IN 1966 90A45

782. **Lokal**- und Provinznachrichten. Czernowitz, 27. Juni. Der 60. Geburstag Prof. Hilbergs. *Ibidem.* 1912. 28. Juni (Nr. 2798, Jg. 10). S. 3.

Participation of University Professor Dr. Ehrlich in the celebration of the 60th birthday of Professor Dr. Isidor Hilberg.

IN 1978 90A45

783. **Lokal**- und Provinznachrichten. Czernowitz, 11. Juni. Seminar für lebendes Recht. *Ibidem.* 1910. 12. Juni (Nr. 2193, Jg. 8). S. 5.

About the research trip of the participants of the seminar on "Living Law" under the supervision of University Professor Dr. Eugen Ehrlich together with the lawyer Dr. Dutczak to Lenkivtsi on the 12th of June 1910.

IN 1974 90A45

784. **Lokal**- und Provinznachrichten. Czernowitz, 19. Mai. Seminar für lebendes Recht. *Ibidem.* 1911. 20. Mai (Nr. 2474, Jg. 9). S. 3.

Announcement for the participants of the seminar on "Living Law" by Professor Dr. Ehrlich to be held on the 21st of May 1911.

IN 1976 90A45

785. **Lokal**- und Provinznachrichten. Czernowitz, 12. November. Seminar für lebendes Recht des Herrn Universitätsprofessors Dr. Eugen Ehrlich und sozialwissenschaftlicher akademischer Verein. *Ibidem.* 1913. 13. Nov. (Nr. 3213, Jg. 11). S. 4.

Announcement for the participants of the seminar on "Living Law" by Professor Dr. Ehrlich to be held on the 14th of May 1911.

IN 1983 90A45

786. **Lokal**- und Provinznachrichten. Czernowitz, 23. November. "Soziale Heimat der Heilsarmee". *Ibidem.* 1910. 24. Nov. (Nr. 2329, Jg. 8). S. 4.

About the meeting of Social-Scientific Academic Society in which Professor Dr. Ehrlich presented the brochure by Professor Schumpeter entitled "Wie studiert man Sozialwissenschaft" ["How to study Social Science"]; the future presentation of the works by Ehrlich was announced.

IN 1975 90A45

787. **Lokal**- und Provinznachrichten. Czernowitz, 1. Dezember. "Sozialismus und Marxismus ". *Ibidem.* 1910. 2. Dez. (Nr. 2336, Jg. 8). S. 3.

Information of the Social-Scientific Academic Society about the lecture by University Professor Dr. Ehrlich on the topic of "Sozialismus und Marxismus" ("Socialism and Marxism") on the 3rd of December 1910.

IN 1975 90A45

788. **Lokal**- und Provinznachrichten. Czernowitz, 5. Dezember. Sozialpolitik in der Bukowina. *Ibidem.* 1908. 6. Dez. (Nr. 1747, Jg. 6). S. 5.

Information of the Social-Scientific Academic Society about the lecture by University Professor Dr. Ehrlich on the topic of "Sozialpolitik in der Bukowina" ["Social Policy in Bukovina"].

IN 1971 90A45

789. **Lokal**- und Provinznachrichten. Czernowitz, 9. Dezember. "Sozialpolitik in der Bukowina". *Ibidem.* 1908. 10. Dez. (Nr. 1749, Jg. 6). S. 4.

Information of the Social-Scientific Academic Society about the discussion of University Professor Dr. Ehrlich on the topic of social policy in Bukovina.

IN 1971 90A45

790. **Lokal**- und Provinznachrichten. Czernowitz, 13. Dezember. Sozialpolitik in der Bukowina. *Ibidem.* 1909. 14. Dez. (Nr. 2048, Jg. 7). S. 3–4.

Information of the Social-Scientific Academic Society about the discussion of University Professor Dr. Ehrlich on the topic of social policy in Bukovina.

IN 1973 90A45

791. **Lokal**- und Provinznachrichten. Czernowitz, 28. Juni. Sozialpolitische Aufgaben in der Bukowina. *Ibidem.* 1909. 29. Juni (Nr. 1909, Jg. 7). S. 4. Die Unterschrift : Dr. M. E.

Information about the initiative of the Social-Scientific Academic Society to publish the lectures of University Professor Dr. Ehrlich which he read last winter on the topic of social policy in Bukovina.

IN 1972 90A45

792. **Lokal**- und Provinznachrichten. Czernowitz, 30. Mai. Sozialwissenschaftlich akademischer Verein. *Ibidem.* 1912. 31. Mai (Nr. 2775, Jg. 10). S. 4.

About the excursion for the seminar members and the members of the Social Scientific Academic Society led by University Professors Ehrlich, Last and Dungern.

IN 1978 90A45

793. **Lokal**- und Provinznachrichten. Czernowitz, 28. Oktober. Sozialwissenschaftlicher akademische Verein... *Ibidem.* 1909. 29. Okt. (Nr. 2011, Jg. 7). S. 4.

About the event of conferring an honorary membership of the Social Scientific Academic Society to University Professor Dr. Eugen Ehrlich in recognition of the merits for the Society, on the 24th of October 1909.

IN 1973 90A45

794. **Lokal**- und Provinznachrichten. Czernowitz, 21. November. Sozialwissenschaftlicher akademischer Verein. *Ibidem.* 1908. 22. Nov. (Nr. 1735, Jg. 6). S. 5.

Information of the Social-Scientific Academic Society about the report of University Professor Dr. Ehrlich on the topic of "Sozialpolitik in der Bukowina" ["Social Policy in Bukovina"].

IN 1971 90A45

795. **Lokal**- und Provinznachrichten. Czernowitz, 28. November. Sozialwissenschaftlicher akad. Verein. *Ibidem.* 1908. 29. Nov. (Nr. 1741, Jg. 6). S. 5.

Information of the Social-Scientific Academic Society about the report of University Professor Dr. Ehrlich on the topic of "Sozialpolitik in der Bukowina" ["Social Policy in Bukovina"].

IN 1971 90A45

796. **Lokal**- und Provinznachrichten. Czernowitz, 3. Dezember. Sozialwissenschaftlicher akademischer Verein. *Ibidem.* 1908. 4. Dez. (Nr. 1745, Jg. 6). S. 4.

Information of the Social-Scientific Academic Society about the report of University Professor Dr. Ehrlich on the topic of "Sozialpolitik in der Bukowina" ["Social Policy in Bukovina"].

IN 1971 90A45

797. **Lokal**- und Provinznachrichten. 7. Dezember. Sozialwissenschaftlicher akad. Verein. *Ibidem.* 1908. 8. Dez. (Nr. 1748, Jg. 6). S. 4.

Information of the Social-Scientific Academic Society about the continuation of the discussion of University Professor Dr. Ehrlich on the topic of social policy in Bukovina.

IN 1971 90A45

798. **Lokal**- und Provinznachrichten. Czernowitz, 22. April. Sozialwissenschaftlicher akadem. Verein. *Ibidem.* 1909. 23. Apr. (Nr. 1856, Jg. 7). S. 4.

Information about the first meeting of "Juden- und Bauernfrage in der Bukowina" ("Issues of Jews and Peasants in Bukovina") under the supervision of University Professor Dr. Ehrlich onthe 25th of April 1909.

IN 1972 90A45

799. **Lokal**- und Provinznachrichten. Czernowitz, 13. Mai. Sozialwissenschaftlicher akademischer Verein. *Ibidem.* 1909. 14. Mai (Nr. 1873, Jg. 7). S. 4.

Information about the lecture by University Professor Dr. E. Ehrlich on the topic of "Das englische und festländische System der Altersfürsorge" in "National House" ["Continental and English Retirement Systems"].

IN 1972 90A45

800. **Lokal**- und Provinznachrichten. Czernowitz, 21. Mai. Sozialwissenschaftlicher akad. Verein. *Ibidem.* 1909. 22. Mai (Nr. 1879, Jg. 7). S. 4.

Information about the first meeting of "Sektion zum Studium der Bauernfrage" ("Section for the Study of Issues of Peasants") under the super vision of University Professor Dr. E. Ehrlich.

IN 1972 90A45

801. **Lokal**- und Provinznachrichten. Czernowitz, 24. Mai. Sozialwissenschaftlicher akademischer Verein. *Ibidem.* 1909. 25. Mai (Nr. 1881, Jg. 7). S. 3.

About the excursion "Landwirtschaftlichen Mittelschule" ["Agricultural middle school"] for the members of the Social Scientific Academic Society led by University Professors Dr. Ehrlich and Dr. Kogler on the 26th of May 1909.

IN 1972 90A45

802. **Lokal**- und Provinznachrichten. Czernowitz, 19. Juni. Sozialwissenschaftlicher akad. Verein. *Ibidem.* 1909. 20. Juni (Nr. 1902, Jg. 7). S. 4.

About the excursion to the brewery for the members of the Social Scientific Academic Society led by University Professors Dr. Ehrlich and Dr. Kogler on the 16th of June 1909.

IN 1972 90A45

803. **Lokal**- und Provinznachrichten. Czernowitz, 3. Jänner. Sozialwissenschaftlicher akademischer Verein. *Ibidem.* 1910. 4. Jänner (Nr. 2064, Jg. 8). S. 3–4.

About the mutual decision of University Professors Dr. Eugen Ehrlich and Dr. Joseph Schumpeter to announce the best three papers a teach meeting of the Social-Scientific Academic Society.

IN 1974 90A45

804. **Lokal**- und Provinznachrichten. Czernowitz, 19. Februar. Sozialwissenschaftlicher akad. Verein. *Ibidem*. 1910. 20. Febr. (Nr. 2103, Jg. 8). S. 4.

Information about the lecture by University Professor Dr. Ehrlich on the topic of "Lebendes Recht" ("Living Law") to be held in the hall of "kaufmännischen Vereines" on Petersplatz 2 on the 23rd of February 1910.

IN 1974 90A45

805. **Lokal**- und Provinznachrichten. Czernowitz, 22. Februar. Sozialwissenschaftlicherakad. Verein. *Ibidem*. 1910. 23. Febr. (Nr. 2105, Jg. 8). S. 4.

Information about the lecture followed by the discussion by University Professor Dr. Ehrlich on the topic of "Lebendes Recht" ("Living Law") to be held in the hall of "kaufmännischen Vereines"on Petersplatz 2 on the 23rd of February 1910.

IN 1974 90A45

806. **Lokal**- und Provinznachrichten. Czernowitz, 3. Dezember. Sozialwissenschaftlicher akad. Verein. *Ibidem*. 1910. 4. Dez. (Nr. 2338, Jg. 8). S. 5.

About the change of the date of the earlier announced lecture by University Professor Dr. Ehrlich on "Marxismus und Sozialismus" ("Marxism and Socialism") to the 6th of December 1910.

IN 1975 90A45

807. **Lokal**- und Provinznachrichten. Czernowitz, 5. Dezember. Sozialwissenschaftlicher akad. Verein. *Ibidem*. 1910. 6. Dez. (Nr. 2339, Jg. 8). S. 3.

Information about the lecture by University Professor Dr. Eugen Ehrlich on "Marxismus und Sozialismus" ("Marxism and Socialism") to be held in the hall of "kaufmännischen Hauses" on the 6th of December 1910.

IN 1975 90A45

808. **Lokal**- und Provinznachrichten. Czernowitz, 7. April. Sozialwissenschaftlicher Akademischer Verein. *Ibidem*. 1914. 8. Apr. (Nr. 3417, Jg. 12). S. 5.

About the 14th general assembly of the Social-Scientific Academic Society on which Professor Dr. Hans von Frisch was elected the third honorary member of the Society, after the first two being Professors Dr. Eugen Ehrlich and Dr. Joseph Schumpeter.

IN 1985 90A45

809. **Lokal**- und Provinznachrichten. Czernowitz, 17. Jänner 1905. "Soziologie und Jurisprudenz". *Ibidem.* 1905. 18. Jänner (Nr. 590, Jg. 3). S. 4.

About the lecture by Professor Dr. Eugen Ehrlich at the Faculty of Philosophy at the University of Vienna on "Soziologie und Jurisprudenz" on the 15th of January 1905.

IN 1964 90A45

810. **Lokal**- und Provinznachrichten. Czernowitz, 23. Dezember. Eine Studentenversammlung. *Ibidem.* 1905. 24. Dez. (Nr. 869, Jg. 3). S. 8.

About the General Assembly of Students at Czernowitz University with the participation of Professor Dr. Ehrlich. The text of the speech by Dr. Ehrlich is provided.

IN 1965 90A45

811. **Lokal**- und Provinznachrichten. Czernowitz, 21. Juni. Eine stürmische Rektorswahl. *Ibidem.* 1913. 22. Juni (Nr. 3094, Jg. 11). S. 3.

Election of the Rector of Czernowitz University for the academic year 1913/1914. Professor Dr. Eugen Ehrlich elected the Rector.

IN 1981 90A45

812. **Lokal**- und Provinznachrichten. Czernowitz, 10. Oktober. Trauerkommers der "Akademischen Lesehalle". *Ibidem.* 1906. 11. Okt. (Nr. 1104, Jg. 4). S. 4.

Information about memorial service held in the "Academic Reading Hall" on the 6th of October 1906, in honour of Honorary Adviser University Professor Dr. Zieglauer von Blumenthal and Honorary Mayor Kochanowski von Stawczan, including the information about the participation and speech of the Rector University Professor Dr. Eugene Ehrlich in the funeral service.

IN 1967 90A45

813. **Lokal**- und Provinznachrichten. Czernowitz, 3. Juni. Trauerkommers für weiland Dr. Eduard Reiss. *Ibidem.* 1907. 4. Juni (Nr. 1292, Jg. 5). S. 3–4.

Participation of the University Rector Dr. Ehrlich in the mourning service for Eduard Reiss, former Mayor and Deputy-Mayor of Czernowitz held on the 1st of June 1907.

IN 1968 90A45

814. **Lokal**- und Provinznachrichten. Czernowitz, 7. November. Trauerkundgebungen anlätzlich des Ablebens des Erzherzogs Otto. *Ibidem.* 1906. 8. Nov. (Nr. 1127, Jg. 4). S. 4.

Participation of the Rector Professor Dr. Ehrlich, together with the deans, in the memorial service dedicated to the late Archduke Otto in the Cathedral Church on the 6th of November 1906.

IN 1967 90A45

815. **Lokal-** und Provinznachrichten. Czernowitz, 21. Februar. Universitätsjubiläum. *Ibidem.* 1914. 22. Febr. (Nr. 3380, Jg. 12). S. 4.

Information about the celebration of the 300th anniversary of the foundation of the University of Groningen in July 1614. Czernowitz University represented by Professor Dr. Eugen Ehrlich.

IN 1984 90A45

816. **Lokal-** und Provinznachrichten. Czernowitz, 21. Juni. Universitätsprofessor a. D. Dr. Wrobel. *Ibidem.* 1909. 22. Juni (Nr. 1903, Jg. 7). S. 3.

About the funeral of University Professor Dr. Johann Wrobel with the participation of the Dean Dr. Ehrlich.

IN 1972 90A45

817. **Lokal-** und Provinznachrichten. Czernowitz, 25. November. Die Vergangenheit und Zukunft der Sozialwissenschaften : Abschiedsvortrag Prof. Schumpeter. *Ibidem.* 1911. 26. Nov. (Nr. 2627, Jg. 9). S. 4–5.

About the farewell lecture by University Professor Dr. Joseph Schumpeter organized by the Social-Scientific Academic Society on the 21st of November 1911 on the topic of "The Past and Future of Social Sciences" ("Vergangenheit und Zukunft der Sozialwissenschaften").

Also the content of speeches by the members of the Society at the farewell banquet in the hotel "Schwarzer ler" ("Black Eagle") is provided including the speech of Professor Dr. Ehrlich – p. 5.

IN 1977 90A45

818. **Lokal-** und Provinznachrichten. Czernowitz, 11. Februar. Volkstümliche Universitätskurse. *Ibidem.* 1905. 12. Febr. (Nr. 611, Jg. 3). S. 5.

The schedule of courses held by professors and associate professors of Czernowitz University in March and April of the current year including the information about the lecture on "General Theory of Law" ("Allgemeine Rechtslehre") by Professor Dr. Eugen Ehrlich.

IN 1964 90A45

819. **Lokal-** und Provinznachrichten. Czernowitz, 28. Juni. Volkstümliche Universitätskurse. *Ibidem.* 1905. 29. Juni (Nr. 722, Jg. 3). S. 4.

The schedule of courses and the numbers of students in the courses held by professors and associate professors of

Czernowitz University in March and April of the current year including the information about the number of students of the lecture course on "General Theory of Law" ("Ueber allgemeine Rechtslehre") by Professor Dr. Eugen Ehrlich.

IN 1964 90A45

820. **Lokal**- und Provinznachrichten. Czernowitz, 10. Oktober. Volkstümliche Universitätskurse. *Ibidem.* 1905. 11. Okt. (Nr. 807, Jg. 3). S. 3–4.

The schedule of courses held by professors and associate professors in the academic year 1905/1906 including the information about the course on "General Theory of Law" ("Allgemeine Rechtslehre") by Professor Dr. Eugen Ehrlich – p. 3.

IN 1965 90A45

821. **Lokal**- und Provinznachrichten. Czernowitz, 18. Oktober. Volkstümliche Universitätskurse. *Ibidem.* 1905. 19. Okt. (Nr. 814, Jg. 3). S. 5.

Information about the opening of the popular university lecture series by the lecture on "General Theory of Law" ("Allgemeine Rechtslehre") by Professor Dr. Eugen Ehrlich that will take place on Friday, the 20th of October 1905 in the lecture hall Nr. 5.

IN 1965 90A45

822. **Lokal**- und Provinznachrichten. Czernowitz, 13. November. Volkstümliche Universitätskurse. *Ibidem.* 1905. 14. Nov. (Nr. 835, Jg. 3). S. 4.

Information about the lecture on "General Theory of Law" ("Allgemeine Rechtslehre") by Professor Dr. Eugen Ehrlich to be held on the 17th of November 1905.

IN 1965 90A45

823. **Lokal**- und Provinznachrichten. Czernowitz, 16. November. Volkstümliche Universitätskurse. *Ibidem.* 1905. 17. Nov. (Nr. 838, Jg. 3). S. 4.

Information about the lecture on "General Theory of Law" ("Allgemeine Rechtslehre") by Professor Dr. Eugen Ehrlich to be held in the lecture hall Nr. 5 on the 17th of November 1905.

IN 1965 90A45

824. **Lokal**- und Provinznachrichten. Czernowitz, 31. Mai. Volkstümliche Universitätskurse. *Ibidem.* 1906. 1. Juni (Nr. 997, Jg. 4). S. 3.

The schedule of courses held by professors and associate professors in the academic year 1905/1906 including the information about the course on "General Theory of Law" ("Allgemeine Rechtslehre") by Professor Dr. Ehrlich.

IN 1966 90A45

825. **Lokal**- und Provinznachrichten. Czernowitz, 6. September. Volkstümliche Universitätskurse. *Ibidem.* 1911. 7. Sept. (Nr. 2562, Jg. 9). S. 3.

Information about the first series of th epopular university courses for the academic year 1911/1912 beginning on the 21st of October 1911 including four stages of the course on "Die Theorien von Karl Marx im Lichte der wirtschaftlichen Entwicklung der Gegenwart" ["Karl Marx's Theories in the Light of Economic Development of the Present Times"] by Professor Dr. Eugen Ehrlich.

IN 1977 90A45

826. **Lokal**- und Provinznachrichten. Czernowitz, 20. Oktober. Volkstümliche Universitätskurse. *Ibidem.* 1911. 21. Okt. (Nr. 2597, Jg. 9). S. 3.

Notice about the first lecture within the series on "Die Theorien von Karl Marx im Lichte der wirtschaftlichen Entwicklung" ["Karl Marx's Theories in the Light of Economic Development"] by Professor Dr. Eugen Ehrlich in the lecture hall Nr. 7.

IN 1977 90A45

827. **Lokal**- und Provinznachrichten. Czernowitz, 27. Oktober. Volkstümliche Universitätskurse. *Ibidem.* 1911. 28. Okt. (Nr. 2603, Jg. 9). S. 4.

Notice about the second lecture within the series on "Die Theorien von Karl Marx im Lichte der wirtschaftlichen Entwicklung" ["Karl Marx's Theories in the Light of Economic Development"] by Professor Dr. Eugen Ehrlich in the lecture hall Nr. 7.

IN 1977 90A45

828. **Lokal**- und Provinznachrichten. Czernowitz, 9. November. Volkstümliche Universitätskurse. *Ibidem.* 1911. 10. Nov. (Nr. 2613, Jg. 9). S. 3.

Information about the lecture by Professor Dr. Eugen Ehrlich announced for the 11th of November 1911 on "Die Theorien von Karl Marx im Lichte der wirtschaftlichen Entwicklung der Gegenwart" ["Karl Marx's Theories in the Light of Economic Development of the Present Times"] that had to be cancelled due to his business trip. The new date will be announced in newspapers.

IN 1977 90A45

829. **Lokal**- und Provinznachrichten. Czernowitz, 24. November. Volkstümliche Universitätskurse. *Ibidem.* 1911. 25. Nov. (Nr. 2626, Jg. 9). S. 3–4.

Information about the time and place of the lecture by Professor Dr. Eugen Ehrlich on "Die Theorien von Karl Marx im Lichte der wirtschaftlichen Entwicklung der Gegenwart" ["Karl Marx's Theories in the Light of Economic Development of the Present Times"] on the 30th of November 1911 and the 7th of December 1911.

IN 1977 90A45

830. **Lokal**- und Provinznachrichten. Czernowitz, 20. Oktober. Vom Studentenheim. *Ibidem.* 1905. 22. Okt. (Nr. 817, Jg. 3). S. 5.

Election of University Professor Dr. Ehrlich a member of Board of Trustees replacing Professor Dr. von Halban.

IN 1965 90A45

831. **Lokal**- und Provinznachrichten. Czernowitz, 31. Jänner. Von der Universität. *Ibidem.* 1903. 1. Febr. (Nr. 5, Jg. 1). S. 3.

Professor Dr. Ehrlich – promoter of the graduation ceremony of a new doctor of law at Czernowitz University – Selig Horowitz.

IN 1960 90A45

832. **Lokal**- und Provinznachrichten. Czernowitz, 16. Juli 1903. Von der Universität. *Ibidem.* 1903. 17. Juli (Nr. 140, Jg. 1). S. 3.

Information about vacations of the Rector Professor Dr. Scharitzer, the Dean Professor Dr. Adler, and the Vice-Dean Professor Dr. Ehrlich. Management of the rectorate is taken by the Vice-Rector Professor Dr. Emilian Wojucki, and management of the dean's office of the Faculty of Law and Public Administration is taken by the Advisor Professor Dr. Kleinwächter.

IN 1961 90A45

833. **Lokal**- und Provinznachrichten. Czernowitz, 28. September. Von der Universität. *Ibidem.* 1903. 29. Sept. (Nr. 201, Jg. 1). S. 3.

Composition of the Academic Senate of Czernowitz University in the current academic year. Dr. Eugen Ehrlich – Vice-Dean of the Faculty of Law and Public Administration.

IN 1961 90A45

834. **Lokal**- und Provinznachrichten. Czernowitz, 6. Juli 1904. Von der Universität. *Ibidem.* 1904. 7. Juli (Nr. 430, Jg. 2). S. 4.

Information about the co-authorship by Dr. Eugen Ehrlich of the Address to Professor of German University in

Prague Dr. Anton von Randa by the Faculty of Law and Public Administration of Czernowitz University.

IN 1963 90A45

835. **Lokal**- und Provinznachrichten. Czernowitz, 5. Oktober. Von der Universität. *Ibidem.* 1905. 6. Okt. (Nr. 803, Jg. 3). S. 3–4.

On the appointment of members of the State Judicial Examination Boards in Czernowitz for the period of the academic years 1905/1906 to 1907/1908 by the Minister of Cultus and Education including the appointment of University Professor Dr. Eugen Ehrlich a member of the State Judicial Examination Board by the end of September 1908 – p. 3.

IN 1965 90A45

836. **Lokal**- und Provinznachrichten. Czernowitz, 24. November. Von der Universität. *Ibidem.* 1906. 25. Nov. (Nr. 1142, Jg. 4). S. 5.

Information about the 2nd of December 1906, the day of the anniversary of the government of the Emperor Franz Joseph I, when the solemn inauguration of the Rector for the academic year 1906/1907 will be held at 11 am with the Rector Professor Dr. Eugen Ehrlich's inaugural address on the subject of "Die Tatsachen des Gewohnheitsrechts" ("Facts of Customary Law").

IN 1967 90A45

837. **Lokal**- und Provinznachrichten. Czernowitz, 1. Februar. Von der Universität. *Ibidem.* 1907. 2. Febr. (Nr. 1197, Jg. 5). S. 4.

Information that the Academic Senate entrusted the Vice-Rector Professor Dr. Sigmund Herzberg-Fränkel to represent Czernowitz University in the Council of Curators of Regional Museums and the Vice-Rector Professor Dr. Eugen Ehrlich to represent Czernowitz University in the Council of Curators of Crafts Museum in Bukovina.

IN 1968 90A45

838. **Lokal**- und Provinznachrichten. Czernowitz, 20. November. Von der Universität. *Ibidem.* 1907. 21. Nov. (Nr. 1435, Jg. 5). S. 4.

Information about the report on the previous academic year by the Vice-Rector of Czernowitz University Professor Dr. Eugen Ehrlich on the occasion of the inauguration of the Rector Dr. Eugen Kozak for the academic year 1907/1908 on the 2nd of December 1907.

IN 1969 90A45

839. **Lokal**- und Provinznachrichten. Czernowitz, 22. August. Von der Universität. *Ibidem.* 1912. 24. Aug. (Nr. 2845, Jg. 10). S. 4.

The list of public lectures for the winter semester of the academic year 1912/1913 issued by the Academic Senate, including a note about Professor Ehrlich's vacation in this semester, and indicating that information about the lecture course on Roman law will be published later.

IN 1979 90A45

840. **Lokal**- und Provinznachrichten. Czernowitz, 12. Juli. Von unserer Universität. *Ibidem.* 1907. 13. Juli (Nr. 1325, Jg. 5). S. 4.

Information about the decision of the Academic Senate of Czernowitz University related to the 300th anniversary of the University of Hessen to be held in Hessen from the 31st of July 1907 to the 3rd of August 1907. As part of the celebration events the Rector Professor Dr. Eugen Ehrlich will represent Czernowitz University at the second meeting of the rectors of German universities.

IN 1969 90A45

841. **Lokal**- und Provinznachrichten. Czernowitz, 23. Sept. Von unserer Universität. *Ibidem.* 1907. 24. Sept. (Nr. 1386, Jg. 5). S. 5.

Information related to the death of the Rector Elect Dr. Basil Gaina: until the new elections, the acting Rector Professor Dr. Eugen Ehrlich and the acting Vice-Rector Professor Dr. Sigmund Herzberg-Fränkel, remain in their positions with the possibility of re-election to their positions.

IN 1969 90A45

842. **Lokal**- und Provinznachrichten. Czernowitz, 25. Juni. Von unserer Universität. *Ibidem.* 1908. 26. Juni (Nr. 1612, Jg. 6). S. 4.

Election of the Dean of the Faculty of Law of Czernowitz University for the academic year 1908/1909. Professor of Roman law Dr. Eugen Ehrlich elected the Dean.

IN 1970 90A45

843. **Lokal**- und Provinznachrichten. Czernowitz, 27. Juni. Von unserer Universität. *Ibidem.* 1908. 28. Juni (Nr. 1614, Jg. 6). S. 5.

Composition of the Academic Senate of Czernowitz University for the academic year 1908/1909. Dr. Eugen Ehrlich – the Dean of the Faculty of Law.

IN 1970 90A45

844. **Lokal**- und Provinznachrichten. Czernowitz, 27. Juli. Von unserer Universität. *Ibidem.* 1908. 28. Juli (Nr. 1638, Jg. 6). S. 3.

About the verification of the academic officials of Czernowitz University by the Decree of the Ministry of Cultus and Education of the 21st of July 1908 including the Dean of *the Faculty of Law and Public Administration Professor Dr. Eugen Ehrlich.*

IN 1971 90A45

845. **Lokal**- und Provinznachrichten. Czernowitz, 30. Dezember. Von unserer Universität. *Ibidem.* 1908. 31. Dez. (Nr. 1765, Jg. 6). S. 3.

On the appointment of Professor Dr. Eugen Ehrlich the second Vice-President of the State Judicial Examination Board at Czernowitz University by the Minister of Cultus and Education.

IN 1971 90A45

846. **Lokal**- und Provinznachrichten. Czernowitz, 9. Oktober. Von unserer Universität. *Ibidem.* 1909. 10. Okt. (Nr. 1995, Jg. 7). S. 5.

Information about the seminars in the winte rsemester of the current year conducted by Professor Dr. Eugen Ehrlich, including the seminar for certified lawyers conducted together with Professor Dr. Ferdinand Kogler entitled "Für lebendes Recht" ("On Living Law").

IN 1973 90A45

847. **Lokal**- und Provinznachrichten. Czernowitz, 21. Juni. Von unserer Universität. *Ibidem.* 1911. 22. Juni (Nr. 2498, Jg. 9). S. 4.

Election of the Dean of the Faculty of Law of Czernowitz University for the academic year 1911/1912. Professor of Roman law Dr. Eugen Ehrlich elected the Dean.

IN 1976 90A45

848. **Lokal**- und Provinznachrichten. Czernowitz, 27. Jänner. Von unserer Universität. *Ibidem.* 1912. 28. Jänner (Nr. 2665, Jg. 10). S. 4.

Participation of the Dean of the Faculty of Law Professor Dr. Eugen Ehrlich in the Matriculation ceremony for the new students of the university registered for the winter semester of the academic year 1911/1912.

IN 1978 90A45

849. **Lokal**- und Provinznachrichten. Czernowitz, 17. August. Von unserer Universität. *Ibidem.* 1913. 17. Aug. (1. Beibl. zu Nr. 3141, Jg. 11). S. [9].

Information about the approval of the project of public lectures at Czernowitz University in the winter semester of the academic year 1913/1914 by the Decree of the Ministry of Cultus and Education of the 15 of July 1913, including the information that Dr. Ehrlich will read the following lectures: "Römisches Recht mit Ausnahme der Quellen und Verfassungsgeschichte" ("Roman Law with the Exception of Sources and Constitutional History") 8, "Römisches Recht in seinen

Grundzügen mit Berücksichtigung der byzantinischen Fortentwicklung" ("Roman Law in its Principles, Considering the Byzantine Development") 4, and "Seminar für lebendes Recht" ("Seminar on Living Law") 2.

IN 1982 90A45

850. **Lokal-** und Provinznachrichten. Czernowitz, 20. Oktober. Vorlesungen über lebendes Recht. *Ibidem.* 1909. 21. Okt. (Nr. 2004, Jg. 7). S. 3.

Information about the seminar on "Lebendes Recht" ("Living Law") to be conducted by Professor Dr. Eugen Ehrlich and Professor Dr. Ferdinand Kogler for certified lawyers (advocates, notaries, candidate notaries and advocates) on the 28th of October 1909.

IN 1973 90A45

851. **Lokal-** und Provinznachrichten. Czernowitz, 25. Oktober. Vorlesungen über die Soziologie des Rechts. *Ibidem.* 1913. 26. Okt. (Nr. 3199, Jg. 11). S. 5.

About the appeal of the Sociological Society in Vienna to the Ministry of Education with the requirement to introduce the lectures on sociology to university studies. It also refers to Professor of Czernowitz University Dr. Ehrlich who holds lectures on sociology.

IN 1983 90A45

852. **Lokal-** und Provinznachrichten. Czernowitz, 8. März. Vortrag. *Ibidem.* 1909. 9. März (Nr. 1820, Jg. 7). S. 3.

Information about the lecture by University Professor Dr. Eugen Ehrlich on the topic of "Streifzüge durch Grossbritannien" ["Trips through Great Britain"], to be held in the Town Hall.

IN 1972 90A45

853. **Lokal-** und Provinznachrichten. Czernowitz, 15. November. Vortrag Eugen Ehrlich. *Ibidem.* 1913. 16. Nov. (Nr. 3216, Jg. 11). S. 3.

Information about the lecture by University Professor Dr. Eugen Ehrlich on the topic of "Nationalität und se" ["Nationality and Race"] on the 28th of November 1913.

IN 1983 90A45

854. **Lokal-** und Provinznachrichten. Czernowitz, 4. Dezember. Vortrag Eugen Ehrlich. *Ibidem.* 1913. 5. Dez. (Nr. 3232, Jg. 11). S. 4.

About the time and place of the second lecture by University Professor Dr. Eugen Ehrlich on "Nationalität und Rasse" ["Nationality and Race"].

IN 1983 90A45

855. **Lokal**- und Provinznachrichten. Czernowitz, 26. November. Vortrag des Universitätsprofessors Dr. Eugen Ehrlich. *Ibidem.* 1913. 27. Nov. (Nr. 3225, Jg. 11). S. 4.

About the time and place of these cond lecture on the 28th of November 1913 by University Professor Dr. Eugen Ehrlich on "Nationalität und Rasse" ["Nationality and Race"].

IN 1983 90A45

856. **Lokal**- und Provinznachrichten. Czernowitz, 1. April. Ein Vortrag des Univ.-Prof. Dr. Eugen Ehrlich. Der Ruf nach Lordrichtern für Oesterreich. *Ibidem.* 1914. 2. Apr. (Nr. 3412, Jg. 12). S. 3–4.

About the report by University Professor Dr. Eugen Ehrlich provided to the Society of Austrian Judges in Vienna. The text of the report is also provided.

IN 1985 90A45

857. **Lokal**- und Provinznachrichten. Czernowitz, 30. Jänner. Vortrag Ludo M. Hartmann. *Ibidem.* 1911. 31. Jänner (Nr. 2384, Jg. 9). S. 3–4.

About the event organized on the 26th of January 1911 by the Social-Scientific Academic Society in honour of Ludo M. Hartmann who presented the lecture on "Christianity and Socialism" ("Christentum und Sozialismus"). The event was attended, among other honorary members of the Society, by Professor Dr. Ehrlich who also spoke at the organized party – p. 4.

IN 1976 90A45

858. **Lokal**- und Provinznachrichten. Czernowitz, 15. November. Vorträgedes Prof. Ehrlich. *Ibidem.* 1910. 16. Nov. (Nr. 2322, Jg. 8). S. 4.

Information about the intention of University Professor Dr. Ehrlich to hold a series of lectures for the Juridical-Political Scientific Society entitled "Science of Law" ("Rechtswissenschaft"). It also points out that the first lecture will be on the 18th of November 1910 in the large hall of the Palace of Justice.

IN 1975 90A45

859. **Lokal**- und Provinznachrichten. Czernowitz, 4. Februar. Der Wärmestubenball. *Ibidem.* 1907. 5. Febr. (Nr. 1198, Jg. 5). S. 2–3.

Participation of the University Rector Dr. Ehrlich in the charity ball – p. 2.

IN 1968 90A45

860. **Lokal**- und Provinznachrichten. Czernowitz, 15. Jänner 1907. Dr. Wilhelm R. v. Hartel. *Ibidem.* 1907. 16. Jänner (Nr. 1182, Jg. 5). S. 3.

Participation of Professor Dr. Eugen Ehrlich in the Czernowitz University delegation at the funeral of Honorary Doctor of Czernowitz University Dr. Hartel.

IN 1968 90A45

861. **Lokal**- und Provinznachrichten. Czernowitz, 1. Februar. Zum Vortrag Ludo M. Hartmann. *Ibidem.* 1911. 2. Febr. (Nr. 2386, Jg. 9). S. 3–4.

About three major presentations organized by the Social-Scientific Academic Society in honour of Dr. Ludo M. Hartmann: the Rector Dr. Friedwagner, Professors Dr. Adler and Dr. Ehrlich.

IN 1976 90A45

862. **Lokal**- und Provinznachrichten. Czernowitz, 24. September. Zur Anerkennung der jüdischen Nationalität. *Ibidem.* 1907. 25. Sept. (Nr. 1387, Jg. 5). S. 4.

Participation of the Rector Professor Dr. Ehrlich in the dispute about the recognition of Jews at Czernowitz University.

IN 1969 90A45

863. **Lokal**- und Provinznachrichten. Czernowitz, 12. Dezember. Zur Gemeinderatskrise. *Ibidem.* 1905. 13. Dez. (Nr. 859, Jg. 3). S. 4.

About the participation of Professor Ehrlich in the solution of municipal crisis.

IN 1965 90A45

864. **Lokal**- und Provinznachrichten. Czernowitz, 6. Juli. Zur Sprachenfrage an der Universität. *Ibidem.* 1905. 7. Juli (Nr. 728, Jg. 3). S. 3–4.

Participation of Professor Dr. E. Ehrlich in dispute of the language issue at Czernowitz University – p. 3.

IN 1965 90A45

865. **Lokal**-und Provinznachrichten. Czernowitz, 19. Mai. Zur Wiedereröffnung der Universität. *Ibidem.* 1916. 19. Mai (Nr. 3862, Jg. 14). S. 3.

About the resumption of daily lectures at the University in Czernowitz. It is pointed out that the permission not to teach is given to those professors engaged in military service and to group of teachers, including Professor Dr. Ehrlich.

IN 1988 90A45

866. **Lokal**- und Provinznachrichten. Czernowitz, 9. Februar. II. internationaler Kongress für Schulhygiene in London. *Ibidem.* 1907. 10. Febr. (Nr. 1203, Jg. 5). S. 5.

Election of the University Rector Professor Dr. Eugen Ehrlich the Deputy-Head of the Regional Committee that will *organize the II International Congress of the School of Hygiene that will take place in London in the period from the 5th to the 10th of August 1907.*

IN 1968 90A45

867. **Lokal**- und Provinznachrichten. Zweiter Vortrag Eugen Ehrlich. *Ibidem.* 1913. 30. Nov. (Nr. 3228, Jg. 11). S. 3–4.

On the decision of University Professor Dr. Eugen Ehrlich to repeat the lecture on "Nationalität und Rasse" ["Nationality and Race"], because the number of those who wanted to attend the first lecture exceeded the number of available seats in the lecture hall.

IN 1983 90A45

868. **Ludwig, Markus.** *Sein und Sollen : eine Untersuchung zur Abgrenzung der Rechtsnormen von den sozialen Normen bei Max Weber und Eugen Ehrlich.* Marburg : Tectum Verl., 1999. 178 S. (*Wissenschaftliche Beiträge aus dem Tectum Verlag. Reihe Politikwissenschften*; Bd. 2). Lit.-Verz.: S. 171–178.

Information about the research into distinction of legal norms from social norms performed by Eugen Ehrlich.

869. **Maliska, Marcos Augusto.** *Introdução à sociologia do direito de Eugen Ehrlich : aportes para uma reflexão atual sobre pluralismo e Constituição. 2ª ed.* Curitiba : Juruá, 2015. 172 p.

Introduction into Sociology of Law by Eugen Ehrlich.

870. **Michaels, Ralf.** "The Re-Statement of Non-State Law: The State, Choice of Law, and the Challenge from Global Legal Pluralism." *The Wayne Law Review.* 2005. Vol. 51. P. 1209–1259.

E. Ehrlich. – pp. 1222–1224, 1232, 1233, 1244–1246.

871. **Minerva** : Jahrbuch der gelehrten Welt. Jg. 4, *"1894–1895"*, hrsg. von R. Kukula, und K. Trübner. Strassburg : Karl J. Trübner, 1895. XVI, 930, 80 S.

Information about Professor Eugen Ehrlich in the publication – p. 767.

IN 256926 60H22

Jg. 5, *"1895–1896"*, hrsg. von R. Kukula, und K. Trübner. Strassburg : Karl J. Trübner, 1896. XIX, 989 S.

Information about Professor Eugen Ehrlich in the publication – p. 820.

IN 256927 60H22

Jg. 6, *"1896–1897"*, hrsg. von K. Trübner. Strassburg : Karl J. Trübner, 1897. XIV, 1082, 76 S.

Information about Professor Eugen Ehrlich in the publication – p. 900.

IN 256928 60H22

Jg. 9, *"1899–1900"*, hrsg. von K. Trübner, und F. Mentz. Strassburg : Karl J. Trübner, 1900. XXXII, 1167, 77 S.

Information about Professor Eugen Ehrlich in the publication – p. 231.

IN 256929 60H22

Jg. 10, *"1900–1901"*, hrsg. von K. Trübner. Strassburg : Karl J. Trübner, 1901. XXVIII, 1244 S.

Information about Professor Eugen Ehrlich in the publication – p. 248.

IN 256930 60H22

Jg. 12, *"1902–1903"*, hrsg. von K. Trübner. Strassburg : Karl J. Trübner, 1903. XL, 1347 S.

Information about Professor Eugen Ehrlich in the publication – p. 270.

IN 256931 60H22

Jg. 15, *"1905–1906"*, hrsg. von K. Trübner. Strassburg : Karl J. Trübner, 1906. XLIII, 1493, 71 S.

Information about Professor Eugen Ehrlich in the publication – p. 295.

IN 256932 60H22

Jg. 17, *"1907–1908"*, hrsg. von K. Trübner. Strassburg : Karl J. Trübner, 1908. XXXI, L, 1612, 71 S.

Information about Professor Eugen Ehrlich in the publication – pp. 320, 321.

IN 256933 60H22

Jg. 18, *"1908–1909"*, hrsg. von K. Trübner. Strassburg : Karl J. Trübner, 1909. XXXIX, LIV, 1360, 69 S.

Information about Professor Eugen Ehrlich in the publication – p. 277.

IN 256934 60H22

Jg. 19, *"1909–1910"*, begr. von K. Trübner. Strassburg : Karl J. Trübner, 1910. XXXIX, LVIII, 1512, 67 S.

Information about Professor Eugen Ehrlich in the publication – p. 313.

IN 256935 60H22

Jg. 21, *"1911–1912"*, begr. von R. Kukula, und K. Trübner. Strassburg : Karl J. Trübner, 1912. LI, LXXXVIII, 1699, 71 S.

Information about Professor Eugen Ehrlich in the publication – p. 353.

IN 256936 60H22

Jg. 22, *"1912–1913"*, begr. von R. Kukula, und K. Trübner. Strassburg : Karl J. Trübner, 1913. LI, LXIV, 1822, 83 S.

Information about Professor Eugen Ehrlich in the publication – p. 373.

IN 256937 60H22

Jg. 23, *"1913–1914"*, begr. von R. Kukula, und K. Trübner. Strassburg : Karl J. Trübner, 1914. XLVI, LXXXV, 1889, 75 S.

Information about Professor Eugen Ehrlich in the publication – p. 389.

IN 256938 60H22

872. **Muñoz de Baena Simón, José Luis.** El lugar de Ehrlich en el debate sobre la ciencia juridical. In Ehrlich, Eugen. *Escritos sobre sociología y jurisprudencia.* Madrid : Marcial Pons, 2005. pp. 27–50. (*Politopías* ; 3).

Information about Professor Eugen Ehrlich in the publication.

873. **Nachrichten** aus Stadt und Land. Czernowitz, den 27. Juni. Der akademische Senat... *Bukowiner Nachrichten.* 1908. 28. Juni (Nr. 5902, Jg. 21). S. 4.

Composition of the Academic Senate of Czernowitz University for the academic year 1908/1909. Dr. Eugen Ehrlich – the Dean of the Faculty of Law.

IN 2038 90J6

874. **Nachrichten** aus Stadt und Land. Czernowitz, 3. September. 31. Deutscher Juristentag. *Ibidem.* 1912. 4. Sept. (Nr. 6904, Jg. 25). S. 4.

Departure of University Professor Dr. Ehrlich to participate in the 31st Assembly of German Lawyers.

IN 2045 90J6

875. **Nachrichten** aus Stadt und Land. Czernowitz, den 16. Dezember. Fremde Orden. *Ibidem.* 1907. 17. Dez. (Nr. 5745, Jg. 20). S. 2.

University Professor Dr. Eugen Ehrlich from Czernowitz awarded the Commander's Cross of the Greek Order of the Saviour by Kaiser.

IN 2037 90J6

876. **Nachrichten** aus Stadt und Land. Czernowitz, den 20. November. K. k. Franz Josefs-Universität. *Ibidem.* 1907. 21. Nov. (Nr. 5723, Jg. 20). S. 4.

Information about the report on the previous academic year by the Vice-Rector of Czernowitz University Professor Dr. Eugen Ehrlich on the occasion of the inauguration of the Rector Dr. Eugen Kozak for the academic year 1907/1908.

IN 2037 90J6

877. **Nachrichten** aus Stadt und Land. Czernowitz, den 13. Februar. Karnevalfest "Die Welt auf Reisen". *Ibidem.* 1908. 14. Febr. (Nr. 5792, Jg. 21). S. 3.

About financial contributions to Karnevalfest "Die Welt auf Reisen" ("World Travel"), including the contribution of 20 crowns by Professor Dr. Ehrlich.

IN 2038 90J6

878. **Nachrichten** aus Stadt und Land. Czernowitz, den 9. Dezember. Rektorsinauguration. *Ibidem.* 1907. 10. Dez. (Nr. 5739, Jg. 20). S. 2.

Information about the report on the previous academic year by the Vice-Rector of Czernowitz University Professor Dr. Eugen Ehrlich on the occasion of the inauguration of the Rector Dr. Eugen Kozak for the academic year 1907/1908.

IN 2037 90J6

879. **Nachrichten** aus Stadt und Land. Czernowitz, den 27. Juli. Von der Universität. *Ibidem.* 1908. 28. Juli (Nr. 5926, Jg. 21). S. 2.

About the verification of the academic officials of Czernowitz University by the Ministry of Culture and Education, including the Dean of the Faculty of Law and Public Administration Professor Dr. Eugen Ehrlich.

IN 2039 90J6

880. **Nachrichten** aus Stadt und Land. Czernowitz, 29. Aug. Von der Universität. *Ibidem.* 1912. 30. Aug. (Nr. 6902, Jg. 25). S. 2–3.

The list of public lectures for the winter semester of the academic year 1912/1913 issued by the Academic Senate, including a note about Professor Ehrlich's vacation in this semester, and indicating that information about the lecture course on Roman law will be published later.

IN 2045 90J6

881. **Nelken, David.** "Ane-mail from Global Bukowina." *International Journal of Law in Context.* 2007. Vol. 3, Iss. 3. P. 189–202.

882. **Nelken, David.** "Eugen Ehrlich, Living Law, and Plural Legalities." *Theoretical Inquiries in Law.* 2008. Vol. 9, Nr. 2 (Juli). P. 443–471.

883. **Nelken, David.** Pound and Ehrlich on the Living Law. In *Soziologische Jurisprudenz und realistische Theorien des Rechts = Sociological jurisprudence and realist theories of law,* hrsg. von Eugene Kamenka, Robert S. Summers, and William L. Twining ; Vorw. Aleksander Peczenik. Berlin : Duncker & Humnblot, 1986. S. 175–187. (*Rechtstheorie* ; Beih. 9).

884. **Neueres** von deutschen und auswärtigen Hochschulen. *Hochschul-Nachrichten.* 1896. Nov. (Nr. 74). S. 11–20.

Information about Professor Eugen Ehrlich in the publication – pp.17, 18.

IN 19432 60A15

885. **Norst, Anton.** *Alma mater Francisco-Josephina : Festschrift zu deren – 25 jährigen Bestande.* Czernowitz : [Pardini], 1900. 136 S. + 1 Tab.

Information about Professor Eugen Ehrlich in the publication – p. 51.

IN 107071 90B6

886. **Notizen** und Vermischtes. Universitäts-Nachrichten. *Juristisches Litteraturblatt.* 1900. 15. März (Nr. 113 ; Bd. 12, Nr. 3). S. 76.

Appointment of Dr. E. Ehrlich from Czernowitz a Full Professor.

IN 19794 86B2

887. **Obstgarten, Isidor.** "Zum 25-jährigen Jubiläum der Franz-Josephs-Universität in Czernowitz." *Theater-, Kunst- und Literatur-Zeitung.* 1900. 30. Nov. (Jg. 6). S. 2.

Information about Professor Eugen Ehrlich in the publication.

IN 330 84A9

888. **Oeffentliche** Vorlesungenander k. k. Universität zu Wien im Sommer-Semester 1895. *Hochschul-Nachrichten.* 1895. März (Nr. 54). Anh. S. 13–28.

Information about Professor Eugen Ehrlich's public lecture – p. 13.

IN 19430 60A15

889. **Oeffentliche** Vorlesungenander k. k. Universität zu Wien im Winter-Semester 1895/1896. *Ibidem.* 1895. Aug. (Nr. 59). Anh. S. 23–29.

Information about Professor Eugen Ehrlich's public lecture – p. 24.

IN 19430 60A15

890. **Oeffentliche** Vorlesungenander k. k. Universität zu Wien im Sommer-Semester 1896. *Ibidem.* 1896. März (Nr. 66). Anh. S. 21–26.

Information about Professor Eugen Ehrlich's public lecture – p. 22.

IN 19431 60A15

891. **Oeffentliche** Vorlesungen an der k. k. Universität zu Wien im Winter-Semester 1896/1897. *Ibidem.* 1896. Aug./Sept. (Nr. 71/72). Anh. S. 20–27.

Information about Professor Eugen Ehrlich's public lecture – p. 21.

IN 19431 60A15

892. **Ortsnachrichten.** Czernowitz, 18. März. Archäologischer Kongress. *Bukowiner Nachrichten.* 1905. 19. März (Nr. 4929, Jg. 18). S. 3.

Information about the departure of University Professor Dr. Ehrlich for Athens where he will participate in the discussions of the Archaeological Congress.

IN2035 90J6

893. **Ortsnachrichten.** Czernowitz, 4. Februar. Aus Anlass des Scheidens... *Ibidem.* 1907. 5. Febr. (Nr. 5485, Jg. 20). S. 3.

Participation of University Professor Dr. Ehrlich in a farewell dinner of Divisional General Major von Hornik.

IN 2037 90J6

894. **Ortsnachrichten.** Czernowitz, 5. Februar. Burschenschafter kränzchen. *Ibidem.* 1907. 6. Febr. (Nr. 5486, Jg. 20). S. 3.

Participation of the University Rector Dr. Ehrlich in the charity ball of the Academic Societies "Arminia" and "Teutonia".

IN 2037 90J6

895. **Ortsnachrichten.** Czernowitz, 15. März. Denkmalausschuss. *Ibidem.* 1907. 16. März (Nr. 5519, Jg. 20). S. 3.

On the inaugural meeting of the Committee for the installation of the monument for Professor Johann von Mikulicz-Radecki in his birthplace of Czernowitz (based on the initiative of the Rector of the local University Professor Dr. Eugen Ehrlich). The text of speech of Dr. Ehrlich presented at the meeting is also provided.

IN 2037 90J6

896. **Ortsnachrichten.** Czernowitz, 21. Dezember. Hausindustrieausstellung in Wien. *Ibidem.* 1905. 22. Dez. (Nr. 5155, Jg. 18). S. 3.

Participation of University Professor Dr. Ehrlich in the exhibition of the handicraft production and folk art in Vienna.

IN 2035 90J6

897. **Ortsnachrichten.** Czernowitz, 3. Dezember. Die Inauguration des neuen Rektors… *Ibidem.* 1906. 4. Dez. (Nr. 5436, Jg. 19). S. 2.

About the ceremonial inauguration of the new Rector of Czernowitz University Professor Dr. Ehrlich.

IN 2036 90J6

898. **Ortsnachrichten.** Czernowitz, 4. Februar. Die juristisch-staatswissenschaftliche Gesellschaft… *Ibidem.* 1905. 5. Febr. (Nr. 4893, Jg. 18). S. 2.

Notice that University Professor Dr. Eugen Ehrlich will read a lecture on "Sociologie und Rechtswissenschaft" ("Sociology and Science of Law") in the Town Hall on the 15th of February 1905.

IN 2035 90J6

899. **Ortsnachrichten.** Czernowitz, 13. Februar. Juristisch-staatswissenschaftliche Gesellschaft. *Ibidem.* 1905. 14. Febr. (Nr. 4900, Jg. 18). S. 2.

Notice that University Professor Dr. Eugen Ehrlich will read a lecture on "Sociologie und Jurisprudenz" ("Sociology and Jurisprudence") in the Town Hall on the 15th of February 1905.

IN 2035 90J6

900. **Ortsnachrichten.** Czernowitz, 13. Februar. Juristisch-staatswissenschaftliche Gesellschaft. *Ibidem.* 1906. 14. Febr. (Nr. 5196, Jg. 19). S. 2.

Information about the commemorative speech by University Professor Dr. Eugen Ehrlich for the late Honorary Professor of the University of Vienna Dr. Anton Menger on the 14th of February 1906 at 7 pm.

IN2036 90J6

901. **Ortsnachrichten.** Czernowitz, 4. März. Juristisch-staatswissenschaftliche Gesellschaft. *Ibidem.* 1907. 5. März (Nr. 5509, Jg. 20). S. 3.

Information about the report of Professor Dr. Eugen Ehrlichon "Zur Lehre von den juristischen Personen" ("The Doctrine of Legal Persons") to be provided in the hall of the Privincial Court (Civil Law Chamber) on the 8th of March 1907.

IN 2037 90J6

902. **Ortsnachrichten.** Czernowitz, 9. Februar. Kongress für Schulhygiene in London. *Ibidem.* 1907. 10. Febr. (Nr. 5490, Jg. 20). S. 5.

Election of the University Rector Professor Dr. Eugen Ehrlich the Deputy-Head of the Regional Committee that will organize the II International Congress of the School of Hygiene that will take place in London in the period from the 5th to the 10th of August 1907.

IN 2037 90J6

903. **Ortsnachrichten.** Czernowitz, 9. Februar. Die konservativen Studenten... *Ibidem.* 1907. 10. Febr. (Nr. 5490, Jg. 20). S. 5.

Decisions of the Academic Senate signed by the Rector Dr. Ehrlich related to the academic student societies.

IN 2037 90J6

904. **Ortsnachrichten.** Czernowitz, 3. November. Promotion. *Ibidem.* 1905. 4. Nov. (Nr. 5115, Jg. 18). S. 2.

Professor Dr. Ehrlich – promoter of the graduation ceremony of a new doctor of law at Czernowitz University – Julius Brüll.

IN 2035 90J6

905. **Ortsnachrichten.** Czernowitz, 11. Oktober. Volkstümliche Universitätskurse. *Ibidem.* 1905. 12. Okt. (Nr. 5096, Jg. 18). S. 2.

The schedule of courses held by professors and associate professors in the academic year 1905/1906 including the information about the course on "General Theory of Law" by Professor Dr. Eugen Ehrlich.

IN 2035 90J6

906. **Ortsnachrichten.** Czernowitz, 23. Oktober. Volkstümliche Universitätskurse. *Ibidem.* 1905. 24. Okt. (Nr. 5106, Jg. 18). S. 2.

Notice about the second lecture within the series on "General Theory of Law" to be held by Professor Dr. Eugen Ehrlich on the 27th of October 1905 in the lecture hall Nr. 5.

IN 2035 90J6

907. **Ortsnachrichten.** Czernowitz, 11. November. Volkstümliche Universitätskurse. *Ibidem.* 1905. 12. Nov. (Nr. 5122, Jg. 18). S. 4.

Information about the fifth lecture on "General Theory of Law" by Professor Dr. Eugen Ehrlich to be held in the lecture hall Nr. 5 on the 17th of November 1905.

IN 2035 90J6

908. **Ortsnachrichten.** Czernowitz, 15. November. Volkstümliche Universitätskurse. *Ibidem.* 1905. 16. Nov. (Nr. 5125, Jg. 18). S. 3.

Information about the fifth lecture by Professor Dr. Eugen Ehrlich to be held in the lecture hall Nr. 5 on the 17th of November 1905.

IN 2035 90J6

909. **Ortsnachrichten.** Czernowitz, 24. November. Von der Universität. *Ibidem.* 1906. 25. Nov. (Nr. 5429, Jg. 19). S. 4.

Information about the inauguration ceremony of the Rector Professor Dr. Eugen Ehrlich for the academic year 1906/1907 held on the 2nd of December 1906 with the Rector's inaugural address on the subject of "Die Tatsachen des Gewohnheitsrechts" ["Facts of Customary Law"].

IN 2036 90J6

910. **Ortsnachrichten.** Czernowitz, 13. Dezember. Von der Universität. *Ibidem.* 1906. 14. Dez. (Nr. 5444, Jg. 19). S. 3.

Participation of the Rector of Czernowitz University Professor Dr. Eugen Ehrlich in the Matriculation ceremony of the new students of the University.

IN 2036 90J6

911. **Ortsnachrichten.** Czernowitz, 1. Februar. Von der Universität. *Ibidem.* 1907. 2. Febr. (Nr. 5484, Jg. 20). S. 3.

Information that the Academic Senate entrusted the Vice-Rector Professor Dr. Sigmund Herzberg-Fränkel to represent Czernowitz University in the Council of Curators of Regional Museums and the Vice-Rector Professor Dr. Eugen Ehrlich to represent Czernowitz University in the Council of Curators of Crafts Museum in Bukovina.

IN 2037 90J6

912. **Ortsnachrichten.** Czernowitz, 26. Juni. Von der Universität. *Ibidem.* 1907. 27. Juni (Nr. 5600, Jg. 20). S. 4.

Composition of the Academic Senate for the academic year 1907/1908. Professor Dr. Eugen Ehrlich – the Vice-Rector of Czernowitz University.

IN 2037 90J6

913. **Ortsnachrichten.** Czernowitz, 6. Februar. Zum Burschenschafter kränzchen. *Ibidem.* 1907. 7. Febr. (Nr. 5487, Jg. 20). S. 4.

On the financial contributions by distinguished persons of the region to finance the study of a student of German nationality including the contribution of the University Rector Dr. Ehrlich.

IN 2037 90J6

914. **Page, Herbert William.** "Professor Ehrlich's Czernowitz Seminar of the Living Law." *Northern Kentucky Law Rewiew.* 1977. Nr. 1, Vol. 4.

S. 37–63 ; *Proceedings of the 14th Annual Meeting of the Association of American Law Schools.* 1914. P. 46–75.

915. **Papendorf, Knut,** Stefan Machura, and Anne Hellum, Eds. *Eugen Ehrlich's Sociology of Law.* Wien ; Zürich ; Berlin ; Münster : LIT Verl., 2014. II, 259 p. (*Society and Law* ; Vol. 8).

Contents:

Stefan Machura, Anne Hellum, Knut Papendorf. Introduction. p. 1;

EHRLICH'S LEGACY. Klaus A. Ziegert. Beyond "Living Law": Eugen Ehrlich's General Theory of Law. p. 17; Stefan Machura. Eugen Ehrlich's Legacy in Contemporary German Sociology of Law. p. 39; Franz and Keebet von Benda-Beckmann. "Living Law" as a Political and Analytical Concept. p. 69;

EHRLICH IN SCANDINAVIA.

Anne Hellum. Legal Pluralist Perspectives in Scandinavian and African Women's Law. p. 95; Knut Papendorf. A Voyage of Discovery: Eugen Ehrlich in Scandinavia. p. 115; Hanne Petersen. Sociology of Law at "the Edge of Empires and Eras" – Reflections on Lawyers and Living Law 65 Years after the Legal Expedition to Greenland. p. 133;

EHRLICH'S CONCEPT APPLIED TO NON-WESTERN COUNTRIES.

Olga Litvinova, Stefan Machura. Organizing a Community: The "Living Law" of the Don Cossacks. p. 157; Monika Lindbekk. Between the Power of the State and the Guardianship of the Church: Orthodox Copts Seeking Divorce. p. 179; Rustamjon Urinboyev, Måns Svensson. Rethinking Corruption in Post-Soviet Uzbekistan: Ethnography of "Living Law". p. 209;

EUGEN EHRLICH'S PASSION.

Olga Litvinova. Ehrlich's Passion: Bukovina Traditional Textiles. p. 241.

916. **Pattai, Robert.** *Der Kampf um die Rechtswissenschaft und die Freirechtsbewegung : Vortag, gehalten am 6. Dezember 1912 im Festsaale der Urania zu Wien.* Wien : Manz, 1913. 60 S.

Information about Professor Eugen Ehrlich in the publication – pp. 25, 27, 52–55.

IN 240651 17D12

917. **Paulson, Stanley L.,** Hrsg. *Hans Kelsen und die Rechtssozioligie : Auseinandersetzungen mit Hermann U. Kantorowicz, Eugen Ehrlich und Max Weber.* Aalen : Scientia Verl., 1992. [XIII, 119 S.].

Information about Eugen Ehrlich in the publication.

918. **Personalnachrichten**. Auf das Amt haben verzichtet. *Verordnungsblatt des k. k. Justizministeriums.* 1896. 31. Dez. (Stück 24, Jg. 12). S. 275.

Official information of the Imperial and Royal Ministry of Justice about the refusal of Dr. Eugen Ehrlich to have a post in the town of Schwechat.

IN 2921 13K1

919. **Personalnachrichten**. In die Advocatenliste wurde eingetragen. *Verordnungsblatt des k. k. Justizministeriums.* 1893. 14. Juli (Stück 15, Jg. 9). S. 120.

Official information of the Imperial and Royal Ministry of Justice about Dr. Eugen Ehrlich from Schwechat being included into the list of advocates.

IN 2929 13K1

920. **Personalstand** der k. k. Franz-Josephs-Universität zu Czernowitz im Studienjahre 1906/1907. Czernowitz : Verl. des akademischen Senates, [s. a.]. 22 S.

Information about Professor Eugen Ehrlich as a staff member at Franz Joseph University in Czernowitz – pp. 3, 9.

IN 193739 90T814

921. **Personalstand** der k. k. Franz-Josephs-Universität zu Czernowitz im Studienjahre 1907/1908. Czernowitz : Verl. des akademischen Senates, [s. a.]. 22 S.

Information about Professor Eugen Ehrlich as a staff member at Franz Joseph University in Czernowitz – pp. 3, 4, 9.

IN 194746 90T814

922. **Personalstand** der k. k. Franz-Josephs-Universität zu Czernowitz im Studienjahre 1908/1909. Czernowitz : Verl. des akademischen Senates, [s. a.]. 22 S.

Information about Professor Eugen Ehrlich as a staff member at Franz Joseph University in Czernowitz – pp. 3, 4, 8, 9.

IN 193750 90T814

923. **Personalstand** der k. k. Franz-Josephs-Universität zu Czernowitz im Studienjahre 1909/1910. Czernowitz : Verl. des akademischen Senates, [s. a.]. 22 S.

Information about Professor Eugen Ehrlich as a staff member at Franz Joseph University in Czernowitz – pp. 3, 4, 8, 9.

IN 193752 90T814

924. **Personalstand** der k. k. Franz Josephs-Universität zu Czernowitz im Studienjahre 1910/1911. Czernowitz : Verl. des akademischen Senates, [s. a.]. 22 S.

Information about Professor Eugen Ehrlich as a staff member at Franz Joseph University in Czernowitz – pp. 4, 9.

IN 193754 90T814

925. **Personalstand** der k. k. Franz Josephs-Universität zu Czernowitz im Studienjahre 1911/1912. Czernowitz : Verl. Des akademischen Senates, [s. a.]. 23 S.

Information about Professor Eugen Ehrlich as a staff member at Franz Joseph University in Czernowitz – pp. 3, 8–9.

IN 193756 90T814

926. **Personalstand** der k. k. Franz Josephs-Universität zu Czernowitz im Studienjahre 1912/1913. Czernowitz : Verl. des akademischen Senates, [s. a.]. 24 S.

Information about Professor Eugen Ehrlich as a staff member at Franz Joseph University in Czernowitz – pp. 3, 8, 9.

IN 193757 90T814

927. **Personalstand** der k. k. Franz Josephs-Universität zu Czernowitz im Studienjahre 1913/1914. Czernowitz : Verl. des akademischen Senates, [s. a.]. 24 S.

Information about Professor Eugen Ehrlich as a staff member at Franz Joseph University in Czernowitz – p. 8.

IN 193758 90T814

928. **Personalstand** der k. k. Franz Josephs-Universität zu Czernowitz im Studienjahre 1918/1919. Czernowitz : Verl. des akademischen Senates, [s. a.]. 24 S.

Information about Professor Eugen Ehrlich as a staff member at Franz Joseph University in Czernowitz – p. 9.

IN 193760 90T814

929. **Porsche-Ludwig, Markus.** Ehrlich, Eugen. In *Biographisch-Bibliographisches Kirchenlexikon: ein theologisches Nachschlagewerk,* hrsg. Traugott Bautz. Nordhausen: Traugott Bautz, 2011. Bd. 32, Erg. 19. S. 288–292.

930. **Porsche-Ludwig, Markus.** *Eugen Ehrlich interkulturell gelesen.* Nordhausen : Traugott Bautz, 2011. 21 S. (*Interkulturelle Bibliothek*; Bd. 127).

Information about Professor Eugen Ehrlich in the publication.

931. **Pound, Roscoe.** "An Appreciation of Eugen Ehrlich." *Harvard Law Review.* 1922. Vol. 36, No. 2 (Dec.). P. 129–130.

Information about Professor Eugen Ehrlich in the publication.

932. **Pound, Roscoe.** "The Scope and Purpose of Sociological Jurisprudence." *Harvard Law Review.* 1911. Vol. 24, No. 8 (June). P. 591–619 ; 1912. – Vol. 25, No. 6 (Apr.). P. 489–516.

Information about Professor Eugen Ehrlich in the publication – pp. 614, 512–513, 515.

933. **Promotion** sub auspiciis imperatoris. *Bukowinaer Post.* 1907. 17. Nov. (Nr. 2150, Jg. 15). S. 4.

On the solemn promotion at Czernowitz University. The text of the speech by the Vice-Rector Dr. Ehrlich is also provided.

IN 2061 90J26

934. **Pulzer, Peter.** The Contemporary Relevance of Joseph Schumpeter. In *Die Bukowina: Vergangenheit und Gegenwart : eine Veröffentlichung des Österreichischen Ost- und Südosteuropa-Instituts,* hrsg. von Ilona Slawinski, and Joseph P. Strelka. Bern ; Berlin ; Frankfurt a. M. ; New York ; Paris ; Wien : Peter Lang, 1995. S. 155–170.

Note about Professor Eugen Ehrlich in the publication – p. 158.

ЦБЗ 7623 BB

935. **Rădulescu, C.** "Cuvântul nostrum." *Bucovina : revistă lunară de drept, socioligie şi criminologie.* 1927. Anul 1, No. 1 (mar.). P. I–IV.

Note about Professor Eugen Ehrlich in the publication – p. II.

IN 30231 16C46

936. **Raiser, Thomas.** *Grundlagen der Rechtssoziologie.* 6., durchges. und erw. Aufl. Tübingen : Mohr Siebeck, 2013. XXI, 388 S.

Information about Eugen Ehrlich as a founder of the Sociology of Law and his views – pp. III, XX, 6–8, 11–12. 16, 26, 31, 37, 43, 56, 68, 71–85, 178, 182, 312.

937. **Raiser, Thomas.** *Das lebende Recht: Rechtssoziologie in Deutschland.* 3., überbearb. Aufl. Baden-Baden : Nomos-Verl.-Ges., 1999. 438 S.

Information about Eugen Ehrlich's views on 'living law' – pp. 94–107.

938. **Rehbinder, Manfred.** Aus den letzten Jahren im Leben und Schaffen von Eugen Ehrlich. In *Jus humanum : Grundlagen des Rechts und Strafrecht : Festschrift für Ernst-Joachim Lampe zum 70. Geburstag.* hrsg. von Dieter Dölling. Berlin : Duncker & Humblot, 2003. S. 199–210.

939. **Rehbinder, Manfred.** *Die Begründung der Rechtssoziologie durch Eugen Ehrlich*, mit einem Geleitw. von René König. Berlin : Duncker & Humblot, 1967. 122 S. (*Schriftenreihe des Instituts für Rechtssoziologie und Rechtstatsachenforschung der Freien Universität Berlin*; Bd. 6). Bibliogr.: S. 121–122.

940. **Rehbinder, Manfred.** *Die Begründung der Rechtssoziologie durch Eugen Ehrlich.* 2., völlig neu bearb. Aufl. Berlin: Duncker und Humblot, 1986. 147 S. (*Schriftenreihe zur Rechtssoziologie und Rechtstatsachenforschung*; Bd. 6). Bibliogr.: S. 143–147.

IN 387174 316R36

941. **Rehbinder, M.** Eugen Ehrlich als Rechtslehrer. В *Проблеми філософії права.* Київ ; Чернівці : Рута, 2005. Т. 3, № 1/2. С. 140–146. [Rehbinder, M. Eugen Ehrlich als Rechtslehrer. In *Problems of the philosophy of law.* Kyiv ; Czernowitz : Ruta, 2005. Volume 3, Nr. 1/2. pp. 140–146.]

B 70701 34П781

942. **Rehbinder, Manfred.** "Eugen Ehrlich, dem Begründer der deutschen Rechtssoziologie, zum 100. Geburtstag." *Juristenzeitung.* 1962. Bd. 17. S. 613–614.

943. **Rehbinder, Manfred.** Eugen Ehrlichs Plädoyer für ein soziales Vertragsrecht. In *Aktuelle Aspekte des Schuld- und Sachenrechts : Festschrift für Heinz Rey zum 60. Geburtstag*, hrsg. von Heinrich Honsell, Wolfgang Portmann, Roger Zäch, und Dieter Zobl. Zürich : Schulthess Verl., 2003. S. 279–283.

944. **Rehbinder, M.** Eugen Ehrlichs Seminar für Lebendes Recht : eine Einrichtung für die Weiterbildung von Rechtspraktikern. В *Проблеми філософії права.* Київ ; Чернівці : Рута, 2005. Т. 3, № 1/2. С. 135–139. [Rehbinder, M. Eugen Ehrlichs Seminar für Lebendes Recht : eine Einrichtung für die Weiterbildung von Rechtspraktikern. In *Problems of the philosophy of law.* Kyiv ; Czernowitz : Ruta, 2005. Volume 3, Nr. 1/2. pp. 135–139.]

B 70701 34П781

945. **Rehbinder, Manfred.** "Die Grundlegung der Rechtssoziologie durch Eugen Ehrlich." *Kölner Zeitschrift für Sociologie und Socialpsychologie.* 1963. Jg. 15. S. 338–353.

946. **Rehbinder, Manfred.** "Internationales Privatrecht als Weltrecht. Das Plädoyer des Rechtssoziologen Eugen Ehrlich für die Lehre von Ernst Zitelmann." *Milletlerarası Hukuk ve Milletlerarası Özel Hukuk Bülteni.* 2003. Yıl 23, Sayi 1/2. S. 619–641.

947. **Rehbinder, M.** Neues über Leben und Werk von Eugen Ehrlich. In *Recht und Gesellschaft: Festschrift für Helmut Schelsky zum 65. Geburtstag*, hrsg. von Friedrich Kaulbach, und Werner Krawietz. Berlin : Duncker und Humblot, 1978. S. 403–418.

948. **Rehbinder, M.** Der Pluralismus des Rechts im Zeitalter der Globasierung. Zum Rechtsbegriff in der Rechtssoziologie. В *Проблеми філософії права.* Київ ; Чернівці : Рута, 2005. Т. 3, № 1/2. С. 227–232. [Rehbinder, M. Der Pluralismus des Rechts im Zeitalter der Globasierung. Zum Rechtsbegriff in der Rechtssoziologie. In *Problems of the philosophy of law.* Kyiv ; Czernowitz : Ruta, 2005. Volume 3, Nr. 1/2. pp. 227–232.]

E. Ehrlich. – pp. 227–229.

B 70701 34П781

949. **Rehbinder, Manfred.** "Die politischen Schriften des Rechtssoziologen Eugen Ehrlich auf dem Hintergrund seines bewegten Lebens." *Anuarul Institutului de Istorie "George Bariţiu" din Cluj-Napoca. Series Historica.* 2007. T. 46. P. 269–271.

950. **Rehbinder, Manfred.** Die rechts- und staatswissenschaftliche Fakultät der Franz-Josephs-Universität in Czernowitz. Ihr Beitrag zur Erforschung des Rechts in einer multikulturellen Gesellschaft. In *Festschrift für Hans Stoll zum 75. Geburtstag,* hrsg. von Gerhard Hohloch, Rainer Frank, und Peter Schlechtriem. Tübingen : Mohr Siebeck, 2001. S. 327–344 ; *Kaindl-Archiv.* 2001. Heft 46. S. 51–66 ; *Anuarul Institutului de Istorie "George Bariţiu" din Cluj-Napoca. Series Historica.* 2008. T. 47. P. 199–217.

951. **Rehbinder, Manfred.** *Rechtssoziologie.* 4., neu bearb. Aufl. München : C. H. Beck, 2000. IX, 261 S. *(Juristische Kurz-Lehrbücher).*

E. Ehrlich. – pp. 2, 16, 31, 46, 49–51, 71, 80–81, 83–84, 87–89, 117, 141–142, 161, 220.

IN387173316R36

952. **Rehbinder, Manfred.** *Rechtssoziologie : ein Studienbuch.* 8., neu bearb. Aufl. München : C. H. Beck, 2014. XIV, 222 S. : Ill., graph. Darst. *(Juristische Kurz-Lehrbücher).*

E. Ehrlich. – S. V–VIII, IX, XI, 1–2, 13, 26, 39, 42–43, 45, 59–60, 67–68, 69–70, 73–74, 98, 118–119, 135, 184, 199, 204.

953. **Rehbinder, Manfred.** Richterliche Rechtsfortbildung in der Sicht von Eugen Ehrlich. In Rehbinder, Manfred. *Abhandlungen zur Rechtssoziologie,* ausgew. und eingel. von Thomas Würtenberger. Berlin : Duncker und Humblot, 1995. S. 191–202. (*Schriftenreihe zur Rechtssoziologie und Rechtstatsachenforschung*; Bd. 77).

954. **Rektorsinauguration.** Czernowitz, den 4. Dezember. *Bukowiner Nachrichten.* 1906. 5. Dez. (Nr. 5437, Jg. 19). S. 3–4.

On the procedure for the solemn inauguration of the Rector of Czernowitz University Professor Dr. Eugen Ehrlich for the academic year 1906/1907 and his inaugural address

"Die Tatsachen des Gewohnheitsrechts" ["Facts of Customary Law"].

IN 2036 90J6

955. **Rektorsinstallation** an der k. k. Franz Josephs-Universität. *Czernowitzer Zeitung.* 1906. 4. Dez. (Nr. 277, Jg. 41). S. 3–5.

Information about the procedure of the inauguration ceremony of the Rector of Czernowitz University Professor Dr. Eugen Ehrlich for the academic year 1906/1907 and his inaugural address on the subject of "Die Tatsachen des Gewohnheitsrechts" ["Facts of Customary Law"].

IN 1941 90A1

956. **Rektorsinstallation** an der k. k. Franz Josephs-Universität. *Ibidem.* 1913. 3. Dez. (Nr. 278, Jg. 48). S. 2–4.

On the procedure for the solemn inauguration of the Rector of Czernowitz University for the current academic year, with the report by the Vice-Rector Professor Dr. Kaindl in which, among other important events, the participation of the representatives of Czernowitz University Professors Dr. Eugene Ehrlich and Dr. Otto von Dungern in the International Congress of Historic Sciences held in London from the 3rd to the 9th of April 1913 is mentioned – p. 3.

IN 1955 90A1

957. **Rheinstein, Max.** "Sociology of Law. Apropos Moll's Translation of Eugen Ehrlich's Grundlegung der Soziologie des Rechts." *The International Journal of Ethics.* 1938. Vol. 48, Nr. 2 (Jan.). P. 232–239.

958. **Riebschlager, Klaus.** *Die Freirechtsbewegung: zur Entwicklung einer soziologischen Rechtsschule.* Berlin: Duncker & Humblot, 1968. 124 S. (*Schriftenreihe des Instituts für Rechtssoziologie und Rechtstatsachenforschung der Freien Universität Berlin,* hrsg. Ernst E. Hirsch ; Bd. 11).

Information about Eugen Ehrlich as a founder of the sociological school of law – pp. 33–35.

959. **Röhl, Klaus F.** Die Begründung der Rechtssoziologie durch Eugen Ehrlich. In Röhl, Klaus F. *Rechtssoziologie : ein Lehrbuch.* Köln ; Berlin ; Bonn ; München : Heymann, [1987]. S. 27–33.

960. **Röhl, Klaus F.,** und Stefan Machura. "100 Jahre Rechtssoziologie: Eugen Ehrlichs Rechtspluralismus heute." *Juristen Zeitung.* 2013. Dez. (Nr. 23, Vol. 68). S. 1117–1128.

961. **Röschmann-Hörburg, Julius v.** Bericht über das Studienjahr 1896/1897, erstattet am 4. October 1897 von dem abtretenden Universitätsrector. In *Die feierliche Inauguration des Rectors der k. k. Franz-Josephs-Universität in Czernowitz für das Studienjahr*

1897/1898 am 4. October 1897. Czernowitz: Selbstverl. der k. k. Universität, 1898. S. 3–10.

Appointment of the successor to Professor of Czernowitz University Ernst Hruza – Professor of Roman law Dr. Ehrlich – p. 5.

IN 193487 90K126

962. **Rottleuthner, Hubert.** Drei Rechtssoziologien: Eugen Ehrlich, Hugo Sinzheimer, Max Weber. In *Historische Soziologie der Rechtswissenschaft,* hrsg. Erk Volkmar Heyen. Frankfurt am Main: Vittorio Klostermann, 1986. S. 227–252.

Information about the life the work of Eugen Ehrlich in the publication.

963. **Salagean, Emil.** Leben und Werk von Eugen Ehrlich und Manfred Rehbinder. In *Recht und Psychologie: gelebtes Recht als Objekt qualitativer und quantitativer Betrachtung.* Hrsg. von Raimund Jakob, Martin Usteri, und Rober Weimar. Bern; Berlin; Bruxelles; Frankfurt am Main; New York; Oxford; Wien: Peter Lang, 2006. S. 73–96. Bibliogr.: S. 95–96.

964. **Sinzheimer, Hugo.** *Jüdische Klassiker der deutschen Rechtswissenschaft.* Amsterdam: Menno Hertzberger & Co., 1938. 312 S.

Information about Eugen Ehrlich as one of the Jewish representative of the German science of law – pp. 231–255.

965. **Socaciu, Pantelimon.** *Arboroasa: file din cronica vieţii studenţeşti cernăuţene,* ed. îngr., studiu introd., note şi coment. de Marian Olaru. Rădăuţi: Septentrion, 2009. 336, [18] p.: 40 p. il. (*Colecţia "Hiperion", C. N. "Eudoxiu Hurmuzachi".* Rădăuţi; [Vol.] 1). Bibliogr.: p. 330–333.

Information about Professor Eugen Ehrlich in the publication – pp. 52, 215.

IN 393479 378S70

966. **Sojuz-Ball.** *CzernowitzerTagblatt.* 1911. 7. Febr. (Nr. 2389, Jg. 9). S. 3.

About the Ball of the Rusyn Academic Society "Union" ("Союз"), held in the premises of the German House with the participation of University Professor Dr. Ehrlich including information about his dancing with the wife of Professor Zelinka among other 150 couples participating in the dance of "Patronessen-Quadrill".

IN 1976 90A45

967. **Spiegel, Ludwig.** "Jurisprudenz und Sozialwissenschaft." *Zeitschrift für das Privat- und öffentliche Recht der Gegenwart.* 1909. Bd. 36. S. 1–30.

Note about Professor Eugen Ehrlich in the publication – pp. 8–9, 30.

IN 23066 16F1

968. **Staatsbeamtentag** in Czernowitz. *Bukowiner Beamten-Zeitung.* 1906. 28. Okt. (Nr. 18, Jg. 1). S. 3–7.

About the report on the civil servants in Czernowitz requiring the assistance due to the high cost. The summary of the speech of the Rector University Professor Dr. Ehrlich dedicated to this problem – p. 5.

IN 2164 90A60

969. **Stone, Julius.** *Social Dimensions of Law and Justice.* Stanford : Stanford Univ. Press ; Bombay : N. M. Tripathi ; Sydney : Maitland Publ. ; London : Stevens & Sons Ltd., 1966. XXXV, 933 p.

E. Ehrlich. – pp. 28, 33, 36, 41, 44, 46–47, 52,65, 96, 98, 637.

970. **Die Studentenbewegung.** *Bukowinaer Post.* 1912. 7. Apr. (Nr. 2828, Jg. 19). S. 4–5.

Information about the Student Movement for the Equality of Jews which entered into the active period because of the Decisions of the Academic Senate of Czernowitz University on "Emunah" and "Zephirah", including the informarion about the dispute between the Jewish student speakers and the Dean Professor Ehrlich at the controversial meeting.

IN 2066 90J26

971. **Studenţi mea** cernăuţeană contrad-lor Ehrlich şi Last. *Glasul Bucovinei.* 1921. 15 mar. (Nr. 656, An. 4). p. 2. Semnătură : G. C.

Information about protests of Czernowitz University students against professors Ehrlich and Last.

IN 732 90A89

972. **Ţabrea, Ilie.** "Un protest al studenţi mii române." *Glasul Bucovinei.* 1921. 2 noem. (Nr. 837, An. 4). p. 1.

Information about protests of Czernowitz University students against professors Ehrlich and Last.

IN 733 90A89

973. **Tagesbericht.** Franz-Josefs-Universität. *Bukowinaer Journal.* 1901. 24. Sept. (Nr. 1, Jg. 1). S. 5.

Enrollment of the Dean of the Faculty of Law and Public Administration Professor Dr. Eugen Ehrlich to the composition of the Academic Senate of Czernowitz University in the academic year 1901/1902.

IN 355888 90J56

974. **Tagesbericht.** Aug. Wilhelm Ritter von Hartel... *Bukowiner Nachrichten.* 1907. 16. Jänner (Nr. 5469, Jg. 20). S. 3–4.

Participation of Professor Dr. Eugen Ehrlich in the Czernowitz University delegation at the funeral of Honorary Doctor of Czernowitz University Dr. Hartel in Vienna.

IN 2037 90J6

975. **Tageschronik.** Abschiedsdiner für Divisionär Generalmajor von Hornik. *Czernowitzer Zeitung.* 1907. 5. Febr. (Nr. 29, Jg. 42). S. 3.

Participation of University Professor Dr. Ehrlich in a farewell dinner of Divisional General Major von Hornik on the 3rd of February 1907.

IN 1942 90A1

976. **Tageschronik.** Czernowitz, 11. Juli. 80. Geburstag. *Ibidem.* 1911. 11. Juli (Nr. 156, Jg. 46). S. 3.

Greetings from the Faculty of Law and Public Administration of Czernowitz University to Professor of Law Dr. Hermann Fitting at the University of Halle on the occasion of his 80th birthday signed by the collegium of the Faculty of Law professors including Dr. Eugen Ehrlich.

IN 1951 90A1

977. **Tageschronik.** Czernowitz, 25. Juni. Die akademische Korps "Alemannia"... *Bukowinaer Volks-Zeitung.* 1907. 26. Juni (Nr. 92, Jg. 1). S. 2–3.

About the Rector of Czernowitz University Professor Dr. Ehrlich and the Society "Alemannia".

IN 2166 90A64

978. **Tageschronik.** Czernowitz, 26. Juni. Der akademische Senat unserer Universität... *Ibidem.* 1907. 27. Juni (Nr. 93, Jg. 1). S. 3.

Composition of the Academic Senate for the academic year 1907/1908. Professor Dr. Eugen Ehrlich – the Vice-Rector of Czernowitz University.

IN 2166 90A64

979. **Tageschronik.** Czernowitz, 19. März. Akademische Studienreise. *Czernowitzer Zeitung.* 1912. 19. März (Nr. 64, Jg. 47). S. 3.

Participation of the Dean of the Faculty of Law Professor Dr. Ehrlich in the students' meeting on the 17th of March 1912.

IN 1952 90A1

980. **Tageschronik.** Akademischer Senat. *Ibidem.* 1907. 27. Juni (Nr. 145, Jg. 42). S. 3.

Composition of the Academic Senate for the academic year 1907/1908. Professor Dr. Eugen Ehrlich – the Vice-Rector of Czernowitz University.

IN 1942 90A1

981. **Tageschronik.** Czernowitz, 27. Juni. Akademischer Senat. *Ibidem.* 1909. 22. Juni (Nr. 144, Jg. 44). S. 4.

Composition of the Academic Senate of Czernowitz University for the academic year 1909/1910. Dr. Eugen Ehrlich – the Vice-Dean of the Faculty of Law and Public Administration.

IN 1946 90A1

982. **Tageschronik.** Czernowitz, 25. Juni. Akademischer Senat. *Ibidem.* 1911. 25. Juni (Nr. 144, Jg. 46). S. 3.

Composition of the Academic Senate of Czernowitz University for the academic year 1911/1912. Professor Dr. Eugen Ehrlich – the Dean of the Faculty of Law and Public Administration.

IN 1950 90A1

983. **Tageschronik.** Akademisches Korps "Alemannia". *Ibidem.* 1903. 15. Nov. (Nr. 263, Jg. 38). S. 4.

Participation of University Professor Dr. Ehrlich, among other guests, in the event of the Academic Society "Alemannia" held on the 7th of November 1903.

IN 1935 90A1

984. **Tageschronik.** Allerhöchstes Namensfest. *Ibidem.* 1906. 5. Okt. (Nr. 227, Jg. 41). S. 3.

Participation of the University Rector Professor Dr. Ehrlich, together with academic officials of Czernowitz University, in the worship of His Majesty the Emperor for students of primary and secondary schools in all churches.

IN 1941 90A1

985. **Tageschronik.** Czernowitz, 21. November. Auerkennung der jüd. Nationalität. *Bukowinaer Volks-Zeitung.* 1907. 22. Nov. (Nr. 216, Jg. 1). S. 2.

Professor Dr. Ehrlich about the recognition of Jews at Czernowitz University.

IN 2166 90A64

986. **Tageschronik.** Ausstellung alter Gold- und Silberschmiedearbeiten. *Czernowitzer Zeitung.* 1907. 12. Febr. (Nr. 35, Jg. 42). S. 4.

Information about the University Rector Professor Dr. Ehrlich visiting the exhibition of old golden and silver jewelry organized by the Czernowitz Crafts Museum.

IN 1942 90A1

987. **Tageschronik.** Czernowitz, 20. September. Auszeichnung. *Bukowinaer Volks-Zeitung.* 1907. 21. Sept. (Nr. 164, Jg. 1). S. 2.

The Rector of Czernowitz University Professor Dr. Eugen Ehrlich awarded the Commander's Cross of the Greek Order of the Saviour.

IN 2166 90A64

988. **Tageschronik.** Czernowitz, 16. Dezember. Auszeichnung. *Ibidem.* 1907. 17. Dez. (Nr. 237, Jg. 1). S. 2.

The Rector of Czernowitz University Professor Dr. Eugen Ehrlich awarded the Commander's Cross of the Greek Order of the Saviour.

IN 2166 90A64

989. **Tageschronik.** Ball des akademischen Vereines "Junimea". *Czernowitzer Zeitung.* 1907. 10. Febr. (Nr. 34, Jg. 42). S. 4.

Participation of the Rector of Czernowitz University Professor Dr. Ehrlich in the ball of the Academic Society "Junimea".

IN 1942 90A1

990. **Tageschronik.** Der Ball zu Gunsten des Wärmestuben- und katholischen Wohltätigkeitsvereines. *Ibidem.* 1907. 5. Febr. (Nr. 29, Jg. 42). S. 3.

Participation of the Rector of Czernowitz University Dr. Ehrlich in the charity ball held on the 2nd of February 1907.

IN 1942 90A1

991. **Tageschronik.** Czernowitz, 23. Dezember. Czernowitzer Herrenfecht-Société. *Ibidem.* 1910. 23. Dez. (Nr. 292, Jg. 45). S. 2.

In the election of the 19th of December 1910 University Professor Dr. Ehrlich elected the Head of the Czernowitz Society of Fencing.

IN 1949 90A1

992. **Tageschronik.** Czernowitz, 29. Jänner. Czernowitzer Herrenfecht-Société. *Ibidem.* 1911. 29. Jänner (Nr. 24, Jg. 46). S. 3.

About University Professor Dr. Ehrlich and the Society of Fencing.

IN 1950 90A1

993. **Tageschronik.** Czernowitz, 12. Dezember. Czernowitzer Herrenfecht-Société. *Ibidem.* 1911. 12. Dez. (Nr. 283, Jg. 46). S. 2.

About University Professor Dr. Ehrlich and the Czernowitz Society of Fencing.

IN 1951 90A1

994. **Tageschronik.** Dejeuner beim Herrn Landespräsidenten. *Ibidem.* 1906. 14. Okt.(Nr. 235, Jg. 41). S. 4.

Participation of the Rector Professor Dr. Ehrlich in the Sunday lunch event organized by the Regional President Dr. Octavian von Bleyleben on 12th of October 1906.

IN 1941 90A1

995. **Tageschronik.** Denkmalkomitee. *Ibidem.* 1907. 16. März (Nr. 63, Jg. 42). S. 3.

On the inaugural meeting of the Committee for the installation of the monument for Professor Johann von Mikulicz-Radecki in his birthplace of Czernowitz (based on the initiative of the Rector of the local University Professor Dr. Eugen Ehrlich). The text of speech of Dr. Ehrlich presented at the meeting is also provided.

IN 1942 90A1

996. **Tageschronik.** Diner beim Herrn k. k. Landespräsidenten. *Ibidem.* 1907. 8. Okt. (Nr. 231, Jg. 42). S. 3.

Participation of the Rector Dr. Ehrlich in the Sunday lunch event organized by the Regional President Dr. Octavian von Bleyleben.

IN 1943 90A1

997. **Tageschronik.** Czernowitz, 14. März. Ehrung für den verstorbenen Professor Mikulicz. *Bukowinaer Volks-Zeitung.* 1907. 15. März (Nr. 11, Jg. 1). S. 2–3.

On the inaugural meeting of the Committee for the installation of the monument for Professor Johann von Mikulicz-Radecki in his birth place of Czernowitz (based on the initiative of the Rector of the local University Professor Dr. Eugen Ehrlich who was elected the Chairman of the Committee).

IN 2166 90A64

998. **Tageschronik.** Czernowitz, 31. Mai. Exkursion. *Czernowitzer Zeitung.* 1912. 31. Mai (Nr. 123, Jg. 47). S. 3.

About the excursion for the members of the seminar on living law and the members of the Social Scientific Academic Society led by University Professors Ehrlich, Last and Dungern.

IN 1952 90A1

999. **Tageschronik.** Fremder Orden. *Ibidem.* 1907. 20. Sept. (Nr. 216, Jg. 42). S. 3.

The Rector of Czernowitz University Professor Dr. Eugen Ehrlich awarded the Commander's Cross of the Greek Order of the Saviour.

IN 1943 90A1

1000. **Tageschronik.** Frohnleichnamsfeier. *Ibidem.* 1907. 1. Juni (Nr. 123, Jg. 42). S. 2–3.

Participation of the University Rector Dr. Ehrlich in the religious celebration Corpus Christi.

IN 1942 90A1

1001. **Tageschronik.** 25jähriges Doktorjubiläum. *Ibidem.* 1906. 25. Febr. (Nr. 45, Jg. 41). S. 3.

Participation of University Professor Dr. Ehrlich in the solemn commemoration of the 25th anniversary of awarding the degree of doctor to Professor Emilian Wojucki – the first Doctor of Orthodox Theology.

IN 1940 90A1

1002. **Tageschronik.** Czernowitz, 31. März. 50jähriges Doktorjubiläum. *Ibidem.* 1912. 31. März (Nr. 74, Jg. 47). S. 3.

Participation of the Dean of the Faculty of Law and Public Administration of Franz Joseph University Professor Dr. Ehrlich in the celebration of the 50th anniversary of the promotion of the director of "Bukowinaer Sparkasse" Dr. Friedrich von Kleinwächter to the position of doctor of law at Prague University.

IN 1952 90A1

1003. **Tageschronik.** Czernowitz, 16. Dezember. Für die durch die Hochwasserkatastrophe Geschädigten... *Ibidem.* 1911. 16. Dez. (Nr. 287, Jg. 46). S. 3.

Information about the amount of collected donations for the flood victims including the donation of 10 crowns by University Professor Dr. Eugen Ehrlich.

IN 1951 90A1

1004. **Tageschronik.** Czernowitz, 16. Jänner. Generalversammlung der "Czernowitzer Herrenfecht-Société". *Ibidem.* 1912. 16. Jänner (Nr. 11, Jg. 47). S. 3.

University Professor Dr. Ehrlich – the Head of the Czernowitz Society of Fencing.

IN 1952 90A1

1005. **Tageschronik.** Gratulationen. *Ibidem.* 1908. 1. Febr. (Nr. 26, Jg. 43). S. 4.

About the welcome of the Provincial President and his Deputy by the elite of the region including Professor Dr. Ehrlich.

IN 1944 90A1

1006. **Tageschronik.** Czernowitz, 31. Mai. Gratulationsempfang bei Sr. Exzellenz dem Herrn Landespräsidenten Dr. Freiherrn v. Bleyleben. *Ibidem.* 1911. 31. Mai (Nr. 124, Jg. 46). S. 3.

About the welcome of the Provincial President Dr. von Bleyleben and his Deputy by the elite of the region including Professor Dr. Ehrlich.

IN 1950 90A1

1007. **Tageschronik.** Czernowitz, 22. Juni. Die Gründung einer Ortsgruppe... *Bukowinaer Volks-Zeitung.* 1907. 23. Juni (Nr. 90, Jg. 1). S. 4.

About Professor Dr. Ehrlich and the establishment of the local branch of the Society for the Fight against Sexually Transmitted Deseases.

IN 2166 90A64

1008. **Tageschronik.** Czernowitz, 12. Dezember. Im sozialwissenschaftlich- akademischen Vereine... *Czernowitzer Zeitung.* 1909. 12. Dez. (Nr. 283, Jg. 44). S. 4.

About the lecture by Professor Dr. Ehrlich for the Social-Scientific Academic Society on the topic of "Socialpolitik in der Bukowina" ["Social Policy in Bukovina"].

IN 1947 90A1

1009. **Tages-Chronik.** Czernowitz, 20. März. Historikerkongress in Rom. *Czernowitzer Tagblatt.* 1903. 21. März (Nr. 45, Jg. 1). S. 3.

Information about University Professor Dr. Ehrlich representing Czernowitz at the Congress of Historians in Rome on the 2nd of April 1903.

IN 1960 90A45

1010. **Tages-Chronik.** Czernowitz, 26. März. Historiker-Kongress in Rom. *Ibidem.* 1903. 27. März (Nr. 49, Jg. 1). S. 2.

Information about University Professor Dr. Ehrlich representing Czernowitz at the Congress of Historians in Rome.

IN 1960 90A45

1011. **Tages-Chronik.** Czernowitz, 6. März. Juristische Gesellschaft in Wien. *Ibidem.* 1903. 7. März (Nr. 33, Jg. 1). S. 2.

About the lecture by Czernowitz University Professor Dr. E. Ehrlich provided to the Society of Austrian Judges in Vienna on the 4th of March 1903 on the topic of "Freie

Rechtsfindung und freie Rechtswissenschaft" ["Free Finding of the Law and Free Science of Law"].

IN 1960 90A45

1012. **Tageschronik.** Czernowitz, 5. März. Juristisch-staatswissenschaftliche Gesellschaft. *Bukowinaer Volks-Zeitung.* 1907. 6. März (Nr. 3, Jg. 1). S. 2.

Information about the report of University Professor Dr. Eugen Ehrlich on "Zur Lehre von den juristischen Personen" ("The Doctrine of Legal Persons") to be provided in the hall of the Provincial Court (Civil Law Chamber) on the 8th of March 1907.

IN 2166 90A64

1013. **Tageschronik.** Juristisch-staatswissenschaftliche Gesellschaft. *Czernowitzer Zeitung.* 1903. 10. Febr. (Nr. 32, Jg. 38). S. 5.

Information about the lecture on "Freie Rechtsfindung und freie Rechtswissenschaft" ["Free Finding of the Law and Free Science of Law"] to be delivered by Professor Dr. Ehrlich in the Town Hall on the 11th of February 1903.

IN 1934 90A1

1014. **Tageschronik.** Die juristisch-staatswissenschaftliche Gesellschaft. *Ibidem.* 1904. 26. Jänner (Nr. 20, Jg. 39). S. 3.

Information about the 4th annual meeting of the members of Juridical-Political Scientific Society on the 20th of January 1904 and notification of the lecture and discussion by Professor Dr. Ehrlich on the topic of "Freie Rechtsfindung und freie Rechtswissenschaft" ["Free Finding of the Law and Free Science of Law"].

IN 1936 90A1

1015. **Tageschronik.** Juristisch-staatswissenschaftliche Gesellschaft. *Ibidem.* 1904. 23. Febr. (Nr. 43, Jg. 39). S. 4.

Information about the lecture by Professor Dr. Eugen Ehrlich entitled "Zittelmann, internationales Privatrecht" ["Zittelmann, International Law"], to be held in the Town Hall on the 24th of February 1904.

IN 1936 90A1

1016. **Tageschronik.** Juristisch-staatswissenschaftliche Gesellschaft. *Ibidem.* 1906. 28. Jänner (Nr. 22, Jg. 41). S. 5.

Information of the Juridical-Political Scientific Society about the lecture by University Professor Dr. Eugen Ehrlich on the reform of contract law that will be delivered on the 31st of January 1906.

IN 1940 90A1

1017. **Tageschronik.** Juristisch-staatswissenschaftliche Gesellschaft. *Ibidem.* 1906. 13. Febr. (Nr. 34, Jg. 41). S. 4.

Information about the commemorative speech by University Professor Dr. Eugen Ehrlich for the late Honorary Professor of the University of Vienna Dr. Anton Menger on the 14th of February 1906 at 7 pm.

IN 1940 90A1

1018. **Tageschronik.** Juristisch-staatswissenschaftliche Gesellschaft. *Ibidem.* 1907. 5. März (Nr. 53, Jg. 42). S. 3.

Information about the report of University Professor Dr. Eugen Ehrlich on "Zur Lehre von den juristischen Personen" ["The Doctrine of Legal Persons"] to be provided in the hall of the Privincial Court (Civil Law Chamber) on the 8th of March 1907.

IN 1942 90A1

1019. **Tageschronik.** Juristisch-staatswissenschaftliche Gesellschaft. *Ibidem.* 1908. 18. Nov. (Nr. 266, Jg. 43). S. 4.

Information about the report of University Professor Dr. Eugen Ehrlich on "Englische Rechtspflege" ["English Administration of Justice"] to be provided in the Civil Law Chamber on the 21st of November 1908.

IN 1945 90A1

1020. **Tageschronik.** Czernowitz, 28. Mai. Juristisch-staatswissenschaftliche Gesellschaft. *Ibidem.* 1913. 28. Mai (Nr. 120, Jg. 48). S. 4.

Information about the commemorative speech by University Professor Dr. Ehrlich to be delivered in the House of Civil Justice on the 30th of May 1913.

IN 1954 90A1

1021. **Tageschronik.** Kaiser Franz Joseph-Knabeninternat. *Ibidem.* 1906. 5. Okt. (Nr. 227, Jg. 41). S. 3–4.

Participation of the Rector Professor Dr. Ehrlich in the inauguration of the Romanian Boarding School for boys which was established with the help of charity activities of the Society of Romanian Culture and Literature.

IN 1941 90A1

1022. **Tageschronik.** Kaiser Franz Joseph Universitäts-Studentenheim. *Ibidem.* 1905. 22. Okt. (Nr. 242, Jg. 40). S. 3.

On the appointment of University Associate Professors Dr. Alfred von Halban and Dr. Eugen Ehrlich members of the State Judicial Examination Board in Czernowitz.

IN 1939 90A1

1023. **Tageschronik.** K. k. akademischer Senat. *Ibidem.* 1903. 27. Sept. (Nr. 222, Jg. 38). S. 4.

Composition of the Academic Senate of Czernowitz University for the current academic year. Dr. Eugen Ehrlich – Vice-Dean of the Faculty of Law and Public Administration.

IN 1935 90A1

1024. **Tageschronik.** K. k. Franz Josephs-Universität. *Ibidem.* 1903. 16. Juli (Nr. 161, Jg. 38). S. 4.

Information about vacations of the Rector Professor Dr. Scharizer, the Dean Professor Dr. Adler, and the Vice-Dean Professor Dr. Ehrlich. Management of the rectorate is taken by the Vice-Rector Professor Dr. Wojucki, and management of the dean's office of the Faculty of Law and Public Administration is taken by the Advisor Professor Dr. Kleinwächter.

IN 1935 90A1

1025. **Tageschronik.** K. k. Franz Josephs-Universität. *Ibidem.* 1906. 24. Juni (Nr. 143, Jg. 41). S. 3–4.

The unanimous election of the Professor of Roman law Dr. Eugen Erhlich for the Rector of Czernowitz University for the academic year 1906/1907 on the 23rd of June 1906. The CV of the new Rector is provided.

IN 1940 90A1

1026. **Tageschronik.** K. k. Franz Josephs-Universität. *Ibidem.* 1906. 10. Okt. (Nr. 231, Jg. 41). S. 3.

Information about the 2nd of December 1906, the day of the anniversary of the government of the Emperor Franz Joseph I, when the solemn inauguration of the Rector for the academic year 1906/1907 will be held at 11 am with the Rector Professor Dr. Eugen Ehrlich's inaugural address on the subject of "Die Tatsachendes Gewohnheitsrechts" ("Facts of Customary Law").

IN 1941 90A1

1027. **Tageschronik.** K. k. Franz Josephs-Universität. *Ibidem.* 1906. 24. Nov. (Nr. 269, Jg. 41). S. 3.

Information about the 2nd of December 1906, the day of the anniversary of the government of the Emperor Franz Joseph I, when the solemn inauguration of the Rector for the academic year 1906/1907 will be held at 11 am with the Rector Professor Dr. Eugen Ehrlich's inaugural address on the subject of "Die Tatsachendes Gewohnheitsrechts" ("Facts of Customary Law").

IN 1941 90A1

1028. **Tageschronik.** K. k. Franz Josephs-Universität. *Ibidem.* 1906. 14. Dez. (Nr. 285, Jg. 41). S. 4.

Participation of the Rector of Czernowitz University Professor Dr. Eugen Ehrlich, together with the deans, in the Matriculation ceremony of the new students of the University on the 13th of December 1906. Information about the number of students at each of the three faculties is also provided.

IN 1941 90A1

1029. **Tageschronik.** K. k. Franz Josephs-Universität. *Ibidem.* 1907. 1. Febr. (Nr. 27, Jg. 42). S. 4.

Information that the Academic Senate entrusted the Vice-Rector Professor Dr. Sigmund Herzberg-Fränkel to represent Czernowitz University in the Council of Curators of Regional Museums and the Rector Professor Dr. Eugen Ehrlich to represent Czernowitz University in the Council of Curators of Crafts Museum in Bukovina.

IN 1942 90A1

1030. **Tageschronik.** K. k. Franz Josephs-Universität. *Ibidem.* 1907. 27. Juni (Nr. 145, Jg. 42). S. 3.

Information about the election of the rector for the upcoming academic year on the 26th of June 1907 by the representatives of all faculties supervised by the Rector Professor Dr. Ehrlich. Professor of Theology Dr. Basil Gaina acquired the majority of votes in the first round.

IN 1942 90A1

1031. **Tageschronik.** K. k. Franz Josephs-Universität. Ibidem. 1907. 12. Juli (Nr. 157, Jg. 42). S. 3.

Information about the decision of the Academic Senate of Czernowitz University related to the 300th anniversary of the University of Hessen to be held in Hessen from the 31st of July 1907 to the 3rd of August 1907. As part of the celebration events the Rector Professor Dr. Eugen Ehrlich will represent Czernowitz University at the second meeting of the rectors of German universities.

IN 1943 90A1

1032. **Tageschronik.** K. k. Franz Josephs-Universität. *Ibidem.* 1907. 22. Sept. (Nr. 218, Jg. 42). S. 3.

Information related to the death of the Rector Elect Dr. Basil Gaina: until the new elections, the acting Rector Professor Dr. Eugen Ehrlich and the acting Vice-Rector Professor Dr. Sigmund Herzberg-Fränkel, remain in their positions with the possibility of re-election to their positions.

IN 1943 90A1

1033. **Tageschronik.** K. k. Franz Josephs-Universität. *Ibidem.* 1907. 20. Nov. (Nr. 267, Jg. 42). S. 2.

Information about the report on the previous academic year by the Vice-Rector of Czernowitz University Professor Dr. Eugen Ehrlich on the occasion of the inauguration of the Rector Dr. Eugen Kozak for the academic year 1907/1908.

IN 1943 90A1

1034. **Tageschronik.** K. k. Franz Josephs-Universität. *Ibidem.* 1908. 25. Juni (Nr. 145, Jg. 43). S. 3.

Election of the Dean of the Faculty of Law and Public Administration of Czernowitz University for the academic year 1908/1909. Professor of Roman law Dr. Eugen Ehrlich elected the Dean.

IN 1944 90A1

1035. **Tageschronik.** K. k. Franz Josephs-Universität. *Ibidem.* 1908. 5. Juli (Nr. 153, Jg. 43). S. 3.

Composition of the Academic Senate of Czernowitz University for the academic year 1908/1909. Dr. Eugen Ehrlich – the Dean of the Faculty of Law and Public Administration.

IN 1945 90A1

1036. **Tageschronik.** K. k. Franz Josephs-Universität. *Ibidem.* 1908. 28. Juli (Nr. 172, Jg. 43). S. 2.

About the verification of the academic officials of Czernowitz University by the Decree of the Ministry of Cultus and Education of the 21st of July 1908 including the Dean of the Faculty of Law and Public Administration Professor Dr. Eugen Ehrlich.

IN 1945 90A1

1037. **Tageschronik.** Czernowitz, 9. Oktober. K. k. Franz Josephs-Universität. *Ibidem.* 1909. 9. Okt. (Nr. 230, Jg. 44). S. 2.

Information about the seminar conducted by Professor Dr. Eugen Ehrlich together with Professor Dr. Ferdinand Kogler for lawyers with higher education entitled (especially judges and advocates) entitled "On Living Law".

IN 1947 90A1

1038. **Tageschronik.** Czernowitz, 21. Juni. K. k. Franz Josephs-Universität. *Ibidem.* 1911. 21. Juni (Nr. 140, Jg. 46). S. 3.

Election of the Dean of the Faculty of Law and Public Administration of Czernowitz University for the academic year 1911/1913. Professor Dr. Eugen Ehrlich elected the Dean.

IN 1950 90A1

1039. **Tageschronik.** Czernowitz, 23. Juni. K. k. Franz Josephs-Universität. *Ibidem.* 1912. 23. Juni (Nr. 142, Jg. 47). S. 2–3.

Composition of the Academic Senate of Czernowitz University for the academic year 1912/1913. Dr. Eugen Ehrlich – the Vice-Dean of the Faculty of Law and Public Administration – p. 3.

IN 1952 90A1

1040. **Tageschronik.** Czernowitz, 13. Februar. Karnevalfest "Die Welt auf Reisen". *Bukowinaer Volks-Zeitung.* 1908. 14. Febr. (Nr. 284, Jg. 2). S. 3.

About the donations at the carnival "Die Welt auf Reisen", including the information about 20 crowns being donated by Professor Dr. Ehrlich.

IN 2167 90A64

1041. **Tageschronik.** Kongresse. *Czernowitzer Zeitung.* 1903. 25. März (Nr. 69, Jg. 38). S. 4.

Information about University Professor Dr. Ehrlich representing Czernowitz at the Congress of Historians in Rome from the 2nd to the 9th of April 1903.

IN 1934 90A1

1042. **Tageschronik.** Czernowitz, 17. Juni. Landeszentrale für Kinderschutzund Jugendfürsorge. *Ibidem.* 1911. 17. Juni (Nr. 137, Jg. 46). S. 3.

Participation of University Professor Dr. Ehrlich in the meeting of the Regional Centre for Child Protection.

IN 1950 90A1

1043. **Tageschronik.** Czernowitz, 31. Oktober. "Das lebende Recht". *Ibidem.* 1909. 31. Okt.(Nr. 249, Jg. 44). S. 5.

Information about the seminar on "Living Law" to be conducted by Professor Dr. Eugen Ehrlich and Professor Dr. Ferdinand Kogler for certified lawyers on the 28th of October 1909.

IN 1947 90A1

1044. **Tageschronik.** Czernowitz, 7. November. "Das lebende Recht". *Ibidem.* 1909. 7. Nov. (Nr. 254, Jg. 44). S. 4.

About the second session of the seminar on "Living Law" by Professors Dr. Ehrlich and Dr. Kogler.

IN 1947 90A1

1045. **Tageschronik.** Czernowitz, 9. November. "Das lebende Recht". *Ibidem.* 1909. 9. Nov. (Nr. 255, Jg. 44). S. 2.

About the excursion for the members of the seminar on living law led by Professor Dr. Ehrlich.

IN 1947 90A1

1046. **Tageschronik.** Czernowitz, 2. Februar. "Lebendes Recht". *Ibidem.* 1910. 2. Febr. (Nr. 26, Jg. 45). S. 3.

Information about Professors Dr. Ehrlich and Dr. Kogler resuming classes of the seminar on living law on Thursday for the first time after the Christmas break.

IN 1948 90A1

1047. **Tageschronik.** Die Neugestaltung des Vertragsrechtes. *Ibidem.* 1906. 10. Jänner (Nr. 6, Jg. 41). S. 3.

Information about the speech of Professor of Czernowitz University Dr. Eugen Ehrlich at the plenary session of Lower Austrian Commercial Society in Vienna on the 5th of January entitled "Die Neugestaltung des Vertragsrechtes" ("Restructuring Contract Law"). The summary of the speech is also provided.

IN 1940 90A1

1048. **Tageschronik.** "Ognisko"-Ball. *Ibidem.* 1907. 12. Febr. (Nr. 35, Jg. 42). S. 3–4.

Participation of the University Rector Dr. Ehrlich in the ball of the Polish Academic Society "Ognisko" on the 9th of February 1907.

IN 1942 90A1

1049. **Tageschronik.** Personalnachrichten. *Ibidem.* 1907. 14. Juli (Nr. 159, Jg. 42). S. 3.

Information about a long vacation of the Rector Dr. Eugen Ehrlich as of the 14th of July 1907, and about his trip to Vienna.

IN 1943 90A1

1050. **Tageschronik.** Promotion. *Ibidem.* 1904. 11. Febr.(Nr. 33, Jg. 39). S. 4.

Professor Dr. Ehrlich – promoter of the graduation ceremony of a new doctor of law at Czernowitz University – Felix Reik.

IN 1936 90A1

1051. **Tageschronik.** Promotion. *Ibidem.* 1904. 10. Juli (Nr. 156, Jg. 39). S. 5.

Professor Dr. Ehrlich – promoter of the Czernowitz University graduation ceremony of a new doctor of law Anton Josefowicz.

IN 1937 90A1

1052. **Tageschronik.** Promotion. *Ibidem.* 1904. 16. Dez.(Nr. 287, Jg. 39). S. 4.

Professor Dr. Ehrlich – promoter of the Czernowitz University graduation ceremony of a new doctor of law Leo Löwner.

IN 1937 90A1

1053. **Tageschronik.** Promotion. *Ibidem.* 1905. 18. Febr. (Nr. 40, Jg. 40). S. 5.

Professor Dr. Ehrlich – promoter of the Czernowitz University graduation ceremony of a new doctor of law Max Singer.

IN 1938 90A1

1054. **Tageschronik.** Promotion. *Ibidem.* 1905. 4. Nov. (Nr. 252, Jg. 40). S. 4.

Professor Dr. Ehrlich – promoter of the graduation ceremony of a new doctor of law at Czernowitz University Julius Brüll.

IN 1939 90A1

1055. **Tageschronik.** Promotion. *Ibidem.* 1908. 4. Apr. (Nr. 79, Jg. 43). S. 3.

Professor Dr. Ehrlich – promoter of the graduation ceremony of a new doctor of law at Czernowitz University Lazar Pomeranz.

IN 1944 90A1

1056. **Tageschronik.** Czernowitz, 13. Juli. Promotion. *Ibidem.* 1909. 13. Juli (Nr. 156, Jg. 44). S. 4.

Participation of the Dean Professor Dr. Ehrlich in the defense procedure of Ludwig Kleinwächter applying for the degree of doctor of law.

IN 1947 90A1

1057. **Tageschronik.** Czernowitz, 24. Oktober. Promotion. *Ibidem.* 1909. 24. Okt. (Nr. 243, Jg. 44). S. 4.

Professor Dr. Ehrlich – promoter of the Czernowitz University graduation ceremony of a new doctor of law Max Johann Tarden on the 22nd of October 1909.

IN 1947 90A1

1058. **Tageschronik.** Czernowitz, 17. April. Promotion. *Ibidem.* 1910. 17. Apr. (Nr. 87, Jg. 45). S. 3.

Professor Dr. Eugen Ehrlich – promoter of the Czernowitz University graduation ceremony of a new doctor of law Leopold Sekler on the 14th of April 1910.

IN 1948 90A1

1059. **Tageschronik.** Czernowitz, 24. Februar. Promotion. *Ibidem.* 1911. 24. Febr. (Nr. 45, Jg. 46). S. 2.

Professor Dr. Ehrlich – promoter of the Czernowitz University graduation ceremony of a new doctor of law Romuald von Szymonowitz on the 23rd of February 1911.

IN 1950 90A1

1060. **Tageschronik.** Promotionen. *Ibidem.* 1903. 1. Febr. (Nr. 26, Jg. 38). S. 4.

Professor Ehrlich – promoter of the Czernowitz University graduation ceremony of a new doctor of law Selig Horowitz.

IN 1934 90A1

1061. **Tageschronik.** Promotionen. *Ibidem.* 1903. 17. Okt. (Nr. 238, Jg. 38). S. 5.

Professor Dr. Ehrlich – promoter of the Czernowitz University graduation ceremony of a new doctor of law Edgar Bucksch.

IN 1935 90A1

1062. **Tageschronik.** Promotionen. *Ibidem.* 1905. 1. Juli (Nr. 148, Jg. 40). S. 5.

Professor Dr. Ehrlich – promoter of the Czernowitz University graduation ceremony of a new doctor of law Mordche Deligdisch on the 28th of June 1905.

IN 1939 90A1

1063. **Tageschronik.** Promotionen. *Ibidem.* 1908. 17. März (Nr. 64, Jg. 43). S. 4.

Professor Dr. Ehrlich – promoter of the Czernowitz University graduation ceremony of new doctors of law Meier Kinsbrunner, Moses Fischer and Norbert Sekler on the 17th of March 1908.

IN 1944 90A1

1064. **Tageschronik.** Czernowitz, 8. Dezember. Promotionen. *Ibidem.* 1909. 8. Dez. (Nr. 280, Jg. 44). S. 3.

Professor Dr. Ehrlich – promoter of the Czernowitz University graduation ceremony of a new doctor of law Rubin Lang on the 7th of December 1909.

IN 1947 90A1

1065. **Tageschronik.** Czernowitz, 19. Dezember. Promotionen. *Ibidem.* 1909. 19. Dez. (Nr. 289, Jg. 44). S. 3.

Professor Dr. Ehrlich – promoter of the Czernowitz University graduation ceremony of a new doctor of law Artur Füllenbaum.

IN 1947 90A1

1066. **Tageschronik.** Czernowitz, 11. März. Promotionen. *Ibidem.* 1910. 11. März (Nr. 57, Jg. 45). S. 4.

Professor Dr. Ehrlich – promoter of the Czernowitz University graduation ceremony of new doctors of law Ezechiel Pappaport on the 11th of March 1910 and cand. jur. Apollonarius Argasinski on the 10th of March 1910.

IN 1948 90A1

1067. **Tageschronik.** Czernowitz, 2. Juli. Promotionen. *Ibidem.* 1910. 2. Juli (Nr. 148, Jg. 45). S. 2.

Professor Dr. Ehrlich – promoter of the Czernowitz University graduation ceremony of new doctors of law Richard Poras, Julius Hruder and Moses Krässel on the 7th of July 1910.

IN 1949 90A1

1068. **Tageschronik.** Czernowitz, 6. April. Promotionen. *Ibidem.* 1911. 6. Apr. (Nr. 79, Jg. 46). S. 3.

Professor Dr. Ehrlich – promoter of the Czernowitz University graduation ceremony of new doctors of law Theodor Czechowski, Konstantin Lewandowski, Mendel Sekler and Emilian Berthold Winkler on the 5th of April 1911.

IN 1950 90A1

1069. **Tageschronik.** Czernowitz, 22. Juni. Rektorswahl an der k. k. Franz Josephs-Universität in Czernowitz. *Ibidem.* 1913. 22. Juni (Nr. 142, Jg. 48). S. 4.

Election of the Rector of Czernowitz University for the academic year 1913/1914. Professor Dr. Eugen Ehrlich amongst the candidates representing the Faculty of Law and Public Administration.

IN 1954 90A1

1070. **Tageschronik.** Czernowitz, 19. Mai. Seminar für lebendes Recht. *Ibidem.* 1911. 19. Mai (Nr. 115, Jg. 46). S. 2.

Announcement for the participants of the seminar on living law by Visiting Professor Dr. Ehrlich to be held on the 21st of May 1911.

IN 1950 90A1

1071. **Tageschronik.** Czernowitz, 23. November. Soziale Heimat der Heilsarmee. *Ibidem.* 1910. 23. Nov. (Nr. 267, Jg. 45). S. 3.

Information about the meeting of the Social-Scientific Academic Society where Professor Dr. Ehrlich as its honorary member presented the brochure by Professor Schumpeter entitled "Wie studiert man Sozialwissenschaft" ["How to study Social Science"]; the future presentation of the works by Ehrlich was announced.

IN 1949 90A1

1072. **Tageschronik.** Czernowitz, 27. Oktober. Der „Sozialwissenschaftliche akademische Verein". *Ibidem.* 1909. 27. Okt. (Nr. 245, Jg. 44). S. 2.

About the event of conferring an honorary membership of the Social Scientific Academic Society to University

Professor Dr. Eugen Ehrich in recognition of the merits for the Society, on the 24th of October 1909.

IN 1947 90A1

1073. **Tageschronik.** Czernowitz, 9. Jänner. Sozialwissenschaftlicher akademischer Verein. *Ibidem.* 1910. 9. Jänner (Nr. 6, Jg. 45). S. 3.

About the mutual decision of University Professors Dr. Eugen Ehrlich and Dr. Joseph Schumpeter to announce the best three papers a teach meeting of the Social-Scientific Academic Society.

IN 1948 90A1

1074. **Tageschronik.** Czernowitz, 22. Februar. Sozialwissenschaftlicher akademischer Verein. *Ibidem.* 1910. 22. Febr. (Nr. 42, Jg. 45). S. 3.

Information about the lecture on the topic of "Living Law" by University Professor Dr. Eugen Ehrlich.

IN 1948 90A1

1075. **Tageschronik.** Czernowitz, 6. Dezember. Sozialwissenschaftlicher akademischer Verein. *Ibidem.* 1910. 6. Dez. (Nr. 278, Jg. 45). S. 4.

Information about the lecture by University Professor Dr. Ehrlich on "Marxismus und Sozialismus" ["Marxism and Socialism"] in the hall of "Kaufmännischen Hauses".

IN 1949 90A1

1076. **Tageschronik.** Czernowitz, 27. November. Sozialwissenschaftlicher akademischer Verein. *Ibidem.* 1913. 27. Nov. (Nr. 273, Jg. 48). S. 3.

About the time and place of the lecture on the 28th of November 1913 by University Professor Dr. Eugen Ehrlich on "Nationalität und Rasse" ["Nationality and Race"].

IN 1955 90A1

1077. **Tageschronik.** Czernowitz, 30. November. Sozialwissenschaftlicher akademischer Verein. *Ibidem.* 1913. 30. Nov. (Nr. 276, Jg. 48). S. 3–4.

On the decision of University Professor Dr. Eugen Ehrlich to repeat the lecture on "Nationalität und Rasse" ["Nationality and Race"], because the number of those who wanted to attend the first lecture exceeded the number of available seats in the lecture hall.

IN 1955 90A1

1078. **Tageschronik.** Czernowitz, 5. Dezember. Sozialwissenschaftlich-akademischer Verein. *Ibidem.* 1913. 5. Dez. (Nr. 280, Jg. 48). S. 5.

About the time and place of the second lecture on the 28th of November 1913 by University Professor Dr. Eugen Ehrlich on "Nationalität und Rasse" ["Nationality and Race"].

IN 1955 90A1

1079. **Tageschronik.** Czernowitz, 12. November. Sozialwissenschaftlicher akademischer Verein und Seminar für lebendes Recht des Herrn Professors Dr. Eugen Ehrlich. *Ibidem.* 1913. 12. Nov. (Nr. 260, Jg. 48). S. 3.

Information about seminar on 'living law' and the Sociological Academic Society.

IN 1955 90A1

1080. **Tageschronik.** Czernowitz, 4. März. Eine stürmische Studentenversammlung. *Bukowinaer Volks-Zeitung.* 1907. 5. März (Nr. 2, Jg. 1). S. 2–3.

Information about the participation of the collegium of professors led by the Rector of Czernowitz University Dr. Ehrlich in the meetings of student societies.

IN 2166 90A64

1081. **Tageschronik.** Czernowitz, 4. Juni. Trauerkommers für weiland Dr. Eduard Reiss. *Ibidem.* 1907. 5. Juni (Nr. 74, Jg. 1). S. 2.

Participation of the University Rector Dr. Ehrlich in the mourning service for Eduard Reiss, former Mayor and Deputy-Mayor of Czernowitz held in the grand hall of the Music Society.

IN 2166 90A64

1082. **Tageschronik.** Trauerkommers. *Czernowitzer Zeitung.* 1907. 5. Juni (Nr. 126, Jg. 42). S. 2–3.

Participation of the University Rector Dr. Ehrlich in the mourning service for Eduard Reiss, former Mayor and Deputy-Mayor of Czernowitz held in the grand hall of the Music Society.

IN 1942 90A1

1083. **Tageschronik.** Der Trauerkommers der "Akademischen Lesehalle". *Ibidem.* 1906. 11. Okt. (Nr. 232, Jg. 41). S. 2–3.

Information about memorial service held in the "Academic Reading Hall" on the 6th of October 1906, in honour of Honorary Advisor University Professor Dr. Ferdinand Zieglauer von Blumenthal and Honorary Mayor Anton Kochanowski, including the information about the participation and speech of the Rector University Professor Dr. Eugene Ehrlich in the funeral service.

IN 1941 90A1

1084. **Tageschronik.** Trauerkundgebungen anlässlich des Ablebens Seiner k. und k. Hoheit des durchlauchtigsten Herrn Erzherzogs Otto. *Ibidem.* 1906. 7. Nov. (Nr. 254, Jg. 41). S. 2–3.

Participation of the Rector Professor Dr. Eugen Ehrlich, together with the deans, in the memorial service dedicated to the late Archduke Otto at the Cathedral Church.

IN 1941 90A1

1085. **Tageschronik.** Volkstümliche Universitätskurse. *Ibidem.* 1905. 17. März (Nr. 63, Jg. 40). S. 4.

The schedule of courses held by professors and associate professors of Czernowitz University in March of the current year including the information about the beginning of the lecture course on the general theory of law by Professor Dr. Eugen Ehrlich.

IN 1938 90A1

1086. **Tageschronik.** Volkstümliche Universitätskurse. *Ibidem.* 1905. 12. Nov. (Nr. 259, Jg. 40). S. 4.

Notice about the fifth lecture within the series on "General Theory of Law" to be held by Professor Dr. Eugen Ehrlich on the 17th of November 1905 in the lecture hall Nr. 5.

IN 1939 90A1

1087. **Tageschronik.** Volkstümliche Universitätskurse. *Ibidem.* 1906. 1. Juni (Nr. 125, Jg. 41). S. 5.

The schedule of courses held by professors and associate professors in the academic year 1905/1906 including the information about the course on "General Theory of Law" by Professor Dr. Eugen Ehrlich.

IN 1940 90A1

1088. **Tageschronik.** Czernowitz, 6. September. Volkstümliche Universitätskurse. *Ibidem.* 1911. 6. Sept. (Nr. 204, Jg. 46). S. 3.

Information about the first series of the popular university courses for the academic year 1911/2912 beginning on the 21st of October 1911 including four stages of the course on "Die Theorien von Karl Marx im Lichte der wirtschaftlichen Entwicklung der Gegenwart" by Professor Dr. Eugen Ehrlich.

IN 1951 90A1

1089. **Tageschronik.** Czernowitz, 20. Oktober. Volkstümliche Universitätskurse. *Ibidem.* 1911. 20. Okt. (Nr. 240, Jg. 46). S. 3.

Notice about the first lecture within the series on "Die Theorien von Karl Marx im Lichte der wirtschaftlichen Entwicklung der Gegenwart" by Professor Dr. Eugen Ehrlich in the lecture hall Nr. 7.

IN 1951 90A1

1090. **Tageschronik.** Czernowitz, 28. Oktober. Volkstümliche Universitätskurse. *Ibidem.* 1911. 28. Okt. (Nr. 247, Jg. 46). S. 2.

Notice about the second lecture within the series on "Die Theorien von Karl Marx im Lichte der wirtschaftlichen Entwicklung der Gegenwart" by Professor Dr. Eugen Ehrlich in the lecture hall Nr. 7.

IN 1951 90A1

1091. **Tageschronik.** Czernowitz, 4. November. Volkstümliche Universitätskurse. *Ibidem.* 1911. 4. Nov. (Nr. 252, Jg. 46). S. 2.

Notice about the third lecture within the series on "Die Theorien von Karl Marx im Lichte der wirtschaftlichen Entwicklung der Gegenwart" by Professor Dr. Eugen Ehrlich in the lecture hall Nr. 7.

IN 1951 90A1

1092. **Tageschronik.** Czernowitz, 10. November. Volkstümliche Universitätskurse. *Ibidem.* 1911. 10. Nov. (Nr. 257, Jg. 46). S. 2.

Information about the cancelled lecture by Professor Dr. Eugen Ehrlich announced for the 11th of November 1911 on "Die Theorien von Karl Marx im Lichte der wirtschaftlichen Entwicklung der Gegenwart" due to his business trip. The new date will be announced in newspapers.

IN 1951 90A1

1093. **Tageschronik.** Czernowitz, 25. November. Volkstümliche Universitätskurse. *Ibidem.* 1911. 25. Nov. (Nr. 270, Jg. 46). S. 2.

Information about time and place of the previously cancelled lecture by Professor Dr. Eugen Ehrlich on "Die Theorien von Karl Marx im Lichte der wirtschaftlichen Entwicklung der Gegenwart" set for the 30th of November 1911 andthe 7th of December 1911.

IN 1951 90A1

1094. **Tageschronik.** Czernowitz, 30. November. Volkstümliche Universitätskurse. *Ibidem.* 1911. 30. Nov. (Nr. 274, Jg. 46). S. 4.

Notice about the lecture on "Die Theorien von Karl Marx im Lichte der wirtschaftlichen Entwicklung der Gegenwart" by Professor Dr. Eugen Ehrlich in the lecture hall Nr. 7 on the 30th of November 1911.

IN 1951 90A1

1095. **Tageschronik.** Czernowitz, 7. Dezember. Volkstümliche Universitätskurse. *Ibidem.* 1911. 7. Dez. (Nr. 280, Jg. 46). S. 4.

Notice about the last lecture within the series on "Die Theorien von Karl Marx im Lichte der wirtschaftlichen Entwicklung der Gegenwart" by Professor Dr. Eugen Ehrlich in the lecture hall Nr. 7 on the 9th of December 1911.

IN 1951 90A1

1096. **Tageschronik.** Czernowitz, 15. August. Von der k. k. Franz Josephs-Universität. *Ibidem.* 1913. 15. Aug. (Nr. 188, Jg. 48). S. 4.

Information about the approval of the project of public lectures at Czernowitz University in the winter semester of the academic year 1913/1914 by the Decree of the Ministry of Science Cultus and Education of the 15 of July 1913, including the information that Dr. Ehrlich will read the following lectures: "Römisches Recht mit Ausnahme der Quellen und Verfassungsgeschichte" ("The Roman Law with the Exception of Sources and Constitutional History") 8, "Römisches Recht in seinen Grundzügen mit Berücksichtigung der byzantinischen Fortentwicklung" ("The Roman Law in its Principles, Considering the Byzantine Development") 4, and "Seminar für lebendes Recht" ("The Workshop on Living Law") 2.

IN 1955 90A1

1097. **Tageschronik.** Czernowitz, 22. November. Von der k. k. Franz-Joseph-Universität in Czernowitz. *Bukowinaer Volks-Zeitung.* 1907. 23. Nov. (Nr. 217, Jg. 1). S. 2–3.

Information about the report on the previous academic year by the Vice-Rector of Czernowitz University Professor Dr. Eugen Ehrlich on the occasion of the inauguration of the Rector Dr. Eugen Kozak for the academic year 1907/1908.

IN 2166 90A64

1098. **Tageschronik.** Czernowitz, 21. Oktober. Von der k. k. Universität. *Czernowitzer Zeitung.* 1909. 21. Okt. (Nr. 240, Jg. 44). S. 3.

Information about the seminar on "Living Law" to be conducted by Professor Dr. Eugen Ehrlich and Professor Dr. Ferdinand Kogler for certified lawyers (advocates, notaries, candidate notaries and advocates) ont he 26th of October 1909.

IN 1947 90A1

1099. **Tageschronik.** Czernowitz, 12. Juli. Von unserer Universität. *Bukowinaer Volks-Zeitung.* 1907. 13. Juli (Nr. 106, Jg. 1). S. 2.

Information about the decision of the Academic Senate of Czernowitz University related to the 300th anniversary of the University of Hessen to be held in Hessen from the 31st of July 1907 to the 3rd of August 1907. As part of the celebration events the Rector Professor Dr. Eugen Ehrlich will represent Czernowitz University at the second meeting of the rectors of German universities.

IN 2166 90A64

1100. **Tageschronik.** Czernowitz, 23. September. Von unserer Universität. *Ibidem.* 1907. 24. Sept. (Nr. 166, Jg. 1). S. 3.

Information related to the death of the Rector Elect Dr. Basil Gaina: until the new elections, the acting Rector Professor Dr. Eugen Ehrlich and the acting Vice-Rector Professor Dr. Sigmund Herzberg-Fränkel, remain in their positions with the possibility of re-election to their positions.

IN 2166 90A64

1101. **Tageschronik.** Czernowitz, 28. Oktober. Von unserer Universität. *Ibidem.* 1907. 29. Okt. (Nr. 196, Jg. 1). S. 2.

Composition of the Academic Senate in the current academic year. Dr. Eugen Ehrlich – Vice-Rector of Czernowitz University.

IN 2166 90A64

1102. **Tageschronik.** Vorstellungen bei Sr. Durchlaucht dem Herrn k. k. Landespräsidenten Konrad Prinzen zu Hohenlohe-Schillingsfürst. *Czernowitzer Zeitung.* 1903. 30. Apr. (Nr. 98, Jg. 38). S. 4.

Participation of University Professor Dr. Eugen Ehrlich on behalf of the Dean of the Faculty of Law and Public Administration, among the members of the Academic Senate of Czernowitz University, in the event where the Regional President of Bukovina Prince Konrad zu Hohenlohe-Schillingsfürst presented his speech.

IN 1934 90A1

1103. **Tageschronik.** Czernowitz, 14. November. Vortrag Eugen Ehrlich. *Ibidem.* 1913. 14. Nov. (Nr. 262, Jg. 48). S. 3.

Information about the lecture on the 28th of November 1913 by University Professor Dr. Eugen Ehrlich on "Nationalität und Rasse" ["Nationality and Race"].

IN1955 90A1

1104. **Tageschronik.** Vorträge. *Ibidem.* 1904. 21. Jänner (Nr. 16, Jg. 39). S. 3.

Information about the lecture programme of the Juridical-Political Scientific Society. The lecture by University Professor Dr. Ehrlich to be delivered on the 24th of February 1904.

IN 1936 90A1

1105. **Tageschronik.** Czernowitz, 7. Dezember. Vorträge des Univ.-Prof. Dr. Eugen Ehrlich. *Ibidem.* 1913. 7. Dez. (Nr. 282, Jg. 48). S. 3.

About the lecture on "Nationalität und Rasse" ["Nationality and Race"] by University Professor Dr. Eugen Ehrlich that took place on the 28th of November 1913 and the 5th of December 1913 (repeated).

IN 1955 90A1

1106. **Tageschronik.** Czernowitz, 12. April. Wohltätigkeits-Fechtakademie. *Ibidem.* 1910. 12. Apr. (Nr. 82, Jg. 45). S. 2–3.

Information about the participation of Dr. Ehrlich in the charity event of the Society of Fencing, including his fight with the fencing master Tonioni.

IN 1948 90A1

1107. **Tageschronik.** Czernowitz, 4. Dezember. Zum Versucheder Klerikalisierung der Universitäten. *Bukowinaer Volks-Zeitung.* 1907. 5. Dez. (Nr. 227, Jg. 1). S. 2.

Information about the chapter by the Vice-Rector of Czernowitz University Professor Dr. Eugen Ehrlich entitled "Statistisches zur Universitätsrede des Grafen Thun" ["Statistics on the university speech of Count Thun"] published in the newspaper "Neue Freie Presse".

IN 2166 90A64

1108. **Tageschronik.** II. internationaler Kongress für Schulhygiene in London. *Czernowitzer Zeitung.* 1907. 10. Febr. (Nr. 34, Jg. 42). S. 4.

Election of the University Rector Professor Dr. Eugen Ehrlich the Deputy-Head of the Regional Committee that will organize the II International Congress of the School of Hygiene that will take place in London in the period from the 5th to the 10th of August 1907.

IN 1942 90A1

1109. **Tagespost.** Der akademische Senat unserer Universität. *Bukowinaer Post.* 1909. 27. Juni (Nr. 2400, Jg. 16). S. 6.

Composition of the Academic Senate of Czernowitz University for the academic year 1909/1910. Dr. Eugen Ehrlich – Vice-Dean of the Faculty of Law.

IN 2063 90J26

1110. **Tagespost.** Der akademische Senat unsere... *Ibidem.* 1912. 23. Juni (Nr. 2859, Jg. 19). S. 4.

Composition of the Academic Senate of Czernowitz University for the academic year 1912/1913. Dr. Eugen Ehrlich – Vice-Dean of the Faculty of Law.

IN 2066 90J26

1111. **Tagespost.** Akademischer Senat. *Ibidem.* 1906. 26. Juni (Nr. 1934, Jg. 13). S. 2.

Composition of the Academic Senate of Czernowitz University for the academic year 1906/1907. Dr. Eugen Ehrlich – Rector of the University.

IN 2060 90J26

1112. **Tagespost.** Die Anerkennung der jüdischen Nationalität auf unserer Universität. *Ibidem.* 1907. 26. Febr. (Nr. 2038, Jg. 14). S. 3.

Decision of the Academic Senate of Czernowitz University signed by the Rector Ehrlich on behalf of the Rectorate, to recognize the Jews at Czernowitz University.

IN 2061 90J26

1113. **Tagespost.** Archeologischer Kongress in Athen. *Ibidem.* 1905. 5. Febr. (Nr. 1721, Jg. 12). S. 3.

Information about the Archaeological Congress to be held from the 7th to the 13th of April 1905 in Athens – Czernowitz University will be represented there by Professor Dr. Ehrlich.

IN 2059 90J26

1114. **Tagespost.** "Die Aufgaben der Sozialpolitik in der Bukowina". *Ibidem.* 1909. 1. Aug. (Nr. 2415, Jg. 16). S. 6.

Information about the second edition of the publication of University Professor Dr. Eugen Ehrlich entitled "Die Aufgaben der Sozialpolitik im österreichischen Osten, insbesondere in der Bukowina, mitbesonderer Beleuchtung der Juden- und Bauernfrage" ["Tasks of Social Politicy in Austrian East, especially in Bukovina, with Special Illumination of Issues of Jews and Peasants"] by the Czernowitz Social Scientific Academic Society. It also provides the information about the cost of the brochure and the address where it is available.

IN 2063 90J26

1115. **Tagespost.** Der Ball der akademischen Lesehatle. *Bukowinaer Post.* 1897. 14. Febr. (Nr. 498, Jg. 4). S. 4.

Participation of University Professor Dr. Ehrlich in the ball of the Society "Academic Reading Hall".

IN 2051 90J26

1116. **Tagespost.** Czernowitzer Herrenfecht-Societe. *Ibidem.* 1910. 25. Dez. (Nr. 2630, Jg. 18). S. 6.

In the elections of the 19th of December 1910 University Professor Dr. Ehrlich elected the Head of the Czernowitz Society of Fencing.

IN 2064 90J26

1117. **Tagespost.** Denkmalkomitee. *Ibidem.* 1907. 17. März (Nr. 2046, Jg. 14). S. 5.

On the inaugural meeting of the Committee for the installation of the monument for Professor Johann von Mikulicz-Radecki in his birthplace of Czernowitz (based on the initiative of the Rector of the local University Professor Dr. Eugen Ehrlich).

IN 206190J26

1118. **Tagespost.** Dreihundertjahrfeier der Grooninger Universität. *Ibidem.* 1914. 28. Juni (Nr. 3161, Jg. 21). S. 4.

Information about the celebration of the 300th anniversary of the foundation of the University of Groningen in Amsterdam. Czernowitz University represented by Professor Dr. Eugen Ehrlich.

IN 2068 90J26

1119. **Tagespost**. 31. Deutscher Juristentag. *Ibidem.* 1912. 3. Sept. (Nr. 2890, Jg. 19). S. 3.

Departure of University Professor Dr. Ehrlich to participate in the 31st Assembly of German Lawyers.

IN 2066 90J26

1120. **Tagespost**. Ehrung Professors Dr. Eugen Ehrlich. *Ibidem.* 1910. 29. Nov. (Nr. 2619, Jg. 18). S. 3.

About honoring achievements of Professor Dr. Eugen Ehrlich at the meeting of the Czernowitz Social-Scientific Academic Society.

IN 2064 90J26

1121. **Tagespost.** Erzherzog Otto. *Ibidem.* 1906. 8. Nov. (Nr. 1992, Jg. 13). S. 3.

Participation of the Rector Professor Dr. Eugen Ehrlich, together with the deans, in the memorial service dedicated to the late Archduke Otto at the Cathedral Church on the 7th of November 1906.

IN 2060 90J26

1122. **Tagespost**. Faschingsnachrichten. *Ibidem.* 1898. 6. Febr. (Nr. 648, Jg. 5). S. 5.

Participation of University Professor Dr. Ehrlich in the ball of the Academic Society "Junimea".

IN2052 90J26

1123. **Tagespost**. 50-jähriges Doktorjubiläum. *Ibidem.* 1912. 2. Apr. (Nr. 2826, Jg. 19). S. 2.

Participation of the Dean of the Faculty of Law and Public Administration of Franz Joseph University Professor Dr. Ehrlich in the celebration of the 50th anniversary of the promotion of the director of "Bukowinaer Sparkasse" Dr. Friedrich von Kleinwächter to the position of doctor of law at Prague University.

IN 2066 90J26

1124. **Tagespost.** Fünf-Uhr-Tee an Bord. *Ibidem.* 1914. 25. Jänner (Nr. 3098, Jg. 21). S. 6.

Participation of Professor Dr. Ehrlich in the tea ceremony.

IN 2068 90J26

1125. **Tagespost.** Inauguration des Rektors. *Ibidem.* 1906. 4. Dez. (Nr. 2003, Jg. 14). S. 2–3.

Information about the inauguration ceremony of the Rector Professor Dr. Eugen Ehrlich for the academic year 1907 held on the 2nd of December 1906 with the Rector's inaugural address on the subject of "Die Tatsachen des Gewohnheitsrechts" ("Facts of Customary Law").

IN 2060 90J26

1126. **Tagespost.** Inauguration des Rektors. *Ibidem.* 1907. 10. Dez. (Nr. 2160, Jg. 15). S. 2.

Information about the report on the previous academic year by the former Rector of Czernowitz University Professor Dr. Eugen Ehrlich on the occasion of the inauguration of the Rector Dr. Eugen Kozak for the academic year 1907/1908.

IN 2061 90J26

1127. **Tagespost.** Jubiläum. *Ibidem.* 1902. 23. Febr. (Nr. 1266, Jg. 9). S. 3.

Participation of University Professor Dr. Ehrlich in the Committee for the organization of the grand celebration in the Academic Reading Hall of the 40th anniversary of the award of the doctor of sciences diploma by Prague University to Honorary Professor Dr. Friedrich Kleinwächter.

IN 2056 90J26

1128. **Tagespost.** Der Junimeaball. *Ibidem.* 1897. 7. Febr. (Nr. 495, Jg. 4). S. 4.

Participation of University Professor Dr. Ehrlich in the ball of the Academic Society "Junimea".

IN 2051 90J26

1129. **Tagespost.** Junimeaball. *Ibidem.* 1907. 10. Febr. (Nr. 2031, Jg. 14). S. 5.

Participation of the University Rector Dr. Ehrlich in the traditional ball of the Academic Society "Junimea" – "Junimea-Ball" on the 7th of February 1907.

IN 2061 90J26

1130. **Tagespost.** Juristisch-staatswissenschaftl. Gesellschaft. *Ibidem.* 1903. 10. Febr. (Nr. 1414, Jg. 10). S. 3.

Information of the Juridical-Political Scientific Society about the lecture on "Freie Rechtsfindung und freie Rechtswissenschaft" ["Free Finding of the Law and Free Science of Law"] to be delivered by Professor Dr. Ehrlich in the Town Hall on the 11th of February 1903.

IN 2057 90J26

1131. **Tagespost.** Juristisch-staatswissenschaftl. Gesellschaft. *Ibidem.* 1904. 23. Febr. (Nr. 1574, Jg. 11). S. 3.

Information of the Juridical-Political Scientific Society about the lecture by Professor Dr. Eugen Ehrlich entitled "Zittelmann, internationales Privatrecht" ["Zittelmann, International Law"], to be held in the Town Hall on the 24th of February 1904.

IN 2058 90J26

1132. **Tagespost.** Die juristisch-staatswissenschaftl. Gesellschaft... *Ibidem.* 1905. 5. Febr. (Nr. 1721, Jg. 12). S. 4.

Information about the lecture by Professor Dr. Eugen Ehrlich on "Sociologie und Rechtswissenschaft" ("Sociology and Science of Law"), to be held on the 15th February 1905 in the Town Hall.

IN 2059 90J26

1133. **Tagespost.** Juristisch-staatswissenschaftliche Gesellschaft. *Ibidem.* 1905. 14. Febr. (Nr. 1725, Jg. 12). S. 3.

Notice that University Professor Dr. Eugen Ehrlich will read a lecture on "Sociologie und Jurisprudenz" ("Sociology and Jurisprudence") in the Town Hall on the 15th of February 1905.

IN 2059 90J26

1134. **Tagespost.** Juristisch-staatswissenschaftliche Gesellschaft. *Ibidem.* 1906. 28. Jänner (Nr. 1871, Jg. 13). S. 5.

Information of the Juridical-Political Scientific Society about the lecture by University Professor Dr. Eugen Ehrlich entitled "Reform des Vortragsrechtes" ["Reform of the right to lecture"] to be held in the Town Hall on the 31st of January 1906.

IN 2060 90J26

1135. **Tagespost.** Juristisch-staatswissenschaftliche Gesellschaft. *Ibidem.* 1906. 13. Febr. (Nr. 1878, Jg. 13). S. 3.

Information of the Juridical-Political Scientific Society about the commemorative speech by University Professor Dr. Eugen Ehrlich for the late Honorary Professor of the University of Vienna Dr. Anton Menger on the 14th of February 1906 at 7 pm.

IN 2060 90J26

1136. **Tagespost.** Juristisch-staatswissenschaftliche Gesellschaft. *Ibidem.* 1907. 5. März (Nr. 2041, Jg. 14). S. 2.

Information about the report of Professor Dr. Eugen Ehrlich on "Zur Lehre von den juristischen Personen" ("The

Doctrine of Legal Persons") to be provided in the hall of the Privincial Court (Civil Law Chamber) on the 8th of March 1907.

IN 2061 90J26

1137. **Tagespost**. Kaiser Franz Josef-Universitäts-Studentenheim. *Ibidem.* 1902. 24. Juni (Nr. 1316, Jg. 9). S. 2–3.

Participation of the Dean Professor Dr. Ehrlich in the celebration of the laying the first stone in the foundations of Czernowitz University dormitory on the 20th of June 1902.

IN 2056 90J26

1138. **Tagespost**. Kleinwächter-Commers der "Akademischen Lesehalle". *Ibidem.* 1902. 9. März (Nr. 1272, Jg. 9). S. 5.

Participation of University Professor Dr. Ehrlich in the Committee for the organization of the 15th March 1902 grand celebration in the Academic Reading Hall of the 40th anniversary of the award of the doctor of sciences diploma by Prague University on the 31st of March 1902 to Honorary Professor Dr. Kleinwächter who was popular in all segments of the population of Bukovina.

IN 2056 90J26

1139. **Tagespost**. Kongresse. *Ibidem.* 1903. 29. März (Nr. 1434, Jg. 10). S. 4.

Information about University Professor Dr. Ehrlich representing Czernowitz at the Congress of Historians in Rome from the 2nd to the 9th of April 1903.

IN 2057 90J26

1140. **Tagespost**. Löwl-Feier. *Ibidem.* 1909. 4. Mai (Nr. 2378, Jg. 16). S. 3.

Information about the participation of the Dean of the Faculty of Law Professor Dr. Eugen Ehrlich in the commemorative events dedicated to the University Professor Dr. Ferdinand Löwl von Lenkenthal on the 1st of May 1909.

IN 2063 90J26

1141. **Tagespost**. Personalnachrichten. *Ibidem.* 1899. 5. Febr. (Nr. 800, Jg. 6). S. 3.

Information about the departure of Professor of Czernowitz University Eugen Ehrlich went to Vienna.

IN2053 90J26

1142. **Tagespost**. Personalnachrichten. *Ibidem.* 1900. 25. Febr. (Nr. 961, Jg. 7). S. 4.

Information about the departure of University Professor Dr. Ehrlich went to Vienna.

IN 2054 90J26

1143. **Tagespost**. Personalnachrichten. *Bukowinaer Post.* 1901. 10. März (Nr. 1120, Jg. 8). S. 4.

Information that University Professor Dr. Ehrlich took long vacations.

IN 2055 90J26

1144. **Tagespost**. Personalnachrichten. *Ibidem.* 1901. 25. Apr.(Nr. 1138, Jg. 8). S. 3.

Information about the return of University Professor Dr. Ehrlich from his research trip.

IN 2055 90J26

1145. **Tagespost**. Personalnachrichten. *Ibidem.* 1903. 25. Jänner (Nr. 1407, Jg. 10). S. 3.

Information about participation of Professor Ehrlich from Czernowitz in the Easter Congress of Historians in Rome.

IN 2057 90J26

1146. **Tagespost**. Populär-wissenschaftliche Vorträge. *Ibidem.* 1902. 6. Febr. (Nr. 1259, Jg. 9). S. 7.

Information about the change of the date of the scientific-popular lecture by Professor Dr. Ehrlich on "The Origins of Women's Question" from the 7th of February 1902 to the 14th of March 1902.

IN 2056 90J26

1147. **Tagespost**. Promotion. *Ibidem.* 1900. 28. Juni (Nr. 1012, Jg. 7). S. 3.

Professor Dr. Ehrlich – promoter of the Czernowitz University graduation ceremony of a new doctor of law Dragoş Bumbac.

IN 2054 90J26

1148. **Tagespost**. Promotion. *Ibidem.* 1900. 6. Nov.(Nr. 1068, Jg. 7). S. 3.

Professor Dr. Ehrlich – promoter of the Czernowitz University graduation ceremony of a new doctor of law Carl Franz Bertoni.

IN 2054 90J26

1149. **Tagespost**. Promotion. *Ibidem.* 1904. 11. Febr. (Nr. 1569, Jg. 11). S. 3.

Dr. Ehrlich – promoter of the Czernowitz University graduation ceremony of a new doctor of law journalist from Vienna Felix Reig.

IN 2058 90J26

1150. **Tagespost**. Promotion. *Ibidem.* 1904. 12. Juli (Nr. 1632, Jg. 11). S. 2.

Professor Dr. Ehrlich – promoter of the Czernowitz University graduation ceremony of a new doctor of law Anton Josefowicz.

IN 2058 90J26

1151. **Tagespost**. Promotion. *Ibidem*. 1904. 18. Dez.(Nr. 1701, Jg. 12). S. 3.

Professor Dr. Ehrlich – promoter of the Czernowitz University graduation ceremony of a new doctor of law Leo Löwner.

IN 2058 90J26

1152. **Tagespost**. Promotion. *Ibidem*. 1907. 15. Dez. (Nr. 2162, Jg. 15). S. 6.

Professor Dr. Ehrlich – promoter of the Czernowitz University graduation ceremony of a new doctor of law Moses Bardach.

IN 2061 90J26

1153. **Tagespost**. Promotion. *Ibidem*. 1908. 5. Apr. (Nr. 2210, Jg. 15). S. 5.

Professor Dr. Ehrlich – promoter of the Czernowitz University graduation ceremony of a new doctor of law Lazar Pomeranz.

IN 2062 90J26

1154. **Tagespost**. Promotion. *Ibidem*. 1909. 24. Okt. (Nr. 2451, Jg. 16). S. 4.

Professor Dr. Ehrlich – promoter of the Czernowitz University graduation ceremony of a new doctor of law Johann Max Tarden.

IN 2063 90J26

1155. **Tagespost**. Promotion. *Ibidem*. 1909. 28. Nov. (Nr. 2466, Jg. 17). S. 4.

Professor Dr. Ehrlich – promoter of the Czernowitz University graduation ceremony of a new doctor of law Samuel Rubinger.

IN 2063 90J26

1156. **Tagespost**. Promotion. *Ibidem*. 1909. 9. Dez. (Nr. 2471, Jg. 17). S. 4.

Professor Dr. Ehrlich – promoter of the Czernowitz University graduation ceremony of a new doctor of law Rubin Lang on the 7th of December 1909.

IN 2063 90J26

1157. **Tagespost**. Promotion. *Ibidem*. 1910. 17. Febr. (Nr. 2501, Jg. 17). S. 2.

Professor Dr. Ehrlich – promoter of the Czernowitz University graduation ceremony of a new doctor of law Abraham Ber Tamler on the 15th of February 1910.

IN 2064 90J26

1158. **Tagespost**. Promotionen. *Ibidem*. 1900. 23. Dec. (Nr. 1088, Jg. 8). S. 6.

Professor Dr. Ehrlich – promoter of the Czernowitz University graduation ceremony of a new doctor of law Hugo Badian.

IN 2054 90J26

1159. **Tagespost**. Promotionen. *Ibidem*. 1901. 28. Apr.(Nr. 1139, Jg. 8). S. 4.

Professor Dr. Ehrlich – promoter of the Czernowitz University Faculty of Law graduation ceremony of new doctors of law Bernhard Stecher and Jankel Fleischer.

IN 2055 90J26

1160. **Tagespost**. Promotionen. *Ibidem.* 1903. 1. Febr. (Nr. 1410, Jg. 10). S. 4.

Professor Dr. Ehrlich – promoter of the Czernowitz University graduation ceremony of a new doctor of law Siegmund Horowicz.

IN 2057 90J26

1161. **Tagespost**. Promotionen. *Ibidem.* 1905. 2. Juli (Nr. 1782, Jg. 12). S. 5.

Professor Dr. Ehrlich and Dr. Adler – promoters of the Czernowitz University graduation ceremony of new doctors of law Mordche Deligdisch and Karl Sonnenthal.

IN 2059 90J26

1162. **Tagespost**. Promotionen. *Ibidem.* 1905. 5. Nov. (Nr. 1836, Jg. 12). S. 5.

Professor Dr. Ehrlich – promoter of the Czernowitz University graduation ceremony of a new doctor of law Julius Brüll.

IN 2059 90J26

1163. **Tagespost**. Promotionen. *Ibidem.* 1907. 19. Mai (Nr. 2073, Jg. 14). S. 4.

Professor Dr. Ehrlich – promoter of the Czernowitz University graduation ceremony of a new doctor of law Heinrich Amster.

IN 2061 90J26

1164. **Tagespost**. Promotionen. *Ibidem.* 1908. 2. Febr. (Nr. 2183, Jg. 15). S. 4.

Professor Dr. Ehrlich – promoter of the Czernowitz University graduation ceremony of a new doctor of law Rubin Geringer.

IN 206290J26

1165. **Tagespost**. Promotionen. *Ibidem.* 1908. 19. März (Nr. 2203, Jg. 15). S. 3.

Professor Dr. Ehrlich – promoter of the Czernowitz University graduation ceremony of new doctors of law M. Fischer and Norbert Sekler.

IN 2062 90J26

1166. **Tagespost**. Promotionen. *Ibidem.* 1909. 2. Dez. (Nr. 2468, Jg. 17). S. 3.

Dr. Ehrlich – promoter of the Czernowitz University graduation ceremony of a new doctor of law financial officer Otto Ernst.

IN 2063 90J26

1167. **Tagespost**. Promotionen. Ibidem. 1909. 19. Dez. (Nr. 2475, Jg. 17). S. 4.

Dr. Ehrlich – promoter of the Czernowitz University graduation ceremony of a new doctor of law Artur Füllenbaum.

IN 2063 90J26

1168. **Tagespost**. Promotionen. *Ibidem.* 1910. 8. Febr. (Nr. 2497, Jg. 17). S. 2.

Professor Dr. Ehrlich – promoter of the Czernowitz University graduation ceremony of a new doctor of law Simon Knopf.

IN 2064 90J26

1169. **Tagespost**. Promotionen. *Ibidem.* 1910. 3. Juli (Nr. 2556, Jg. 17). S. 5.

Professor Dr. Ehrlich – promoter of the Czernowitz University graduation ceremony of new doctors of law Julius Hruder and Moses Krässel.

IN 2064 90J26

1170. **Tagespost**. Promotionen. *Ibidem.* 1910. 3. Nov. (Nr. 2608, Jg. 17). S. 3.

Professor Dr. Ehrlich – promoter of the Czernowitz University graduation ceremony of new doctors of law Erich Ebermann and Hermann Altmann.

IN 2064 90J26

1171. **Tagespost**. Promotionen. *Ibidem.* 1911. 19. Febr. (Nr. 2653, Jg. 18). S. 5.

Professor Dr. Ehrlich – promoter of the Czernowitz University graduation ceremony of a new doctor of law David Müller.

IN 2065 90J26

1172. **Tagespost**. Promotionen. *Ibidem.* 1911. 9. Apr. (Nr. 2674, Jg. 18). S. 5.

Dr. Ehrlich – promoter of the Czernowitz University graduation ceremony of new doctors of law Theodor Czechowski, Konstantin Lewandowski, Mendel Sekler and Emilian Berthold Winkler.

IN 2065 90J26

1173. **Tagespost**. Promotionen. *Ibidem.* 1913. 22. Juni (Nr. 3014, Jg. 20). S. 6.

Professor Dr. Ehrlich – promoter of the Czernowitz University graduation ceremony of a new doctor of law Josef Sommer.

IN 2067 90J26

1174. **Tagespost**. Promotionen. *Ibidem*. 1913. 24. Juli (Nr. 3028, Jg. 20). S. 4.

Professor Dr. Ehrlich – promoter of the Czernowitz University graduation ceremony of a new doctor of law Otto Sorda.

IN 2067 90J26

1175. **Tagespost**. Retorswahl an unserer Universität. *Ibidem*. 1906. 24. Juni (Nr. 1933, Jg. 13). S. 5.

Information about the election by the Academic Senate on the 23rd of June 1906 in which Professor of the Faculty of Law and Public Administration Dr. Eugen Ehrlich was unanimously elected the Rector of Czernowitz University for the academic year 1906/1907. The CV of the new Rector taken from the work by Norst "Alma mater" is provided.

IN 2060 90J26

1176. **Tagespost**. Soziale Heimat der Heilsarmee. *Ibidem*. 1910. 27. Nov. (Nr. 2618, Jg. 18). S. 6.

Information about the meeting of the Social-Scientific Academic Society where Professor Dr. Ehrlich as its honorary member presented the brochure by Professor Schumpeter entitled "Wie studiert man Sozialwissenschaft" ["How to study Social Science"]; the future presentation of the works by Ehrlich was announced.

IN 2064 90J26

1177. **Tagespost**. Sozialismus und Marxismus. *Ibidem*. 1910. 4. Dez. (Nr. 2621, Jg. 18). S. 7.

About the change of the date of the lecture by University Professor Dr. Ehrlich on "Marxismus und Sozialismus" ["Marxism and Socialism"] to the 6th of December 1910.

IN 2064 90J26

1178. **Tagespost**. Sozial-wissenschaftliche Akad. Verein. *Ibidem*. 1909. 28. Okt. (Nr. 2453, Jg. 16). S. 4.

About the event of conferring an honorary membership of the Social Scientific Academic Society to University Professor Dr. Eugen Ehrich in recognition of the merits for the Society, on the 24th of October 1909.

IN 2063 90J26

1179. **Tagespost**. Sozialwissenschaftlicher akad. Verein. *Ibidem.* 1909. 23. Mai (Nr. 2386, Jg. 16). S. 5.

Information about the lecture by University Professor Dr. Eugen Ehrlich on the 14th of March 1909 on the topic of "die englische und festländische Altersversorgung" within the lecture course of the current academic year. The summary of the lecture is also provided.

IN 2063 90J26

1180. **Tagespost**. Sozialwissenschaftlicher akademischer Verein. *Ibidem.* 1909. 25. Mai (Nr. 2387, Jg. 16). S. 3.

About the excursion for the members of the Social Scientific Academic Society led by University Professors Dr. Ehrlich and Dr. Kogler on the 26th of May 1909.

IN 2063 90J26

1181. **Tagespost**. Sozialwissenschaftlicher akad. Verein. *Ibidem.* 1910. 10. Jänner (Nr. 2484, Jg. 17). S. 6.

About the mutual decision of University Professors Dr. Eugen Ehrlich and Dr. Joseph Schumpeter to announce the best three papers a teach meeting of the Social-Scientific Academic Society.

IN 2064 90J26

1182. **Tagespost**. Sozialwissenschaftlicher akad. Verein. *Ibidem.* 1910. 29. Nov. (Nr. 2619, Jg. 18). S. 3.

Information about the lecture by University Professor Dr. Ehrlich on "Marxism and Socialism" ("Marxismus und Sozialismus") in the hall of "Kaufmännischen Hauses" on the 4th of December 1910.

IN 2064 90J26

1183. **Tagespost**. Sozialwissenschaftlicher akad. Verein. *Ibidem.* 1910. 1. Dez. (Nr. 2620, Jg. 18). S. 5.

Information about the lecture by University Professor Dr. Ehrlich on "Marxismus und Sozialismus" in the hall of "Kaufmännischen Hauses".

IN 2064 90J26

1184. **Tagespost**. Sozialwissenschaftlicher akademischer Verein und Seminar für lebendes Recht des Herrn Univ. Prof. Dr. Eugen Ehrlich. *Ibidem.* 1913. 6. Nov. (Nr. 3071, Jg. 20). S. 5.

Information about Sociological Academic Society and the seminar on 'living law.'

IN 2067 90J26

1185. **Tagespost**. Sozialwissenschaftlicher akad. Verein. *Ibidem*. 1914. 16. Apr. (Nr. 3131, Jg. 21). S. 5.

About the 14th general assembly of the Social-Scientific Academic Society on which Professor Dr. Hans von Frisch was elected the third honorary member of the Society, after the first two being Professors Dr. Eugen Ehrlich and and Dr. Joseph Schumpeter.

IN 2068 90J26

1186. **Tagespost**. Todesfälle. *Ibidem*. 1907. 17. Jänner (Nr. 2021, Jg. 14). S. 4.

Participation of Professor Dr. Eugen Ehrlich in the Czernowitz University delegation at the funeral of Honorary Doctor of Czernowitz University Dr. Hartel in Vienna.

IN 2061 90J26

1187. **Tagespost**. Ueber die Anfänge der Frauenfrage... *Ibidem*. 1902. 23. Febr. (Nr. 1266, Jg. 9). S. 4.

About the scientific-popular lecture by Professor Dr. Eugen Ehrlich on "the Origins of Women's Question".

IN 2056 90J26

1188. **Tagespost.** Universitätsprofessor Dr. Eugen Ehrlich – Ehrendoktor der Universität Groningen. *Ibidem*. 1914. 2. Juli (Nr. 3165, Jg. 21). S. 3.

Information about the celebration of the 300th anniversary of the foundation of the University of Groningen in Amsterdam where Professor Dr. Eugen Ehrlich representing Czernowitz University was awarded the honorary doctorate.

IN 2068 90J2

1189. **Tagespost**. Universitäts-Studentenheim. *Ibidem*. 1905. 22. Okt. (Nr. 1830, Jg. 12). S. 4.

Election of Professor Dr. Ehrlich a member of Board of Trustees of the Faculty of Law.

IN 2059 90J26

1190. **Tagespost**. Volkstümliche Universitätskurse. *Ibidem*. 1905. 12. Okt. (Nr. 1826, Jg. 12). S. 4.

The schedule of courses held by professors and associate professors in the academic year 1905/1906 including the information about the course on "General Theory of Law" by Professor Dr. Eugen Ehrlich.

IN 2059 90J26

1191. **Tagespost**. Volkstümliche Universitätskurse. *Ibidem*. 1905. 24. Okt. (Nr. 1831, Jg. 12). S. 3.

Notice about the second lecture within the series on "General Theory of Law" to be held by Professor Dr. Eugen Ehrlich on the 27th of October 1905 in the lecture hall Nr. 5.

IN 2059 90J26

1192. **Tagespost.** Volkstümliche Universitätskurse. *Ibidem.* 1905. 7. Dez. (Nr. 1850, Jg. 13). S. 5.

Notice about the fifth lecture within the series on "General Theory of Law" to be held by Professor Dr. Eugen Ehrlich on the 17th of November 1905 in the lecture hall Nr. 5.

IN 2059 90J26

1193. **Tagespost.** Volkstümliche Universitätskurse. *Ibidem.* 1911. 26. Sept. (Nr. 2747, Jg. 18). S. 3.

Information about the first series of the popular university courses for the academic year 1911/1912 beginning on the 21st of October 1911 including four stages of the course on "Die Theorien von Karl Marx im Lichte der wirtschaftlichen Entwicklung der Gegenwart" ["Karl Marx's Theories in the Light of Economic Development of the Present Times"] by Professor Dr. Eugen Ehrlich.

IN 2065 90J26

1194. **Tagespost.** Volkstümliche Universitätskurse. *Ibidem.* 1911. 7. Dez. (Nr. 2778, Jg. 19). S. 4.

Notice about the last lecture within the series on "Die Theorien von Karl Marx im Lichte der wirtschaftlichen Entwicklung der Gegenwart" ["Karl Marx's Theories in the Light of Economic Development of the Present Times"] by Professor Dr. Eugen Ehrlich on the 9th of December 1911.

IN 2065 90J26

1195. **Tagespost.** Von der Staatsprüfungscommission. *Ibidem.* 1897. 29. Apr. (Nr. 529, Jg. 4). S. 3.

On the appointment of University Associate Professors Dr. Alfred von Halban and Dr. Eugen Ehrlich members of the State Judicial Examination Board in Czernowitz.

IN 2051 90J26

1196. **Tagespost.** Von der Universität. *Ibidem.* 1896. 29. Oct. (Nr. 453, Jg. 3). S. 3.

Information about the appointment of the lawyer from Vienna and at the same time the privatdozent Dr. Ehrlich who will become a member of the Department of Roman law at the local university, on the request of the Senate of our Alma Mater to the Ministry of Education.

IN 2050 90J26

1197. **Tagespost.** Von der Universität. *Ibidem.* 1896. 15. Nov. (Nr. 460, Jg. 3). S. 3.

Information about the appointment of the lawyer from Schwechat and at the same time the privatdozent of the University of Vienna Dr. Eugen Ehrlich an associate professor of Roman law at Czernowitz University on the 25th of October 1896. It is pointed out that the birthplace of the newly appointed Professor is Bukovina.

IN 2050 90J26

1198. **Tagespost**. Von der Universität. *Ibidem.* 1896. 24. Nov. (Nr. 464, Jg. 3). S. 2.

Announcement of the beginning of the lecture courses of the 1st of December 1896 by the newly appointed Associate Professor of Roman law at Czernowitz University Dr. Eugen Ehrlich.

IN 2050 90J26

1199. **Tagespost**. Von der Universität. *Ibidem.* 1900. 15. Febr. (Nr. 957, Jg. 7). S. 4.

Notice of the official information in the Austrian newspaper "Wiener Zeitung" about the appointment of Dr. E. Ehrlich a Full Professor of Roman law at Czernowitz University.

*IN 2054 90J26***Tagespost**. Von der Universität. *Ibidem.* 1901. 23. Juni (Nr. 1162, Jg. 8). S. 4.

Elections of the 19th of June of the Dean of the Faculty of Law of Czernowitz University for the academic year 1901/1902 – Professor Dr. Eugen Ehrlich.

IN 2055 90J26

1200. **Tagespost**. Von der Universität. *Ibidem.* 1901. 24. Sept. (Nr. 1202, Jg. 8). S. 3.

Election of the academic officials of Czernowitz University for the academic year 1901/1902 on the 23rd of September 1901, including the Dean of the Faculty of Law and Public Administration Professor Dr. Eugen Ehrlich.

IN 2055 90J26

1201. **Tagespost**. Von der Universität. *Ibidem.* 1902. 11. Mai (Nr. 1298, Jg. 9). S. 4.

Information about the return of the Dean Professor Dr. Ehrlich from the vacations on the 9th of May 1902.

IN 2056 90J26

1202. **Tagespost**. Von der Universität. *Ibidem.* 1906. 11. Okt. (Nr. 1980, Jg. 13). S. 3.

Information about the 2nd of December 1906, the day of the anniversary of the government of the Emperor Franz Joseph I, when the solemn inauguration of the Rector for the *academic year 1906/1907 will be held at 11 am with the Rector Professor Dr. Eugen Ehrlich's inaugural address on the subject of "Die Tatsachendes Gewohnheitsrechts" ("Facts of Customary Law").*

IN 2060 90J26

1203. **Tagespost**. Von der Universität. *Ibidem*. 1906. 25. Nov. (Nr. 1999, Jg. 14). S. 6.

Information about the inauguration ceremony of the Rector Dr. Ehrlich on the 2nd of December 1906 with his inaugural address on the subject of "Die Tatsachendes Gewohnheitsrechts" ("Facts of Customary Law").

IN 2060 90J26

1204. **Tagespost**. Von der Universität. *Ibidem*. 1907. 2. Febr. (Nr. 2028, Jg. 14). S. 4.

Information that the Academic Senate entrusted the Vice-Rector Professor Dr. Sigmund Herzberg-Fränkel to represent Czernowitz University in the Council of Curators of Regional Museums and the Rector Professor Dr. Eugen Ehrlich to represent Czernowitz University in the Council of Curators of Crafts Museum in Bukovina.

IN 2061 90J26

1205. **Tagespost**. Von der Universität. *Ibidem*. 1907. 27. Juni (Nr. 2089, Jg. 14). S. 4.

Composition of the Academic Senate in the academic year 1907/1908. Dr. Eugen Ehrlich – Vice-Rector of Czernowitz University.

IN 2061 90J26

1206. **Tagespost**. Von der Universität. *Ibidem*. 1907. 14. Juli (Nr. 2096, Jg. 14). S. 4.

Information about the decision of the Academic Senate of Czernowitz University related to the 300th anniversary of the University of Hessen to be held in Hessen from the 31st of July 1907 to the 3rd of August. As part of the celebration events the Rector Professor Dr. Eugen Ehrlich will represent Czernowitz University at the second meeting of the rectors of German universities.

IN 206190J26

1207. **Tagespost**. Von der Universität. *Ibidem*. 1907. 24. Sept. (Nr. 2127, Jg. 14). S. 2.

Information related to the death of the Rector Elected Dr. Basil Gaina: until the newelections, the acting Rector Professor Dr. Eugen Ehrlich and the acting Vice-Rector Professor

Dr. Sigmund Herzberg-Fränkel, remain in their positions with the possibility of re-election to their positions.

IN 2061 90J26

1208. **Tagespost**. Von der Universität. *Ibidem.* 1907. 29. Okt. (Nr. 2142, Jg. 14). S. 2.

Composition of the Academic Senate for the current academic year. Dr. Eugen Ehrlich – the Vice-Rector of Czernowitz University.

IN 2061 90J26

1209. **Tagespost**. Von der Universität. *Ibidem.* 1907. 21. Nov. (Nr. 2152, Jg. 15). S. 3.

Information about the report on the previous academic year by the Vice-Rector of Czernowitz University Professor Dr. Eugen Ehrlich on the occasion of the inauguration of the Rector Dr. Eugen Kozak for the academic year 1907/1908.

IN 2061 90J26

1210. **Tagespost**. Von der Universität. *Ibidem.* 1908. 28. Juli (Nr. 2257, Jg. 15). S. 3.

About the verification of the academic officials of Czernowitz University by the Ministry of Cultus and Education, including the Dean of the Faculty of Law and Public Administration Professor Dr. Eugen Ehrlich.

IN 2062 90J26

1211. **Tagespost**. Von der Universität. *Ibidem.* 1909. 10. Okt. (Nr. 2445, Jg. 16). S. 5.

Information about the seminars in the winter semester of the current academic yearby Professor Dr. Eugen Ehrlich including the seminar on "Living Law" to be coconducted by Professor Dr. Ferdinand Kogler for certified lawyers.

IN 2063 90J26

1212. **Tagespost**. Von der Universität. *Ibidem.* 1909. 21. Okt. (Nr. 2450, Jg. 16). S. 3.

Information about the seminar on "Living Law" to be conducted by Professor Dr. Eugen Ehrlich and Professor Dr. Ferdinand Kogler for certified lawyers (advocates, notaries, candidate notaries and advocates) on the 26th of October 1909.

IN 2063 90J26

1213. **Tagespost**. Von der Universität. *Ibidem.* 1911. 1. Nov. (Nr. 2763, Jg. 18). S. 3.

On the appointment of University Professor Dr. Eugen Ehrlich a member of the State Judicial Examination Board and the examiner of the Austrian private law, commercial law, and exchange law in Czernowitz for the period of the academic years 1911/1912 to 1913/1914 by the Minister of Cultus and Education. It also includes information about the appointment by the Minister of Professor Dr. Eugen Ehrlich a member of the State Historic-Legal Examination Board with the powers of the examiner of German law.

IN 2065 90J26

1214. **Tagespost**. Von unserer Universität. *Ibidem.* 1911. 22. Juni (Nr. 2706, Jg. 18). S. 4.

In the elections of the 20th June 1911 Professorof Roman law Dr. Eugen Ehrlich elected the Dean of the Faculty of Law of Czernowitz University for the academic year 1911/1912.

IN 2065 90J26

1215. **Tagespost**. Von unserer Universität. *Ibidem.* 1912. 28. Jänner (Nr. 2798, Jg. 19). S. 4.

Participation of the Dean of the Faculty of Law Professor Dr. Eugen Ehrlich in the Matriculation ceremony for the new students of the university registered for the winter semester of the academic year 1911/1912.

IN 2066 90J26

1216. **Tagespost**. Vorlesungen über die Soziologie des Rechts. *Ibidem.* 1913. 30. Okt. (Nr. 3068, Jg. 20). S. 4–5.

About the appeal of the Sociological Society in Vienna to the Ministry of Education with the requirement to introduce the lectures on sociology to university studies. It also refers to Professor of Czernowitz University Dr. Ehrlich who holds lectures on sociology.

IN 2067 90J26

1217. **Tageschronik.**Czernowitz, 28. Oktober. Vorlesungen über die Soziologie des Rechts. *Czernowitzer Zeitung.* 1913. 28. Okt. (Nr. 248, Jg. 48). S. 3.

About the appeal of the Sociological Society in Vienna to the Ministry of Education with the requirement to introduce the lectures on sociology to university studies. It also refers to Professor of Czernowitz University Dr. Ehrlich who holds lectures on sociology.

IN 1955 90A1

1218. **Tagespost**. Vortrag. *Bukowinaer Post.* 1905. 31. Dez. (Nr. 1859, Jg. 13). S. 4.

Information about the speech of Professor of Czernowitz University Dr. Eugen Ehrlich in Vienna on the 5th of January 1905 entitled "Restructuring Contract Law" ("neugestaltung des Vertragsrechtes").

IN 2059 90J26

1219. **Tagespost**. Vorträge des Professor Ehrlich. *Ibidem*. 1910. 17. Nov. (Nr. 2614, Jg. 18). S. 4.

Information about the intention of University Professor Dr. Ehrlich to hold a series of lectures for the Juridical-Political Scientific Society entitled "Ueber Rechtswissenschaft" ("Science of Law"). It also points out that the first lecture will be on the 18th of November 1910 in the large hall of the Palace of Justice.

IN 2064 90J26

1220. **Tagespost**. Vortrag Ludo M. Hartmann. *Ibidem*. 1911. 2. Febr. (Nr. 2646, Jg. 18). S. 3–4.

About the event organized on the 26th of January 1911 by the Social-Scientific Academic Society in honour of Ludo M. Hartmann who presented the lecture on "Christianity and Socialism" ("Christentum und Sozialismus"). The event was attended, among other honorary members of the Society, by Professor Dr. Ehrlich who also spoke at the organized party.

IN 2065 90J26

1221. **Tagespost**. Zur Anerkennung der jüdischen Nationalität. *Ibidem*. 1907. 24. Sept. (Nr. 2127, Jg. 14). S. 3.

Participation of the Rector Professor Dr. Ehrlich in the dispute about the recognition of Jews at Czernowitz University.

IN 2061 90J26

1222. **Tagespost**. Zur Einführung der neuen Civilprocessordnung. *Ibidem*. 1898. 1. Febr. (Nr. 646, Jg. 5). S. 2.

Participation of Professor Dr. Ehrlich in the first meeting with the discussion of the new civil procedure law on the 31st of January 1898.

IN 2052 90J26

1223. **Tagespost**. Zur Konzipientensperre. *Ibidem*. 1905. 24. Dez. (Nr. 1857, Jg. 13). S. 5.

Participation of Professor Dr. Ehrlich in the students' meetings.

IN 2059 90J26

1224. **Tagespost**. Zur ruthenischen Universitätsfrage… *Ibidem*. 1907. 3. März (Nr. 2040, Jg. 14). S. 5.

Participation of the Rector Dr. Ehrlich in th econsideration of Rusyn issue at Czernowitz University.

IN 2061 90J26

1225. **Die Tagung** des Deutschen Juristentages. *Czernowitzer Zeitung.* 1912. 30. Aug. (Nr. 198, Jg. 47). S. 3.

About the scheduled 31st assembly of the German Lawyers in Vienna on the 4th of September 1912. The programme of the meeting includes the participation of Czernowitz Professor Dr. Ehrlich.

IN 1953 90A1

1226. **Takahashi, Hiroshi,** hrsg. *Manfred Rehbinder zum 60. Geburtstag.* Hiroshima : Nakamoro Sogo Printing Co., Ltd., 1995. 114 S.

E. Ehrlich. – pp.11, 23, 27, 28, 32, 40, 52, 55, 59.

1227. **Tamanaha, Brian Z.** *A General Jurisprudence of Law and Society.* Oxford ; New York : Oxford University Press Inc., 2001. XX, 284 p. *(Oxford socio-legal studies).*

E. Ehrlich. – pp. 2, 224–227.

1228. **Tamanaha, Brian Z.** "A Vision of Socio-Legal Change: Rescuing Ehrlich from "Living Law". *Law and Social Inquiry.* 2011. Vol. 36. Nr. 1. p. 297–318.

1229. **Tarnawski, Theodor.** Bericht über das Studienjahr 1904/1905 : erstattet am 2. Dezember 1905 von dem abtretenden Rektor. In *Die feierliche Inauguration des Rectors der k. k. Franz-Josephs-Universität in Czernowitz für das Studienjahr 1905/1906 am 2. Dezember 1905.* Czernowitz : Selbstverl. der k. k. Universität, 1906. S. 3–14 ; *Czernowitzer Zeitung.* 1905. 14. Dez. (Nr. 285, Jg. 40). S. 3–4 ; 15. Dez. (Nr. 286, Jg. 40). S. 4.

Number of students of the course "General Theory of Law" by Professor Dr. Eugen Ehrlich – p. 10.

IN 193508 90K126

IN 1939 90A1

1230. **Tedeschi, Guido (Gad).** Ehrlich, Eugen. In *Encyclopaedia Judaica,* ed. : Fred Skolnik, und Michael Berenbaum. 2 ed. Detroit ; New York ; London : Thomson Gale, 2007. Vol. 6, *"Dr–Feu."* p. 243.

1231. **Teubner, Gunther.** Global Bukowina: Legal Pluralism in the World Society. In *Global Law Without a State,* ed. Gunther Teubner. Aldershot ; Brookfield ; Singapore ; Sydney : Dartmouth, 1997. pp. 3–28.

E. Ehrlich. – pp. 3, 5–6, 9, 11, 20.

1232. **Timasheff, N. S.** *An Introduction to the Sociology of Law.* Cambridge : Harvard Univ. Comm. on Research in the Social Sciences, 1939. XIV, 418 p., (*Harvard sociological studies* ; vol. 3). Bibliogr.: pp. 381–403.

E. Ehrlich. – pp. 12, 25–27, 30, 50, 53, 54, 58, 59, 83, 111, 121–122, 132, 133, 137, 140, 156, 163, 165, 191, 250, 272, 296–298, 312, 315, 318, 324, 325, 337, 353, 366, 385, 390, 396.

1233. **Timasheff, Nicholas S.** *An Introduction to the Sociology of Law,* with a new introd. by A. Javier Treviño. New Brunswick ; London : Trans. Publ., 2009. XLIII, 418 p. Bibliogr.: pp. 381–403.

E. Ehrlich. – pp. IX, XII, XV-XVI, XXI, XXXVII, 12, 25–27, 30, 50, 53, 54, 58, 59, 83, 111, 121–122, 132, 133, 137, 140, 156, 163, 165, 191, 250, 272, 296–298, 312, 315, 318, 324, 325, 337, 353, 366, 385, 390, 396.

1234. **Timasheff, N. S.** Ehrlich, Eugen. In *International Encyclopedia of the Social Sciences,* ed. by David L. Sills. New York : Macmillan, 1968. Vol. 4, *"Cumu–Elas."* – pp. 540–542.

1235. **Timasheff, Nicholas S.** Growth and Scope of Sociology of Law. In *Modern Sociological Theory in Continuity and Change,* ed. by Howard Becker, and Alvin Boskoff. New York : The Dryden Press, 1957. pp. 424–449.

1236. **Timasheff, N. S.** "What is "Sociology of Law"?" *The American Journal of Sociology.* 1937. Vol. 43, Nr. 2 (Sept.). pp. 225–235.

1237. **Treiber, Hubert.** "Max Weber and Eugen Ehrlich: On the Janus-headed Construction of Weber's Ideal Type in the Sociology of Law." *Max Weber Studies.* 2008. Vol. 8, Iss. 2. pp. 225–246.

1238. **Uebersicht** der Akademischen Behörden Professoren, Privatdocenten, Lehrer, Beamten etc. an der k. k. Franz-Josephs-Universität zu Czernowitz im Studienjahre 1897 / 1898. Czernowitz : Verl. des akademischen Senates, [s. a.]. 19 S.

Overview of the leading academic authorities, professors, associate professors, lecturers, officials, etc. at Czernowitz University in the academic year 1897/1898.

E. Ehrlich. – p. 8.

IN 194022 90T817

1239. **Uebersicht** der Akademischen Behörden Professoren, Privatdocenten, Lehrer, Beamten etc. an der k. k. Franz-Josephs-Universität zu Czernowitz im Studienjahre 1898 / 1899. Czernowitz : Verl. des akademischen Senates, [s. a.]. 16 S.

Overview of the leading academic authorities, professors, associate professors, lecturers, officials, etc. at Czernowitz University in the academic year 1898/1899.

E. Ehrlich. – p. 7.

IN 377222 90T817

1240. **Uebersicht** der Akademischen Behörden Professoren, Privatdocenten, Lehrer, Beamten etc. an der k. k. Franz-Josephs-Universität zu Czernowitz im Studienjahre 1899 / 1900. Czernowitz : Verl. des akademischen Senates, [s. a.]. 18 S.

Overview of the leading academic authorities, professors, associate professors, lecturers, officials, etc. at Czernowitz University in the academic year 1899/1900.

E. Ehrlich. – p. 8.

IN 359437 90T817

1241. **Uebersicht** der Akademischen Behörden Professoren, Privatdocenten, Lehrer, Beamten etc. an der k. k. Franz-Josephs-Universität zu Czernowitz im Studienjahre 1901/1902. Czernowitz: Verl. des akademischen Senates, [s. a.]. 19 S.

Overview of the leading academic authorities, professors, associate professors, lecturers, officials, etc. at Czernowitz University in the academic year 1901/1902.

E. Ehrlich. – pp. 3, 7, 8.

IN 194032 90T817

1242. **Uebersicht** der Akademischen Behörden Professoren, Privatdocenten, Lehrer, Beamten etc. an der k. k. Franz-Josephs-Universität zu Czernowitz im Studienjahre 1902/1903. Czernowitz: Verl. des akademischen Senates, [s. a.]. 20 S.

Overview of the leading academic authorities, professors, associate professors, lecturers, officials, etc. at Czernowitz University in the academic year 1902/1903.

E. Ehrlich. – pp. 3, 7, 8.

IN 194036 90T817

1243. **Uebersicht** der Akademischen Behörden Professoren, Privatdocenten, Lehrer, Beamten etc. an der k. k. Franz-Josephs-Universität zu Czernowitz im Studienjahre 1903/1904. Czernowitz: Verl. des akademischen Senates, [s. a.]. 19 S.

Overview of the leading academic authorities, professors, associate professors, lecturers, officials, etc. at Czernowitz University in the academic year 1903/1904.

E. Ehrlich. – p. 8.

IN 194039 90T817

1244. **Uebersicht** der Akademischen Behörden Professoren, Privatdocenten, Lehrer, Beamten etc. an der k. k. Franz-Josephs-Universität zu Czernowitz im Studienjahre 1904/1905. Czernowitz: Verl. des akademischen Senates, [s. a.]. 20 S.

Overview of the leading academic authorities, professors, associate professors, lecturers, officials, etc. at Czernowitz University in the academic year 1904/1905.

E. Ehrlich. – p. 8.

IN 194043 90T817

1245. **Uebersicht** der Akademischen Behörden Professoren, Privatdocenten, Lehrer, Beamten etc. an der k. k. Franz-Josephs-Universität zu Czernowitz im Studienjahre 1905/1906. Czernowitz: Verl. des akademischen Senates, [s. a.]. 19 S.

Overview of the leading academic authorities, professors, associate professors, lecturers, officials, etc. at Czernowitz University in the academic year 1905/1906.

E. Ehrlich. – p. 8.

IN 194049 90T817

1246. **Universitätsprofessor** Dr. Johann Wrobel. *Czernowitzer Zeitung.* 1909. 22. Juni (Nr. 139, Jg. 44). S. 3–4.

Information about the funeral of University Professor Dr. Johann Wrobel attended by the Dean Dr. Ehrlich.

IN 1946 90A1

1247. **Varga, Csaba.** *A jog mint folyamat.* Budapest: Szent István Társulat, 2002. 430 o. [Varga, Csaba. *Law as a process.* Budapest: Szent István Publisher, 2002. 430 p.]

Information about scientific views of Eugen Ehrlich – pp. 31, 76, 152, 181, 187–188, 218–219.

1248. **Varga, Csaba.** *Law and philosophy: Selected papers in legal theory.* Budapest: [s. n.], 1994. XI, 530 p. *(Philosophiae iuris: publications of the project on comparative legal cultures of the Faculty of law of Loránd Eötvös University in Budapest).* Bibliogr.: pp. 493–513.

Information about scientific views of Eugen Ehrlich – pp. 41, 48, 52, 69, 70, 108, 189, 284, 439–440, 452, 455

IN 389191 340V29

1249. **Varga, Csaba.** "Macrosociological Theories of Law: A Survey and Appraisal." *Tidskrift för rättssociologi.* 1986. Vol. 3. Nr. 3/4. pp. 165–198.

Information about scientific views of Eugen Ehrlich – pp. 170, 174, 191, 192.

1250. **Verhandlungen** der Gesellschaft Österreichischer Volkswirte: [E. Ehrlich. LIII. Plenarversammlung vom 29. Jänner 1895. S. 261–267; E. Ehrlich. LIV. Plenarversammlung vom 5. Februar 1895. S. 267–271; E. Ehrlich. LV. Plenarversammlung vom 12. Februar 1895. S. 271–278]. *Zeitschrift für Volkswirtschaft, Socialpolitik und Verwaltung.* 1895. Bd. 4, [Heft 1]. S. 103–123; Bd. 4, [Heft 2]. S. 250–278; Bd. 4, [Heft 3]. S. 459–480.

Information about the participation of Eugen Ehrlich in the negotiations of the Association of Austrian Economists.

IN 244215 14R8

1251. **Die "Verjudung"** der Universität. Czernowitz, 4. Dezember. *Czernowitzer Tagblatt.* 1907. 5. Dez. (Nr. 1447, Jg. 5). S. 1–2.

Information about the chapter by the Vice-Rector of Czernowitz University Professor Dr. Eugen Ehrlich entitled "Statistisches zur Universitätsrede des Grafen Thun" ["Statistics on the university speech of Count Thun"] published in the newspaper "Neue Freie Presse" related to the "Judaisation" of university. The summary of the chapter is also provided.

IN 1969 90A45

1252. **Vermeşan, Vasile.** "Domnii Ehrlich şiLast." *Glasul Bucovinei.* 1921. 13 mar. (Nr. 655, An. 4). p. 2.

Criticim of Ehrlich and Last by Romanian nationalist in the newspaper Glasul Bucovinei.

IN 732 90A89

1253. **Vermeşanu.** "Moţiunea studenttimii române în chestia Ehrlich-Last." *Ibidem.* 1921. 15 mar. (Nr. 656, An. 4). p. 1.

Information about criticism of professors Ehrlich and Last by Romanian students.

IN 732 90A89

1254. **Verschiedenes.** Allerhöchstes Namensfest. *Bukowiner Beamten-Zeitung.* 1906. 7. Okt. (Nr. 15, Jg. 1). S. 7.

Participation of the University Rector Professor Dr. Ehrlich, together with academic officials of Czernowitz University, in the worship of His Majesty the Emperor for students of primary and secondary schools in all churches.

IN 2164 90A60

1255. **Verschiedenes.** Fremde Orden. *Ibidem.* 1907. 1. Okt. (Nr. 59, Jg. 2). S. 10.

The Rector of Czernowitz University Professor Dr. Eugen Ehrlich awarded the Commander's Cross of the Greek Order of the Saviour.

IN 2162 90A60

1256. **Verschiedenes.** Fremde Orden. *Ibidem.* 1908. 1. Jänner (Nr. 1, Jg. 3). S. 6.

The Rector of Czernowitz University Professor Dr. Eugen Ehrlich awarded the Commander's Cross of the Greek Order of the Saviour.

IN 2163 90A60

1257. **Verschiedenes.** Rektorswahl. *Ibidem.* 1909. 1. Juli (Nr. 13, Jg. 4). S. 4.

Composition of the Academic Senate of Czernowitz University for the academic year 1909/1910. Dr. Eugen Ehrlich – Vice-Dean of the Faculty of Law and Public Administration.

IN 2160 90A60

1258. **Verschiedenes.** Wilhelm v. Hartel. *Ibidem.* 1907. 20. Jänner (Nr. 30, Jg. 2). S. 9.

Participation of the Rector Professor Dr. Eugen Ehrlich in the Czernowitz University delegation at the funeral of the Minister of Education and Honorary Doctor of Czernowitz University Dr. Wilhelm von Hartel in Vienna.

IN 2162 90A60

1259. **Verzeichnis** der öffentlichen Vorlesungen an der k. k. Franz-Josephs-Universität zu Czernowitz im Sommersemester 1897. Beginn : 1. März 1897. – Ende : 31. Juli 1897. Czernowitz : Verl. des akademischen Senates, [s. a.]. 27 S.

List of public lectures at Czernowitz University.

E. Ehrlich. – pp. 8, 20, 21, 25.

IN 193852 90T815

1260. **Verzeichnis** der öffentlichen Vorlesungen an der k. k. Franz-Josephs-Universität zu Czernowitz im Wintersemester 1897/1898. Beginn : 1. October 1897. – Ende : 28. Februar 1898. Czernowitz : Verl. des akademischen Senates, [s. a.]. 25 S.

List of public lectures at Czernowitz University.

E. Ehrlich. – pp. 7, 17, 18, 21.

IN 193857 90T815

1261. **Verzeichnis** der öffentlichen Vorlesungen an der k. k. Franz-Josephs-Universität zu Czernowitz im Sommersemester 1898. Beginn : 1. März 1898. – Ende : 31. Juli 1898. Czernowitz : Verl. des akademischen Senates, [s. a.]. 27 S.

List of public lectures at Czernowitz University.

E. Ehrlich. – pp. 7, 20, 21.

IN 377232 90T815

1262. **Verzeichnis** der öffentlichen Vorlesungen an der k. k. Franz-Josephs-Universität zu Czernowitz im Wintersemester 1898/1899. Beginn : 1. October 1898. – Ende : 28. Februar 1899. Czernowitz : Verl. des akademischen Senates, [s. a.]. 21 S.

List of public lectures at Czernowitz University.

E. Ehrlich. – pp. 6, 13, 14, 16.

IN 193863 90T815

1263. **Verzeichnis** der öffentlichen Vorlesungen an der k. k. Franz-Josephs-Universität zu Czernowitz im Sommersemester 1899. Beginn : 1. März 1899. – Ende : 31. Juli 1899. Czernowitz : Verl. des akademischen Senates, [s. a.]. 21 S.

List of public lectures at Czernowitz University.

E. Ehrlich. – pp. 6, 14, 18.

IN 193864 90T815

1264. **Verzeichnis** der öffentlichen Vorlesungen an der k. k. Franz-Josephs-Universität zu Czernowitz im Wintersemester 1899/1900. Beginn : 1. October 1899. – Ende : 28. Februar 1900. Czernowitz : Verl. des akademischen Senates, [s. a.]. 23 S.

List of public lectures at Czernowitz University.

E. Ehrlich. – pp. 7, 15, 16, 19.

IN 193866 90T815

1265. **Verzeichnis** der öffentlichen Vorlesungen an der k. k. Franz-Josephs-Universität zu Czernowitz im Sommersemester 1900. Beginn : 1. März 1900. – Ende : 31. Juli 1900. Czernowitz : Verl. des akademischen Senates, [s. a.]. 23 S.

List of public lectures at Czernowitz University.

E. Ehrlich. – pp. 7, 15, 16, 17.

IN 193869 90T815

1266. **Verzeichnis** der öffentlichen Vorlesungen an der k. k. Franz-Josephs-Universität zu Czernowitz im Wintersemester 1900/1901. Beginn : 1. October 1900. – Ende : 28. Februar 1901. Czernowitz : Verl. des akademischen Senates, [s. a.]. 23 S.

List of public lectures at Czernowitz University.

E. Ehrlich. – pp. 7, 16, 17.

IN 377233 90T815

1267. **Verzeichnis** der öffentlichen Vorlesungen an der k. k. Franz-Josephs-Universität zu Czernowitz im Sommersemester 1901. Beginn : 1. März 1901. – Ende : 31. Juli 1901. Czernowitz : Verl. des akademischen Senates, [s. a.]. 23 S.

List of public lectures at Czernowitz University.

E. Ehrlich. – pp. 7, 15, 20.

IN 193874 90T815

1268. **Verzeichnis** der öffentlichen Vorlesungen an der k. k. Franz-Josephs-Universität zu Czernowitz im Wintersemester 1901/1902. Beginn : 1. October 1901. – Ende : 28. Februar 1902. Czernowitz : Verl. des akademischen Senates, [s. a.]. 23 S.

List of public lectures at Czernowitz University.

E. Ehrlich. – pp. 7, 15, 16, 17.

IN 193876 90T815

1269. **Verzeichnis** der öffentlichen Vorlesungen an der k. k. Franz-Josephs-Universität zu Czernowitz im Sommersemester 1902. Beginn : 1. März 1902. – Ende : 31. Juli 1902. Czernowitz : Verl. des akademischen Senates, [s. a.]. 25 S.

List of public lectures at Czernowitz University.

E. Ehrlich. – pp. 8, 17, 18, 22.

IN 167898 90T817

1270. **Verzeichnis** der öffentlichen Vorlesungen an der k. k. Franz-Josephs-Universität zu Czernowitz im Wintersemester 1902/1903. Beginn : 1. Oktober1902. – Ende : 28. Februar 1903. Czernowitz : Verl. des akademischen Senates, [s. a.]. 23 S.

List of public lectures at Czernowitz University.

E. Ehrlich. – pp. 7, 14, 16.

IN 193878 90T815

1271. **Verzeichnis** der öffentlichen Vorlesungen an der k. k. Franz-Josephs-Universität zu Czernowitz im Sommersemester 1903. Beginn : 1. März 1903. – Ende : 31. Juli 1903. Czernowitz : Verl. des akademischen Senates, [s. a.]. 25 S.

List of public lectures at Czernowitz University.

E. Ehrlich. – pp. 7, 16, 18, 22.

IN 193879 90T815

1272. **Verzeichnis** der öffentlichen Vorlesungen an der k. k. Franz-Josephs-Universität zu Czernowitz im Wintersemester 1903/1904. Beginn : 1. Oktober 1903. – Ende : 28. Februar1904. Czernowitz : Verl. des akademischen Senates, [s. a.]. 23 S.

List of public lectures at Czernowitz University.

E. Ehrlich. – pp. 7, 14, 15, 17, 20.

IN 191161 90T81

1273. **Verzeichnis** der öffentlichen Vorlesungen an der k. k. Franz-Josephs-Universität zu Czernowitz im Sommersemester 1904. Beginn : 1. März 1904. – Ende : 31. Juli 1904. Czernowitz : Verl. des akademischen Senates, [s. a.]. 23 S.

List of public lectures at Czernowitz University.

E. Ehrlich. – pp. 7, 15, 16, 20.

IN 193890 90T815

1274. **Verzeichnis** der öffentlichen Vorlesungen an der k. k. Franz-Josephs-Universität zu Czernowitz im Wintersemester 1904/1905. Beginn : 1. Oktober 1904. – Ende : 28. Februar 1905. Czernowitz : Verl. des akademischen Senates, [s. a.]. 25 S.

List of public lectures at Czernowitz University.

E. Ehrlich. – pp. 8, 17, 19, 22.

IN 191167 90T815

1275. **Verzeichnis** der öffentlichen Vorlesungen an der k. k. Franz-Josephs-Universität zu Czernowitz im Sommersemester 1905. Beginn : 1. März 1905. – Ende : 31. Juli 1905. Czernowitz : Verl. des akademischen Senates, [s. a.]. 27 S.

List of public lectures at Czernowitz University.

E. Ehrlich. – pp. 8, 18, 19, 23.

IN 191171 90T815

1276. **Verzeichnis** der öffentlichen Vorlesungen an der k. k. Franz-Josephs-Universität zu Czernowitz im Wintersemester 1905/1906. Beginn : 1. Ocktober 1905. – Ende : 28. Februar 1906. Czernowitz : Verl. des akademischen Senates, [s. a.]. 25 S.

List of public lectures at Czernowitz University.

E. Ehrlich. – pp. 8, 17, 19, 22.

IN 191174 90T815

1277. **Verzeichnis** der öffentlichen Vorlesungen an der k. k. Franz-Josephs-Universität zu Czernowitz im Sommersemester 1906. Beginn : 1. März 1906. – Ende : 31. Juli 1906. Czernowitz : Verl. des akademischen Senates, [s. a.]. 27 S.

List of public lectures at Czernowitz University.

E. Ehrlich. – pp. 8, 17, 18, 20, 24.

IN 194181 90T815

1278. **Verzeichnis** der öffentlichen Vorlesungen an der k. k. Franz-Josephs-Universität zu Czernowitz im Wintersemester 1906/1907. Beginn : 1. Ocktober 1906. – Ende : 28. Februar 1907. Czernowitz : Verl. des akademischen Senates, [s. a.]. 25 S.

List of public lectures at Czernowitz University.

E. Ehrlich. – pp. 8, 17, 19, 22.

IN 359798 90T815

1279. **Verzeichnis** der öffentlichen Vorlesungen an der k. k. Franz-Josephs-Universität zu Czernowitz im Sommersemester 1907. Beginn : 1. März 1907. – Ende : 31. Juli 1907. Czernowitz : Verl. des akademischen Senates, [s. a.]. 27 S.

List of public lectures at Czernowitz University.

E. Ehrlich. – pp. 8, 18, 19, 20, 23.

IN 359804 90T815

1280. **Verzeichnis** der öffentlichen Vorlesungen an der k. k. Franz-Josephs-Universität zu Czernowitz im Winter-Semester 1907/1908. Beginn : 1. Oktober1907. – Ende : 28. Februar 1908. Czernowitz : Verl. des akademischen Senates, [s. a.]. 29 S.

List of public lectures at Czernowitz University.

E. Ehrlich. – pp. 9, 21, 23, 27.

IN 193925 90T815

1281. **Verzeichnis** der öffentlichen Vorlesungen an der k. k. Franz-Josephs-Universität zu Czernowitz im Sommersemester 1908. Beginn : 1. März 1908. – Ende : 31. Juli 1908. Czernowitz : Verl. des akademischen Senates, [s. a.]. 29 S.

List of public lectures at Czernowitz University.

E. Ehrlich. – pp. 8, 19, 20, 25.

IN 194189 90T815

1282. **Verzeichnis** der öffentlichen Vorlesungen an der k. k. Franz-Josephs-Universität zu Czernowitz im Winter-Semester 1908/1909. Beginn: 1. Oktober 1908. – Ende: 28. Februar 1909. Czernowitz : Verl. des akademischen Senates, [s. a.]. 29 S.

List of public lectures at Czernowitz University.

E. Ehrlich. – pp. 9, 21, 22, 23, 26.

IN 194197 90T815

1283. **Verzeichnis** der öffentlichen Vorlesungen an der k. k. Franz-Josephs-Universität zu Czernowitz im Sommersemester 1909. Beginn : 1. März 1909. – Ende : 31. Juli 1909. Czernowitz : Verl. des akademischen Senates, [s. a.]. 29 S.

List of public lectures at Czernowitz University.

E. Ehrlich. – pp. 8, 20, 21, 26.

IN 193936 90T815

1284. **Verzeichnis** der öffentlichen Vorlesungen an der k. k. Franz-Josephs-Universität zu Czernowitz im Winter-Semester 1909/1910. Beginn: 1. Oktober 1909. – Ende: 28. Februar 1910. Czernowitz : Verl. des akademischen Senates, [s. a.]. 29 S.

List of public lectures at Czernowitz University.

E. Ehrlich. – pp. 9, 21, 23, 27.

IN 193938 90T815

1285. **Verzeichnis** der öffentlichen Vorlesungen an der k. k. Franz-Josephs-Universität zu Czernowitz im Sommersemester 1910. Beginn : 1. März 1910. – Ende : 31. Juli 1910. Czernowitz : Verl. des akademischen Senates, [s. a.]. 31 S.

List of public lectures at Czernowitz University.

E. Ehrlich. – pp. 9, 21, 22.

IN 193940 90T815

1286. **Verzeichnis** der öffentlichen Vorlesungen an der k. k. Franz-Josephs-Universität zu Czernowitz im Wintersemester 1910/1911. Beginn: 1. Oktober 1910. – Ende: 28. Februar 1911. Czernowitz : Verl. des akademischen Senates, [s. a.]. 27 S.

List of public lectures at Czernowitz University.

E. Ehrlich. – pp. 8, 19, 21, 24.

IN 193343 90T815

1287. **Verzeichnis** der öffentlichen Vorlesungen an der k. k. Franz-Josephs-Universität zu Czernowitz im Sommersemester 1911. Beginn : 1. März 1911. – Ende : 31. Juli 1911. Czernowitz : Verl. des akademischen Senates, [s. a.]. 29 S.

List of public lectures at Czernowitz University.

E. Ehrlich. – pp. 8, 18, 19.

IN 193944 90T815

1288. **Verzeichnis** der öffentlichen Vorlesungen an der k. k. Franz-Josephs-Universität zu Czernowitz im Wintersemester 1911/1912. Beginn : 1. Oktober 1911. – Ende : 28. Februar 1912. Czernowitz : Verl. des akademischen Senates, [s. a.]. 35 S.

List of public lectures at Czernowitz University.

E. Ehrlich. – pp. 8, 21, 22, 25, 32.

IN 193948 90T815

1289. **Verzeichnis** der öffentlichen Vorlesungen an der k. k. Franz-Josephs-Universität zu Czernowitz im Sommersemester 1912. Beginn : 1. März 1912. – Ende : 31. Juli 1912. Czernowitz : Verl. des akademischen Senates, [s. a.]. 33 S.

List of public lectures at Czernowitz University.

E. Ehrlich. – pp. 8, 22, 29.

IN 358387 90T815

1290. **Verzeichnis** der öffentlichen Vorlesungen an der k. k. Franz-Josephs-Universität zu Czernowitz im Wintersemester 1912/1913. Beginn : 1. Oktober 1912. – Ende : 28. Februar 1913. Czernowitz : Verl. des akademischen Senates, [s. a.]. 31 S.

List of public lectures at Czernowitz University.

E. Ehrlich. – p. 8.

IN 358390 90T815

1291. **Verzeichnis** der öffentlichen Vorlesungen an der k. k. Franz-Josephs-Universität zu Czernowitz im Sommersemester 1913. Beginn : 1. März 1913. – Ende : 31. Juli 1913. Czernowitz : Verl. des akademischen Senates, [s. a.]. 33 S.

List of public lectures at Czernowitz University.

E. Ehrlich. – pp. 8, 21, 30.

IN 358392 90T815

1292. **Verzeichnis** der öffentlichen Vorlesungen an der k. k. Franz-Josephs-Universität zu Czernowitz im Wintersemester 1913/1914. Beginn : 1. Oktober 1913. – Ende : 28. Februar 1914. Czernowitz : Verl. des akademischen Senates, [s. a.]. 39 S.

List of public lectures at Czernowitz University.

E. Ehrlich. – pp. 8, 22, 24, 27, 34.

IN 193953 90T815

1293. **Verzeichnis** der öffentlichen Vorlesungen an der k. k. Franz-Josephs-Universität zu Czernowitz im Sommersemester 1914. Beginn : 1. März 1914. – Ende : 31. Juli 1914. Czernowitz : Verl. des akademischen Senates, [s. a.]. 35 S.

List of public lectures at Czernowitz University.

E. Ehrlich. – pp. 8, 20, 32.

IN 358396 90T815

1294. **Verzeichnis** der öffentlichen Vorlesungen an der k. k. Franz-Josephs-Universität zu Czernowitz im Sommersemester 1919. Beginn : 1. März 1919. – Ende : 22. September 1919. Czernowitz : Verl. des akademischen Senates, [s. a.]. 15 S.

List of public lectures at Czernowitz University.

E. Ehrlich. – p. 7.

IN 193955 90T815

1295. **Verzeichnis** der öffentlichen Vorlesungen an der k. k. Franz-Josephs-Universität zu Czernowitz im Sommersemester 1897. Beginn : 1. März 1897. – Ende : 31. Juli 1897. *Hochschul-Nachrichten.* 1897. Febr. (Nr. 77). Anh. S. 26.

List of public lectures at Czernowitz University.

IN 19432 60A15

1296. **Verzeichnis** der öffentlichen Vorlesungen an der k. k. Franz-Josephs-Universität zu Czernowitz im Wintersemester 1897/1898. *Ibidem.* 1897. Aug./Sept. (Nr. 83/84). Anh. S. 17.

List of public lectures at Czernowitz University.

IN 19432 60A15

1297. **Verzeichnis** der öffentlichen Vorlesungen an der k. k. Franz-Josephs-Universität zu Czernowitz im Wintersemester 1902/1903. *Ibidem.* 1902. Aug./Sept. (Heft 143/144, Jg. 12, Nr. 11/12). Anh. S. 17.

List of public lectures at Czernowitz University.

IN 19437 60A15

1298. **Verzeichnis** der öffentlichen Vorlesungen an der k. k. Franz-Josephs-Universität zu Czernowitz im Sommersemester 1909. Beginn : 1. März 1909. – Ende : 31. Juli 1909. *Ibidem.* 1909. Jan. (Heft 220, Jg. 19, Nr. 4). Anh. S. 14–15.

List of public lectures at Czernowitz University.

E. Ehrlich. – p. 14.

IN 19444 60A15

1299. **Verzeichnis** der öffentlichen Vorlesungen an der k. k. Franz-Josephs-Universität zu Czernowitz im Winter-Semester 1909/1910. Beginn : 1. Oktober 1909.–Ende : 28. Februar 1910. *Ibi-*

dem. 1909. Aug./Sept. (Heft 227/228, Jg. 19, Nr. 11/12). Anh. S. 15–16.

List of public lectures at Czernowitz University.

E. Ehrlich. – p. 15.

IN 19444 60A15

1300. **Verzeichnis** der öffentlichen Vorlesungen an der k. k. Franz-Josephs-Universität zu Czernowitz im Sommer-Semester 1911. Beginn: 1. März 1911. – Ende: 31. Juli 1911. *Ibidem.* 1911. März (Heft 246, Jg. 21, Nr. 6). Anh. S. 13–14.

List of public lectures at Czernowitz University.

E. Ehrlich. – p. 13.

IN 19445 60A15

1301. **Verzeichnis** der öffentlichen Vorlesungen an der k. k. Franz-Josephs-Universität zu Czernowitz im Winter-Semester 1911/1912. Beginn: 1. Oktober 1911. – Ende: 28. Februar 1912. *Ibidem.* 1911. Aug./Sept. (Heft 251/252, Jg. 21, Nr. 11/12). S. 438–439.

List of public lectures at Czernowitz University.

E. Ehrlich. – p. 438.

IN 19446 60A15

1302. **Verzeichnis** der öffentlichen Vorlesungen an der k. k. Franz-Josephs-Universität zu Czernowitz im Sommer-Semester 1912. Beginn: 1. März 1912. – Ende: 31. Juli 1912. *Ibidem.* 1912. März (Heft 258, Jg. 22, Nr. 6). S. 221–222.

List of public lectures at Czernowitz University.

E. Ehrlich. – p. 222.

IN 19447 60A15

1303. **Verzeichnis** der öffentlichen Vorlesungen an der k. k. Franz-Josephs-Universität zu Czernowitz im Winter-Semester 1912/1913. Beginn: 1. Oktober 1912. – Ende :2 8. Februar 1913. *Ibidem.* 1912. Aug./Sept. (Heft 263/264, Jg. 22, Nr. 11/12). S. 481–482.

List of public lectures at Czernowitz University.

E. Ehrlich. – p. 482.

IN 19447 60A15

1304. **Verzeichnis** der öffentlichen Vorlesungen an der k. k. Franz-Josephs-Universität zu Czernowitz im Sommer-Semester 1913. Beginn: 1. März 1913. – Ende: 31. Juli 1913. *Ibidem.* 1913. März (Heft 270, Jg. 23, Nr. 6). S. 236–237.

List of public lectures at Czernowitz University.

E. Ehrlich. – p. 236.

IN 19445 60A15

1305. **Verzeichnis** der Vorlesungen, welche der Studierende zu hören beabsichtigt. Jüristische Fakultät. Winter Semester 1905/06. Czernowitz, 1905/1906. 375 Bl. Ms.

Information about the students of the Faculty of Law of Czernowitz University (on the individual standard sheets, filled in by hand, containing bibliographic data of each student, and the list of courses attended with surnames of lecturers). Winter semester of the academic year 1905/1906.

E. Ehrlich. – pp. 1, 6, 8, 9, 11–13, 16–18, 20–22, 27, 30, 32–34, 37, 42, 43, 45, 49, 52–56, 59–63, 66, 70, 73, 74, 76, 81, 83, 85, 86, 89, 90, 93, 95–98, 104, 106, 110–112, 114, 116, 118–120, 122, 130, 132, 134, 135, 140, 143, 144, 147, 148, 152, 154, 160–162, 164, 165, 167, 168, 171, 176–179, 181, 183, 184, 188–190, 192–197, 203–206, 208, 212, 215, 221–223, 225, 227–229, 233, 242, 250, 252–253, 256, 261, 265, 273, 276, 277, 281–283, 288, 294, 295, 297–300, 302–305, 307–309, 311, 315, 319, 322, 329, 330, 333, 335, 337, 339, 343, 347, 349, 354, 360, 362, 363, 367.

IN Ms.

1306. **Verzeichnis** der Vorlesungen, welche der Studierende zu hören beabsichtigt. Jüristische Fakultät. Sommer Semester 1912/13. Czernowitz, 1912/1913. 273 Bl. Ms.

Information about the students of the Faculty of Law of Czernowitz University (on the individual standard sheets, filled in by hand, containing bibliographic data of each student, and the list of courses attended with surnames of lecturers). Summer semester of the academic year 1912/1913.

E. Ehrlich. – pp. 4, 5, 7, 13, 16, 18, 22, 24, 25, 28, 29, 31, 34, 41, 45, 46, 58, 61, 62, 68, 70, 71, 74, 77, 79, 80, 81, 88, 90, 96, 97, 100, 101, 103–105, 109, 111, 114, 119, 125, 136, 138, 140–144, 154, 155, 162, 165–167, 170, 173, 175, 178, 181, 182, 185, 186, 189, 193, 200, 203–205, 208, 213, 221, 222, 224, 231, 233, 237–239, 241, 244, 246, 250, 255, 256. 261–263, 268, 273.

IN Ms.

1307. **Verzeichnis** der Vorlesungen, welche der Studierende zu hören beabsichtigt. Jüristische Fakultät. Winter Semester 1913/14. Czernowitz, 1913/1914. 276 Bl. Ms.

Information about the students of the Faculty of Law of Czernowitz University (on the individual standard sheets, filled in by hand, containing bibliographic data of each student, and the list of courses attended with surnames of lecturers). Winter semester of the academic year 1913/1914.

E. Ehrlich. – pp. 1, 7, 9, 12, 16, 18, 23, 30, 31, 33, 36, 42, 43, 45–48, 50–52, 55, 58, 60, 65, 67, 69, 75, 76, 79, 81, 82, 84, 85, 88, 90, 93, 99–101, 105, 108, 114, 122–124, 127–130, 134, 138–140, 142–145, 148, 151, 153–157, 159, 160, 162, 164–167,

171–174, 177, 179–181, 184–188, 190, 192, 196, 199–201, 206–208, 210, 212, 213, 222–225, 231–233, 236–240, 246, 250.

IN Ms.

1308. **Vinogradoff, Paul.** Modern tendencies in jurisprudence. In *Historical jurisprudence = Történeti jogtudomány,* [ed. József Szabadfalvi]. Budapest: [s. n.], 2000. pp. 235–250. *(Philosophiae iuris,* red. Csaba Varga).

E. Ehrlich. – p. 242.

IN 394043 34H69

1309. **Vogl, Stefan.** *Soziale Gesetzgebungspolitik, freie Rechtsfindung und soziologische Rechtswissenschaft bei Eugen Ehrlich.* Baden-Baden: Nomos-Verl.-Ges., 2003. 396 S. (*Fundamenta Juridica*; Bd. 46).

Information about scientific views of Eugen Ehrlich.

1310. **Volkswirtschaft.** Czernowitz, 8. Jänner. Die Neugestaltung des Vertragsrechtes. *Czernowitzer Tagblatt.* 1906. 9. Jänner (Nr. 878, Jg. 4). S. 4–5.

Information about the speech of Professor of Czernowitz University Dr. Eugen Ehrlich at the plenary session of Lower Austrian Commercial Society in Vienna onthe 8th of January 1906 entitled "Die Neugestaltung des Vertragsrechtes" ("Restructuring Contract Law"). The summary of the speech is also provided.

IN 1966 90A45

1311. **Vorlesungen** an der k. k. Franz-Josephs-Universität zu Czernowitz. Sommersemester 1898. *Hochschul-Nachrichten.* 1898. Febr. (Nr. 89, Jg. 8. Nr. 5). Anh. S. 30.

List of public lectures at Czernowitz University.

IN 19433 60A15

1312. **Vorlesungen**ander k. k. Franz-Josephs-Universität zu Czernowitz. Wintersemester 1898/1899. Beginn: 1. October 1898. – Ende: 28. Februar 1899. *Ibidem.* 1898. Juli (Nr. 94, Jg. 8. Nr. 10). Anh. S. 36–37.

List of public lectures at Czernowitz University.

E. Ehrlich. – p. 37.

IN 19433 60A15

1313. **Vorlesungen** an der k. k. Franz-Josephs-Universität zu Czernowitz im Wintersemester 1900/1901. Beginn: 1. October 1900. – Ende: 26. Februar 1901. *Ibidem.* 1900. Jg. 10, *"Winter-Semester 1899/1900 und Sommer-Semester 1900."* Anh. S. 12.

List of public lectures at Czernowitz University.

IN 360375 60A15

1314. **Vorlesungen** an der k. k. Franz-Josephs-Universität zu Czernowitz im Wintersemester 1901/1902. Beginn: 1. October1901.–Ende: 28. Februar 1902. *Ibidem.* 1901. Aug./Sept. (Heft 131/132, Jg. 11, Nr. 11/12). Anh. S. 7–8.

List of public lectures at Czernowitz University.

E. Ehrlich. – p. 8.

IN 19436 60A15

1315. **Vorlesungen** an unserer Universität. *Bukowinaer Post.* 1913. 24. Aug. (Nr. 3041, Jg. 20). S. 3–4.

Information about the approval of the project of public lectures at Franz Joseph University in Czernowitz in the winter semester of the academic year 1913/1914 by the Decree of the Ministry of Cultus and Education of the 15 of July 1913, including the information that Dr. Ehrlich will read the following lectures: "Römisches Recht mit Ausnahme der Quellen und Verfassungsgeschichte" ("Roman Law with the Exception of Sources and Constitutional History"), "Römisches Recht in seinen Grundzügen mit Berücksichtigung der byzantinischen Fortentwicklung" ("Roman Law in its Principles, Considering the Byzantine Development"), and "Seminar für lebendes Recht" ("Seminar on Living Law").

IN 2067 90J26

1316. **Wagner, Rudolf,** hrsg. *Alma Mater Francisco Josephina: die deutschsprachige Nationalitäten-Universität in Czernowitz: Festschriftzum 100. Jahrestag ihrer Eröffnung 1875.* [2. Aufl.]. München: Hans Meschendörfer, 1979. 427 S.

Information about Eugen Ehrlich, the Rector of Czernowitz University in the publication – pp. 24, 124, 130, 132, 333, 387.

IN 392715 378A39

1317. **Wagner, Rudolf.** "Die Rechts- und Staatswissenschaftliche Fakultät der Franz-Josephs-Universität in Czernowitz: Ihr Beitrag zur Erforschung des Rechts in einer multikulturellen Gesellschaft." *Anuarul Institutului de Istorie "G. Bariţiu" din Cluj-Napoca.* 2008. T. 42. pp. 199–217.

Information about Professor Eugen Ehrlich in the publication – pp. 200–217.

1318. **Wagner, Rudolf.** *Vom Halbmond zum Doppeladler: ausgewählte Beiträge zur Geschichte der Bukowina und Czernowitzer Universität "Francisco-Josephina": Festgabezum 120. Jahrestag 1995.* Augsburg: Der Südostdeutsche, 1996. [X], 535 S.

Information about Professor Eugen Ehrlich in the publication – pp. 67, 76, 264, 296–323.

IN 384051 9(c287)W14

1319. **Wagner, Rudolf.** *Vom Moldauwappen zum Doppeladler: ausgew. Beiträge zur Geschichte der Bukowina; Festgabe zu seinem 80. Geburtstag,* hrsg. i. A. der Landsmannschaft der Buchenland-deutschen von Paula Tiefenthaler, und Adolf Armbruster. Augsburg : Hofmann-Verl., 1991. XXIV, 625 S.

Information about Professor of Czernowitz University Eugen Ehrlich – pp. 105, 277, 284.

IN 386613 9(c287)W14

1320. **Weber, Max.** *Economy and Society: an Outline of Interpretive Sociology,* ed. by Guenther Roth, and Claus Wittich. Berkeley; Los Angeles ; London : Univ. of California Press, 1978. CX, 1469, LXIV.

E. Ehrlich. – pp. 659, 753, 776, 777, 854, 898, 899.

1321. **Welan, Manfried.** Eugen Ehrlich: Eingrosser europäischer Rechtsdenker aus Czernowitz. In *Die Bukowina: Vergangenheit und Gegenwart: eine Veröffentlichung des Österreichischen Ost- und Südosteuropa-Instituts,* hrsg. von Ilona Slawinski, und Joseph P. Strelka. Bern ; Berlin ; Frankfurt a. M. ; New York ; Paris ; Wien : PeterLang, 1995. S. 191–199.

Information about Professor of Czernowitz University Eugen Ehrlich.

ЦБЗ 7623

1322. **Die Wiener** Tagung des Deutschen Juristentages. *Czernowitzer Tagblatt.* 1912. 30. Aug. (Nr. 2850, Jg. 10). S. 1–2.

About the scheduled 31st assembly of the German Lawyers in Vienna on the 4th of September 1912. The programme of the meeting includes the participation of Czernowitz Professor Dr. Ehrlich – p. 2.

IN 1979 90A45

1323. **Ziegert, Klaus Alex.** "A note on Eugen Ehrlich and the Production of Legal Knowledge." *The Sydney Law Review.* 1998. Vol. 20, Nr. 1 (Mar.). pp. 108–125.

1324. **Ziegert, Klaus A.** On Eugen Ehrlich, Fundamental Principles of the Sociology of Law. In *Classic Writings in Law and Society,* ed. by A. Javier Treviño. New Brunswick; London: Trans. Publ., 2006. pp. 103–130. *(Contemporary Comments and Criticisms).*

1325. **Ziegert, Klaus A.** On Eugen Ehrlich, Fundamental Principles of the Sociology of Law. In *Classic Writings in Law and Society,* ed. by A. Javier Treviño. 2nd ed., rev. and expanded. New Brunswick ; London : Trans. Publ., 2011. pp. 123–149.

1326. **Ziegert, Klaus A.** Sociological Jurisprudence. In *The Philosophy of Law : An Encyclopedia,* ed. by Christopher Berry Gray. New York ;

London: Garland Publ., 1999. Vol. 2, *"K–Z."* pp. 814–817. (*Garland Reference Library of the Humanities*; Vol. 1743).

E. Ehrlich. – pp. 815–817.

1327. **Ziegert, Klaus A.** "The Sociology behind Eugen Ehrlich's Sociology of Law." *International Journal of the Sociology of Law.* 1979. Vol. 7. pp. 225–273.

1328. **Zipprian, Heinz.** Eugen Ehrlich und die Bukowina: Die Entstehung der Rechtssoziologie aus der kulturellen Vielfalt menschlicher Verbände. In *Nation und Nationalismus in wissenschaftlichen Standardwerken Österreich-Ungarns, ca. 1867–1918.* Hrsg. von Endre Kiss, Csaba Kiss, and Justin Stagl. Wien; Köln; Weimar: Böhlau Verl., 1997. S. 112–126. (*Ethnologica austriaca*; 2).

Eugen Ehrlich as a founder of the Sociology of Law.

1329. **Zur Eröffnung** des Justizpalais. Czernowitz, 8. Oktober. *Czernowitzer Tagblatt.* 1906. 9. Okt. (Nr. 1102, Jg. 4). S. 1–4.

Participation of the Rector Dr. Ehrlich in the celebration of the opening of the new Palace of Civil Justice – p. 1.

IN 1967 90A45

1330. **Zur Gemeinderatskrise.** Czernowitz, 13. Dezember. *Ibidem.* 1905. 14. Dez. (Nr. 860, Jg. 3). S. 1–4.

Participation of Professor Ehrlich in solving a municipality crisis – p. 1.

IN 1965 90A45

APPENDICES: DOCUMENTS FROM CHERNIVTSI UNIVERSITY SCIENTIFIC LIBRARY HOLDINGS

Appendix A: Eugen Ehrlich's works: covers and title pages

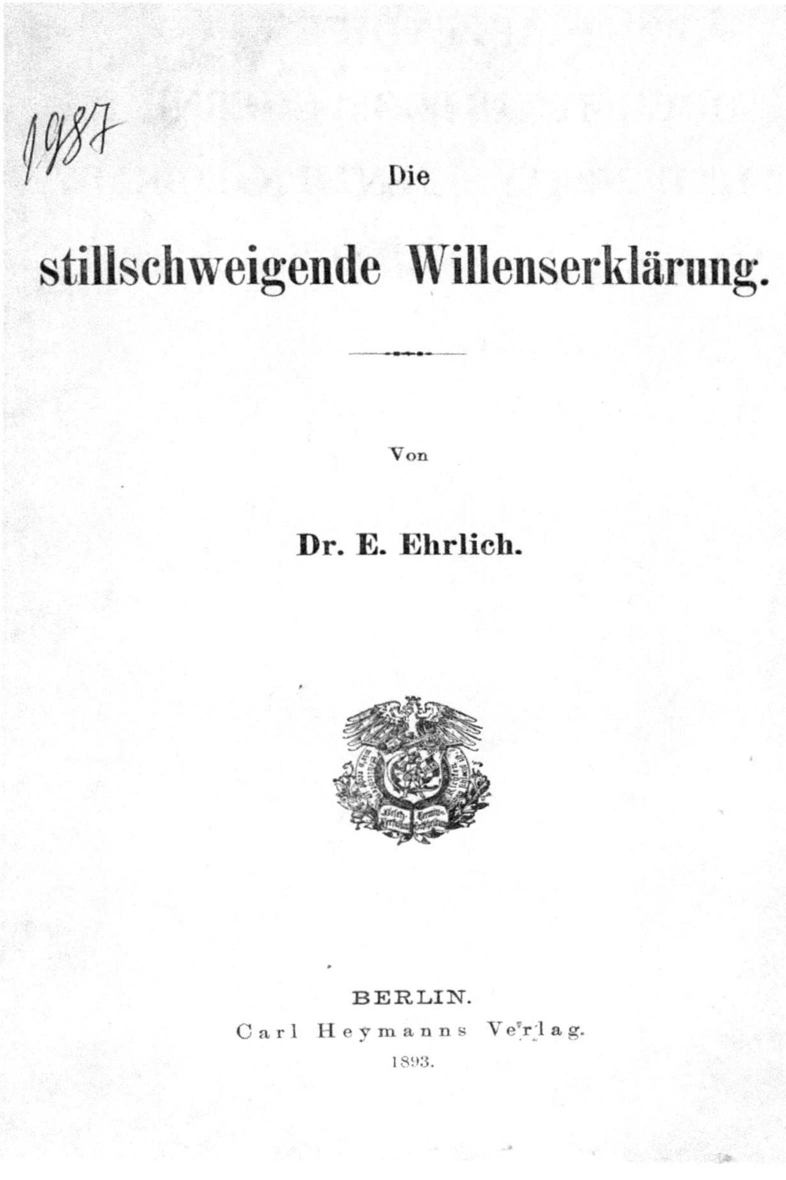

Die

stillschweigende Willenserklärung.

Von

Dr. E. Ehrlich.

BERLIN.
Carl Heymanns Verlag.
1893.

Picture 7. *Tacit Consent*

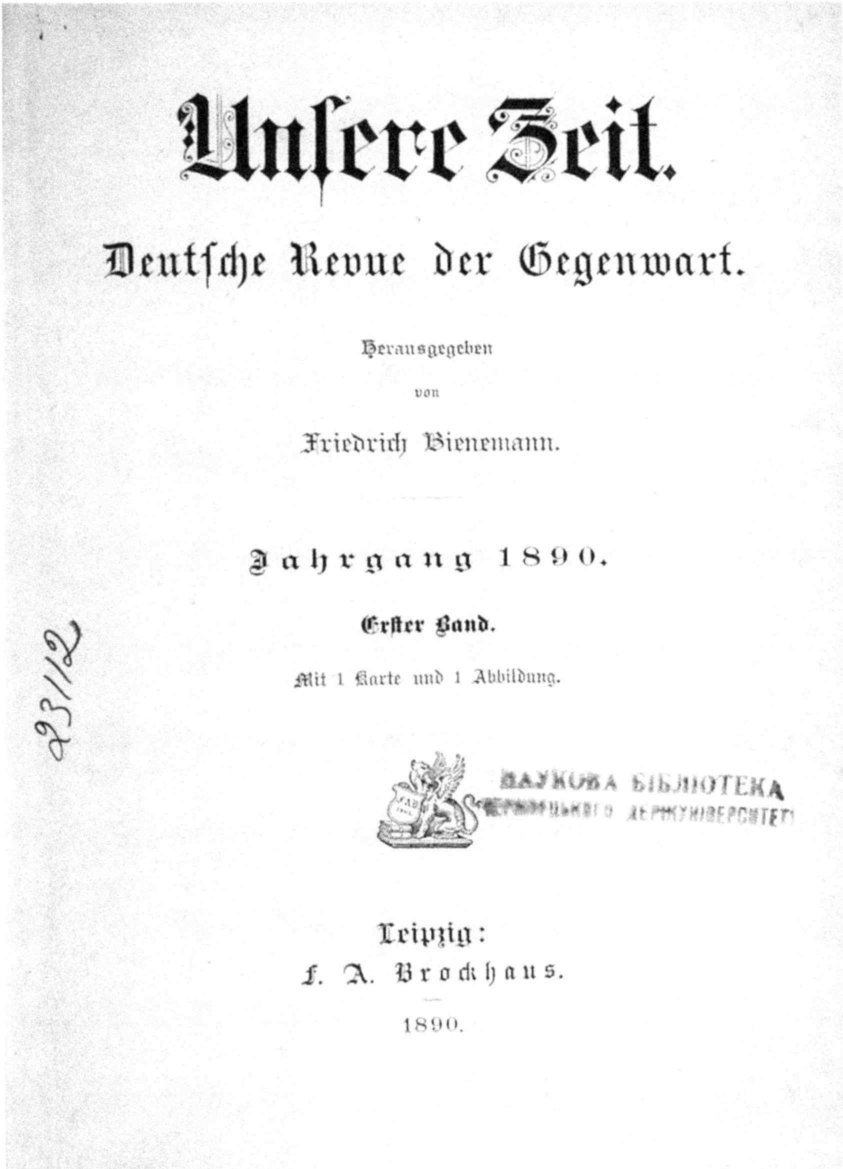

Unsere Zeit.

Deutsche Revue der Gegenwart.

Herausgegeben

von

Friedrich Bienemann.

Jahrgang 1890.

Erster Band.

Mit 1 Karte und 1 Abbildung.

Leipzig:

F. A. Brockhaus.

1890.

Kriegsmacht in dem der Betrachtung gewidmeten Zeitabschnitte mannichfaltig und zum Theile groß, so finden wir einen Abschluß nirgends erreicht, denn auch die Verausgabung der neuen Infanteriewaffe an die Truppen befindet sich erst in den Anfängen. Es liegt die Unfertigkeit der Verhältnisse eben im Charakter unserer Zeit. Aber nicht nur ein materielles und äußerliches, sondern auch ein innerliches und geistiges Werden sehen wir vor uns, zu dem die an das Heer gerichteten kaiserlichen Erlasse den Ausgangspunkt bilden.

Sociale Gesetzgebungspolitik auf dem Gebiete des Deutschen Privatrechts.

Von **Dr. E. Ehrlich** in Wien.

I.

Die ursprüngliche gesellschaftliche Organisation des deutschen Volkes war, wie die aller andern Völker, die Römer nicht ausgenommen, die Gentilverfassung. Das ganze Volk zerfiel, wie auch sonst überall während dieser Entwickelungsperiode, in Geschlechter, Clans (Gentes), welche nach innen mehr oder weniger communistisch organisirt, nach außen nur lose in Hundertschaften und Gaue (Curien und die alten römischen Tribus) verbunden waren. Aber schon in den ältesten Quellen des deutschen Rechtes finden wir die Zersetzung der alten Geschlechterordnung im vollen Zuge, sodaß dieselbe uns auch im entferntesten nicht mehr in jener Geschlossenheit entgegentritt wie etwa in den Familiencommunionen der Südslawen oder dem russischen Mir: nur ganz ausnahmsweise haben sich hie und da in weltentlegenen Theilen Deutschlands fossile Ueberreste derselben bis auf den heutigen Tag erhalten. Der Feudalismus des Mittelalters verzerrte vollends die Geschlechterordnung noch lange vor der Aufnahme des römischen Rechts in ihr Gegentheil, es schwand die alte Freiheit der Geschlechter, ihre communistische Organisation löste sich auf, und, wenn derselbe auch manche gentilicischen Grundsätze in sich aufnahm, so hätte er sie in Deutschland wahrscheinlich ebenso wenig vor dem Untergange bewahren können wie in England, wo er sich mit der Zeit, ohne römisch-rechtliche Einflüsse, ebenfalls als unhaltbar erwies und die gentilicischen und feudalen Rechtselemente zu einem lächerlichen, kostspieligen, unverständlichen Formelkrame wurden. Der Grund des Verfalles der alten Geschlechterordnung und mit ihr des mittelalterlichen deutschen Rechts lag also keineswegs, wie man häufig annimmt, außerhalb derselben, in der Reception des römischen Rechts, sondern darin, daß sie den an die Gesellschaft nunmehr herantretenden Aufgaben nicht mehr gewachsen war.

Gleichzeitig mit dem im 15. Jahrhundert beginnenden Verfalle der Feudalverfassung in Deutschland tritt die Reception des römischen Rechts ein. Dieses „große Räthsel" der deutschen Rechtsentwickelung ist eigentlich nichts weniger als ein Räthsel. Wie sich im individuellen Leben ein Mensch die Er-

Pictures 8, 9. ***Social Legislative Policy in the Field of German Private Law***

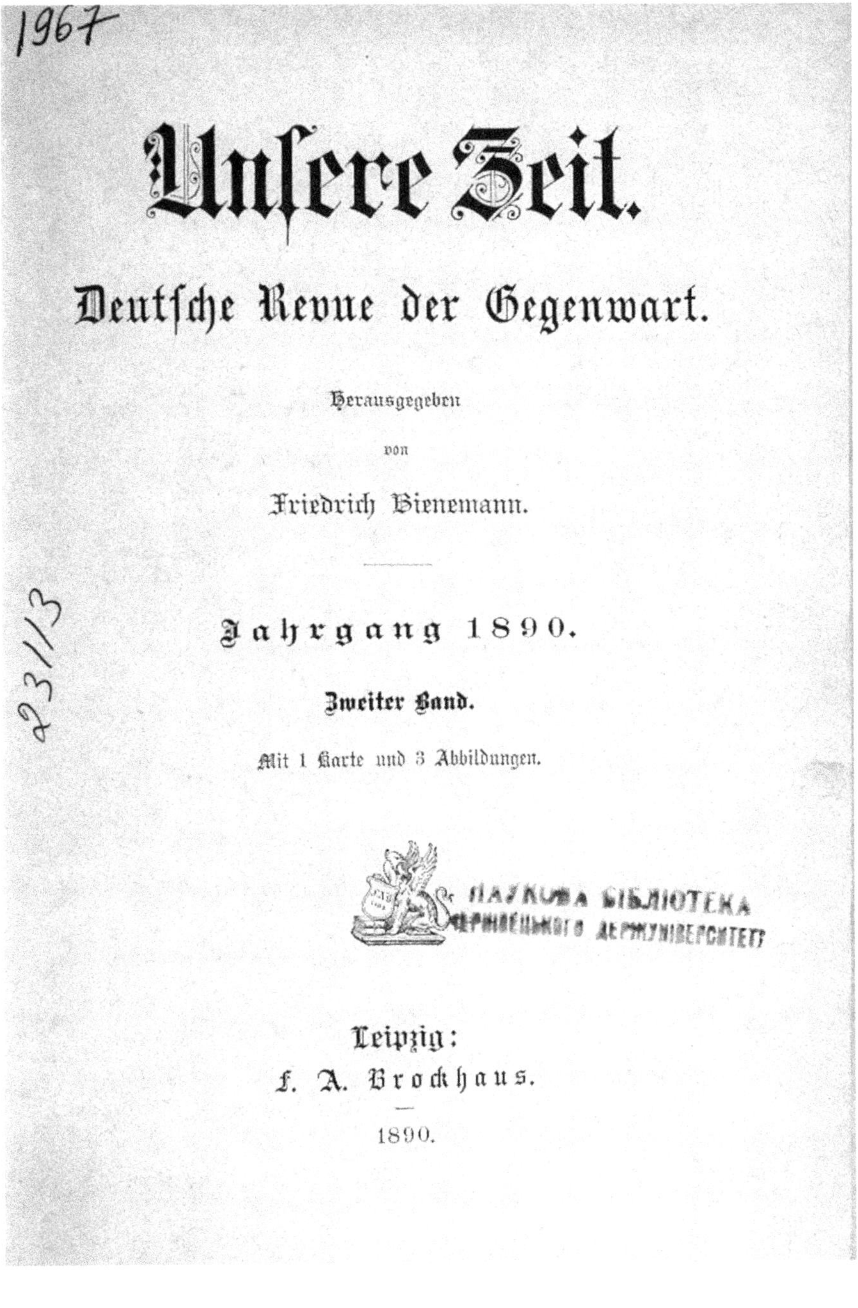

Unsere Zeit.

Deutsche Revue der Gegenwart.

Herausgegeben

von

Friedrich Bienemann.

Jahrgang 1890.

Zweiter Band.

Mit 1 Karte und 3 Abbildungen.

Leipzig:
F. A. Brockhaus.

1890.

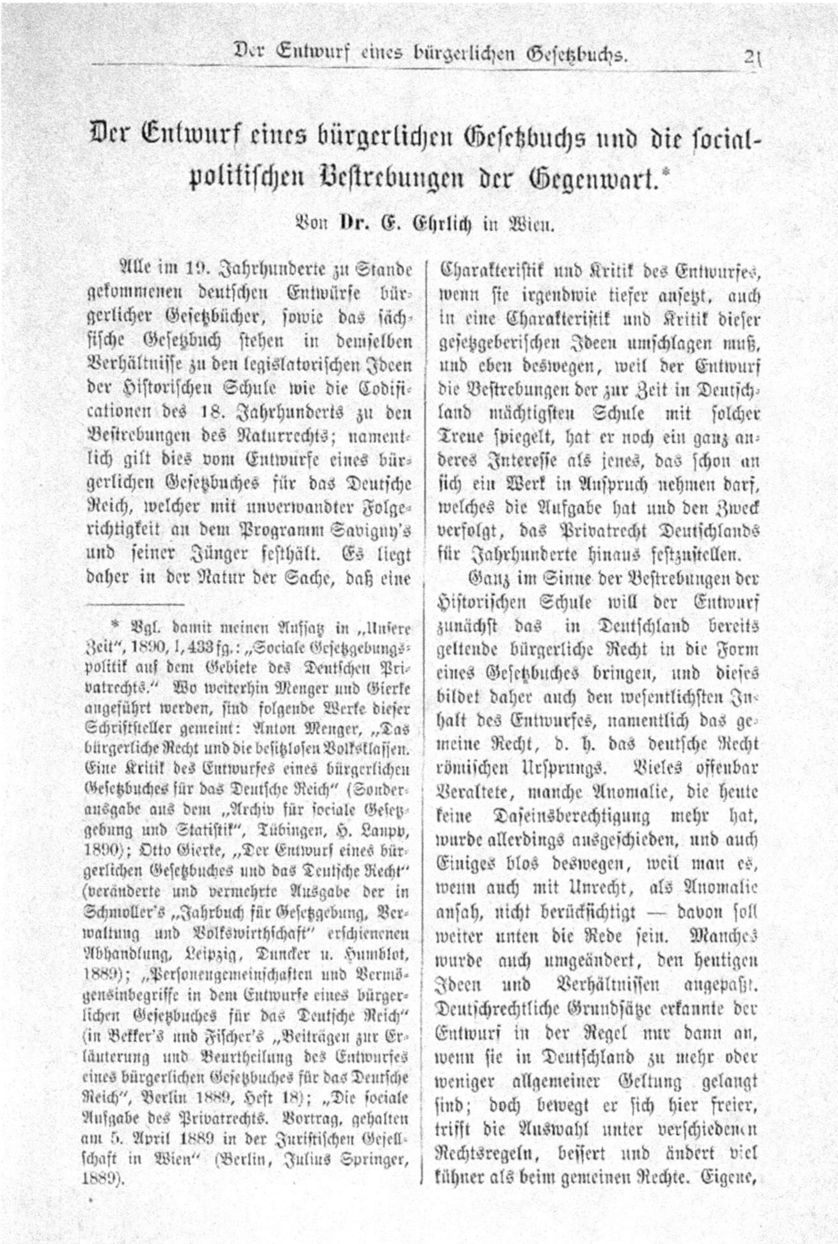

Der Entwurf eines bürgerlichen Gesetzbuchs. 21

Der Entwurf eines bürgerlichen Gesetzbuchs und die socialpolitischen Bestrebungen der Gegenwart.*

Von **Dr. E. Ehrlich** in Wien.

Alle im 19. Jahrhunderte zu Stande gekommenen deutschen Entwürfe bürgerlicher Gesetzbücher, sowie das sächsische Gesetzbuch stehen in demselben Verhältnisse zu den legislatorischen Ideen der Historischen Schule wie die Codificationen des 18. Jahrhunderts zu den Bestrebungen des Naturrechts; namentlich gilt dies vom Entwurfe eines bürgerlichen Gesetzbuches für das Deutsche Reich, welcher mit unverwandter Folgerichtigkeit an dem Programm Savigny's und seiner Jünger festhält. Es liegt daher in der Natur der Sache, daß eine Charakteristik und Kritik des Entwurfes, wenn sie irgendwie tiefer ansetzt, auch in eine Charakteristik und Kritik dieser gesetzgeberischen Ideen umschlagen muß, und eben deswegen, weil der Entwurf die Bestrebungen der zur Zeit in Deutschland mächtigsten Schule mit solcher Treue spiegelt, hat er noch ein ganz anderes Interesse als jenes, das schon an sich ein Werk in Anspruch nehmen darf, welches die Aufgabe hat und den Zweck verfolgt, das Privatrecht Deutschlands für Jahrhunderte hinaus festzustellen.

Ganz im Sinne der Bestrebungen der Historischen Schule will der Entwurf zunächst das in Deutschland bereits geltende bürgerliche Recht in die Form eines Gesetzbuches bringen, und dieses bildet daher auch den wesentlichsten Inhalt des Entwurfes, namentlich das gemeine Recht, d. h. das deutsche Recht römischen Ursprungs. Vieles offenbar Veraltete, manche Anomalie, die heute keine Daseinsberechtigung mehr hat, wurde allerdings ausgeschieden, und auch Einiges blos deswegen, weil man es, wenn auch mit Unrecht, als Anomalie ansah, nicht berücksichtigt — davon soll weiter unten die Rede sein. Manches wurde auch umgeändert, den heutigen Ideen und Verhältnissen angepaßt. Deutschrechtliche Grundsätze erkannte der Entwurf in der Regel nur dann an, wenn sie in Deutschland zu mehr oder weniger allgemeiner Geltung gelangt sind; doch bewegt er sich hier freier, trifft die Auswahl unter verschiedenen Rechtsregeln, bessert und ändert viel kühner als beim gemeinen Rechte. Eigene,

* Vgl. damit meinen Aufsatz in „Unsere Zeit", 1890, I, 433 fg.: „Sociale Gesetzgebungspolitik auf dem Gebiete des Deutschen Privatrechts." Wo weiterhin Menger und Gierke angeführt werden, sind folgende Werke dieser Schriftsteller gemeint: Anton Menger, „Das bürgerliche Recht und die besitzlosen Volksklassen. Eine Kritik des Entwurfes eines bürgerlichen Gesetzbuches für das Deutsche Reich" (Sonderausgabe aus dem „Archiv für sociale Gesetzgebung und Statistik", Tübingen, H. Laupp, 1890); Otto Gierke, „Der Entwurf eines bürgerlichen Gesetzbuches und das Deutsche Recht" (veränderte und vermehrte Ausgabe der in Schmoller's „Jahrbuch für Gesetzgebung, Verwaltung und Volkswirthschaft" erschienenen Abhandlung, Leipzig, Duncker u. Humblot, 1889); „Personengemeinschaften und Vermögensinbegriffe in dem Entwurfe eines bürgerlichen Gesetzbuches für das Deutsche Reich" (in Bekker's und Fischer's „Beiträgen zur Erläuterung und Beurtheilung des Entwurfes eines bürgerlichen Gesetzbuches für das Deutsche Reich", Berlin 1889, Heft 18); „Die sociale Aufgabe des Privatrechts. Vortrag, gehalten am 5. April 1889 in der Juristischen Gesellschaft in Wien" (Berlin, Julius Springer, 1889).

Pictures 10, 11. ***The Draft of Civil Code and Social-Political Aspirations of the Present Times***

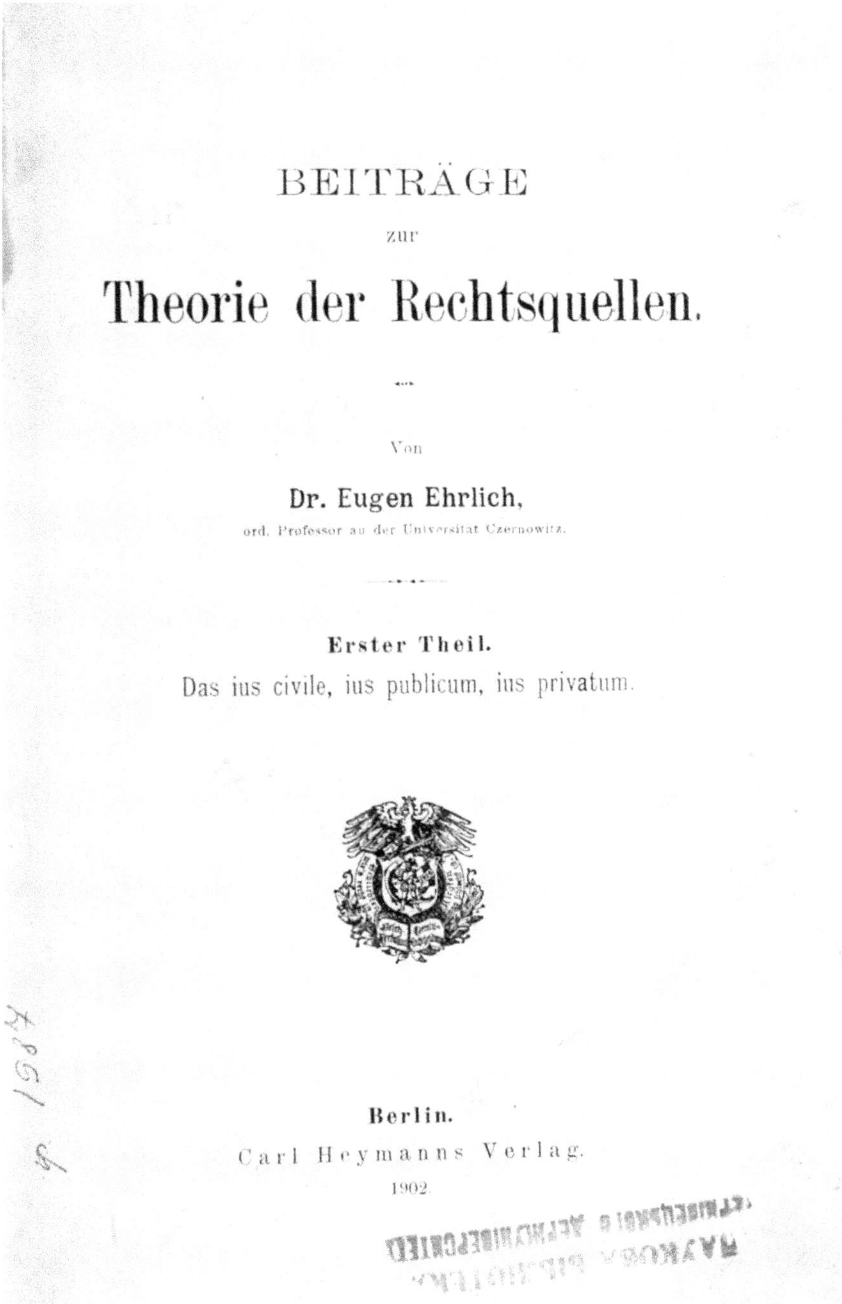

BEITRÄGE

zur

Theorie der Rechtsquellen.

Von

Dr. Eugen Ehrlich,

ord. Professor an der Universität Czernowitz.

Erster Theil.

Das ius civile, ius publicum, ius privatum.

Berlin.

Carl Heymanns Verlag.

1902.

Picture 12. ***Contribution to the Theory of Sources of Law***

FREIE RECHTSFINDUNG

UND

FREIE RECHTSWISSENSCHAFT.

VORTRAG

GEHALTEN IN DER JURISTISCHEN GESELLSCHAFT IN WIEN AM 4. MÄRZ 1903

VON

Dr. EUGEN EHRLICH

PROFESSOR DER RECHTE IN CZERNOWITZ.

LEIPZIG,
VERLAG VON C. L. HIRSCHFELD,
1903.

Picture 13. ***Free Finding of the Law and Free Science of Law***

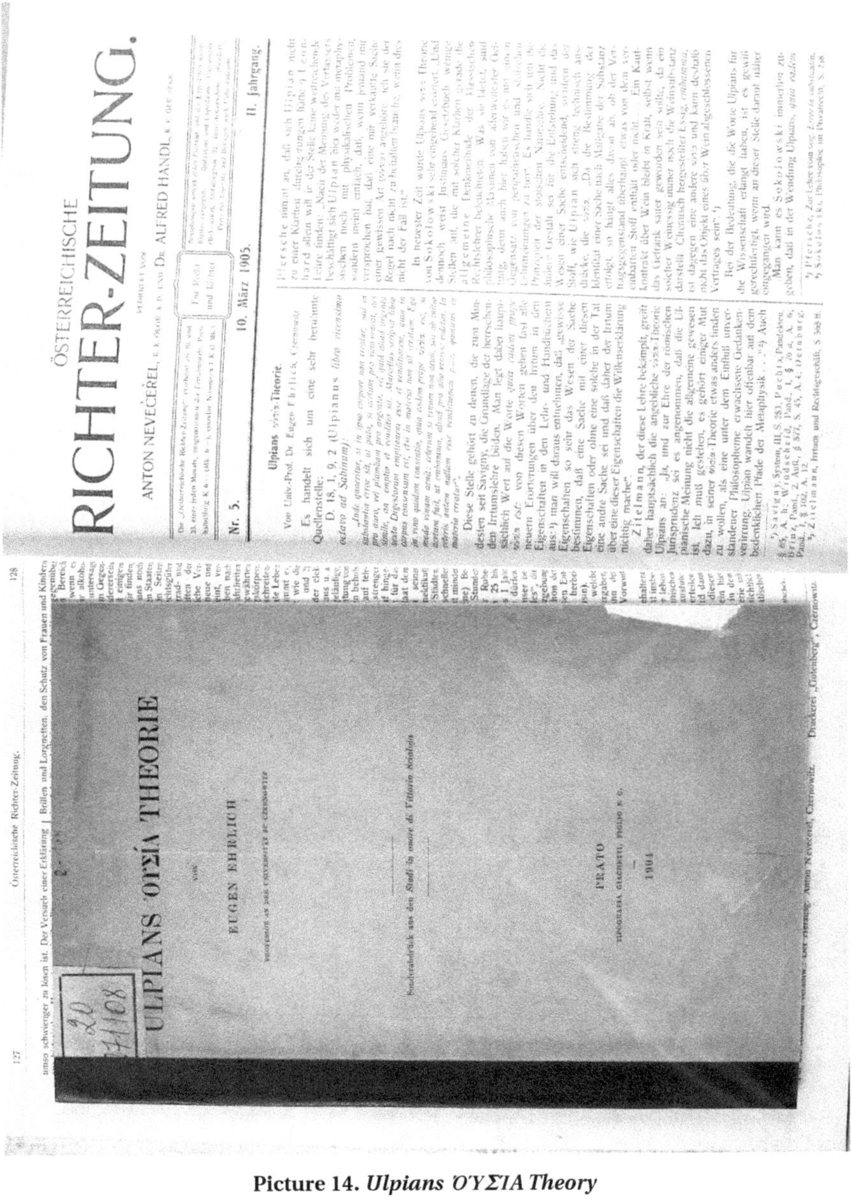

Picture 14. ***Ulpians ΌΥΣΙΑ Theory***

VORTRÄGE UND ABHANDLUNGEN
herausgegeben vom Sozialwissenschaftlichen akademischen Vereine
IN CZERNOWITZ
Nr. I.

DIE AUFGABEN DER SOZIAL-
POLITIK IM ÖSTERR. OSTEN
INSBESONDERE IN DER BUKOWINA

MIT BESONDERER BELEUCHTUNG
DER JUDEN- UND BAUERNFRAGE

VON

PROF. DR. EUGEN EHRLICH

○○○

VORTRAG
GEHALTEN IM SOZIALWISSENSCHAFTLICHEN AKADEM. VEREINE
AN DER CZERNOWITZER UNIVERSITÄT IM WINTERSEMESTER 1908/9

○○○

PREIS 40 HELLER

CZERNOWITZ
IM SELBSTVERLAGE DES VEREINES
1909
BUCHDRUCKEREI „GUTENBERG“

Picture 15. ***The Tasks of Social Policy in the Austrian East, especially in Bukovina***

ÖSTERREICHISCHE

RICHTER-ZEITUNG.

REDIGIERT VON

ANTON NEVEČEŘEL, K. K. OLGR. A. D. UND DR. ALFRED HANDL, K. K. LGR.

Die „Oesterreichische Richter-Zeitung" erscheint am 10. und 25. eines jeden Monats, ausgenommen die Ferialmonate. Preis der Ausgabe für Zivilrecht 8 K (8 Mk.) jährlich, der Ausgabe für Strafrecht 5 K (5 Mk.) jährlich, beider Ausgaben halbjährlich 6 K (6 Mk.), einzelne Nummern 1 K (1 Mk.)

Für Recht und Richter.

Bestellungen nimmt jedes Postamt und die Expedition dieses Blattes entgegen. — Redaktion und Expedition: Czernowitz (Bukowina), Stefaniegasse 22. Inseratenannahme: ebendort. Preis für Inserate und Beilagen nach Uebereinkunft.

Nr. 3. 10. März 1906. III. Jahrgang.

Soziologie und Jurisprudenz.*)

Von Professor Eugen Ehrlich, Czernowitz.

Jedem, der ein Gesetz mit einem darüber geschriebenen juristischen Werk verglichen hat, wird aufgefallen sein, daß das Buch das Gesetz um ein vielfaches, manchmal sogar um mehrhundertfaches übersteigt. Es liegt gewiß sehr nah, nach dem Grunde dieser Erscheinung zu fragen. Wie konnte über ein so kurzes Gesetz ein so dickes Buch geschrieben werden? Wird diese Frage gestellt, so haben die Juristen eine ganz annehmbare Antwort gleich bei der Hand. Jedes Gesetz, es mag noch so klar und ausführlich sein, läßt noch vielen Zweifeln Raum; diese Zweifel zu lösen, sei die Aufgabe der juristischen Literatur. Nun, die Zweifel müssen recht ausgiebig sein, wenn sie nur in Werken zu lösen sind, die viel umfangreicher sind als die Gesetze selbst. Da ist doch wohl die andere Frage berechtigt: warum werden denn die Gesetze nicht so gefaßt, daß keine Zweifel übrig bleiben? Gewonnen ist doch bei der heutigen Methode nichts, wenn man, um sich über alles, was das Gesetz anordnet, Klarheit zu verschaffen, erst nach einem Buch greifen muß, das darüber geschrieben worden ist. Entweder sollten also die Gesetze ausführlicher sein oder die juristische Literatur ist überflüssig.

Einst dachten auch die Juristen so. Sie suchten die Gesetze so ausführlich zu fassen, daß Zweifel über ihren Sinn gar nicht mehr möglich wären. Der Erfolg war zunächst, daß die Gesetze dicker wurden; aber die juristischen Bücher wurden deshalb nicht dünner. Mit der Zeit kam man darauf, daß jedes Wort, das man einem Gesetz hinzufügt, eben nur zu neuen Zweifeln Anlaß gibt. Heute neigen fast alle einsichtigen Juristen der Ansicht zu, je kürzer, je wortkarger ein Gesetz, um so besser sei es. Die landläufige Antwort auf die Frage, warum das, was die juristischen Bücher bringen, nicht schon im Gesetz enthalten sei, kann daher unmöglich befriedigen.

Bei tieferm Eindringen überzeugt man sich in der Tat, daß der Unterschied zwischen Gesetz und einem Werk, das sich mit dem Gesetz befaßt, nicht ein quantitativer, sondern ein qualitativer ist: nicht ein Mehr, sondern ein Anderes bringen die juristischen Bücher. Sie enthalten eben die juristische Wissenschaft. Die Wissenschaft gehört nicht in das Gesetz. Nimmt man sie in das Gesetz auf, wie von denen versucht worden ist, die alles im Gesetz selbst geben wollten, so verliert sie sofort ihre Eigenart: ein Zwitterding entsteht, das die Wissenschaft nicht fördert, das Gesetz aber verunstaltet und nicht selten auch in seiner Wirkung schädigt.

Wenn bisher immer vom Gesetz gesprochen wurde, so liegt der Grund darin, daß es die anschaulichste und auch dem Laien geläufigste Form des Rechtes ist. Dasselbe gilt aber von jeder andern Form, insbesondere auch vom Gewohnheitsrecht. Die Frage, die hier aufgeworfen wird, ist die nach dem Verhältnis der juristischen Wissenschaft zur Rechtsnorm. Es ist eine der schwierigsten Fragen, die eine Wissenschaft überhaupt bieten kann.

Ein Beispiel soll zunächst zeigen, was ich meine. Das Familienrecht des österreichischen bürgerlichen Gesetzbuches ist bekanntlich streng individualistisch, vielleicht das individualistischeste unter allen, die heute in Europa gelten. Die Frau steht dem Mann und die Kinder stehen den Eltern im allgemeinen selbständig gegenüber, fast als ob sie einander ganz fremd wären. Das Kind kann eigenes Vermögen haben und verfügt dann darüber ebenso frei, wie die Eltern über das ihrige; jedes Einkommen des Kindes kommt dem Kinde selbst, nicht den Eltern zugute. Das Kind hat volles Selbstbestimmungsrecht und kann auch seine Arbeitskraft mit voller Freiheit für sich selbst verwerten. Nur so lange das Kind minderjährig ist, steht es unter väterlicher Gewalt; aber der Vater, der Inhaber dieser Gewalt, ist nicht viel mehr als ein Vormund: seine Aufgabe besteht ausschließlich in der Vorsorge, daß das Kind sich nicht durch Unerfahrenheit, Leichtsinn oder

*) Diese Abhandlung wurde zunächst in Hardens ‚Zukunft' veröffentlicht. Da der Herausgeber jedoch mehrere Kürzungen vorgenommen hat, so wird sie hier in der ursprünglichen Fassung nochmals abgedruckt.

Picture 16. ***Sociology and Jurisprudence***

Internationales Privatrecht.

Von

Prof. Dr. **Eugen Ehrlich.**

I.

Es scheint uns selbstverständlich, daß ein deutsches Gericht die Rechtsstreitigkeiten, für die es zuständig ist, nach deutschem Recht entscheidet. Trotzdem ist es nicht immer so. Schon die natürliche Empfindung sagt uns, daß ein in Frankreich von einem Engländer errichtetes Testament, die in England abgeschlossene Ehe zweier Amerikaner, der Kauf eines in Rußland gelegenen Gutes unmöglich nach deutschem Rechte beurteilt werden können. Sollten daher deutsche Gerichte darüber erkennen — und das ist aus verschiedenen Gründen möglich — dann werden sie nicht deutsches, sondern fremdes Recht anwenden müssen. Die Rechtsgrundsätze, die bestimmen, ob in einem Falle das eigene Recht des erkennenden Richters oder ein fremdes Recht, allenfalls welches fremde Recht, anzuwenden sei, bilden, wie man gewöhnlich annimmt, das internationale Privatrecht.

Man würde kaum glauben, wie modern das ganze Rechtsgebilde des internationalen Privatrechts ist. Weder das Altertum noch das deutsche Mittelalter kennt es. Der Grund ist, daß selbst hochentwickelte Völker noch dem Angehörigen eines fremden Volkes kein Recht zubilligen. Das Recht ist bloß um der Angehörigen des eigenen Volkes willen da, der Fremde ist rechtlos. Nur ein Ausdruck der Rechtlosigkeit der Fremden ist die uns im Altertum und im Mittelalter überall begegnende Sklaverei: der rechtlose Mann verfällt dem, der sich seiner bemächtigt. Dieser könnte ihn ja auch töten, ohne daß sich darüber jemand beschweren dürfte.

Eine Folge davon ist, daß auf dieser Entwicklungsstufe jedes Volk sein Recht nur auf die Volksgenossen anwendet. Einem Volke ist sein Recht ebenso eigentümlich wie seine Sprache oder seine Religion. Diese Auffassung klebt jedem primitiven Rechte an; selbst die modernen Kolonialstaaten tragen ihr Rechnung, die den Eingeborenen in ihren Angelegenheiten ihre Rechte lassen, während die in den Kolonien ansässigen Fremden, sie mögen

27*

Picture 17. ***International Private Law***

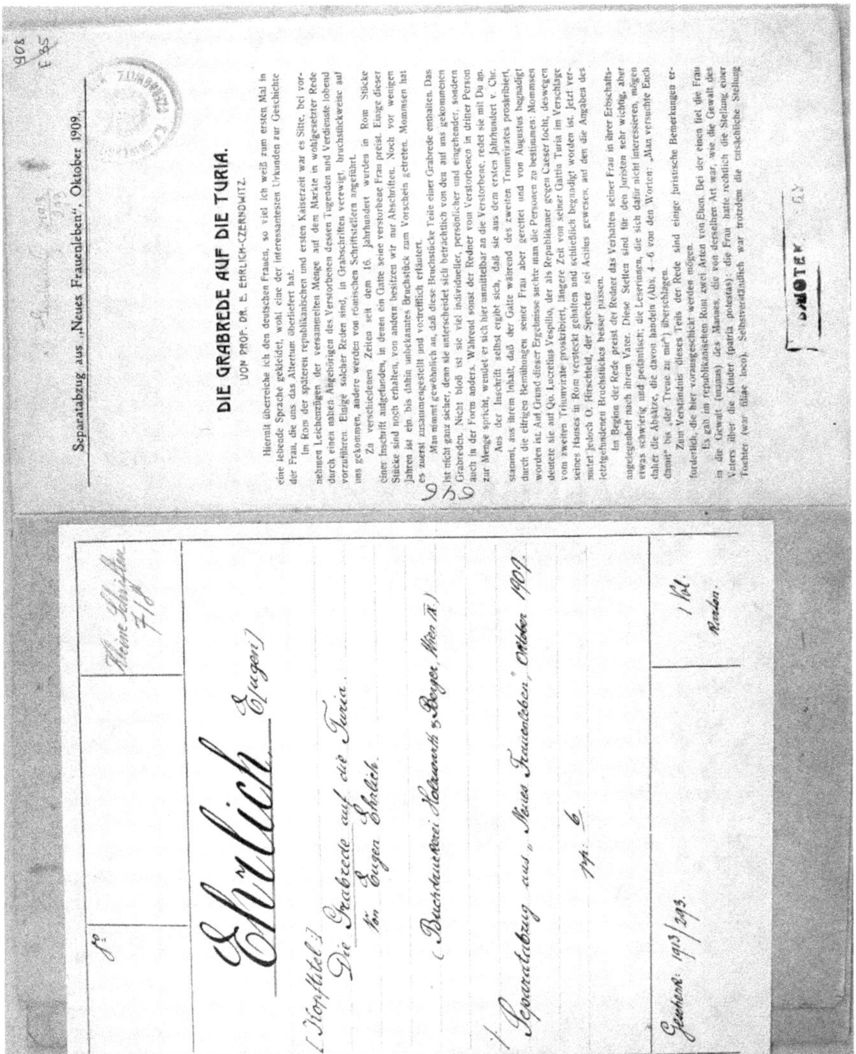
Separatabzug aus „Neues Frauenleben", Oktober 1909.

DIE GRABREDE AUF DIE TURIA.

VON PROF. DR. E. EHRLICH-CZERNOWITZ.

Picture 18. ***Funeral Speech on Turia***

DAS RECHT

Sammlung von Abhandlungen für Juristen und Laien

Herausgegeben von Dr. FRANZ KOBLER

BAND I

EUGEN EHRLICH

DIE RECHTS-FÄHIGKEIT

P M

BERLIN

PUTTKAMMER & MÜHLBRECHT

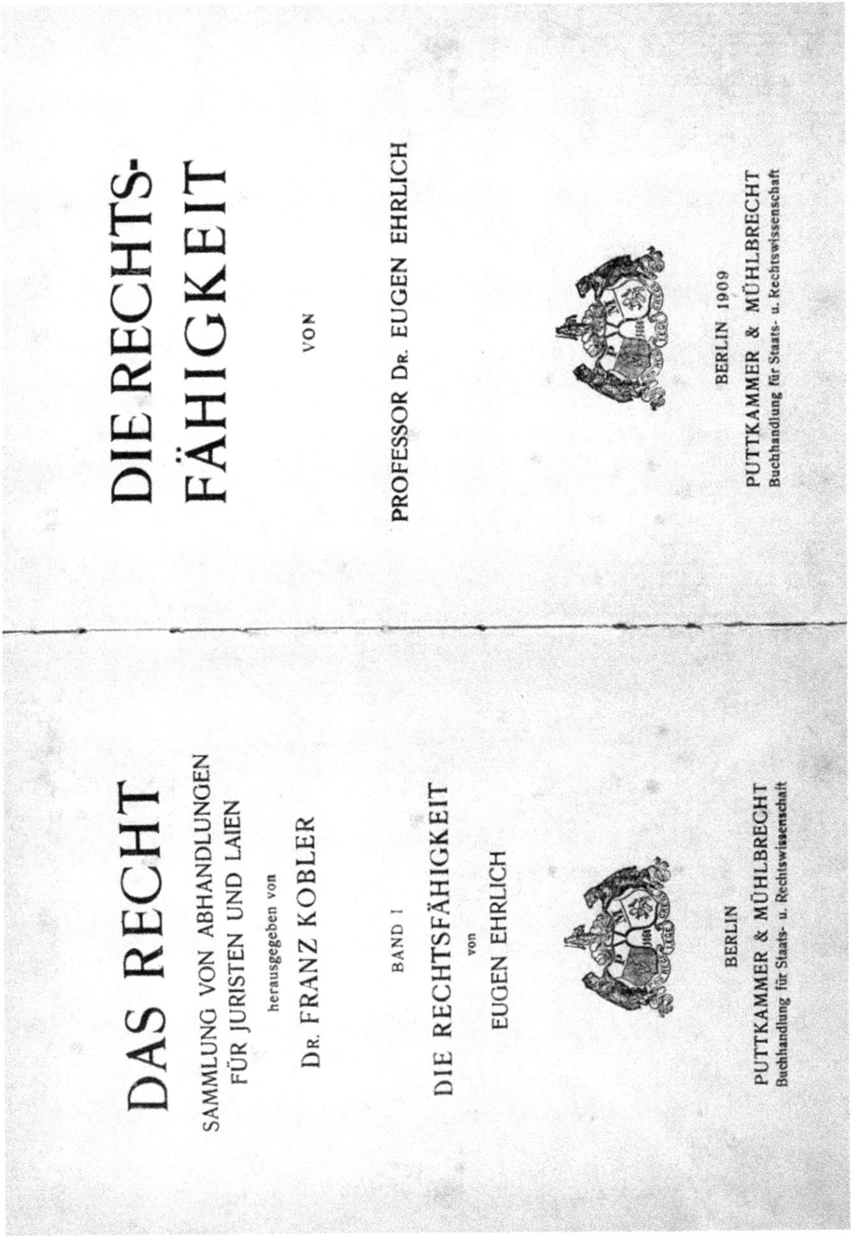

DAS RECHT

SAMMLUNG VON ABHANDLUNGEN
FÜR JURISTEN UND LAIEN

herausgegeben von

DR. FRANZ KOBLER

BAND I

DIE RECHTSFÄHIGKEIT

von

EUGEN EHRLICH

BERLIN

PUTTKAMMER & MÜHLBRECHT
Buchhandlung für Staats- u. Rechtswissenschaft

DIE RECHTS-
FÄHIGKEIT

VON

PROFESSOR DR. EUGEN EHRLICH

BERLIN 1909

PUTTKAMMER & MÜHLBRECHT
Buchhandlung für Staats- u. Rechtswissenschaft

Pictures 19, 20. ***Capability of Law***

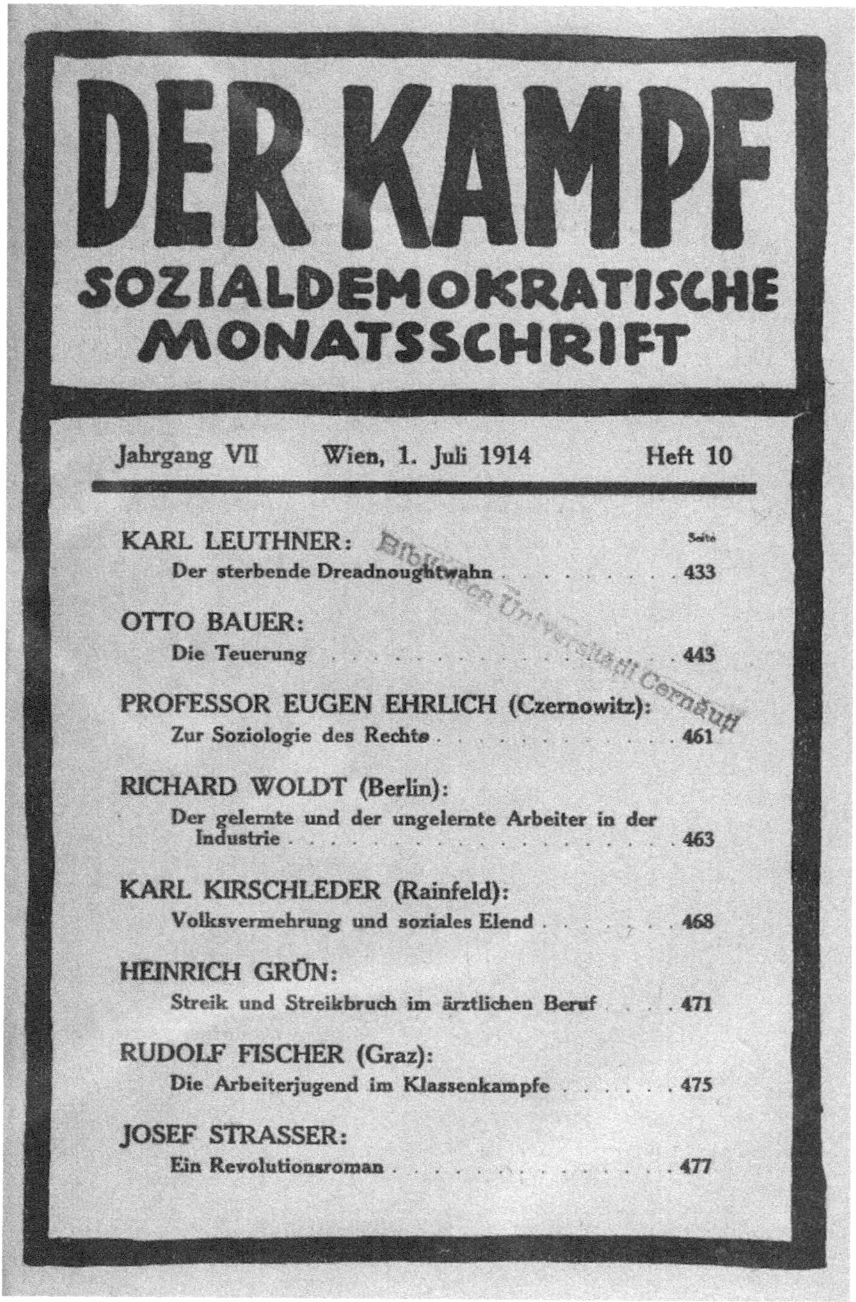

DER KAMPF

SOZIALDEMOKRATISCHE MONATSSCHRIFT

Jahrgang VII Wien, 1. Juli 1914 Heft 10

Zur Soziologie des Rechts 461

Von 1890 bis 1900 sind die Reallöhne schnell und um ein bedeutendes gestiegen. Nach 1900 ist das Bild verändert. Seither zeigen die Reallöhne in Frankreich und in Spanien verlangsamtes Wachstum, in Belgien, Grossbritannien und Preussen absoluten Rückgang!

Die Verschlechterung der Lebenshaltung hat die Volksmassen in einen Zustand der Unruhe und Erregung versetzt. Grossbritannien steht unter dem Druck des „labour unrest", der „Unruhe der Arbeit". In den Vereinigten Staaten von Amerika hat die Unzufriedenheit der Volksmassen die republikanische Partei von der Macht gestossen und gespalten, die bürgerliche Demokratie im Wesen verändert, den Sozialismus gestärkt. Im Deutschen Reich ist die Teuerung die Grundursache der grossen Machtverschiebung, die bei den Reichstagswahlen von 1912 sichtbar wurde. In Frankreich und in Oesterreich hat die Teuerung im Jahre 1911 zu Strassenrevolten geführt. In Italien war sie ein Ferment der grossen sozialen Gärung, die in den häufigen Massenstreiks ihren Ausdruck findet. Aber auch ausserhalb der kapitalistischen Industriestaaten ist sie eine treibende Kraft sozialer und nationaler Bewegungen. In der Literatur über die revolutionären Bewegungen in der Türkei, in Persien, in Indien, in China wird die Teuerung immer wieder als eine der wichtigsten Ursachen der allgemeinen Unzufriedenheit bezeichnet.

Die Teuerung zwingt die Arbeiterklasse zum Kampf um höheren Lohn. Die Unternehmer schaffen immer gewaltigere Organisationen, den Arbeitern entgegenzutreten. Die Bedingungen des gewerkschaftlichen Kampfes sind verändert. Riesenhafte Streiks und Aussperrungen erschüttern alle Länder.

Während so die Klassengegensätze innerhalb der kapitalistischen Länder verschärft werden und die Erhebung der Kolonialländer den europäischen Kapitalismus mit neuen Gefahren bedroht, werden zugleich die Vorbedingungen der Ueberwindung der Kapitalsherrschaft geschaffen. Die Teuerung erhöht die Grundrente und den Profit des kartellierten und vertrusteten Kapitals. Schnell wachsende Reichtümer sammeln sich in den Händen einer kleinen Minderheit der Völker. In den grossen Kartellen und Trusts wird die Produktion vergesellschaftet. Die Voraussetzungen für die Ueberführung der Produktionsmittel in das Eigentum und die Verwaltung des Gemeinwesens werden durch die kapitalistische Entwicklung selbst in beschleunigtem Tempo geschaffen.

Die Teuerung, selbst das Ergebnis einer schnelleren Entwicklung des Kapitalismus, beschleunigt ihrerseits diese Entwicklung. Sie revolutioniert die Arbeit und sie konzentriert das Kapital. So nähert sie uns mit Riesenschritten dem Augenblick, in dem die organisierte Arbeiterklasse sich der organisierten Kapitalsmacht bemächtigen wird, um mit allen Folgewirkungen des kapitalistischen Eigentums auch die Teuerung auszurotten.

Professor Eugen Ehrlich (Czernowitz):

Zur Soziologie des Rechts[1]

Sehr geehrter Herr! Soeben habe ich die Kritik meines Buches: „Grundlegung der Soziologie des Rechts" in Ihrer Zeitschrift gelesen. Ich werde auf die kritischen Urteile darin nicht mit einem Wort erwidern, denn ich liebe nicht die Gegenkritiken. Aber ich glaube nicht, dass ich verpflichtet bin, es ruhig hinzunehmen, wenn mein Kritiker mich das Gegenteil von dem sagen lässt, was ich in dem Buch tatsächlich gesagt habe. Ich bitte Sie daher, diese Antwort in Ihre Zeitschrift aufzunehmen und mir so zu gestatten, Ihren Lesern mitzuteilen, dass sie der Kritiker über den Inhalt meines Buches ganz falsch unterrichtet hat.

Mein Kritiker meint, die Soziologie des Rechts habe „in jeder Gesellschaftsordnung den Zusammenhang des Rechts mit seinem wirtschaftlichen Substrat aufzudecken

[1] Professor Ehrlich, der Verfasser der „Grundlegung der Soziologie des Rechtes" sendet uns vorliegende Entgegnung auf den Artikel von Friedr. Hahn, der im letzten Heft des „Kampf" (S. 401 ff.) erschien.

Pictures 21, 22. *On the Sociology of Law*

Die Valutaschwierigkeiten der Schweiz.

Von Prof. Dr. Eugen Ehrlich, früher in Cernovitz, z. Z. in Bern.*)

Wo immer man gegenwärtig in der Schweiz hinhorcht, in der Gesellschaft, im Theater, im Caféhaus, in der Strassenbahn, überall hört man Klagen über den hohen Stand der Schweizer Valuta: «Unsere Valuta richtet uns zu Grunde,» «wir können wegen der Valuta nichts ausführen,» «wir ersticken in unserem Fett.» Sogar die sehr verdienstliche Darstellung der wirtschaftlichen und finanziellen Lage der Schweiz, die die Banque Suisse jüngst veröffentlicht hat, gibt der Valuta die Schuld an den Schwierigkeiten, mit denen die Schweiz jetzt zu kämpfen hat. Darin liegt etwas Paradoxes. Eine hohe Valuta gilt doch stets als Zeichen des Reichtums, mindestens eines relativen Reichtums, im Verhältnis zu andern Staaten, und über Reichtum pflegt man sich sonst nicht zu beklagen. Sollte nicht eine Unklarheit dahinter stecken, eine Unklarheit des Ausdrucks, die immer auf eine Unklarheit des Gedankens hinweist? So ist es in der Tat. Die Uebelstände von denen man spricht, sind zweifellos vorhanden und die Schweizer Valuta steht gegenwärtig im Verhältnis zu der der meisten europäischen Staaten sehr hoch, aber daraus ergibt sich noch nicht, dass die Uebelstände eine Folge der hohen Valuta wären.

Dem Fehlschluss liegt der sehr alte und sehr verbreitete Irrtum zu Grunde, dass der Reichtum eines Menschen oder eines Volkes auf

*) Wir sind nicht mit allen in dieser Abhandlung verfochtenen Ansichten des Verfassers einverstanden. Für die Aufnahme derselben war für uns vor allem der von uns seit jeher befolgte Grundsatz massgebend, wonach in unserer Zeitschrift die verschiedenen volkswirtschaftspolitischen Anschauungen zum Ausdruck kommen sollten. In diesem Falle kam noch hinzu der wissenschaftliche Ruf des Verfassers und die grosse Wichtigkeit der von ihm angeschnittenen Probleme. Es würde uns sehr freuen, wenn dieser Aufsatz zu einer weiteren Erörterung des Gegenstandes führen sollte, wozu wir Sachverständigen gerne die Spalten unserer Zeitschrift zur Verfügung stellen. *Die Redaktion.*

21

Picture 23. ***Foreign Currency Difficulties in Switzerland***

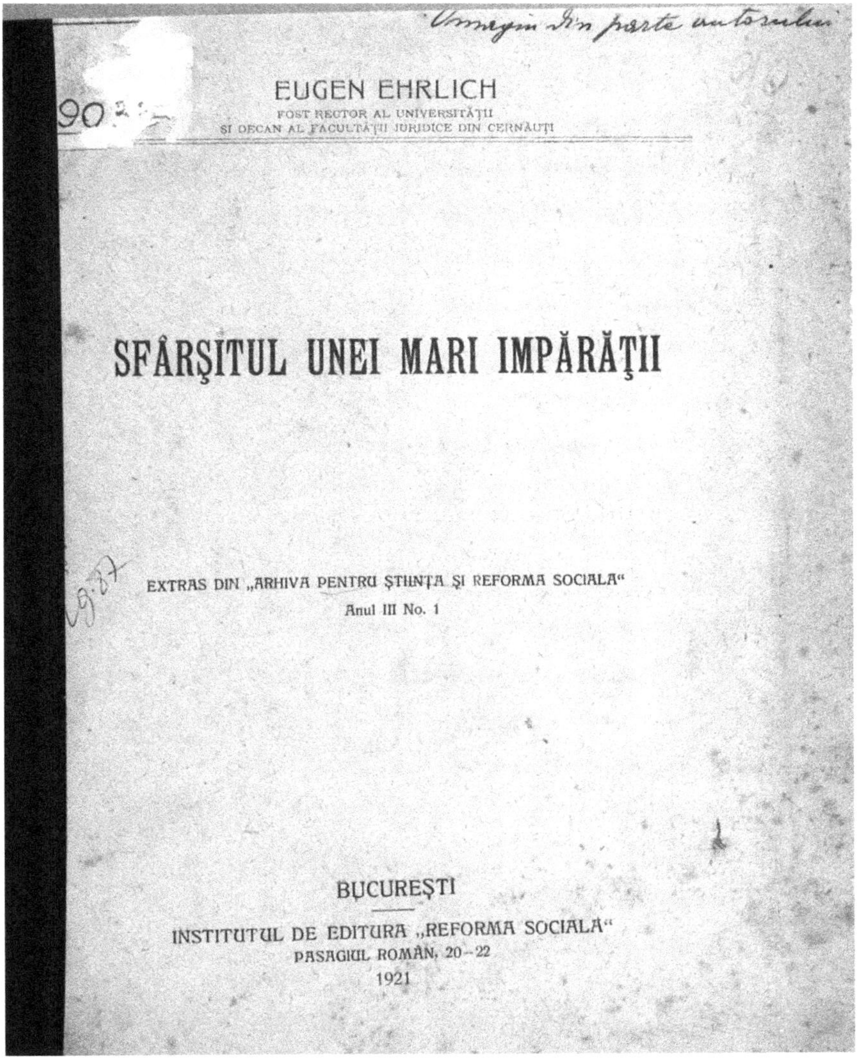

Picture 24. ***The End of Great Empire***

Picture 25. ***The Juridical Logic***

291377
GEN EHRLICH
GRUNDLEGUNG
DER SOZIOLOGIE
DES RECHTS
Vincit Veritas
D&H

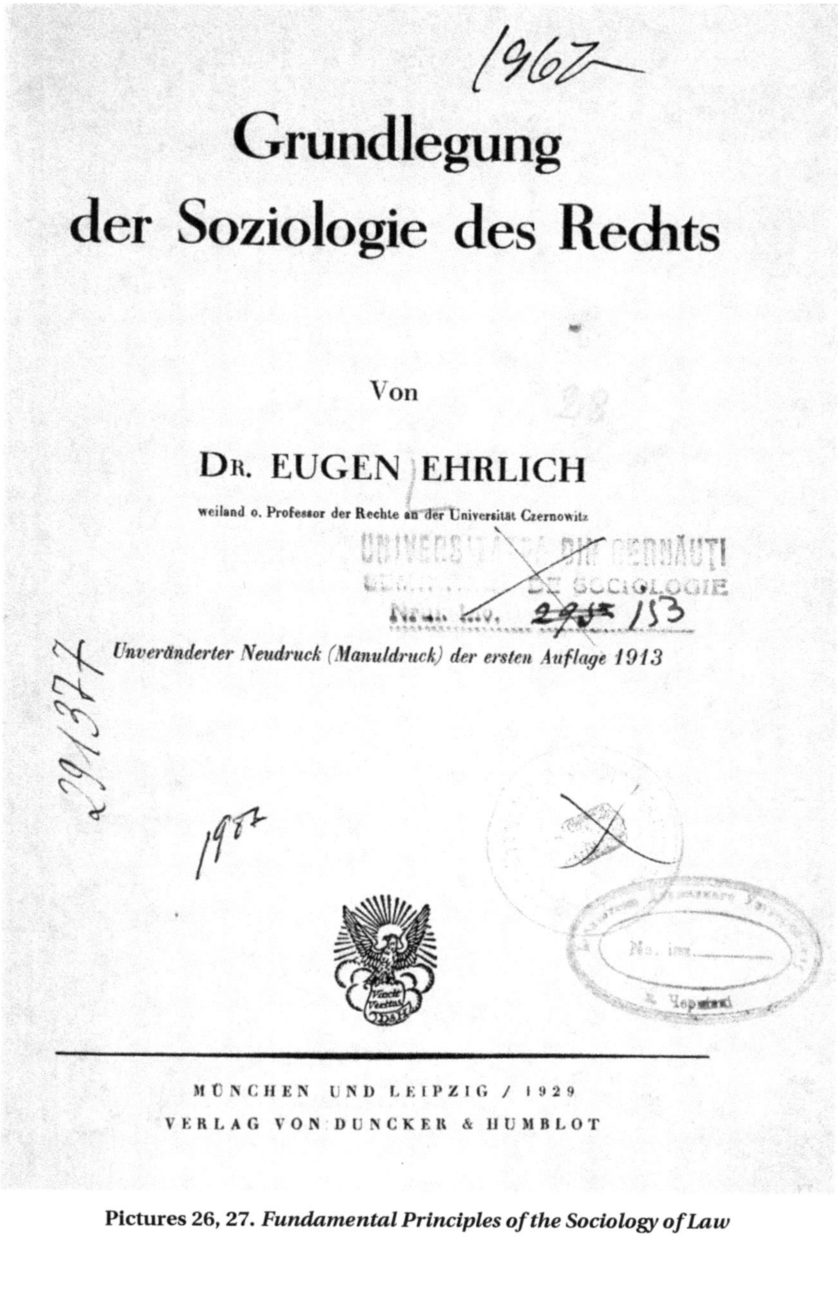

Grundlegung der Soziologie des Rechts

Von

DR. EUGEN EHRLICH

weiland o. Professor der Rechte an der Universität Czernowitz

Unveränderter Neudruck (Manuldruck) der ersten Auflage 1913

MÜNCHEN UND LEIPZIG / 1929

VERLAG VON DUNCKER & HUMBLOT

Pictures 26, 27. ***Fundamental Principles of the Sociology of Law***

Appendix B:
Sources about Eugen Ehrlich's research and education activities at Czernowitz University

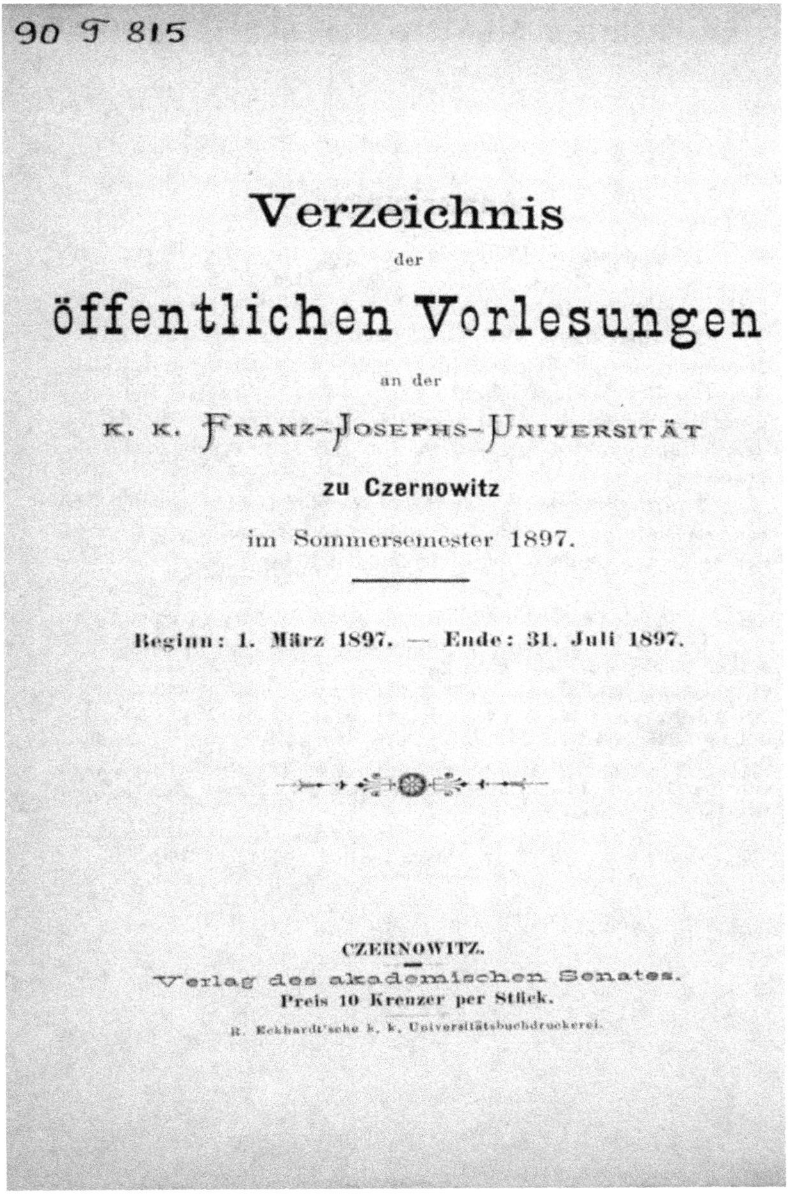

Verzeichnis

der

öffentlichen Vorlesungen

an der

K. K. Franz-Josephs-Universität

zu Czernowitz

im Sommersemester 1897.

Beginn: 1. März 1897. — Ende: 31. Juli 1897.

CZERNOWITZ.

Verlag des akademischen Senates.

Preis 10 Kreuzer per Stück.

R. Eckhardt'sche k. k. Universitätsbuchdruckerei.

8

B. Rechts- u. staatswissenschaftl. Facultät.

Professor Dr. Eugen **Ehrlich**:

*Pandecten: Personen- und Vermögensrecht, sechsstündig, Montag bis Samstag von 8—9 Uhr Vormittags. Saal V.

*Pandecten: Recht des Verkehrs unter Lebenden, fünfstündig, Montag bis Freitag von 9—10 Uhr Vormittags. Saal V.

*Römisches Familienrecht, zweistündig, Samstag von 9—11 Uhr Vormittags. Saal V.

Romanistisches Seminar, zweistündig. (Tag und Stunde nach Uebereinkunft.) Saal V. (Unentgeltlich.)

Professor Dr. Alfred von **Halban**:

*System des deutschen Privatrechtes, dreistündig, Montag bis Mittwoch von 11—12 Uhr Vormittags. Saal V.

*Oesterreichische Reichsgeschichte, fünfstündig, Montag bis Freitag von 10—11 Uhr Vormittags. Saal V.

*Neuere deutsche Rechts- und Wirthschaftsgeschichte, zweistündig, Donnerstag und Freitag von 11—12 Uhr Vormittags. Saal V.

*Geschichte und System des deutschen und österreichischen Bergrechts, dreistündig, Montag bis Mittwoch von 9—10 Uhr Vormittags. Saal VII.

21

Stunden	Theologie	Rechts- und Staatswissenschaften	Philosophie
9—10	v. Onciul: Bibelstudium des A. B., isagogischer Theil, Mo., Mi. u. Fr. — Orientalische Sprachen, Di. u. Sa.	Ehrlich: Pandekten Recht des Verkehrs unter Lebenden, Mo.—Fr. Saal V. Halban: Geschichte u. System des deutschen und österreichischen Bergrechtes. Mo – Mi. Saal VII. Hiller: Gefängniskunde, M. u. Fr. Saal IV. — Seminarübungen Mi. Saal IV.	Herzberg-Fränkel: Das Zeitalter Ludwigs XIV. Mo., Mi. u. Fr. Saal II. — Humanismus u. Renaissance, Di. u. Do. Saal IV. Hilberg: Auswahl u. Seneca's Briefen, fr. Saal I. Tumlirz: Theorie der Wärme, Mo. bis Do. — Dioptrik fr. Tangl: Allgemeine Botanik, Mo.—Mi. — Systematik der Phanerogamen Do. u. Fr. Löwl: Das böhmische Massiv und die Ostalpen, Mo.—Do.
9—11		Ehrlich: Römisches Familienrecht, Sa. Saal V.	
9—12			Přibram: Chemische Übungen im Laboratorium (für Anfänger) Mo.—Fr. — Anleitung zur Ausführung wissenschaftlicher Untersuchungen. Mo.—Fr.
10—11	Gaina: Specielle dogmatische Theologie, Mo., Di, Mi., Fr., Sa. v. Onciul: Lectüre und Erklärung ausgewählter Stücke aus den historischen Büchern des A. B., nach dem Originaltexte, Mo., Di., Mi., Fr, Sa. Eus. Popowicz: Bibelstudium des N. B.: Allgemeine Einleitung in die Bücher des N. B., Mo., Mi. und Fr.	Halban: Österreichische Reichsgeschichte, Mo.—Fr. Saal V. Hiller: Österr. Strafprocessrecht, Mo. bis Fr. Saal IV. Grawein: Österr. allg. Privatrecht. Mo.—Sa. Saal III.	v. Zieglauer: Österr. Reichsgeschichte: Geschichte der Staatsbildung u. des öffentl. Rechtes, Mo.—Fr. Saal VII. Wrobel: Griechische Alterthümer, Mo. u. Do. Saal I. Löwl: Einführung der geographischen Literatur, Mo.

Pictures 28, 29, 30. List of public lectures at Franz Joseph University in Czernowitz.
Summer semester of the year 1897.
Beginning on the 1st of March 1897 – end on the 31st of July 1897.

Verzeichnis

der

öffentlichen Vorlesungen

an der

K. K. FRANZ-JOSEPHS-UNIVERSITÄT

zu Czernowitz

im Wintersemester 1897/98.

Beginn: 1. October 1897. — Ende: 28. Februar 1898.

CZERNOWITZ.

Verlag des akademischen Senates.

Preis 10 Kreuzer per Stück.

R. Eckhardt'sche k. k. Universitätsbuchdruckerei.

B. Rechts- u. staatswissenschaftl. Facultät.

Professor Dr. **Ehrlich**:

*Geschichte und Institutionen des römischen Rechtes, neunstündig, Montag und Samstag von 8—10 Uhr, Dienstag von 9—11 Uhr, dann Mittwoch bis Freitag von 9—10 Uhr Vormittags. Saal V.

*Römisches Erbrecht, dreistündig, Mittwoch, Donnerstag und Freitag von 10—11 Uhr Vormittags. Saal V.

*Uebung in der Exegese der römischen Rechtsquellen, zweistündig, Tag und Stunde nach Uebereinkunft. Saal V.

Professor Dr. Alfred von **Halban**:

*Deutsches Recht, zehnstündig, Montag bis Samstag von 10—11 Uhr Vormittags, Donnerstag, Freitag, Samstag von 9—10 Uhr Vormittags und Mittwoch von 12—1 Uhr Nachmittags. Saal V.

*Oesterreichische Reichsgeschichte, fünfstündig, Montag, Dienstag, Donnerstag, Freitag und Samstag von 12—1 Uhr Nachmittags. Saal V.

Professor Dr. Walter von **Hörmann** zu **Hörbach**:

*System des Kirchenrechtes, siebenstündig, von Montag bis Samstag von 9—10 Uhr und Mittwoch von 10—11 Uhr Vormittags. Saal VII.

Regierungsrath Professor Dr. Carl **Hiller**:

*Oesterreichisches materielles Strafrecht, fünfstündig, Montag bis Freitag von 10—11 Uhr Vormittags. Saal IV.

17

Uebersicht

der

Vorlesungen nach Stunden, in welchen sie gehalten werden.

Abkürzungen: Mo. = Montag, Di. = Dienstag, Mi. = Mittwoch, Do. = Donnerstag, Fr. = Freitag, Sa. = Samstag.

Stunden	Theologie	Rechts- und Staatswissenschaften	Philosophie
8–9		Hauke: Allg. u. österr. Staatsrecht, Mo. bis Fr. Saal II. Skedl: Oesterr. civilgerichtliches Verfahren ausser Streitsachen, Mo., Di. Saal II.	Wahle: Praktische Philosophie, Di. bis Fr. Saal V. Herzberg-Fränkel: Das Zeitalter der Glaubenskämpfe, Mo. bis Fr. Saal IV. Hilberg: Geschichte der röm. Beredsamkeit bis auf Cicero, Fr. Saal I. Puchta: Anwendung der Differential- und Integralrechnung auf die Untersuchung v. Curven und Flächen. Mo.—Mi. Saal VI.
8–10		Ehrlich: Geschichte u. Institutionen des röm. Rechtes, Mo. u Sa. Saal V.	Hilberg: Geschichte der röm. Beredsamkeit bis auf Cicero, Mo. und Mi. Saal I. — Lateinisches Seminar, Di. — Lateinisches Proseminar, Do. Saal I. Puchta: Seminar für Mathematik. Fr. Saal VI. — Proseminar für Mathematik, Sa. Saal VI.
8–12			Scharizer: Mineralogisches Prakticum, Sa.
9–10	Eus. Popowicz: Biblische Hermeneutik, Do.	Ehrlich: Geschichte u. Institutionen des röm. Rechtes, Mi. bis Fr. Saal V.	Herzberg-Fränkel: Historisches Seminar, Di. und Fr.

Pictures 31, 32, 33. List of public lectures at Franz Joseph University in Czernowitz.
Winter semester of the academic year 1897/1898.
Beginning on the 1st of October 1897 – end on the 28th of February 1898.

Verzeichnis

der

öffentlichen Vorlesungen

an der

k. k. Franz-Josephs-Universität

zu Czernowitz

im Wintersemester 1900/1901.

Beginn: 1. October 1900. — Ende: 28. Februar 1901.

CZERNOWITZ.

Verlag des akademischen Senates.

Preis 20 h per Stück.

Rudolf Eckhardt'sche k. k. Universitäts-Buchdruckerei.

B. Rechts- und staatswissenschaftliche Facultät.

Professor Dr. Eugen **Ehrlich**: **Römisches Recht: Römische Rechtsgeschichte; Personen und Vermögensrecht, die historische Darstellung mit der dogmatischen verbunden,* eilfstündig, Montag bis Samstag von 9—10 Uhr und Montag bis Freitag von 10—11 Uhr Vormittags. Saal V.

**Römisches Recht in seinen Grundzügen mit Berücksichtigung der byzantinischen Fortentwicklung,* vierstündig, Samstag von 10—11 Uhr, und Montag bis Mittwoch von 11—12 Uhr Vormittags. Saal V.

Professor Dr. Alfred von **Halban**: **Deutsches Recht, I. Theil (Geschichte der Quellen und des öffentlichen Rechtes),* fünfstündig, Montag bis Freitag von 11—12 Uhr Vormittags. Saal V.

**Geschichte und System des deutschen und österreichischen Bergrechtes,* dreistündig, Dienstag bis Donnerstag von 10—11 Uhr Vormittags. Saal IV.

Professor Dr. Walther von **Hörmann zu Hörbach**: **System des Kirchenrechtes,* siebenstündig, Montag bis Samstag von 9—10 Uhr und Mittwoch von 10—11 Uhr Vormittags. Saal VII.

**Allgemeine Rechtslehre (jur. Encyclopädie),* dreistündig, Saal und Stunde nach Vereinbarung.

Professor Dr. Hans **Gross**: **Materielles Strafrecht,* fünfstündig, Montag bis Freitag von 10—11 Uhr Vormittags. Saal VI.

**Gefängniskunde,* zweistündig, Donnerstag und Freitag von 11—12 Uhr Vormittags. Saal VI.

Professor Dr. Karl **Adler**: **Österreichisches Privatrecht, Allgemeiner Theil und Sachenrecht,* sechsstündig, Donnerstag bis Samstag von 4—6 Uhr Nachmittags. Saal IV.

**Handels- und Wechselrecht,* siebenstündig, Tag und Stunde nach Vereinbarung. Saal IV.

16

Stunden	Theologie	Rechts- und Staatswissenschaften	Philosophie
10--11	Eus. Popowicz: Kirchengeschichte, I. Hälfte 8 st., Mo., Di., Mi., Fr. u. Sa., siehe 3—4. Const. Popowicz: Gr.-or. Kirchenrecht, I. Hälfte 8 st., Mo., Di., Mi., Fr. u. Sa., siehe 5—6. Kozak: Kirchenslavische Grammatik, I. Th. 2 st., Mo. u. Mi.	Ehrlich: Römisches Recht in seinen Grundzügen mit Berücksichtigung der byzantinischen Fortentwicklung 4 st., Sa. Saal V, siehe 11—12. v. Halban: Geschichte u System des deutschen und österr. Bergrechtes 3 st., Di.—Do. Saal IV. v. Hörmann: System des Kirchenrechtes 7 st., Mo. Saal VII, siehe 9 bis 10. Gross: Materielles Strafrecht 5 st., Mo. bis Fr. Saal VI. Kleinwächter: Finanzwissenschaft 5 st., Mo.—Fr. Saal III.	Kalinka: Einführung in die Alterthumswissenschaft 3 st., Mo, Di. u. Fr., Saal II. — Philologisches Proseminar 1 st., Do. Saal II. Handl: Experimentalphysik 5 st, Mo. bis Fr. Tumlirz: Theorie der Capillarität 1 st., Fr. Tangl: Pharmacognosie 5 st., Mo.—Fr.
10—12			Judeich: Einführung in die griechische Inschriftenkunde 3 st., Do., Saal I, siehe 11—12. Wrobel: Encyklopädie der Philologie 2 st, Sa. Saal I. Zelinka: Mikroskopisch-zoologischer Cursus für Anfänger. Mo.—Fr.
11—12	Wojucki: Hebräische Sprache 5 st., Mo., Di., Mi., Fr. u. Sa. Eus. Popowicz: Bibelstudium des N. B.: Specielle Einleitung in die Bücher des N. B. 3 st., Mo. Mi. u. Fr.	Ehrlich: Römisches Recht in seinen Grundzügen mit Berücksichtigung der byzantinischen Fortentwicklung 4 st., Mo. u. Mi., siehe 10—11. v. Halban: Deutsches Recht, I. Theil 5 st., Mo —Fr. Saal V.	Judeich: Einführung in die griechische Inschriftenkunde 3 st., Di. Saal I, siehe 10—12. Kalinka: Thukydides 2 st., Mo. u. Di. Saal II — Philologisches Seminar 2 st., Di. u. Fr. Saal II.

Pictures 34, 35, 36. List of public lectures at Franz Joseph University in Czernowitz.
Winter semester of the academic year 1900/1901.
Beginning on the 1st of October 1900 – end on the 28th of February 1901.

Verzeichnis

der

öffentlichen Vorlesungen

an der

k. k. Franz Josephs-Universität

zu Czernowitz

im Sommersemester 1906.

Beginn: 1. März 1906. — Ende: 31. Juli 1906.

Preis 20 h per Stück.

Czernowitz.

Verlag des akademischen Senates.

R. Eckhardt'sche k. k. Universitäts-Buchdruckerei (J. Mucha).

8

B. Rechts- und staatswissenschaftliche Fakultät.

I. Rechtsphilosophie, Allgemeine Rechtslehre, Vergleichende Rechtswissenschaft.

Geschichte der Rechtsphilosophie*, vierstündig, Dienstag bis Freitag von 12—1 Uhr vormittags, von Professor Dr. Adolf **Lenz; Saal VI.

Allgemeine Rechtslehre auf rechtsvergleichender Grundlage*, dreistündig, von Professor Dr. Walther von **Hörmann zu **Hörbach**. (Tag und Stunde nach Übereinkunft.)

Eine Skizze des englischen Privatrechtes*, zweistündig, von Professor Dr. Eugen **Ehrlich. (Tag und Stunde nach Übereinkunft.)

II. Römisches Recht.

Römisches Recht, II. Teil: Vermögens- und Verkehrsrecht, die historische Darstellung mit der dogmatischen verbunden*, neunstündig, Mittwoch bis Samstag von 9—11 Uhr und Samstag von 11—12 Uhr vormittags, von Professor Dr. Eugen **Ehrlich; Saal V.

**Romanistisches Seminar: Übungen über das Edictum perpetuum an der Hand des Lenel'schen Rekonstruktionsversuches*, zweistündig, von demselben. (Nur für Hörer, welche das Kolleg im Wintersemester belegt haben. Unentgeltlich. Tag und Stunde nach Übereinkunft. Im Seminarsaal.)

III. Deutsches Recht und österreichische Reichsgeschichte.

Österreichische Reichsgeschichte*, fünfstündig, Montag bis Freitag von 11—12 Uhr vormittags, von Professor Dr. Ferdinand **Kogler; Saal V.

**Bergrecht*, dreistündig, von demselben. Nach Übereinkunft.

Seminarübungen aus deutschem Recht und österreichischer Reichsgeschichte, zweistündig, von demselben. (Tag und Stunde nach Übereinkunft.) Seminarlokal.

24

Stunden	Theologie	Rechts- und Staatswissenschaften	Philosophie
Tag und Stunde nach Übereinkunft.	B. Tarnawski: Orientalische Sprachen, II. Kursus, 3 st.	v. Hörmann: Allgemeine Rechtslehre, 3 st. Ehrlich: Romanistisches Seminar, 2 st. — Eine Skizze des englischen Privatrechtes, 2 st. Kogler: Seminarübungen aus deutschem Recht und österr. Reichsgeschichte. 2 st. Im Seminarlokal. — Bergrecht, 3 st. Skedl: System des österr. Zivilprozesses II. Teil, 6 st. Mayer: Gerichtliche Medizin, 4 st.	v. Daublebsky: Algebraische Zahlen, 2 st. — Mathematisches Seminar, 2 st. Pribram: Pharmazeutische Chemie, 5 st. Luksch: Methodik der Bakteriologie, 2 st. In der Prosektur der Landeskrankenanstalt. Scharizer: Das Mikroskop und seine Verwendung in der Mineralogie, 2 st. Gruber: Lektüre moderner franz. Autoren und Übersetzungen aus dem Deutschen ins Französische, 3 st. Saal I.

Pictures 37, 38, 39. List of public lectures at Franz Joseph University in Czernowitz.
Summer semester of the year 1906.
Beginning on the 1st of March 1906 – end on the 31st of July 1906.

Verzeichnis

der

öffentlichen Vorlesungen

an der

k. k. Franz Josephs-Universität

zu Czernowitz

im Wintersemester 1906/1907.

Beginn: 1. Oktober 1906. — Ende: 28. Februar 1907.

Preis 20 h per Stück.

Czernowitz.

Verlag des akademischen Senates.

R. Eckhardt'sche k. k. Universitäts-Buchdruckerei (J. Mucha).

B. Rechts- und staatswissenschaftliche Fakultät.

I. Römisches Recht.

Römisches Recht: Römische Rechtsgeschichte, Personen- und Vemögensrecht, die historische Darstellung mit der dogmatischen verbunden*, elfstündig, Montag bis Freitag von 9—11 Uhr und Samstag von 10—11 Uhr vormittags, von Professor Dr. Eugen **Ehrlich; Saal I.

**Römisches Recht in seinen Grundzügen, mit Berücksichtigung der byzantinischen Fortentwicklung*, vierstündig, Montag bis Donnerstag von 12—1 Uhr nachmittags, von demselben; Saal II.

Romanistisches Seminar: Das Edictum perpetuum an der Hand des Lenelschen Rekonstruktionsversuches, zweistündig, von demselben. (Unentgeltlich, Aufnahme durch den Seminarleiter, Tag und Stunde nach Uebereinkunft.)

II. Deutsches Recht.

Deutsches Recht, I. Teil, Geschichte der Rechtsquellen und des öffentlichen Rechtes*, fünfstündig, Montag bis Freitag von 11—12 Uhr vormittags, von Professor Dr. Ferdinand **Kogler; Saal V.

**Deutsches Recht, II. Teil (Geschichte und System des deutschen Privatrechtes)*, fünfstündig, Montag bis Freitag 10—11 Uhr vormittags, von demselben; Saal IV.

III. Kirchenrecht.

System des Kirchenrechtes*, siebenstündig, Montag bis Freitag von 8—9 Uhr und Samstag von 8—10 Uhr vormittags, von Professor Dr. Walther von **Hörmann zu Hörbach; Saal IV.

17

Stunden	Theologie	Rechts- und Staatswissenschaften	Philosophie
9—10	B. Tarnawski: Arabische Sprache, 3 st., Di., Do. u. Sa. Gaina: Apologetisches Repetitorium, 2 st., Mo. u. Di.	Kleinwächter: Finanzwissenschaft, 5 st., Mo. bis Fr. Saal III.	Jüthner: Griechisches Proseminar, 2 st., Fr. Saal V (siehe 11—12). Radaković: Mechanik, 5 st., Mo. bis Fr. Im math. phys. Inst.
9—10	Gaina: Ausgewählte Kapitel aus der christlichen Philosophie, 2 st., Fr u. Sa. Jeremijczuk: Einleitung in die praktische Theologie u. Homiletik, 3 st., Mi. u. Fr. (siehe 4—5). — Liturgik I. Teil, 5 st., Mo. Di. u. Sa. (siehe 4—5). Kozak: Praktische Übungen im Kirchenslavischen I. Abt., 2 st., Mo. u. Fr. — dto. II. Abt., 1 st., Mi.		Czapek: Physiologische Botanik, 5 st., Mo. bis Fr. Im bot. Institut. Zelinka: Spezielle Zoologie, 5 st., Mo. bis Fr. Im zoologischen Institut. Löwl: Klimatologie, 3 st., Mo., Mi. u. Fr. Saal IV. — Kartenkunde, 2 st., Di. u. Do. Saal IV. — Geograph. Übungen, 1 st., Sa. Saal IV.
9—11		Ehrlich: Röm. Recht, 11 st., Mo. bis Fr. Saal V (siehe 10—11).	Jüthner: Griechisches Seminar, 2 st., Sa. Saal V. Radaković: Seminar für mathematische Physik, 2 st., Sa. Im math. phys. Institut. Czapek: Botanisches Praktikum, 2. st., Sa. Im botanischen Institut.
10—11	B. Tarnawski: Bibelstudium des A. B., archäologischer Teil, 3 st., Di., Fr. u. Sa. Eus. Popowicz: Kirchengeschichte I. Hälfte, 8 st., Mo. bis Mi., Fr. bis Sa. (siehe 3—4).	Ehrlich: Röm. Recht, 11 st., Sa. Saal I (siehe 9—11). Kogler: Deutsches Recht, II. Teil, 5 st., Mo. bis Fr. Saal IV.	Kromayer: Geschichte Alexanders des Großen und des Hellenismus, 3 st., Mo., Mi. und Do. Saal V. — Die Entwicklung der antiken Historiographie, 2 st., Di. u. Fr. Saal V.

Pictures 40, 41, 42. List of public lectures at Franz Joseph University in Czernowitz.
Winter semester of the academic year 1906/1907.
Beginning on the 1st of October 1906 – end on the 28th of February 1907.

Verzeichnis

der

öffentlichen Vorlesungen

an der

k. k. Franz Josephs-Universität

zu Czernowitz

im Sommersemester 1907.

Beginn: 1. März 1907. — Ende: 31. Juli 1907.

Preis 20 h per Stück.

CZERNOWITZ.

Verlag des akademischen Senates.

R. Eckhardt'sche Universitätsbuchdruckerei (J. Mucha).

8

B. Rechts- und staatswissenschaftliche Fakultät.

I. Rechtsphilosophie, allgemeine Rechtslehre, vergleichende Rechtswissenschaft.

Geschichte der Rechtsphilosophie*, vierstündig, Dienstag bis Freitag von 12—1 Uhr vormittags, von Professor Dr. Adolf **Lenz; Saal VI.

Allgemeine Rechtslehre auf rechtsvergleichender Grundlage*, dreistündig, von Professor Dr. Walther von **Hörmann zu **Hörbach.** (Tag und Stunde nach Übereinkunft.)

II. Römisches Recht.

Römisches Recht, II. Teil: Vermögens- und Verkehrsrecht, die historische Darstellung mit der dogmatischen verbunden, mit Ausnahme des Obligationsrechtes, besonderer Teil*, siebenstündig, Donnerstag bis Samstag von 9—11 Uhr und Samstag von 10—12 Uhr vormittags, von Professor Dr. Eugen **Ehrlich; Saal V.

Romanistisches Seminar: Übungen über das Edictum perpetuum an der Hand des Lenel'schen Rekonstruktionsversuches, zweistündig, von demselben. (Nur für Hörer, welche das Kolleg im Wintersemester belegt haben. Unentgeltlich. Tag und Stunde nach Übereinkunft. Im Seminarsaal.)

Römisches Recht, III. Teil: Obligationenrecht spezieller Teil*, zweistündig, Dienstag und Mittwoch von 9—10 Uhr vormittags, von Professor Dr. Robert Ritter von **Mayr; Saal V.

III. Deutsches Recht und österreichische Reichsgeschichte.

Österreichische Reichsgeschichte*, fünfstündig, Montag bis Freitag von 8—9 Uhr vormittags, von Professor Dr. Ferdinand **Kogler; Saal IV.

**Bergrecht*, dreistündig, von demselben. Nach Übereinkunft.

Seminarübungen aus deutschem Recht und österreichischer Reichsgeschichte, zweistündig, von demselben. (Tag und Stunde nach Übereinkunft.) Seminarlokal. (Hörer des I. Jahrganges ausgeschlossen).

18

Stunden	Theologie	Rechts- und Staatswissenschaften	Philosophie
8—9		6 st., Mo., Mi. u. Fr. Saal II (siehe 7—8). — Die rechtliche Stellung des österr. Staatsbeamten, 1 st., Sa. Saal III.	
8—12			v. Geitler: Anleitung zu wissenschaftl. Untersuchungen. Pomeranz: Chemische Übungen, 15 st., Mo. bis Fr. — Anleitung zur Durchführung wissenschaftl. Arbeiten, 20 st., Mo. bis Fr. im chem. Laboratorium (siehe 12—1).
9—10	Gaina: Fundamentaltheologie, 5 st., Mo., Di., Fr. und Sa. Jeremijczuk: Homiletische Übungen, 1 st., Mi. — Pastoral, 2 st., Di. und Fr. Kozak: Praktische Übungen im Kirchenslavischen, I. Abt., 2 st., Mo. und Fr. — dto. II. Abt., 1 st., Mi. B. Tarnawski: Syrische Sprache, 2 st., Di. und Do. — Biblisch-Aramäisch, 1 st., Mi. B. Gheorghiu: Geschichte und Kritik des biblischen Rationalismus, 1 st., Do.	Ehrlich: Röm. Recht, II. T., 7 st., Do., Fr. u. Sa. Saal V (siehe 10—11 u. 11—12). Adler: Österr. Obligationenrecht, 6 st., Mo. bis Sa. Saal IV. Kleinwächter: Österr. Finanzrecht, 3 st., Mo. bis Mi. Saal III. v. Mayr: Röm. Recht, III. T., 2 st., Di. u. Do. Saal V.	Jüthner: Euripides Kyklops, 2 st., Sa. im griech. Seminar (siehe 10—11) Saal I. — Griech. Stilübungen, 1 st., Fr. im griech. Proseminar, Saal I. Hilberg: Die scenische Poesie der Römer zur Zeit der Republik, 5 st., Mo. u. Mi. Saal I (siehe 8—9). — Auswahl aus Ausonius, 2 st., Di. im lat. Seminar (siehe 8—9) Saal I. Czapek: Morphologische Botanik, II. Teil, 5 st., Mo. bis Fr. im bot. Institut. — Botanisches Praktikum, 3 st., Sa. im bot. Institut (siehe 10—12). Radaković: Seminar für mathem. Physik, 2 st., Sa. im Institut für mathem. Physik (siehe 10—11).

Pictures 43, 44, 45. List of public lectures at Franz Joseph University in Czernowitz.
Summer semester of the year 1907.
Beginning on the 1st of March 1907 – end on the 31st of July 1907.

Verzeichnis

der

öffentlichen Vorlesungen

an der

k. k. Franz Josephs-Universität

zu Czernowitz

im Sommersemester 1914.

Beginn: 1. März 1914. — Ende: 31. Juli 1914.

Die Frist zur Inskription beginnt am 21. Februar und dauert bis einschließlich 8. März.

Nachträgliche Inskriptionen werden nur ganz ausnahmsweise bewilligt, wenn für dieselben die im § 32 der Studienordnung angeführten Gründe in unzweifelhafter Art nachgewiesen werden und die Vorlesungen nicht schon zu weit vorgerückt sind, um mit gehörigem Erfolge gehört zu werden. Gesuche um nachträgliche Inskription, welche im Sommersemester nach dem 15. Mai und im Wintersemester nach dem 15. Dezember eingereicht werden, finden keine Berücksichtigung (Senats-Beschluß vom 5. Februar 1902).

Czernowitz.

Verlag des akademischen Senates.

R. Eckhardt'sche Universitäts-Buchdruckerei (J. Brüll).

Preis 20 h per Stück.

8

B. Rechts- und staatswissenschaftliche Fakultät.

I. Soziologie, Seminar für lebendes Recht.

Ehrlich Eugen, o. ö. Prof., Dr.: *Übungen aus der Soziologie des Rechts*, 1stündig, Tag und Stunde nach Vereinbarung; Saal VII.

Seminar für lebendes Recht, 2stündig, Tag und Stunde nach Vereinbarung; Seminarlokal.

II. Römisches Recht.

Ehrlich Eugen, o. ö. Prof., Dr.: **Römisches Recht, Obligationen, Erbrecht*, 4stündig, Mittwoch bis Samstag 9—10; Saal VII.

Last Adolf, o. ö. Prof., Dr.: **Römisches Recht: Sachenrecht*, 4stündig, Montag bis Donnerstag 8—9; Saal VII.

**Romanistisches Seminar*, 1stündig, Montag 4—5; Saal II.

III. Deutsches Recht und österreichische Reichsgeschichte.

Kogler Ferdinand, o. ö. Prof., Dr.: **Österreichische Reichsgeschichte*, 5stündig, Montag bis Freitag 10—11; Saal V.

**Geschichte des deutschen Strafrechtes und Rechtsganges*, 3stündig, Montag bis Mittwoch 11—12; Saal VII.

**Bergrecht*, 3stündig, Montag 4—6, Dienstag 5—6; Saal II.

Seminarübungen aus deutschem Recht und österreichischer Reichsgeschichte, 2stündig, Mittwoch 4—6; Seminarlokal. (Hörer des I. Jahrganges ausgeschlossen.)

Traversa Eduard, Privatdozent, Dr.: **Die Theresianisch-Josefinische Reformepoche (1740—1790)*, 2stündig, Freitag 8—10; Saal IV. (Für Hörer aller Fakultäten.)

**Die Verfassungsgeschichte der südösterreichischen Länder: der gefürsteten Grafschaft Görz-Gradisca, der Markgrafschaft Istrien und des Königreiches Dalmatien*, 2stündig, Tag und Stunde nach Vereinbarung; Saal IV. (Für Hörer aller Fakultäten.)

20

Stunden	Theologie	Rechts- und Staatswissenschaften	Philosophie
8-9			Conrad: Kosmische Physik: Meteorologie, 4st., Mo.—Do. 8-9; Inst. f. kosm. Physik. Lindner Josef: Enzyme u. Enzymwirkungen, 1st., Sa. 8—9; chem. Inst. (verlegbar). Bauer: Pharm. Botanik, 5st., Mo.—Fr. 8-9; botan. Inst. Stark: Lötrohranalyse, 4st., Mo., Mi. 7-9; mineralog. Inst. Kellner: Engl. Sem., 2st., Mi. 8 bis 10; Saal I. Pomeranz: Pharmaz. Chemie, 3 st., Di., Do., Fr. 8-9; chem. Inst. — Chem. Übungen f. Vorgeschr., 20st., Mo.—Fr. 8-1 und 3-5; chem. Inst. — Anleitung zu wissenschaftl. Arbeiten, 20st., Mo.—Sa. 8 bis 12 u. 3-6; chem. Inst.
9—10	V. Tarnavschi: Erklärung des Buches Genesis n. d. Originaltexte, 5st., Mo. bis Mi., Fr., Sa. 9 bis 10. Gheorghiu: Erklärung d. I. Korintherbriefes, 3st., Di. u. Sa. 9—10, Mi., 3—4. Saghin: Fundamentaltheologie, 5st., Mo., Di., Mi., Fr., Sa. 9—10.	Ehrlich: Röm. Recht, 4st., Mi.—Sa. 9—10; Saal VII. Traversa: Die Theresianisch-Josephinische Reformepoche, 2st., Fr. 8—10; Saal IV. Leder: Kirchliche Rechtsgesch., 2 st., Mo., Di. 9—10; Saal V. — Kirchenrechtl. Seminar, 1st., Mi. 9 bis 10; Saal V.	Hilberg: Statius' Silvae, 5st., Mo., Mi. 8-10; Fr. 8—9; Saal I. — Im philolog. Sem.: Interpret. des Culex, 2st., Di. 8—10; Saal I. — Im philolog. Prosem.: Lat. Stil- u. Sprechübungen, 2st., Do. 8—10; Saal I. Plemelj: Funktionentheorie (Forts.), 5st., Mo.—Fr. 9—10; Geolog. Inst.

Pictures 46, 47, 48. List of public lectures at Franz Joseph University in Czernowitz.
Summer semester of the year 1914.
Beginning on the 1st of March 1914 – end on the 31st of July 1914.

Verzeichnis

der

öffentlichen Vorlesungen

an der

Franz Josephs-Universität

zu Czernowitz

im Sommersemester 1919.

Beginn: 1. März 1919. — Ende: 22. September 1919.

Die Frist zur Inskription beginnt am 23. Februar 1919 und dauert bis einschließlich 8. März 1919.

Nachträgliche Inskriptionen werden nur ganz ausnahmsweise bewilligt, wenn für dieselben die im § 32 der Studienordnung angeführten Gründe in unzweifelhafter Art nachgewiesen werden und die Vorlesungen nicht schon zu weit vorgerückt sind, um mit gehörigem Erfolge gehört zu werden. Gesuche um nachträgliche Inskription, welche im Wintersemester nach dem 15. Dezember und im Sommersemester nach dem 15. Mai eingereicht werden, finden keine Berücksichtigung (Senats-Beschluß vom 5. Februar 1902).

Czernowitz.

Verlag des akademischen Senates.

R. Eckhordt'sche Universitäts-Buchdruckerei (J. Brüll).

Preis per Stück: 1 K.

B. Rechts- und staatswissenschaftliche Fakultät.

I. Einführungskollegien.

Leder Paul, o. ö. Prof., Dr.: *Übungen aus der Gesellschaftslehre,* 1stündig, Tag und Stunde nach Vereinbarung; Saal VII (unentgeltlich).

II. Römisches Recht.

Ehrlich Eugen, o. ö. Prof., Dr.: Wird später ankündigen.
Last Adolf, o. ö. Prof., Hofrat, Dr.: Wird später ankündigen.

III. Deutsches Recht und österreichische Reichsgeschichte.

Kogler Ferdinand, o. ö. Prof., Dr.: **Geschichte des deutschen Straf- und Prozeßrechtes,* 3stündig, Montag bis Mittwoch 9—10; Saal V.

**Bergrecht,* 3stündig; nach Vereinbarung.

**Österreichische Reichsgeschichte,* 5stündig, Montag bis Freitag 8—9; Saal V.

IV. Kirchenrecht.

Leder Paul, o. ö. Prof., Dr.: **Kirchliche Rechtsgeschichte,* 2stündig, Montag und Dienstag 9—10; Saal V.

V. Bürgerliches Recht.

Adler Karl, o. ö. Prof., Hofrat, Dr.: **Oesterr. Obligationenrecht,* 6stündig, Montag bis Samstag 10—11; Saal VI.

Uebungen über das Recht des Handelskaufs mit besonderer Rücksicht auf das Kriegsrecht (nur für praktische Juristen), 2stündig, Donnerstag 5—7; Hörsaal IV (unentgeltlich).

Wolff Karl, o. ö. Prof., Dr.: **Oesterr. Familien- und Erbrecht,* 4stündig, Dienstag bis Freitag 9—10; Saal V.

Pictures 49, 50. List of public lectures at Franz Joseph University in Czernowitz.
Summer semester of the year 1919.
Beginning on the 1st of March 1919 – end on the 22 of July 1919

Uebersicht

der

AKADEMISCHEN BEHÖRDEN

Professoren, Privatdocenten, Lehrer, Beamten etc.

an der

k. k. Franz-Josephs-Universität zu Czernowitz

im Studienjahre 1897/98.

CZERNOWITZ.

Verlag des akademischen Senates.

Preis 10 Kreuzer per Stück.

R. Eckhardt'sche k. k. Universitätsbuchdruckerei.

8

Commission, Reichsrathsabgeordneter, im Jahre 1892/93 Decan der rechts- und staatswissenschaftlichen Facultät, im Jahre 1896/97 Rector magnificus der hiesigen k. k. Universität. (Franzensgasse Nr. 43 a.)

Arthur **Skedl,** Doctor der Rechte, k. k. o. ö. Professor des österreichischen Civilprocesses, Mitglied der judiciellen und rechtshistorischen k. k. Staatsprüfungs-Commission, im Jahre 1893/94 Decan der rechts- und staatswissenschaftlichen Facultät. (Austriaplatz Nr. 2.)

Franz **Hauke,** Doctor der Rechte, k. k. o. ö. Professor des allgemeinen und des österreichischen Staatsrechtes, Mitglied der k. k. staatswissenschaftlichen und der rechtshistorischen Staatsprüfungs-Commission. (Roschergasse Nr. 9.)

Ausserordentliche Professoren:

Alfred von **Halban,** Doctor der Rechte, k. k. a. ö. Professor des deutschen Rechtes, Mitglied der rechtshistorischen und judiciellen k. k. Staatsprüfungs-Commission. (Nicolausgasse Nr. 9.)

Walther v. **Hörmann** zu **Hörbach,** Doctor der Rechte, k. k. a. ö. Professor des Kirchenrechtes.

Eugen **Ehrlich,** Doctor der Rechte, k. k. a. ö. Professor des römischen Rechtes, Mitglied der rechtshistorischen und judiciellen k. k. Staatsprüfungs Commission. (Steingasse Nr. 28.)

Docenten:

Basil **Wolan,** Doctor der Medicin und Chirurgie, tit. a. ö. Universitäts-Professor, honorirter Docent der gerichtlichen Medicin, Landes-Sanitätsrath, Director der allgemeinen öffentlichen Landes-Krankenanstalt in Czernowitz, correspon-

Pictures 51, 52. Supervision of leading academic authorities, professors, associate professors, lecturers, officials, etc. at Franz Joseph University in Czernowitz in the academic year 1897/1898.

Uebersicht

der

AKADEMISCHEN BEHÖRDEN

Professoren, Privatdocenten, Lehrer, Beamten etc.

an der

k. k. Franz-Josephs-Universität zu Czernowitz

im Studienjahre 1901/1902.

CZERNOWITZ.

Verlag des akademischen Senates.

Preis 20 h per Stück.

Rudolf Eckhardt'sche k. k. Universitäts-Buchdruckerei (Josef Mucha).

3

A. K. k. akademischer Senat.

Rector magnificus:

Dr. Emilian **Wojucki,** S. 5.

Prorector:

Dr. Franz **Hauke,** S. 7.

Decane:

Gr.-or. theologische Facultät:

Eus. **Popowicz,** S. 4.

Rechts- u. staatswissenschaftliche Facultät:

Dr. Eugen **Ehrlich,** S. 8.

Philosophische Facultät:

Dr. Carl **Zelinka,** S. 12.

Prodecane:

Gr.-or. theologische Facultät:

Dr. Theodor **Tarnawski,** S. 5.

Rechts- u. staatswissenschaftliche Facultät:

Dr. Walther v. **Hörmann** zu **Hörbach,** S. 8.

Philosophische Facultät:

Dr. Sigmund **Herzberg-Fränkel,** S. 12.

Senatoren:

Gr.-or. theologische Facultät:

Dr. Basil **Gaina,** S. 5.

Rechts- u. staatswissenschaftliche Facultät:

Dr. Julius v. **Roschmann-Hörburg,** S. 7.

Philosophische Facultät:

Dr. Ernst **Kalinka,** S. 12.

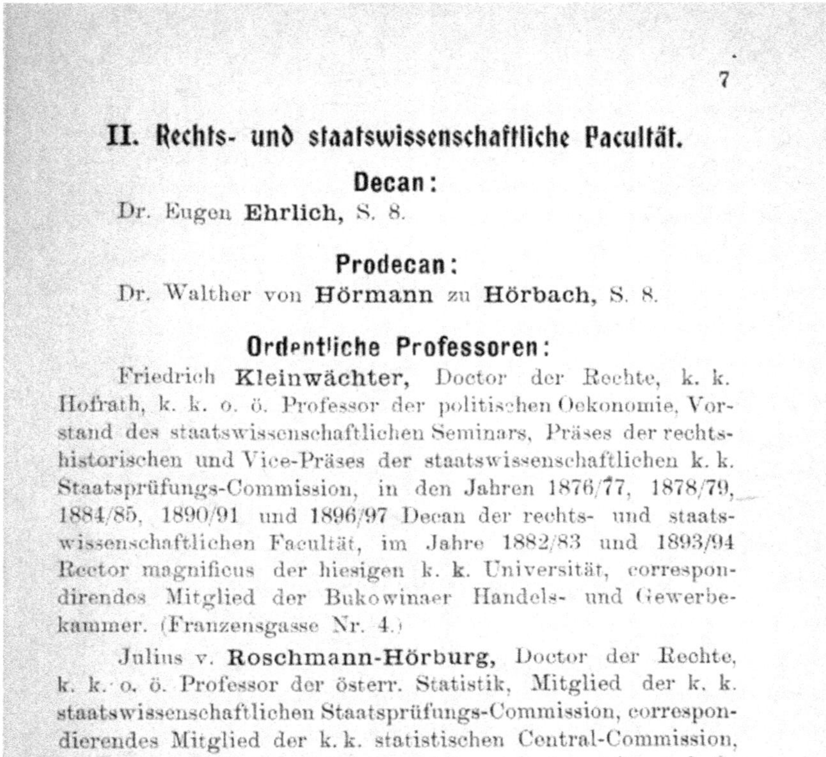

7

II. Rechts- und staatswissenschaftliche Facultät.

Decan:

Dr. Eugen **Ehrlich**, S. 8.

Prodecan:

Dr. Walther von **Hörmann** zu **Hörbach**, S. 8.

Ordentliche Professoren:

Friedrich **Kleinwächter**, Doctor der Rechte, k. k. Hofrath, k. k. o. ö. Professor der politischen Oekonomie, Vorstand des staatswissenschaftlichen Seminars, Präses der rechtshistorischen und Vice-Präses der staatswissenschaftlichen k. k. Staatsprüfungs-Commission, in den Jahren 1876/77, 1878/79, 1884/85, 1890/91 und 1896/97 Decan der rechts- und staatswissenschaftlichen Facultät, im Jahre 1882/83 und 1893/94 Rector magnificus der hiesigen k. k. Universität, correspondirendes Mitglied der Bukowinaer Handels- und Gewerbekammer. (Franzensgasse Nr. 4.)

Julius v. **Roschmann-Hörburg**, Doctor der Rechte, k. k. o. ö. Professor der österr. Statistik, Mitglied der k. k. staatswissenschaftlichen Staatsprüfungs-Commission, correspondierendes Mitglied der k. k. statistischen Central-Commission, im Jahre 1892/93 Decan der rechts- und staatswissenschaftlichen Facultät, im Jahre 1896/97 Rector magnificus der hiesigen k. k. Universität. (Franzensgasse Nr. 43 a.)

Arthur **Skedl**, Doctor der Rechte, Ritter des Ordens der eisernen Krone III. Cl., k. k. o. ö. Professor des österreichischen Civilprocessrechtes, Vicepräses der judiciellen und Mitglied der rechtshistorischen k. k. Staatsprüfungs-Commission, Vorstand des rechtswissenschaftlichen Seminars, Reichsraths- und Landtagsabgeordneter, im Jahre 1893/94 Decan der rechts- und staatswissenschaftlichen Facultät, im Jahre 1898/99 Rector magnificus der hiesigen k. k. Universität. (Rathhausstrasse Nr. 33.)

Franz **Hauke**, Doctor der Rechte, k. k. o. ö. Professor des allgemeinen und des österreichischen Staatsrechtes, Vice-

Pictures 53, 54, 55. Supervision of leading academic authorities, professors, associate professors, lecturers, officials, etc. at Franz Joseph University in Czernowitz in the academic year 1901/1902.

Übersicht

der

AKADEMISCHEN BEHÖRDEN

Professoren, Privatdozenten, Lehrer, Beamten etc.

an der

k. k. Franz-Josephs-Universität zu Czernowitz

im Studienjahre 1902/1903.

CZERNOWITZ.
Verlag des akademischen Senates.
Preis 20 h per Stück.
Rudolf Eckhardt'sche k. k. Universitätsbuchdruckerei (Josef Mucha).

3

A. K. k. akademischer Senat.

Rektor magnificus:

Dr. Rudolf **Scharizer,** S. 12.

Prorektor:

Dr. Emilian **Wojucki,** S. 5.

Dekane:

Gr.-or. theologische Fakultät:

Dr. Theodor **Tarnawski,** S. 5.

Rechts- u. staatswissenschaftliche Fakultät:

Dr. Karl **Adler,** S. 8.

Philosophische Fakultät:

Dr. Ernst **Kalinka,** S. 13.

Prodekane:

Gr.-or. theologische Fakultät:

Eusebius **Popowicz,** S. 4.

Rechts- und staatswissenschaftliche Fakultät:

Dr. Eugen **Ehrlich,** S. 8.

Philosophische Fakultät:

Dr. Karl **Zelinka,** S. 12.

Senatoren:

Gr.-or. theologische Fakultät:

Dr. Basil **Gaina,** S. 5.

Rechts- u. staatswissenschaftliche Fakultät:

Dr. Franz **Hauke,** S. 8.

Philosophische Fakultät:

Dr. Mathias **Friedwagner,** S. 13.

7

gionsprofessor a. D., Mitglied der systematisch-praktischen Abteilung der k. k. Prüfungskommission für Studierende der gr.-or. Theologie, Besitzer der königl. rum. Medaille I. Classe „Bene merenti". (Josefsgase Nr. 9.)

II. Rechts- und staatswissenschaftliche Fakultät.

Dekan:

Dr. Karl **Adler**, S. 8.

Prodekan:

Dr. Eugen **Ehrlich**, S. 8.

Ordentliche Professoren:

Friedrich **Kleinwächter**, Doktor der Rechte, k. k. Hofrat, k. k. o. ö. Professor der politischen Ökonomie, Vorstand des staatswissenschaftlichen Seminars, Präses der rechtshi torischen und Vizepräses der staatswissenschaftlichen k. k. Staatsprüfungs-Kommission, in den Jahren 1876/77, 1878/79, 1884/85, 1890/91 und 1896/97 Dekan der rechts- und staatswissenschaftlichen Fakultät, in den Jahren 1882/83 und 1893/94 Rektor magnificus der hiesigen k. k. Universität, korrespondierendes Mitglied der Bukowiner Handels- und Gewerbekammer. (Franzensgasse Nr. 4.)

Julius v. **Roschmann-Hörburg**, Doktor der Rechte, k. k. o. ö. Professor der österr. Statistik, Mitglied der k. k. staatswissenschaftlichen Staatsprüfungs-Kommission, korrespondierendes Mitglied der k. k. statistischen Zentral-Kommission, im Jahre 1892/93 Dekan der rechts- und staatswissenschaftlichen Fakultät, im Jahre 1896/97 Rektor magnificus der hiesigen k. k. Universität. (Franzensgasse Nr. 43 a.)

Arthur **Skedl**, Doktor der Rechte, Ritter des Ordens der eisernen Krone III. Kl., k. k. o. ö. Professor des österreichischen Zivilprozeßrechtes, Vizepräses der judiziellen und Mitglied der rechtshistorischen k. k. Staatsprüfungs-Kommission,

Pictures 56, 57, 58. Supervision of leading academic authorities, professors, associate professors, lecturers, officials, etc. at Franz Joseph University in Czernowitz in the academic year 1902/1903.

PERSONALSTAND

der

k. k. Franz Josephs-Universität

zu Czernowitz

im Studienjahre 1906/1907.

Czernowitz.

Verlag des akademischen Senates.

R. Eckhardt'sche k. k. Universitätsbuchdruckerei (Josef Mucha).

I. Akademischer Senat.

Rektor magnificus.

Dr. Eugen **Ehrlich**, S. 9.

Prorektor.

Dr. Sigmund **Herzberg-Fränkel**, S. 13.

Dekane.

Dr. Eugen **Kozak** (theolog. Fakultät) S. 6.
Dr. Walther von **Hörmann** zu **Hörbach** (rechts- und staatsw. Fakultät) S. 9.
Dr. Raimund Friedrich **Kaindl** (philosoph. Fakultät) S. 14.

Prodekane.

Dr. Basil **Gaina** (theolog. Fakultät) S. 6.
Dr. Julius von **Roschmann-Hörburg** (rechts- und staatsw. Fakultät) S. 8.
Dr. Johannes **Kromayer** (philosoph. Fakultät) S. 14.

Senatoren.

Dr. Stefan **Saghin** (theolog. Fakultät) S. 7.
Dr. Josef **Lukas** (rechts- und staatsw. Fakultät) S. 9.
Dr. Julius **Jüthner** (philosoph. Fakultät) S. 14.

4

Ständige Kommissionen und Referate des Senates.

Disziplinar-Kommission:

Die drei Dekane.

Stipendien-Kommission:

Die drei Prodekane.

Bibliotheks-Kommission:

Die Professoren: Dr. Stefan **Saghin**, Dr. Karl **Adler**, Dr. Josef **Lukas**, Dr. Sigmund **Herzberg-Fränkel**, Dr. Matthias **Friedwagner** (Obmann), Dr. Karl **Zelinka**. (1 Stelle unbesetzt.)

Im Kuratorium der Kaiser Franz Joseph-Universitäts-Studentenheimstiftung und der Mensa academica:

Dr. Emilian **Wojucki** (theolog. Fakultät).
Dr. Eugen **Ehrlich** (rechts- und staatsw. Fakultät).
Dr. Emil **Kałużniacki** (philosoph. Fakultät).

Ausschuß der volkstümlichen Hochschulkurse:

Dr. Basil **Gaina** und Dr. Eugen **Kozak** (theolog. Fakultät).
Dr. Karl **Adler** und Dr. Adolf **Lenz** (rechts- und staatsw. Fakultät).
Dr. Sigmund **Herzberg-Fränkel** und Dr. Wladimir **Milkowicz** (philosoph. Fakultät).
Dr. Anton **Norst**, Universitätssekretär.

II. Fakultäten.

A. Gr.-or. theologische Fakultät.

Dekan.

Dr. Eugen **Kozak**, S. 6.

Prodekan.

Dr. Basil **Gaina**, S. 6.

Pictures 59, 60, 61. Staff members at Franz Joseph University in Czernowitz in the academic year 1906/1907.

PERSONALSTAND

der

k. k. Franz Josephs-Universität

zu Czernowitz

im Studienjahre 1907/1908.

Czernowitz.

Verlag des akademischen Senates.

R. Eckhardt'sche k. k. Universitätsbuchdruckerei (Josef Mucha).

I. Akademischer Senat.

Rektor.

Dr. Eugen **Kozak,** S. 6.

Prorektor.

Dr. Eugen **Ehrlich,** S. 9.

Dekane.

Dr. Stefan **Saghin** (theolog. Fakultät) S. 7.
Dr. Karl **Adler** (rechts- und staatsw. Fakultät) S. 9.
Dr. Michael **Radaković** (phil. Fakultät) S. 14.

Prodekane.

Eusebius **Popowicz** (theolog. Fakultät) S. 5.
Dr. Walther von **Hörmann** zu **Hörbach** (rechts- und staatsw. Fakultät) S. 9.
Dr. Raimund Friedrich **Kaindl** (philosoph. Fakultät) S. 14.

Senatoren

(gewählt für die Jahre 1905/06—1907/08).

Dr. Basil **Tarnawski** (theolog. Fakultät) S. 7.
Dr. Josef **Lukas** (rechts- und staatsw. Fakultät) S. 9.
Dr. Julius **Jüthner** (philosoph. Fakultät) S. 14.

9

Walther von **Hörmann** zu **Hörbach**, Doktor der Rechte, o. ö. Professor des Kirchenrechtes, Mitglied der rechtshistorischen, judiziellen und staatswissenschaftlichen k. k. Staatsprüfungs-Kommission, Vorstand-Stellvertreter des rechtswissenschaftlichen Seminars, in den Jahren 1900/1 und 1906/7 Dekan der rechts- und staatswissenschaftlichen Fakultät, im Jahre 1903/4 Rektor der Universität. (Sterngasse Nr. 6.)

Eugen **Ehrlich**, Doktor der Rechte, Kommandeur des griech. Erlöserordens, o. ö. Professor des römischen Rechtes, Mitglied der rechtshistorischen und judiziellen k. k. Staatsprüfungs-Kommission, im Jahre 1901/2 Dekan der rechts- und staatswissenschaftlichen Fakultät, im Jahre 1906/7 Rektor der Universität. (Steingasse Nr. 28.)

Karl **Adler**, Doktor der Rechte, o. ö. Professor des österreichischen Zivil-, Handels- und Wechselrechtes, Vizepräses der rechtshistorischen und Mitglied der judiziellen k. k. Staatsprüfungs-Kommission, im Jahre 1902/3 und dz. Dekan der rechts- und staatswissenschaftlichen Fakultät. (Russischegasse Nr. 13.)

Adolf **Lenz**, Doktor der Rechte, o. ö. Professor des österreichischen Strafrechtes und Strafprozesses, Mitglied der judiziellen k. k. Staatsprüfungs-Kommission, im Jahre 1900/1 Dekan der rechts- und staatswissenschaftlichen Fakultät der Universität in Freiburg (Schweiz) und im Jahre 1903/4 Dekan der rechts- und staatswissenschaftlichen Fakultät der hiesigen k. k. Universität. (Universitätsgasse Nr. 24.)

Außerordentliche Professoren:

Josef **Lukas**, Doktor der Rechte, a. ö. Professor des österreichischen Staats- und Verwaltungsrechtes, Mitglied der staatswissenschaftlichen k. k. Staatsprüfungs-Kommission. (Residenzgasse Nr. 1 a.)

Robert Ritter von **Mayr**, Doktor der Rechte, a. ö. Professor des österreichischen Zivilrechtes, Mitglied der judiziellen und rechtshistorischen k. k. Staatsprüfungs-Kommission. (Enzenberg-Hauptstraße Nr. 16.)

Ferdinand **Kogler**, Doktor der Rechte, a. ö. Professor des deutschen Rechtes und der österr. Reichsgeschichte, Mitglied der rechtshistorischen und judiziellen k. k. Staatsprüfungs-

Pictures 62, 63, 64. Staff members at Franz Joseph University in Czernowitz in the academic year 1907/1908.

PERSONALSTAND

der

k. k. Franz Josephs-Universität

zu Czernowitz

im Studienjahre 1908/1909.

Czernowitz.

Verlag des akademischen Senates.

R. Eckhardt'sche k. k. Universitätsbuchdruckerei (Josef Mucha).

3

I. Akademischer Senat.

Rektor.

Dr. Carl **Zelinka**, S. 13.

Prorektor.

Dr. Eugen **Kozak**, S. 6.

Dekane.

Dr. Basil **Tarnawski** (theolog. Fakultät) S. 7.
Dr. Eugen **Ehrlich** (rechts- und staatsw. Fakultät) S. 9.
Dr. Friedrich **Czapek** (phil. Fakultät) S. 13.

Prodekane.

Dr. Stefan **Saghin** (theolog. Fakultät) S. 7.
Dr. Karl **Adler** (rechts- und staatsw. Fakultät) S. 9.
Dr. Michael **Radaković** (phil. Fakultät) S. 14.

Senatoren

(gewählt für die Jahre 1908/09—1910/11).

Dr. Basil **Gheorghiu** (theolog. Fakultät) S. 7.
Dr. Josef **Lukas** (rechts- und staatsw. Fakultät) S. 9.
Dr. Julius **Jüthner** (philosoph. Fakultät) S. 14.

8

B. Rechts- und staatswissenschaftliche Fakultät.

Dekan.

Dr. Eugen **Ehrlich**, S. 9.

Prodekan.

Dr. Karl **Adler**, S. 9.

Professoren-Kollegium.

Ordentliche Professoren:

Friedrich **Kleinwächter**, Doktor der Rechte, k. k. Hofrat, o. ö. Professor der politischen Ökonomie, Vorstand des staatswissenschaftlichen Seminars, Präses der rechtshistorischen und Vizepräses der staatswissenschaftlichen k. k. Staatsprüfungs-Kommission, Ehrenbürger der Landeshauptstadt Czernowitz, korrespondierendes Mitglied der Bukowiner Handels- und Gewerbekammer, in den Jahren 1876/7, 1878/9, 1884/5, 1890/1, 1896/7 und 1904/5 Dekan der rechts- und staatswissenschaftlichen Fakultät, in den Jahren 1882/3 und 1893/4 Rektor der Universität. (Franzensgasse Nr. 4.)

Julius von **Roschmann-Hörburg**, Doktor der Rechte, o. ö. Professor der Statistik, Präses der k. k. staatswissenschaftlichen Staatsprüfungs-Kommission, korrespondierendes Mitglied der k. k. statistischen Zentralkommission, in den Jahren 1892/3 und 1905/6 Dekan der rechts- und staatswissenschaftlichen Fakultät, im Jahre 1896/7 Rektor der Universität. (Franzensgasse Nr. 52.)

Arthur **Skedl**, Doktor der Rechte, k. k. Hofrat, Ritter des Ordens der Krone III. Klasse, k. und k. n. a. Leutnant beim 12. Korps-Artillerie-Regiment, o. ö. Professor des österreichischen Zivilprozeßrechtes, Vizepräses der judiziellen und Mitglied der rechtshistorischen k. k. Staatsprüfungs-Kommission, Vorstand des rechtswissenschaftlichen Seminars, Reichsrats- und Landtagsabgeordneter, Gemeinderat der Landeshauptstadt Czernowitz, Ehrenbürger der Städte Sereth und Suczawa, im Jahre 1893/4 Dekan der rechts- und staatswissenschaftlichen Fakultät, im Jahre 1898/9 Rektor der Universität. (Rathausstraße Nr. 33.)

Pictures 65, 66, 67. Staff members at Franz Joseph University in Czernowitz in the academic year 1908/1908.

PERSONALSTAND

der

k. k. Franz Josephs-Universität

zu Czernowitz

im Studienjahre 1909/1910.

Czernowitz.

Verlag des akademischen Senates.
R. Eckhardt'sche k. k. Universitätsbuchdruckerei (Josef Mucha).

I. Akademischer Senat.

Rektor.

Dr. Karl **Adler,** S. 9.

Prorektor.

Dr. Carl **Zelinka,** S. 12.

Dekane.

Dr. Basil **Gheorghiu** (theolog. Fakultät) S. 7.
Dr. Ferdinand **Kogler** (rechts- und staatsw. Fakultät) S. 9.
Dr. Julius **Jüthner** (philosoph. Fakultät) S. 14.

Prodekane.

Dr. Basil **Tarnawski** (theolog. Fakultät) S. 7.
Dr. Eugen **Ehrlich** (rechts- und staatsw. Fakultät) S. 9.
Dr. Michael **Radaković** (philosoph. Fakultät) S. 13.

Senatoren

(gewählt für die Jahre 1908/09—1910/11).

Dionys **Jeremijczuk** (theolog. Fakultät) S. 7.
Dr. Georg **Petschek** (rechts- und staatsw. Fakultät) S. 9.
Dr. Josef **R. v. Geitler** (philosoph. Fakultät) S. 14.

8

B. Rechts- und staatswissenschaftliche Fakultät.

Dekan.

Dr. Ferdinand **Kogler,** S. 9.

Prodekan.

Dr. Eugen **Ehrlich,** S. 9.

Professor des Ruhestandes:

Friedrich von **Kleinwächter,** Doktor der Rechte, k. k Hofrat, em. ord. Professor der politischen Ökonomie, Ehrenbürger der Landeshauptstadt Czernowitz, korrespondierendes Mitglied der Bukowiner Handels- und Gewerbekammer, in den Jahren 1876/7, 1878/9, 1884/5, 1890/1, 1896/7 und 1904/5 Dekan der rechts- und staatswissenschaftlichen Fakultät, in den Jahren 1882/3 und 1893/4 Rektor der Universität. (Franzensgasse Nr. 4.)

Professoren-Kollegium.

Ordentliche Professoren:

Julius von **Roschmann-Hörburg,** Doktor der Rechte, o. ö. Professor der Statistik und der politischen Ökonomie, Vorstand des staatswissenschaftlichen Seminars, Präses der k. k. staatswissenschaftlichen Staatsprüfungs-Kommission, korrespondierendes Mitglied der k. k. statistischen Zentralkommission, in den Jahren 1892/3 und 1905/6 Dekan der rechts- und staatswissenschaftlichen Fakultät, im Jahre 1896/7 Rektor der Universität. (Franzengasse N. 52.)

Arthur **Skedl,** Doktor der Rechte, k. k. Hofrat, Ritter des Ordens der eisernen Krone III. Klasse, k. und k. n. a. Leutnant beim 12. Korps-Artillerie-Regiment, o. ö. Professor des österreichischen Zivilprozeßrechtes, Vizepräses der judiziellen und Mitglied der rechtshistorischen k. k. Staatsprüfungs-Kommission, I. Vorstand des rechtswissenschaftlichen Seminars, Reichsrats- und Landtagsabgeordneter, Ehrenbürger der Städte Czernowitz, Sereth und Suczawa, im Jahre 1893/4 Dekan der rechts- und staatswissenschaftlichen Fakultät, im Jahre 1898/9 Rektor der Universität. (Rathausstraße Nr. 33.)

Pictures 68, 69, 70. Staff members at Franz Joseph University in Czernowitz in the academic year 1909/1910.

Appendix C: Eugen Ehrlich in archival documents

Picture 71. Systematic-alphabetical catalogue created in the Austrian-Romanian period of Czernowitz University Library (group of sections of law: 1–19)

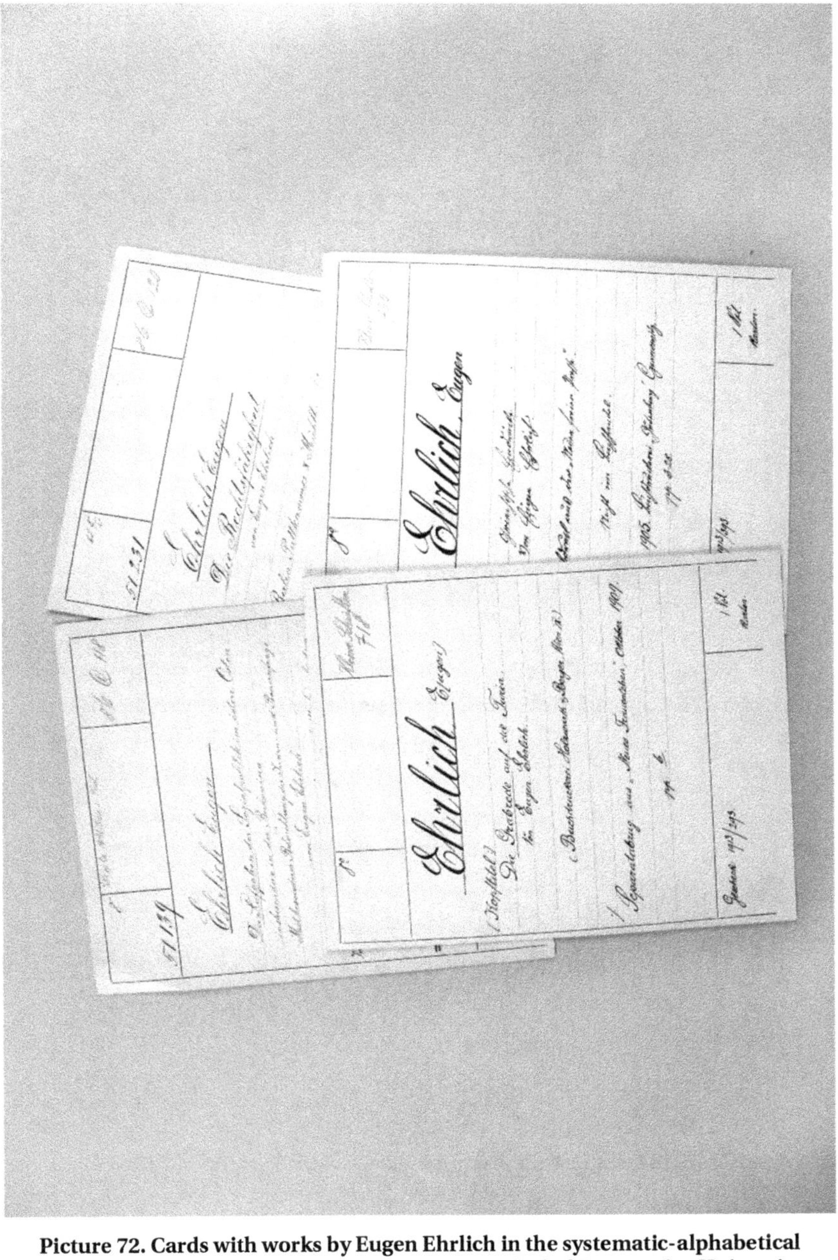

Picture 72. Cards with works by Eugen Ehrlich in the systematic-alphabetical catalogue created in the Austrian-Romanian period of Czernowitz University Library.

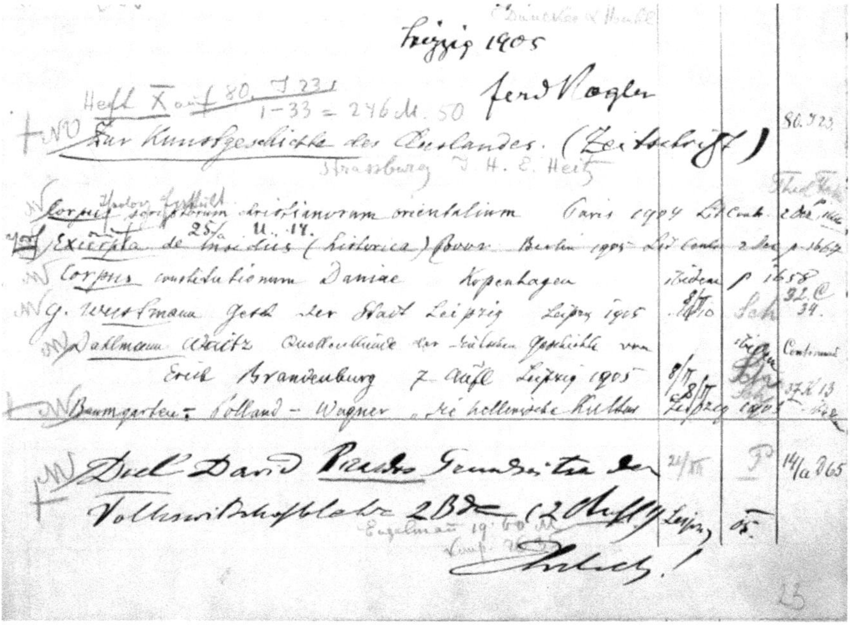

Picture 74. Eugen Ehrlich's pre-order: Czernowitz University: 1905-1911

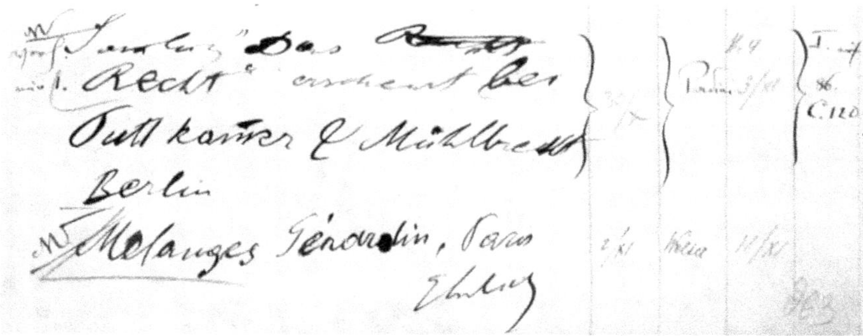

Picture 75. Eugen Ehrlich's pre-order: Czernowitz University: 1905-1911

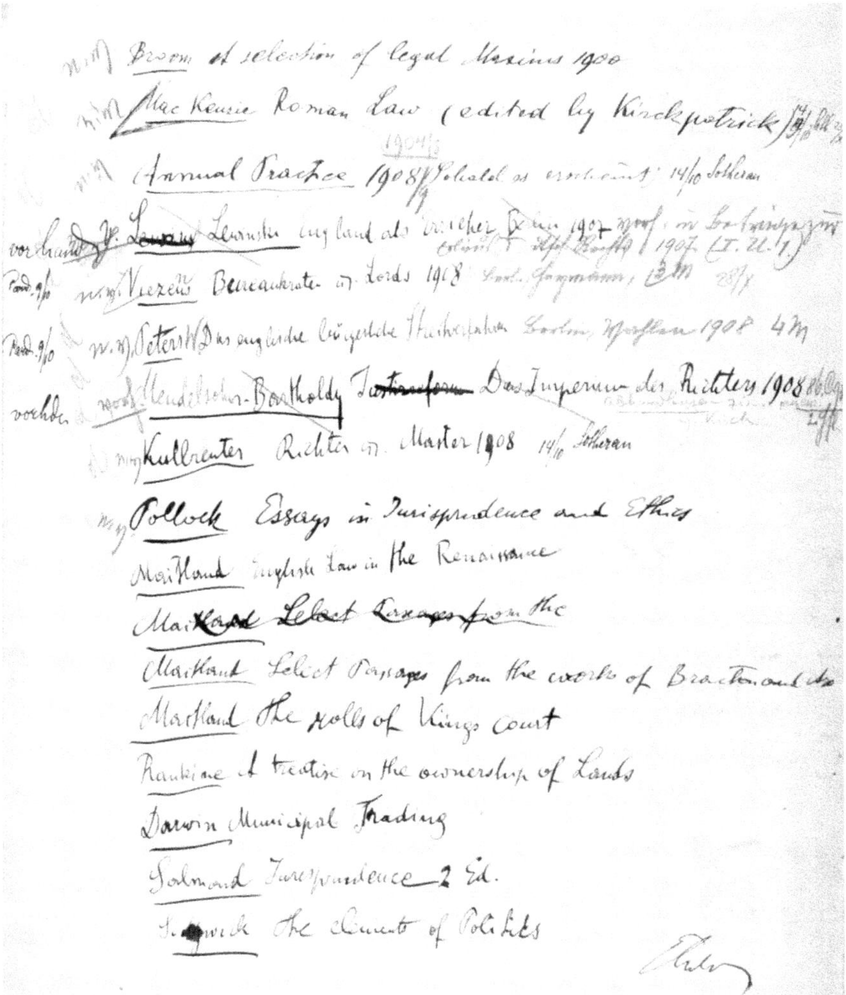

Broom A selection of Legal Maxims 1900

MacKenzie Roman Law (edited by Kirkpatrick [illegible]

Annual Practice 1908 [illegible] 14/10 Sotheran

Lewinski England als Erzieher Berlin 1907 [illegible] 1907

[illegible] Bureaukraten in Lords 1908 [illegible] 28/1

Peters Das englische bürgerliche Streitverfahren Berlin [illegible] 1908 4M

Mendelssohn-Bartholdy Das Imperium des Richters 1908 [illegible]

Kuttreuter Richter und Master 1908 14/10 Sotheran

Pollock Essays in Jurisprudence and Ethics

Maitland English Law in the Renaissance

Maitland Select Passages from the works of Bracton and Azo

Maitland The Rolls of Kings Court

Rankine A treatise on the ownership of Lands

Darwin Municipal Trading

Salmond Jurisprudence 2 Ed.

Sidgwick The elements of Politics

Ehrlich

Picture 76. Eugen Ehrlich's pre-order: Czernowitz University: 1905-1911

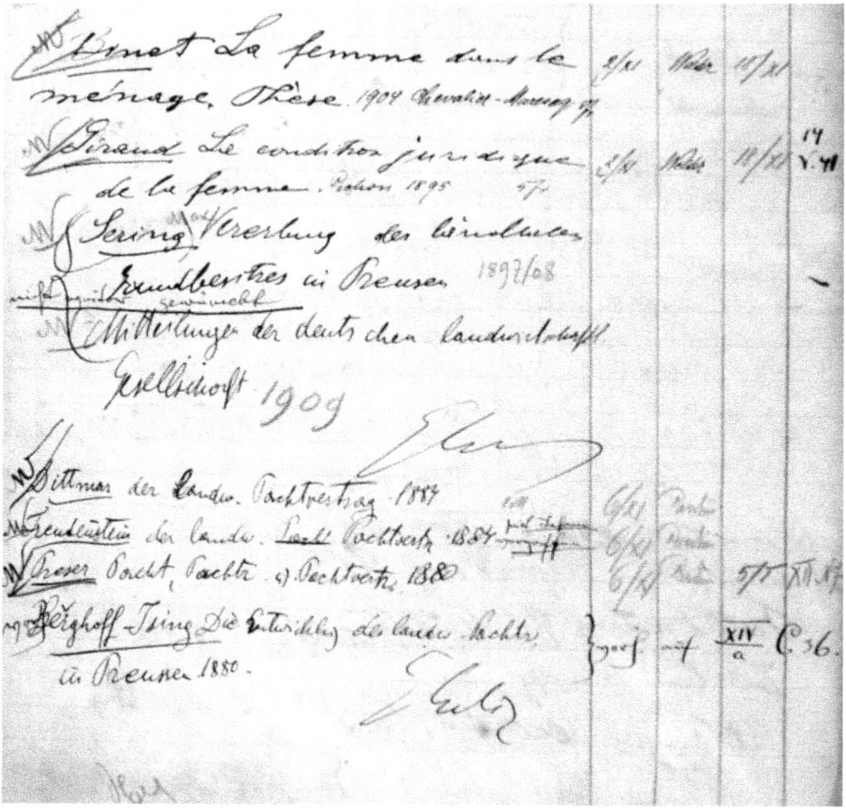

Picture 77. Eugen Ehrlich's pre-order: Czernowitz University: 1905-1911

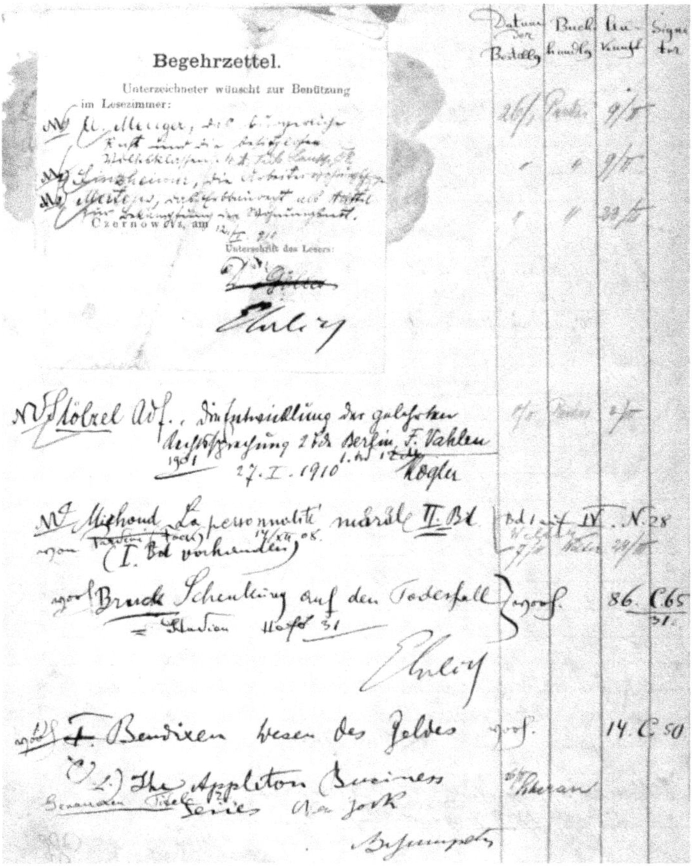
Begehrzettel.

Unterzeichneter wünscht zur Benützung im Lesezimmer:

Czernowitz, am

Unterschrift des Lesers:

Picture 78. Eugen Ehrlich's pre-order: Czernowitz University: 1905-1911

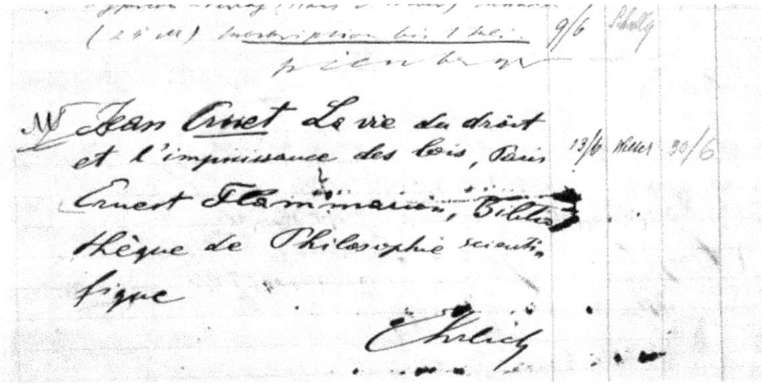

Picture 79. Eugen Ehrlich's pre-order: Czernowitz University: 1905-1911

Picture 80. Journal of addresses to the Academic Senate of Czernowitz University: 1900–1901

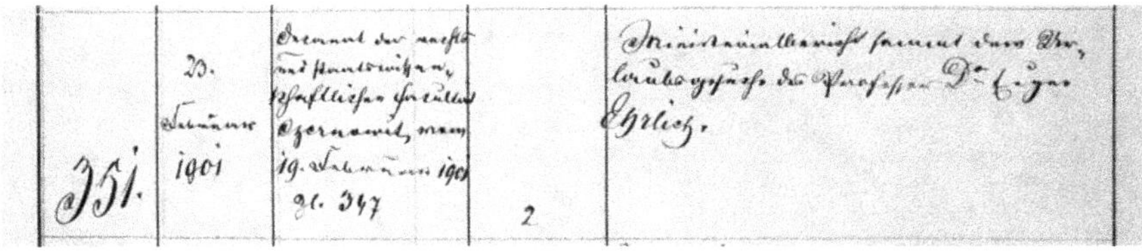

Picture 81. Eugen Ehrlich in Journal of addresses to the Academic Senate of Czernowitz University: 1900–1901

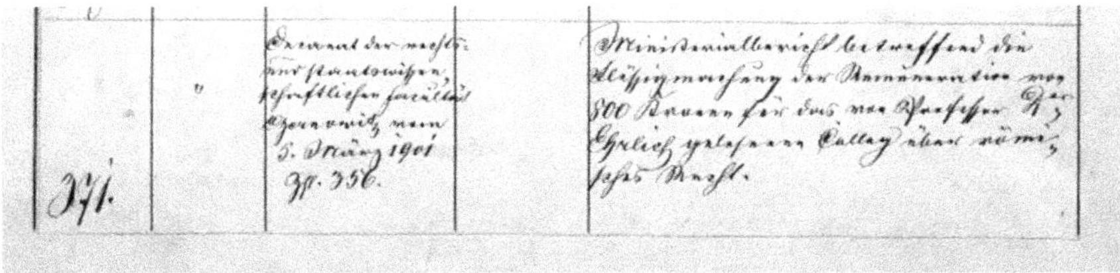

Picture 82. Eugen Ehrlich in Journal of addresses to the Academic Senate of Czernowitz University: 1900–1901

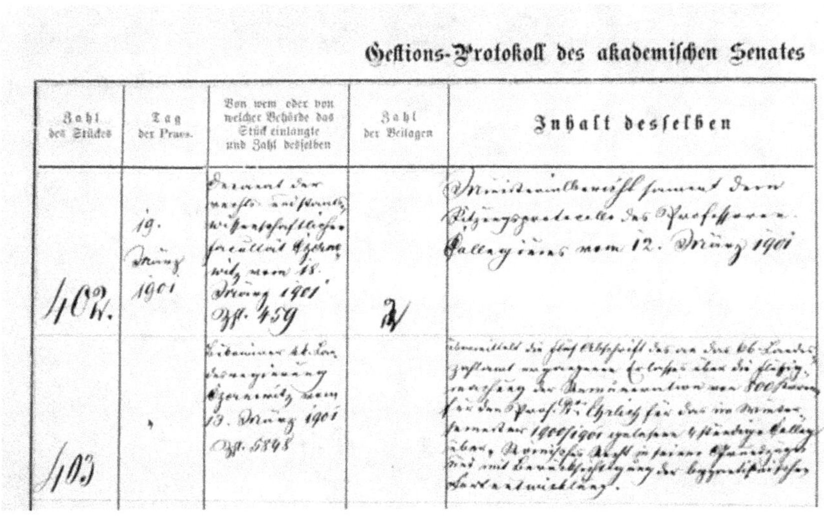

Gestions-Protokoll des akademischen Senates

Zahl des Stückes	Tag der Praes.	Von wem oder von welcher Behörde das Stück einlangte und Zahl desselben	Zahl der Beilagen	Inhalt desselben

Picture 83. Eugen Ehrlich in Journal of addresses to the Academic Senate of Czernowitz University: 1900–1901

Picture 84. Journal of addresses to Czernowitz University: 1910–1911

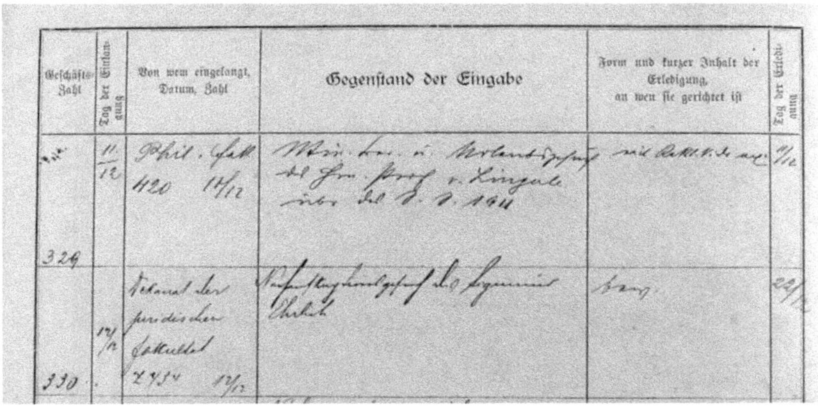

Picture 85. Eugen Ehrlich in Journal of addresses to Czernowitz University: 1910–1911

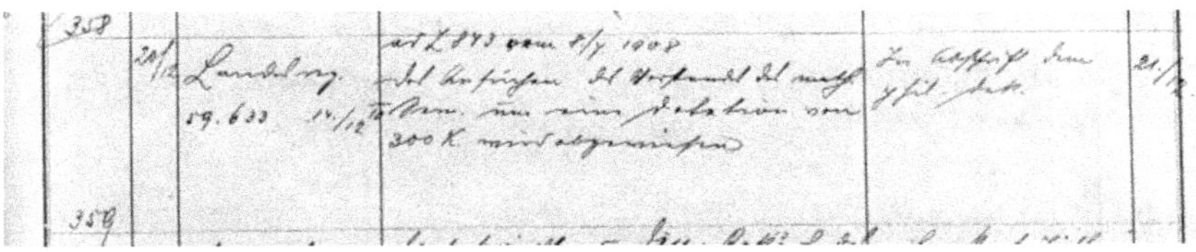

Picture 86. Eugen Ehrlich in Journal of addresses to Czernowitz University: 1910–1911

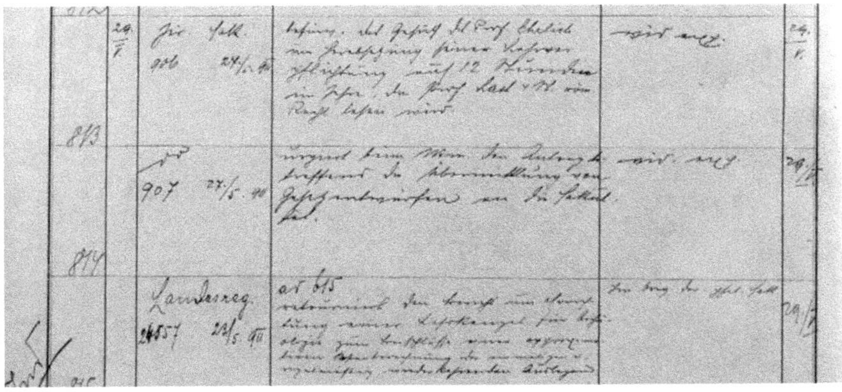

Picture 87. Eugen Ehrlich in Journal of addresses to Czernowitz University: 1910–1911

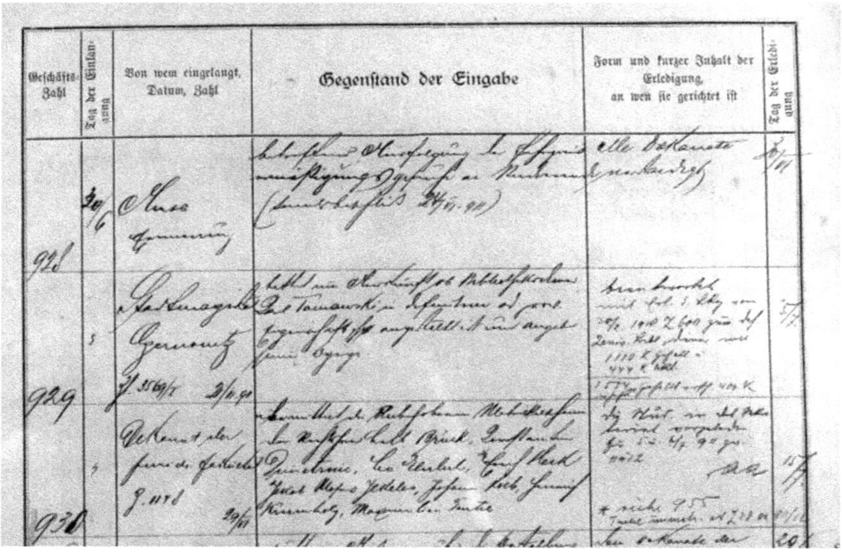

Picture 88. Eugen Ehrlich in Journal of addresses to Czernowitz University: 1910–1911

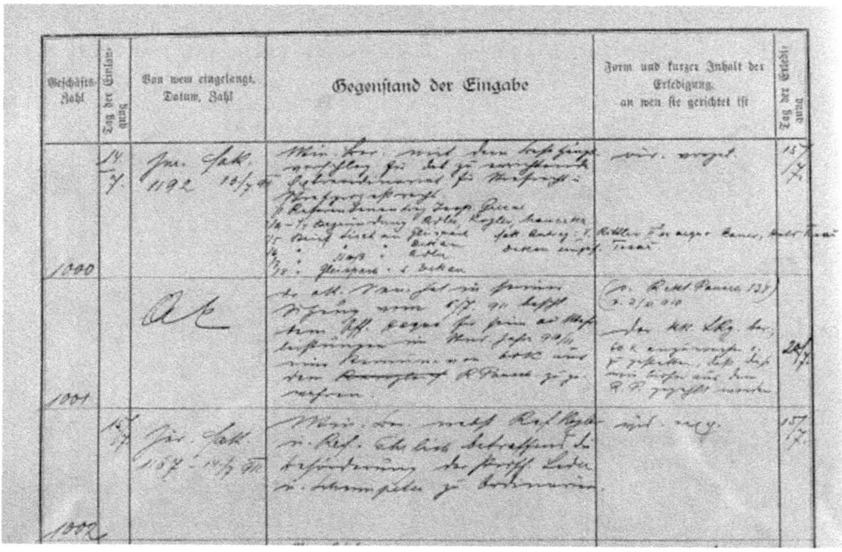

Picture 89. Eugen Ehrlich in Journal of addresses to Czernowitz University: 1910–1911

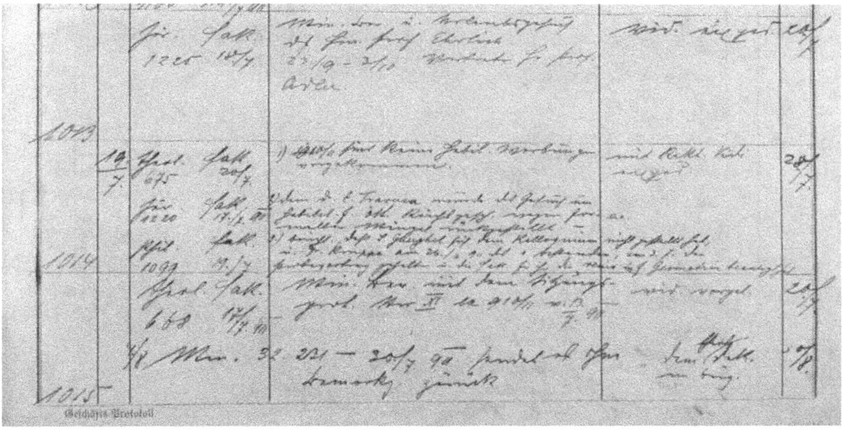

Picture 90. Eugen Ehrlich in Journal of addresses to Czernowitz University: 1910–1911

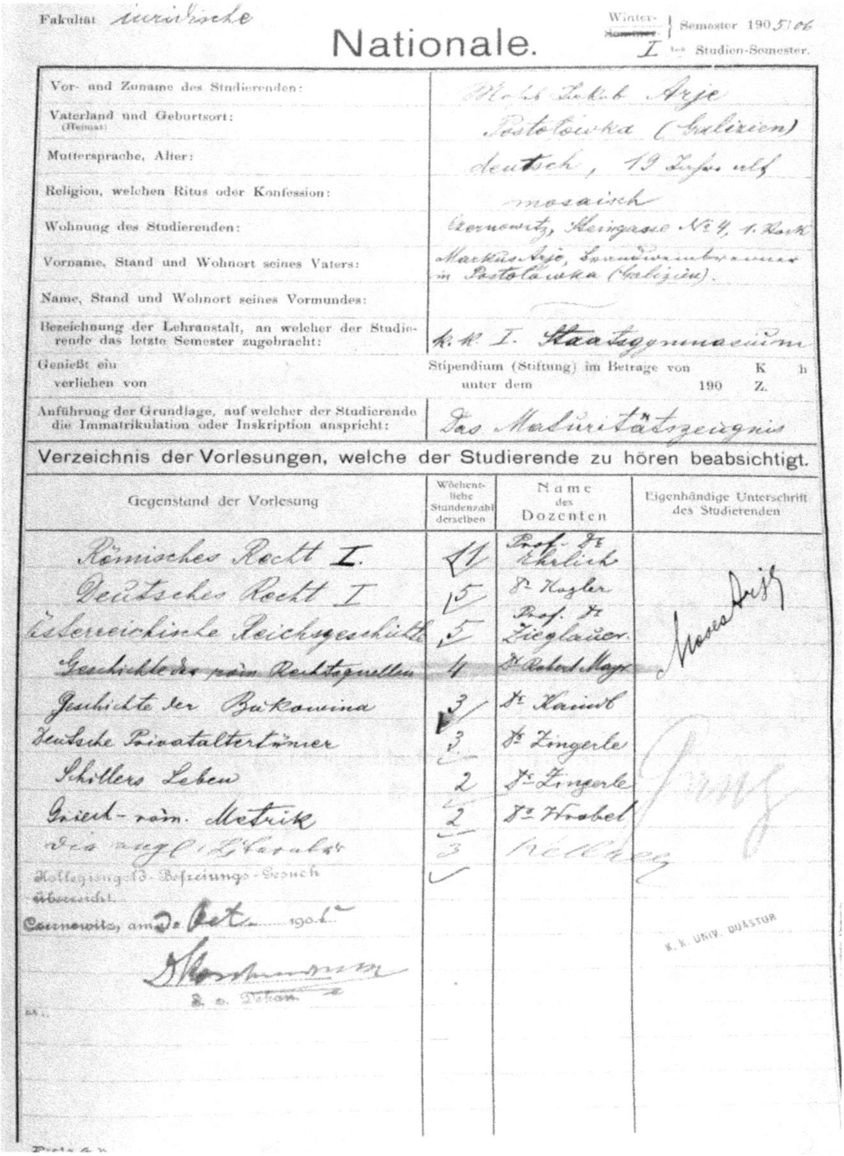

Fakultät juridische

Nationale.

Winter-/Sommer- Semester 1905/06
I tes Studien-Semester.

Vor- und Zuname des Studierenden:	Moses Jakob Arje
Vaterland und Geburtsort: (Heimat)	Postolowka (Galizien)
Muttersprache, Alter:	deutsch, 19 Jahre alt
Religion, welchen Ritus oder Konfession:	mosaisch
Wohnung des Studierenden:	Czernowitz, Herrengasse № 4, 1. Stock
Vorname, Stand und Wohnort seines Vaters:	Markus Arje, [illegible] in Postolowka (Galizien).
Name, Stand und Wohnort seines Vormundes:	—
Bezeichnung der Lehranstalt, an welcher der Studierende das letzte Semester zugebracht:	k. k. I. Staatsgymnasium
Genießt ein verliehen von	Stipendium (Stiftung) im Betrage von K h unter dem 190 Z.
Anführung der Grundlage, auf welcher der Studierende die Immatrikulation oder Inskription anspricht:	Das Maturitätszeugnis

Verzeichnis der Vorlesungen, welche der Studierende zu hören beabsichtigt.

Gegenstand der Vorlesung	Wöchentliche Stundenzahl derselben	Name des Dozenten	Eigenhändige Unterschrift des Studierenden
Römisches Recht I.	11	Prof. Dr. Ehrlich	Moses Arje
Deutsches Recht I	5	Dr. Kogler	
Österreichische Reichsgeschichte	5	Prof. Dr. Zieglauer	
~~Geschichte der röm. Rechtsquellen~~	4	Dr. Robert Mayr	
Geschichte der Bukowina	3	Dr. Kaindl	
Deutsche Privataltertümer	3	Dr. Zingerle	
Schillers Leben	2	Dr. Zingerle	
Griech.-röm. Metrik	2	Dr. Wrobel	
[illegible]	3	[illegible]	

Kollegiengeld-Befreiungs-Gesuch überreicht.

Czernowitz, am 2. Okt. 1905

[illegible signature]

d. z. Dekan

K. K. UNIV. QUÄSTUR

Picture 91. Information about the students of the Faculty of Law of Czernowitz University (on the individual standard sheets, filled in by hand, containing bibliographic data of each student, and the list of courses attended with surnames of lecturers)

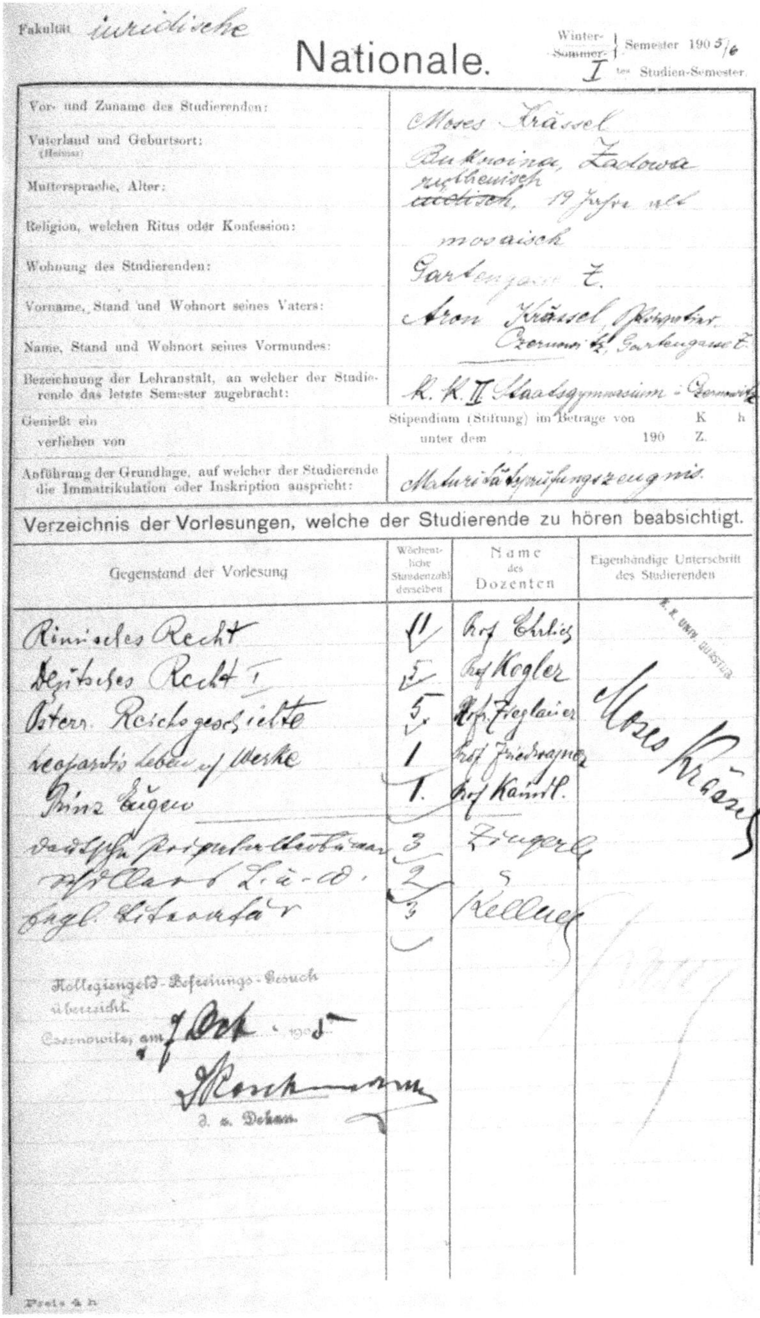

Fakultät *iuridische*

Nationale.

Winter- / ~~Sommer-~~ Semester 190 5/6

I tes Studien-Semester.

Vor- und Zuname des Studierenden:	Moses Kräsel
Vaterland und Geburtsort: (Heimat)	Bukowina, Zadowa
Muttersprache, Alter:	ruthenisch ~~deutsch~~, 19 Jahre alt
Religion, welchen Ritus oder Konfession:	mosaisch
Wohnung des Studierenden:	Gartengasse 7.
Vorname, Stand und Wohnort seines Vaters:	Aron Kräsel, Gutspächter, Czernowitz, Gartengasse 7.
Name, Stand und Wohnort seines Vormundes:	
Bezeichnung der Lehranstalt, an welcher der Studierende das letzte Semester zugebracht:	K. K. II Staatsgymnasium – Czernowitz
Genießt ein verliehen von	Stipendium (Stiftung) im Betrage von K h unter dem 190 Z.
Anführung der Grundlage, auf welcher der Studierende die Immatrikulation oder Inskription anspricht:	Maturitätsprüfungszeugnis.

Verzeichnis der Vorlesungen, welche der Studierende zu hören beabsichtigt.

Gegenstand der Vorlesung	Wöchentliche Stundenzahl derselben	Name des Dozenten	Eigenhändige Unterschrift des Studierenden
Römisches Recht	11	Prof. Ehrlich	Moses Kräsel
Deutsches Recht I	5	Prof. Kogler	
Österr. Reichsgeschichte	5	Prof. Frieglauer	
Leopardis Leben u. Werke	1	Prof. Friedwagner	
Prinz Eugen	1	Prof. Kaindl	
[illegible]	3	[illegible]	
[illegible]	2	[illegible]	
Engl. Literatur	3	Keller	

Kollegiengeld-Befreiungs-Gesuch überreicht.

Czernowitz, am 7 Okt. 1905

[signature]

d. z. Dekan.

Preis 4 h

Picture 92. Ibidem

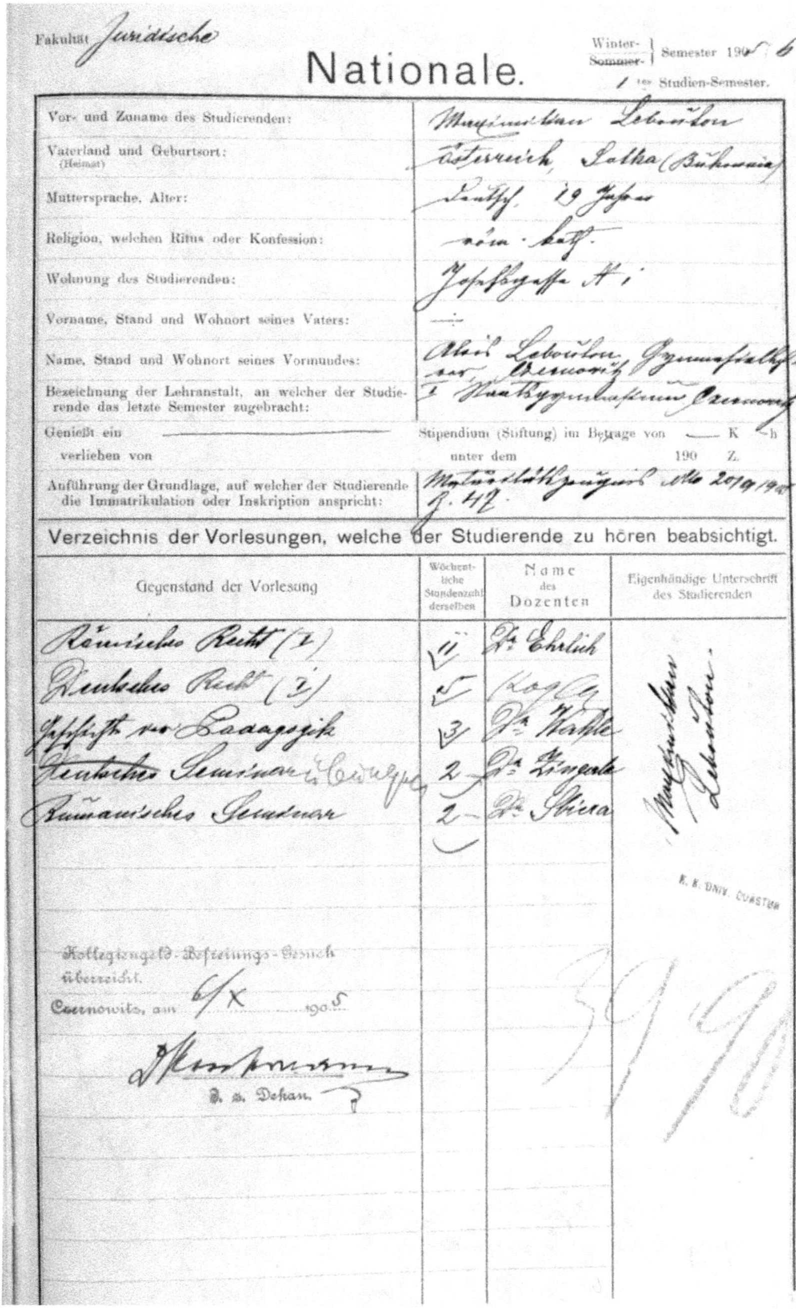

Fakultät Juridische

Nationale.

Winter- ~~Sommer-~~ Semester 1905/6

1 tes Studien-Semester.

Vor- und Zuname des Studierenden:	Maximilian Lebouton
Vaterland und Geburtsort: (Heimat)	Österreich, Satka (Bukowina)
Muttersprache, Alter:	deutsch, 19 Jahre
Religion, welchen Ritus oder Konfession:	röm. kath.
Wohnung des Studierenden:	Josefsgasse 4
Vorname, Stand und Wohnort seines Vaters:	—
Name, Stand und Wohnort seines Vormundes:	Alois Lebouton Gymnasialprof., Czernowitz
Bezeichnung der Lehranstalt, an welcher der Studierende das letzte Semester zugebracht:	I. Staatsgymnasium Czernowitz
Genießt ein ——— verliehen von	Stipendium (Stiftung) im Betrage von — K — h unter dem 190 Z.
Anführung der Grundlage, auf welcher der Studierende die Immatrikulation oder Inskription anspricht:	Maturitätszeugnis dto 20/9 1905 Z. 47

Verzeichnis der Vorlesungen, welche der Studierende zu hören beabsichtigt.

Gegenstand der Vorlesung	Wöchentliche Stundenzahl derselben	Name des Dozenten	Eigenhändige Unterschrift des Studierenden
Römisches Recht (I.)	11	Dr. Ehrlich	Maximilian Lebouton
Deutsches Recht (I.)	5	Kogler	
Geschichte der Pädagogik	3	Dr. Wahle	
Deutsches Seminar	2	Dr. Löwenthal	
Rumänisches Seminar	2	Dr. Stirca	

K. K. UNIV. QUÄSTUR

~~Kollegiengeld-Befreiungs-Gesuch überreicht.~~

Czernowitz, am 6/X 1905

d. z. Dekan.

Picture 93. Ibidem

Appendix D:
Books with commemorative inscriptions for Eugen Ehrlich

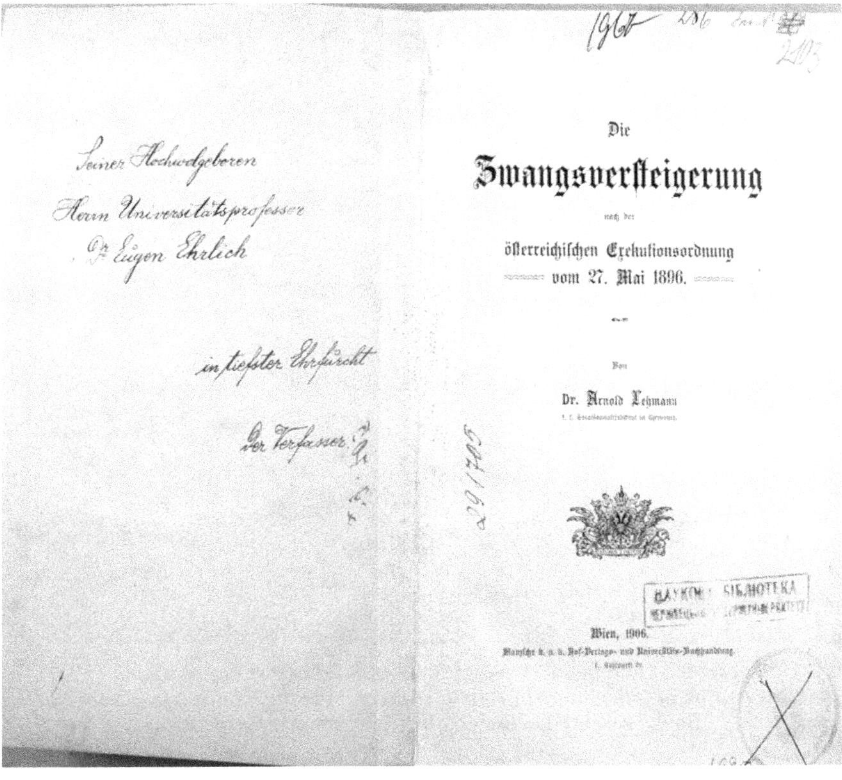

Picture 94. Lehmann, Arnold. *The Forced Sale According to the Austrian Executive Order of May 27, 1896.* Book presented to Eugen Ehrlich by the author.

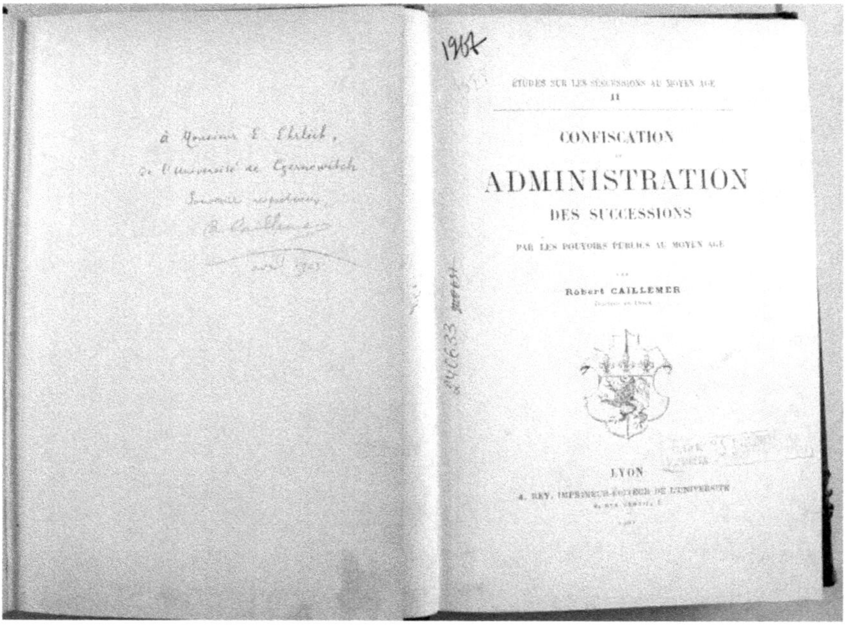

Picture 95. Caillemer de Ferrage, Robert. ***Studies on Confiscation and Administration of Inheritance by Public Authorities in the Middle Ages, Lyon, 1901.*** **Book presented to Eugen Ehrlich by the author in 1903.**

LIST OF WORKS BY EUGEN EHRLICH

PERIODICALS WITH EUGEN EHRLICH'S PUBLICATIONS

Правничий вісник (Львів) [Legal Newsletter (Lviv)]

Allgemeine österreichische Gerichts-Zeitung (Wien)

Arbeiterschutz (Wien)

Archiv für die civilistische Praxis (Tübingen)

Archiv für Rechts- und Wirtschaftsphilosophie (Berlin; Leipzig)

Archiv für soziale Gesetzgebung und Statistik (Berlin)

Archiv für Sozialwissenschaft und Sozialpolitik (Tübingen)

Arhiva pentru ştiinţa şi reforma sociala (Bucureşti)

Bukowinaer Post (Czernowitz)

Bukowinaer Rundschau (Czernowitz)

Bukowiner Beamten-Zeitung (Czernowitz)

Bukowiner Bote (Prag)

Czernowitzer Allgemeine Zeitung (Czernowitz)

Czernowitzer Tagblatt (Czernowitz)

Czernowitzer Zeitung (Czernowitz)

Deutsche Richterzeitung (Hannover)

Deutsche Rundschau (Berlin)

Deutsche Worte (Wien)

Dokumente der Frauen (Wien)

The Economic Review (London)

Der Friede (Wien)

Die Friedens-Warte, Blätter für zwischenstaaliche Organisation (Zürich)

Die Geisteswissenschaften : Wochenschrift für das gesamte Gebiet der Philosophie, Psychologie, Geschichts- und Staatswissenschaften etc. (Leipzig)

Harvard Law Review (Cambridge)

Jahrbuch für Gesetzgebung, Verwaltung und Volkswirtschaft im Deutschen Reich (Leipzig)

Jherings Jahrbücher für die Dogmatik des bürgerlichen Rechts (Jena)

Juristische Blätter (Wien)

Juristisches Litteraturblatt (Berlin)

Der Kampf : Sozialdemokratische Monatsschrift (Wien)

Kaufmännische Zeitschrift (Wien)

Kritische Vierteljahresschrift für Gesetzgebung und Rechtswissenschaft (Freiburg i. B., Leipzig, Tübingen)

Mährisches Tagblatt (Olmütz)

Mitteilungen der Vereinigung der österreichischen Richter (Wien)

Das neue Europa (Zürich)

Neue Freie Presse (Wien)

Neue Revue (Wien)

Die Neue Zeit (Stuttgart)

Neuen Schweizer Zeitung (Zürich)

Neues Frauenleben (Wien)

Neues Wiener Tagblatt (Wien)

Österreichische Richter-Zeitung (Czernowitz)

Österreichische Rundschau (Wien)

Das Recht : volkstümliche Zeitschrift für österreichisches Rechtsleben (Wien)

Recht und Wirtschaft (Berlin)

Revue de droit international privé et de droit pénal international (Paris)

Rivista internazionale di filosofia del diritto (Milano)

Schweizerische Juristen-Zeitung (Zürich)

Schweizerische Zeitschrift für Volkswirtschaft und Sozialpolitik (Bern)

Süddeutsche Monatshefte (Stuttgart)

Unsere Zeit : deutsche Revue der Gegenwart (Leipzig)

Zeitschrift für das Privat- und öffentliche Recht der Gegenwart (Wien)

Zeitschrift für Notariat und freiwillige Gerichtsbarkeit in Österreich (Wien)

Zeitschrift für vergleichende Rechtswissenschaft (Stuttgart)

Die Zukunft (Berlin)

LIST OF USED PERIODICALS

Буковина (Чернівці) [Bukovina (Czernowitz)]

Буковинське віче (Чернівці) [Bukovinian Viche (Chernivtsi)]

Бюлетень Міністерства юстиції України (Київ) [Bulletin of the Ministry of Justice of Ukraine (Kyiv)]

Вестник Коммунистической академии (Москва) [Newsletter of the Communist Academy (Moscow)]

Государство и право (Москва) [State and Law (Moscow)]

Известия высших учебных заведений. Правоведение (Санкт-Петербург) [News of Higher Educational Institutions. Science of Law (Saint-Petersburg)]

Ленинградский юридический журнал (Ленинград) [Leningrad Journal of Law (Leningrad)]

Молодий буковинець (Чернівці) [Young Bukovinian (Chernivtsi)]

Правничий вісник (Львів) [Legal Newsletter (Lviv)]

Право. Журнал Высшей школы экономики (Москва) [Law. Journal of the High School of Economics (Moscow)]

Право України (Київ) [Law of Ukraine (Kyiv)]

Свобода слова (Чернівці) [Freedom of Speech (Chernivtsi)]

Советское государство и право (Москва) [Soviet State and Law (Moscow)]

Соціологія права (Київ) [Sociology of Law (Kyiv)]

Університетський вісник (Чернівці) [University Newsletter (Chernivtsi)]

Філософія права і загальна теорія права (Київ) [Philosophy of Law and General Theory of Law (Kyiv)]

Юридический вестник = Юридичний вісник = Law herald (Одесса) [(Odessa)]

Юридичний вісник України (Київ) [Legal Newsletter of Ukraine (Kyiv)]

Allgemeine Juristen-Zeitung (*früher* "Oesterreichische Advocaten-Zeitung") (Wien)

Allgemeine österreichische Gerichts-Zeitung (Wien)

Allgemeines Literaturblatt (*früher* "Allgemeines Litteraturblatt") (Wien; Stuttgart; Leipzig)

The American Journal of International Law (New York)

The American Journal of Sociology (Chicago)

Annalen der Philosophie und philosophischen Kritik (Leipzig)

Anuarul Institutului de Istorie "George Bariţiu" din Cluj-Napoca. Series Historica (Cluj-Napoca)

Arbeiterschutz (Wien)

Archiv des öffentlichen Rechts (Tübingen)

Archiv für Bürgerliches Recht (Berlin)

Archiv für die civilistische Praxis (Tübingen)

Archiv für Rechts- und Sozialphilosophie = Archives de Philosophie du Droit et de Philosophie Sociale = *Archives for Philosophy of Law and Social Philosophy* = Archivo de Filosofía Jurídica y Social *(Wiesbaden;* Stuttgart; Berlin) (*früher* "Archiv für Rechts- und Wirtschaftsphilosophie" (Berlin; Leipzig)

Archiv für soziale Gesetzgebung und Statistik (Berlin)

Archiv für Sozialwissenschaft und Sozialpolitik (Tübingen)

Arhiva pentru ştiinţa şi reforma sociala (Bucureşti)

Buconina : revistă lunară de drept, socioligie şi criminology (Cernăuţi)

Bukowinaer Rundschau (Czernowitz)

Bukowinaer Journal (Czernowitz)

Bukowinaer Post (Czernowitz)

Bukowinaer Volks- Zeitung (Czernowitz)

Bukowiner Beamten- Zeitung (Czernowitz)

Bukowiner Bote (Prag)

Bukowiner Nachrichten (Czernowitz)

Columbia Law Review (New York)

Czernowitzer Allgemeine Zeitung (Czernowitz)

Czernowitzer Gemeinde-Zeitung (Czernowitz)

Czernowitzer Tagblatt (Czernowitz)

Czernowitzer Zeitung (Czernowitz)

Deutsche Juristen-Zeitung (Berlin)

Deutsche Literaturzeitung (*früher* "Deutsche Litteraturzeitung") (Berlin; Leipzig)

Deutsche Richterzeitung (Hannover)

Deutsche Rundschau (Berlin)

Deutsche Worte (Wien)

Dokumente der Frauen (Wien)

The Economic Review (London)

Der Friede (Wien)

Die Friedens-Warte, Blätter für zwischenstaaliche Organisation (Zürich)

Gazeta Polska (Czerniowce)

Die Geisteswissenschaften : Wochenschrift für das gesamte Gebiet der Philosophie, Psychologie, Geschichts- und Staatswissenschaften etc. (Leipzig)

Giornale degli Economisti e Rivista di Statistica (Roma)

Glasul Bucovinei (Cernăuţi)

Harvard Law Review (Cambridge)

Hochschul-Nachrichten; (*früher* "Hochschul-Nachrichten" : Monats-Berichte von den Deutschen, Oesterreichisch-Ungarischen und Schweizerischen Hochschulen : Als Separat-Abdruck aus der "Academischen Revue" (München)

ICL Journal : Vienna Journal on International Constitutional Law (Vienna)

The International Journal of Ethics (Chicago; London; Tokyo; Shanghai)

International Journal of Law in Context (Cambridge)

International Journal of the Sociology of Law (London)

Jahrbuch für Gesetzgebung, Verwaltung und Volkswirtschaft im Deutschen Reich (Leipzig)

Jherings Jahrbücher für die Dogmatik des bürgerlichen Rechts (Jena)

Journal of Law and Society (Oxford; Malden)

JuristenZeitung (Tübingen)

Juristische Blätter (Wien)

Juristisches Literaturblatt (*früher* "Juristisches Litteraturblatt") (Berlin)

Kaindl-Archiv : Zeitschrift des Bukowina-Instituts für den Kulturaustausch mit den Völkern Mittel- und Osteuropas (Augsburg)

Der Kampf : Sozialdemokratische Monatsschrift (Wien)

Kaufmännische Zeitschrift (Wien)

Kölner Zeitschrift für Sociologie und Socialpsychologie (Köln)

Kritische Vierteljahresschrift für Gesetzgebung und Rechtswissenschaft (Freiburg i. B.; Leipzig; Tübingen)

Law and Social Inquiry (Chicago)

Legea şi viaţa (Закон и жизнь) (Chişinău)

Literarisches Zentralblatt für Deutschland (*früher* "Literarisches Centralblatt für Deutschland" (Leipzig)

Mährisches Tagblatt (Olmütz)

Max Weber Studies (London)

Milletlerarası Hukuk ve Milletlerarası Özel Hukuk Bülteni (İstanbul)

Mitteilungen der Vereinigung der österreichischen Richter (Wien)

The Modern Law Review (London)

Nationaløkonomisk tidsskrift : maanedskrift for samfundsspørgsmaal, økonomi og handel (Kjøbenhavn)

Das neue Europa (Zürich)

Neue Freie Presse (Wien)

Neue Jüdische Monatshefte : Zeitschrift für Politik, Wirtschaft und Literatur in Ost und West (Berlin; München)

Neue Revue (Wien)

Die Neue Zeit (Stuttgart)

Neuen Schweizer Zeitung (Zürich)

Neues Frauenleben (Wien)

Neues Wiener Tagblatt (Wien)

Northern Kentucky Law Rewiew (Highland Heights)

Österreichische Richter-Zeitung (Czernowitz)

Österreichische Rundschau (Wien)

Österreichisches Zentralblatt für die juristische Praxis (Wien)

Proceedings of the 14th Annual Meeting of the Association of American Law Schools (Chicago)

Das Recht : Rundschau für den deutschen Juristenstand (Hannover; Leipzig)

Das Recht : volkstümliche Zeitschrift für österreichisches Rechtsleben (Wien)

Recht und Wirtschaft (Berlin)

Rechtstheorie : Zeitschrift für Logik und Juristische Methodenlehre, Allgemeine Rechts- und Staatslehre, Kommunikations-, Normen- und Handlungstheorie, Soziologie und Philosophie des Rechts (Berlin)

Revista Romana de Sociologie (Bucureşti)

Revue de droit international privé et de droit pénal international (Paris)

Rheinische Zeitschrift für Zivil- und Prozessrecht (Mannheim; Leipzig)

Rivista internazionale di filosofia del diritto (Milano)

Schweizerische Juristen-Zeitung (Zürich)

Schweizerische Zeitschrift für Volkswirtschaft und Sozialpolitik (Bern)

Süddeutsche Monatshefte (Stuttgart)

The Sydney Law Review (Sydney)

Theater-, Kunst- und Literatur-Zeitung (Wien; Czernowitz)

Theoretical Inquiries in Law (Tel Aviv)

Tidskrift för rättssociologi (Lund)

The University of Chicago Law Review (Chicago; Cambridge; Tokyo; Shanghai)

Unsere Zeit. Deutsche Revue der Gegenwart (Leipzig)

Verordnungsblatt des k. k. Justizministeriums (Wien)

Virginia Law Review (Charlottesville)

Die Wahrheit (Czernowitz)

The Wayne Law Review (Detroit)

Weltwirtschaftliches Archiv : Zeitschrift für Allgemeine und Spezielle Weltwirtschaftslehre (Jena)

Wiener Zeitung (Wien)

Zeitschrift der Savigny-Stiftung für Rechtsgeschichte (Wien; Köln; Weimar)

Zeitschrift für das Gesamte Handelsrecht und Konkursrecht (Stuttgart)

Zeitschrift für die gesamte Staatswissenschaft (Tübingen)

Zeitschrift für Notariat und freiwillige Gerichtsbarkeit in Österreich (Wien)

Zeitschrift für das Privat- und öffentliche Recht der Gegenwart (Wien)

Zeitschrift für Rechtssoziologie (Stuttgart)

Zeitschrift für vergleichende Rechtswissenschaft (Stuttgart)

Zeitschrift für Volkswirtschaft, Sozialpolitik und Verwaltung (Prag; Wien; Leipzig)

Zentralblatt für Rechtswissenschaft (*früher* "Centralblatt für Rechtswissenschaft") (Leipzig)

Die Zukunft (Berlin)

NAME INDEX

www.ingramcontent.com/pod-product-compliance
Lightning Source LLC
LaVergne TN
LVHW010722210926
848485LV00007B/1427/J
* 9 7 8 1 6 2 2 7 3 3 7 7 4 *